THE SECURITY OF THE PERSIAN GULF

THE SECURITY OF THE PERSIAN GULF

Edited by
Hossein Amirsadeghi

ST. MARTIN'S PRESS NEW YORK

© 1981 Hossein Amirsadeghi
All rights reserved. For information write:
St. Martin's Press, Inc., 175 Fifth Avenue, New York, N. Y. 10010
Printed in Great Britain
First published in the United States of America in 1981

Library of Congress Cataloging in Publication Data

Main entry under title:
The Security of the Persian Gulf.
  Bibliography: p. 281.
  Includes index.
    1. Persian Gulf region — Politics and government —
Addresses, essays, lectures. 2. Persian Gulf region —
Strategic aspects — Addresses, essays, lectures.
I. Amirsadeghi, Hossein.
DS326.S4 1981   355′.0330536   80-28780

ISBN 0-312-70915-3

CONTENTS

FIGURES AND TABLES

Figure

Tables

ACKNOWLEDGEMENTS

I would like to thank Shahram Chubin and all the other contributors for their worthy efforts in constructing this volume, bearing in mind the time-lag from start to finish, and the unforeseen changes in the political situation brought about by the Iranian Revolution and the Iraq/Iran war. A special word of thanks to my friend John St John for his initial co-operation, and to all those other worthy people upon whom one chances in connection with such projects.

Hossein Amirsadeghi

EDITOR'S PREFACE

Because of my special interest in the politics of my country and the increasingly vital significance of the Persian Gulf in world affairs, and because of the general dearth of material on the Gulf, I set out three years ago to produce a volume of essays not only to help fill this vacuum with a general overview, but also to produce specialist studies that will help shed some light on the intricacies of the politics and society of this most volatile area.

The Persian Gulf, already important because of its vast energy resources, emerged into the limelight of geopolitics at the time of the British Labour government's policy of withdrawal from East of Suez in 1968. Before 1968 it had been recognised that the Gulf lay in the legitimate sphere of influence of Britain, while the United States exerted its influence in the two pivotal littoral states of Iran and Saudi Arabia. The Soviets had been gaining influence in Iraq ever since the overthrow of the monarchy in 1958, and later gained a more secure foothold in South Yemen after the British withdrawal from Aden. The Chinese were also fishing for influence by their support of the Popular Front for the Liberation of the Arabian Gulf, a Marxist guerrilla organisation responsible for the Dhofari rebellion in Oman, and dedicated to the overthrow of the conservative *status quo* of the Gulf countries. But except for some influence in Tehran in the last years of the Shah's regime, the only two remaining arbitrating powers in the Gulf have been the Soviets through their proxies in South Yemen, and to a lesser extent in Iraq and Syria, and the United States, with its increasingly reluctant allies in Riyadh and Muscat.

Since the revolution in Iran and the downfall of the Shah, the whole political balance of the area has been overturned. With their new-found bases on the Iran-Afghan border, the Soviets are only a day's drive from Iran's Gulf ports or the Khuzestan oilfields. With their estimated thirty divisions poised on the Iran-Soviet border, and the continuing turmoil and effective political disintegration of Iran, the Soviet capacity for a direct attack on the Gulf oilfields, and its potential for mischief-making, have increased dramatically. The outcome of the political tug-of-war in Tehran is crucial to the future political map of the Persian Gulf. The collapse of the Khomeini regime will eventually come about; but the question is who or what will replace it. If a moderate regime replaces the present turmoil, the prospects for future stability in the Gulf seem good. If, on the other hand, extremists gain the upper hand, with no doubt a little help from their Soviet mentors, the prospects for an East-West confrontation over the Gulf's vital energy resources become much more likely.

It is with a view to the above dangers that this volume is directed. The various contributors, each distinguished in his or her own area of knowledge, have been assigned to delve into the manifold intricacies of Persian and Arab politics, society and culture. Although the Iranian Revolution caught everybody by surprise, the chapters have been rewritten with the benefit of hindsight, increasing the scope for analysis. But the reader should bear in mind that the volatile political and socio-religious equation in the Gulf precludes any definitive study of this important subject area in just one volume. With due consideration to the in-built limitations of such a broad-based study, this volume attempts to analyse in one place subjects which have hitherto been approached piecemeal. The success will belong to the contributors, and the limitations are the fault of the editor.

Map1: South-West Asia

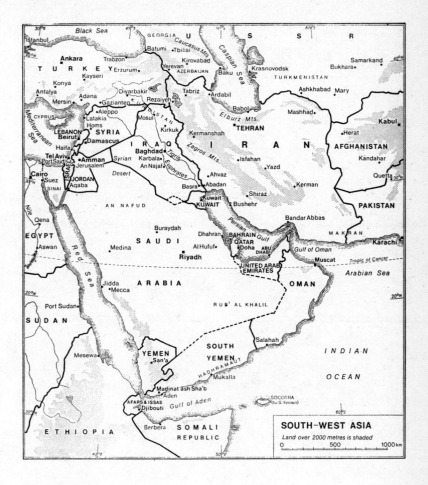

Map2: Persian Gulf and Iran

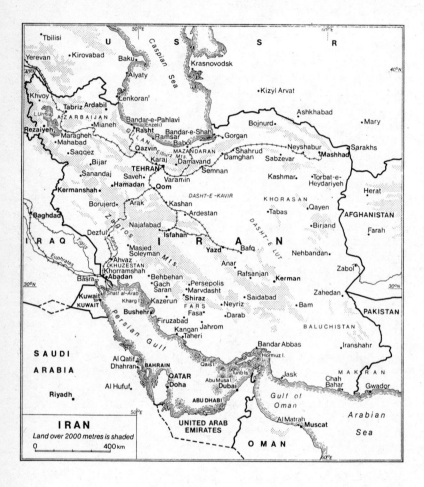

INTRODUCTION

President Eisenhower described the Persian Gulf in 1951 as the most strategically important area in the world. Thirty years and two oil embargoes, a major revolution and a raging war later, there cannot be a more apt description of this most volatile and turbulent area. In terms of sheer riches of petroleum resources, there is no other group of countries that can match it. The eight littoral states of the Gulf hold over 60 per cent of the world's known oil reserves. Their combined petroleum exports in 1978 accounted for 40 per cent of the total world production and their complete shut-off would mean industrial paralysis and devastating economic collapse within a very short time for the industrial nations. The Persian Gulf states' combined imports market represents one of the most lucrative in the world. Vast purchases of armaments, industrial and petroleum plants, manufactured and consumer goods and services are equally vital to the health of world trade. The foreign currency holdings and investments of the Gulf states in Europe and America are becoming staggering. In short, little over 55 million Persians and Arabs hold the free world over the literal barrel.

Little did President Eisenhower imagine how profound his statement at that time would be. Even less could he foresee that thirty years later, and despite America's still awesome power, the value of Washington's friendship would be in such disdain and her ability to influence events in the Gulf so limited. For since the fall of the Shah, with the Carter Administration's muddled abandonment of its long-time Iranian ally, and with its singular ineffectiveness *vis-à-vis* the hostage crisis, all Washington's former friends have scuttled for cover, keeping a safe diplomatic distance, yet demanding increasing security guarantees against encroaching radicalism and the possibilities of direct and indirect aggression by the Soviet Union. Since the Afghan invasion, that threat suddenly seems very real.

In spite of over thirty years of experience in and around the Gulf, the United States seems to have failed in its overall policies. The clear alignments and cold war scenarios began to crumble in the late 1960s, yet Washington could not foresee trends and prepare contingencies to meet inevitable crises with forceful determination. Opportunities were missed and eventually the inability to react with vigour resulted in one of the most devastating post-war reversals for American power and prestige due to the downfall of the Shah. That is not to say that the Iranian revolution was the fault of the United

States, but as the xenophobic hysteria in Iran still points in the direction of the White House, it is only fitting to question why. To have both the remnants of the previous regime and the present Khomeini ensemble blame the US for its demise and troubles does raise disturbing questions.

It is fair to say that Washington was never at home in the 'hotbed' realm of diplomacy and Byzantine intrigue of the Persian Gulf. The British presence up to 1971 ensured a goodly measure of compliance and co-operation, for Whitehall had been at home in the Gulf since the British superseded the Portuguese and the Dutch in the eighteenth century. The Gulf was secured to ensure free passage to India and a British Resident presided over events in the area.

After the discovery of oil at Masjid-e-Suleiman in 1908 in Iran's Khuzistan province, the British looked upon the Gulf as their 'lake' and let it be known to all that it was their 'legitimate' sphere of influence. The Arabian Peninsula was wrested from the Turks, and after the collapse of the Ottoman Empire at the end of the Great War, Mesopotamia was mandated to the British by treaty. Thus, apart from Persia, which was never colonised, the Arab Gulf states were creations of Whitehall and their frontiers drawn up in London. Most became independent states only after the Second World War, and countries like Kuwait have a history of nationhood dating back all of thirty years. The United Arab Emirates was Britain's last imperial hurra, being granted independence in 1971 as Britain finally withdrew from the Gulf.

After their departure, the Shah made it forcefully clear that Iran intended to fill the resultant vacuum and, with the co-operation of the Arab littoral states, to ensure that no foreign power ever again play the dominant role. To thumb his nose at the British, he seized the small islands of the Tumbs and Abu Musa before Whitehall's official date of relinquishment of treaty obligations.

With the advent of the Nixon doctrine of self-help, the Shah soon assumed the mantle of 'policeman of the Gulf' and through Iran's increasing economic, political and military strength — especially after the 1973 OPEC oil price increases — Washington was more than content to let affairs develop and around their 'twin-pillar' strategy of support for Iran and Saudi Arabia. The 1970s saw dramatic economic change in the midst of stability, and the Gulf states managed to sort out their problems with mutual amicability. The threat posed by violent border skirmishing between Iran and Iraq was settled between the Shah and Saddam Hussein at Algiers in 1975, and Iran's increasing military might did not lead her into adventurous or an expansionist foreign policy.

The Shah's forces even put down a long festering Marxist guerrilla war in Oman's Dhofar region, achieving what more limited British and Jordanian forces had not managed in several years of fighting. The political volatility and unreliability of oil supplies was shown up on the two occasions of the Arab-Israeli wars in 1967 and 1973, at which times the Arab Gulf producers boycotted sales to America and Europe. The Palestinian question continued to radicalise Arab politics, and the occupation of Jerusalem became an emotional issue with the Arabs. Gulf politics became entangled with Pan-Arab interests, and Palestinians living in the Gulf mini-states gave cause for conservative alarm. But the enormous wealth brought about by leap-frogging oil prices allowed a measure of relaxation and brought considerable political and international clout. The concept of buying one's stability and bribing other's friendship became a pronounced and effective lever of diplomacy as utilised by the Gulf Arab states. Meanwhile, overall security of the Gulf was assured by Iran's growing military predominance, albeit reluctantly accepted by the Arab Gulf. Threats from radical Iraq were contained, but an unprecedented arms race ensued in the area.

The Soviet Union was meanwhile making the best out of a bad situation, entrenching its position in South Yemen and trying to retain a base with its increasingly reluctant ally, Iraq. Although the Iraqis had depended entirely on the Soviets for their arms, the French began to sell Mirage jets to both Iraq and Kuwait, and Baghdad became increasingly cool towards and independent of Moscow. Communist manufactures and industry proving shoddy, Baghdad moved closer economically to the West while maintaining an outward radical posture. After the loss of Arab prestige by Sadat due to the Camp David accords, Saddam Hussein moved to fill the leadership role. This was made easier by the collapse of the Shah and the decline of Iran's power in the Gulf. Assuming the mantle of leader of the non-aligned movement after Castro, Saddam Hussein, uneasy because of the overspill possibilities of Iran's Shi'ite revolt (as 60 per cent of Iraqis are Shi'ites while the ruling Takrit cabal are Sunnis) and with increasing signs of internal unrest, stumbled into war with Iran. Having failed to achieve a swift victory, or any victory worth mentioning (at the time of writing), the Gulf became for the first time the scene of military conflict. Whatever the outcome of the Iran/Iraq war, the Gulf has been saddled with a perennial future problem more explosive and destructive than the Palestinian issue could ever be.

With the Arab Gulf states siding — somewhat reluctantly — with Iraq, the old ethno-religious battle lines were redrawn, with Persians and Arabs looking across the Gulf at each other as old enemies.

Iran's much larger population and resource potentials will ensure her long-term supremacy — notwithstanding the short-term revolutionary chaos — in the Gulf and its revenge of the Iraqi invasion will not be long in coming. It will be interesting to see where Tehran eventually turns for succour and arms and how the superpowers will be pulled into this new conflict, even if they do not become entangled this time round. The Soviet's assiduous courting of the unpalatable regime of the Mullas is a sign of what they are willing to swallow in the hope of winning over strategically important Iran, and they have shown that they are quite willing and capable of doing a Somalia-Ethiopia flip between Iran and Iraq given half a chance.

At this point in time, Washington's options *vis-à-vis* Tehran seem rather limited, and, unless there is a quick change in regime in Iran, America will find herself ever more visibly entangled with the fate of Saudi Arabia and the sheikhdoms — a fact which will play into the hands of the radicals and inevitably the Soviet Union. For the danger to stability in the area is not so much from overt outside aggression as from subversion, fifth columns and radical *coups d'états*, as happened in Iran. So until the Iranian débâcle is reversed, Washington will become more bogged down than ever in the Gulf through its forward-basing policies designed to protect the *status quo* in Arabia, risking possible military entanglements. The nature of such contingencies and the opposing forces liable to be sucked in are no doubt the subject of much deliberation in both the Kremlin and the Pentagon. It is precisely such possible entanglements that will lead to superpower confrontation and a very real threat to world peace in the critical first years of the 1980s. With the Soviets bogged down in Afghanistan, their long-term energy resource prospects bleak, increasing cracks within their own colonial empire, a cumbersome and inefficient economy on the way to rapid decline, a prospective unsettling battle for leadership after Brezhnev's death and an unprecedented state of strategic parity with and military superiority over the West, it is not just this writer who is anxious about the future of the thirty Soviet divisions straddled along the length of the thousand-mile-long Iran-Soviet border. Whatever happens in Iran will determine the future shape of politics in the Persian Gulf, and possibly the shape of the political map of the world.

1 January 1981

1 THE GULF REGION IN THE GLOBAL SETTING
John C. Campbell

I

It is no new experience for the nations of the Persian Gulf to find their region an arena for the conflicts of the world's great powers. It is a new experience for the great powers themselves, however, to have to come to terms with their own dependence on the resources, and on the decisions, of those nations which in earlier times had been little more than the objects of their strategy and diplomacy. It is this new factor and its interaction with the old one that provide the new global setting for the Gulf region.

The familiar fact of great-power involvement remains, changed in form but not in essence. The United Kingdom, relieved of past concerns for the security of the routes of empire, is no longer the leading actor. Since the Second World War the United States has assumed the major responsibility for the defence of Western interests and for confronting or containing the southward push of Russian power begun under the tsars and continued under the Soviets. With but two great powers, or superpowers, in the world after the Second World War, ideologically hostile and fearful of each other's intentions, it was inevitable that the areas lying between them should be drawn into the global competition known as the Cold War.

The Gulf and the rest of the Middle East had long been labelled as strategically important by contending great powers for elementary reasons of geography. This region lay athwart major routes from Europe to the Far East and from Asia to Africa. It was on Russia's doorstep, a possible launching point for hostile action against Russia or a prime target of Russian expansion. It contained important resources of oil. Domination or control of particular parts of the Gulf region could give one power a decisive military advantage in case of war. Accordingly, no contending power wanted to risk an unfavourable shift of the balance in time of peace.

These considerations were still present in the period of the Cold War. General Eisenhower was only stating a generally accepted proposition when he said in 1951, 'So far as sheer value of territory is concerned there is no more strategically important area in the world.'[1] But in an age in which any general war would be nuclear and

1

enormously destructive through direct exchanges between the principal powers, the military value of peripheral areas did not loom so large. The possibility of limited war in the Middle East or the Gulf was not ignored, but neither the Soviet Union nor the United States appeared to accept the proposition that they could fight each other in that area without becoming involved elsewhere. Nevertheless, each felt it must be prepared. American policy in the 1950s rested on the doctrine of massive retaliation and on the building of a barrier of regional organisation and treaty commitments, backed by the ability to deploy military force along the northern tier (i.e. along the southern border of the USSR). Although this latter capability was never established on a credible scale, the general purpose of American policy remained fixed: to deter any Soviet aggression, limited or general, by the totality of the power of the United States.

In addition, the policy of containment was deliberately applied in a global context. Its high ideological content included the conviction that Communist aggression or expansion must not be allowed to succeed anywhere, lest it eventually succeed everywhere. The Gulf area obviously had weight in the global balance. If an appreciable portion of it should be brought under Soviet control, the political effects on the rest of the world might be disastrous for the West. But Washington did not engage in any fine calculations as to what areas of the 'free world' were important enough to defend. Such was the tension of the Cold War, especially after the attack on South Korea in 1950, that any gain for the Soviets (or Chinese) had to be resisted.

The United States was much concerned with what Secretary Dulles called 'indirect aggression', the taking over of a country through subversive agents, guerrilla movements or local Communist parties, all aided and manipulated from outside. It was not easy to resort to military intervention to deal with those contingencies, but it was important to have every feasible means available to prevent or reverse what the Communist powers might achieve in this way. The situation in Greece which gave rise to the Truman Doctrine was one in which an 'armed minority' aided and allegedly directed from outside was trying to overthrow an elected (and pro-Western) government. American military and economic aid to Turkey, Iraq, Iran and Pakistan was aimed at preventing any success which the Communists might gain by any combination of military threat, subversion and political pressure.

For the USSR, of course, the picture was quite different. The Gulf region was close to Soviet territory and far from the United States. Yet it was the latter which was forming blocs, sending arms and military missions, and setting up military bases that could support attacks on the Soviet Union. As a natural reaction the Soviet leaders could be expected to try to break up the American-sponsored bloc and deny to the United States use of the area for military purposes. To that end they worked to undermine governments which co-operated with the Americans and to encourage those forces which opposed them; that is, they did what the Americans were defining as 'indirect aggression'. That defensive strategy, however, fitted perfectly with an offensive strategy, dating from the Revolution of 1917, of support to local Communist parties and other 'progressive' forces in their efforts to combat Western imperialism and to weaken and replace the existing regimes.

This special pattern of superpower competition, it soon became clear, was less a direct contest of strength than a game in which each had to act through its relations with the local states and in the arena of local politics. Unquestionably the superpowers had a great deal of influence, given the differences in the attributes of power — not only military but others as well — but the local states were not without resources and strengths of their own. They profited from the new atmosphere of the post-war international order, from the existence of the United Nations where they could make their voices heard, and from the anti-colonial revolution then taking place. National sovereignty had acquired a new prestige and could not easily be ignored.

Several other factors, moreover, which marked the historical experience of the Gulf peoples, gave added weight to their ability to cope with outside powers. One was the combination of cultural continuity and tradition, even inertia, that had enabled the peoples of the Ottoman and Persian empires to absorb pressures from outside and survive for centuries despite internal weakness. A second was the fact that British power was for years exerted along the routes important to the Royal Navy and to British commerce in a pattern of treaties and arrangements (unequal ones, to be sure) with local rulers, rather than in the pattern of the conquest of India. The British found no reason to try to dominate the interior of the Arabian Peninsula or to destroy the independence of Persia. A third factor was the room for manoeuvre which the balance between outside powers and the configurations of world politics allowed to smaller states caught in the middle; Iran, for example, was able to play the British against the Russians, and the Germans and later the Americans against both. Finally, with the upheavals of two world wars, the growth of nationalism, the Russian Revolution and its world-wide impact, creation of the mandate system and acceptance of the principle of eventual independence for Iraq and other Arab states, and the increasing influence of the United States as a friend of democracy and self-determination, the basis was laid for the Gulf states to be subjects, not just objects, of the international relations of their region.

The containment policy of the United States, which sprang into being during 1945–6 with diplomatic moves supporting Turkey and Iran against Soviet pressure, and was given solemn official expression in the Truman Doctrine of 1947, was intended not just as an American or Western enterprise but as a collaborative effort with the states of the Middle East and the Gulf. Its purpose, in the genuine belief of the United States, was linked to their vital interest in the maintenance of their integrity and independence. The collaborative aspect of the policy thus rested on the assumption that the governments and peoples of the region saw matters in this light, that they looked upon the Soviet Union and Communism as the main threat to their independence and upon the United States and the West as their natural allies in meeting it.

This assumption was only partially valid. In those countries which bordered on the Soviet Union it was generally accepted. It made possible the formation of the Baghdad Pact, intended as a barrier to Soviet aggression or penetration along the northern tier. It found a mixed and preponderantly negative response in the Arab world, where in the eyes of powerful political forces, in government and outside, the principal threat was not the Soviet Union but Israel, other Arab states, the European colonial powers, or the United States itself. American policy in practice represented an effort to apply a rather simple formula — common defence of the free world against Communism — to a very complex local situation. It involved the United States in the local conflicts of the Middle East and the Gulf and in the internal politics of individual states, for in seeking, finding and aiding friends and allies in the region the Americans became the enemies of all those who for reasons of their own were opposed to those friends and allies. Some of the strongest forces of Arab nationalism, in order to achieve ends of the highest legitimacy to themselves — liberation, independence, unity, recovery of Palestine — turned for help to the only power which could counterbalance American influence, the Soviet Union. It was partly the American policy of containment that opened the doors to a larger role for the Soviet Union in the Middle East. The most dramatic signal of this change in the Eastern Mediterranean was Egypt's turning to the Soviets for arms in 1955, and in the Gulf region was the revolution of 1958 in Iraq.

In the 1950s and 1960s the Soviet Union made extraordinary gains, increasing its political influence and improving its military position. But as one looks back on that period, it is perhaps more extraordinary that the gains were not greater. It could even be said that despite its failures the American policy of containment succeeded, in that no country of the region became a Soviet satellite on the East European model. That result was not due entirely to the skill of American diplomacy. If anything, Soviet diplomacy was even less effective in handling local leaders and exploiting opportunities. The basic reason was that, in situations where the overwhelming force at the disposal of the outside powers was not a viable instrument, the political gains they made were always subject to reversal in any local state by a change in regime or in policy. Governments which showed their independence by calling in the Soviet Union to frustrate the British or the Americans were not of a mind to give up that independence to their new friends.

The relatively stable situation with respect to security in the area of the Gulf and the Arabian Peninsula, in contrast to the Arab-Israel region, was due to a number of favourable factors. One was the continuance of a British role for more than a decade after the Suez affair of 1956 brought British influence in the Eastern Mediterranean area close to the vanishing point. By retaining membership in the Central Treaty Organization (CENTO), a military presence in the Gulf, treaty relations with Oman and the Trucial States, and a security guarantee to Kuwait, the British were a stabilising force even as they debated at length why they were there and whether they could afford to stay. Their departure from Aden in 1968, to be succeeded there by a radical Marxist regime, was no contribution to the stability of the region, but the coming to full independence of Bahrain and the United Arab Emirates was accomplished with a minimum of difficulty.

The British presence in the Gulf could only be effective, however, because of the steadiness of the two large states on either side of the Gulf, Iran and Saudi Arabia. Thanks to oil wealth, firm monarchical leadership (in Iran after 1953 and in Saudi Arabia after 1964), and their ability to contain the expansive thrust of radical Arab nationalism or Marxism — whether from Cairo, Baghdad, Moscow or elsewhere — they laid a basis for regional security that made it possible for the British to withdraw in 1971 without bringing on a period of unrest and crisis or creating a vacuum to be filled by another outside power.

When the United States, in the Nixon Administration, began to talk about a 'two-pillar' system for the security of the Gulf, with Iran and Saudi Arabia as the pillars, there was an element of wishful thinking in the idea, as Saudi Arabia had but a very limited capability and Iran's willingness to co-operate with Arab states was open to question. Yet the American approach, in stressing the responsibility of local states and refraining from moving in to replace the British, was well attuned to the mood of the Gulf rulers and well calculated to keep the Soviets from moving in. It was based also on firmly established relations with both Iran and Saudi Arabia, including security commitments to both of them and a strong mutual interest involving oil, trade and development. It was this 'special relationship' with each of the two Gulf states, rather than the fading CENTO, that the United States saw as offering the best chance for maintaining a stable balance in the Gulf region, keeping Soviet influence to a safe level and preserving the vital Western interest in access to Gulf oil. The events of 1973–4 and then those of 1978–9 put those views and policies to a severe test.

II

In the closing months of 1973, as the October War shook not only the Middle East but the entire world, the oil states of the Gulf asserted a new 'oil power' that neither they nor the industrial countries which were the main consumers of their oil were truly aware they possessed. The Arab states, including America's great friend, Saudi Arabia, restricted the production and export of oil, in order to strike at those countries, primarily the United States, that were aiding Israel. The Arab-Israel conflict and relations with the Gulf states, which American diplomacy for years had tried to keep separated, had now merged indissolubly together. Then OPEC, with the full participation and support of Saudi Arabia and Iran, raised the price of oil fourfold. At the time, this reversal of the historic dependence of the underdeveloped on the developed, loudly applauded by the Third World and by the Soviet Union, seemed to put the vital interests of the West in jeopardy, to break its solidarity, and to call into question the very foundations of American policy in the region. It was at this time, when the Europeans and Japanese were bending over backwards to win the favour of the oil producers, that articles appeared in the American press suggesting the use of force to seize Gulf oilfields, American officials spoke of the need to force down the price of oil, and the Secretary of State said that a nation would inevitably use force if faced with 'strangulation'.[2]

The persisting atmosphere of confrontation, however, did not reflect the underlying long-term interests on both sides. The success of American diplomacy in arranging negotiated truce arrangements which Israel agreed with Egypt and with Syria and in mending American relations with the Arab world gave Saudi Arabia the opportunity to end the oil embargo and restore traditional ties of co-operation with the United States. The oil-consuming countries organised to protect themselves against new interruptions of supply, but at the same time they adjusted as best they could to the new OPEC prices. The practical outcome of the crisis was that the oil states of the Gulf had a great deal more money and a great deal more power. What they wanted to do with it, however, was not to bankrupt the West but to buy the West's goods, skills, technology and arms, and with them to complete the process of emancipation from outside influence and solve their own national and regional problems to their satisfaction.

The general shape of the security problem in the Gulf did not change. Both Iran and Saudi Arabia began to buy American arms in much larger quantities in order to fulfil their expanded roles and ambitions. All the oil states of the Gulf embarked on vast new plans of development, using their expanded revenues to buy capital goods and technology from America, Europe and Japan. Even Iraq, though closely tied to the USSR in economic and military arrangements, sealed by a formal treaty in 1972, turned to the West as the only place it could get what it needed to keep up the pace of development. The *rapprochement* of Iraq with Iran in 1975 was made possible by the former's success against the Kurdish rebellion and the latter's decision to cease aiding the Kurds, but in a larger sense it was the result of the new power and independence of all the Gulf states. They were acting on their own, not as clients of one or another superpower. Whether Moscow approved or disapproved of Iraq's actions is not clear. For public consumption it voiced its approval, but it was evident that Soviet influence in Baghdad and in the region as a whole had not grown as a result of the oil crisis and the change in bargaining power between the Gulf states and the West.[3] Russia's principal gain was economic: its own oil now brought higher prices on the world market.

A major change took place in 1978–9: the revolution in Iran. It grew from internal conditions, not from external stimuli, and the new regime, virulently anti-American, gave no sign of alignment with the USSR. But the change still represented a shift in the superpower balance, whether seen in geopolitical or psychological terms, because of the obvious loss of prestige and position suffered by the United States. The regime of the Shah, who had been a friend and ally, was gone; so were the ties with the Iranian military, the monitoring stations near the Soviet frontier, and the close involvement with the Shah's development projects. Above all, the psychological effects were deep: on Iran, where the victorious revolutionary forces were taking every opportunity to humiliate the United States, the ally and supporter of the hated Shah, even to the point of attacking its embassy in Tehran and holding captive its diplomatic personnel; and on America, whose people had a sense of disaster, of weakness and failure, calling into question the entire basis of policy in the Gulf region.

Iran's future alignment was not clear, because nothing was clear in the chaotic situation that evolved. The Ayatollah Khomeini and the dominant religious elements in the leadership had no sympathy or ties with the USSR, but it was not apparent that the same could be said of Marxist and other radical groups which had shared in the revolution (although the Communist Tudeh Party had a very limited following). Dissidence and separatism among non-Iranian peoples in frontier areas, moreover, were open to exploitation by the Soviets. The latter, using due caution and not undertaking any adventures, were giving verbal encouragement to all Iranian moves directed against America and seeking to improve opportunities for exploitation when the time might be ripe, towards the ultimate aim of a 'friendly' (i.e. compliant) Iran.

The Soviet invasion of Afghanistan in December 1979 was not directly related to the events in Iran. Yet they may have contributed to it in two ways: (1) through the astonishing strength of militant Islam which, in the ascendant in Iran, gave impetus to the resistance to the pro-Soviet regime that had been in power in Kabul since April 1978 and could have repercussions in the Soviet Union itself; and (2) through the obvious weakening of the US position in the region, which may have influenced the decision of the Soviets to move in.

The effect, of course, was a shift in the balance, bringing the Soviet ground and air forces closer to the Indian Ocean and to the oilfields and oil transport routes of the Persian Gulf, and increasing Soviet pressure on Iran and Pakistan. Whether the move into Afghanistan was primarily defensive, to save a satellite regime and avert an intolerable blow to Soviet prestige, or to counter manoeuvres by China, or was a step towards further expansion, the rest of the world had to deal with the fact that the military frontier of the USSR had been moved southward and that a former buffer state had been absorbed.

III

The present security problems are of three kinds: (1) those stemming from the global concerns of the superpowers which extend to the Gulf region, and in a sense are imposed on its peoples, just as they extend to other regions of the world; (2) those related to the policies of the regional state towards outside powers, whether based on fear or confidence, economic strength or economic need, ideological affinity or cultural aversion; and (3) those arising from the local and regional aims and policies of the Gulf states within and among themselves.

Let us consider for a moment, perhaps in too mechanistic a way but as a necessary means of capturing their primary concerns, how the problem looks to the two superpowers. The peace of the world, in default of an accepted working system of international law and security, depends on the balance of military power between them: the global balance in strategic weapons, which provides mutual deterrence on that level, supplemented by a balance at a lower level in regions where both powers have vital interests and where military action could either immediately provoke global nuclear war or set in motion a series of actions and counteractions leading to the same result. These are truisms that have been accepted for so long that people tend to forget them. In the Gulf area the two superpowers have been and are in competition with each other, but they have had a common interest in keeping that competition below the level of military conflict and presumably wish to continue to do so. But neither knows what risks the rival power will take, and neither wishes by displaying weakness to encourage risk-taking by the other.

To preserve the military stand-off, each power has to have the capability of bringing military force to bear in the Gulf region. It is by no means clear on the Western side how much military force, and in what locations, is necessary for this purpose. It may be that in a crisis that threatened to attain global proportions the United States would not wish to commit forces to this region at all. The main purpose is not to be sure of winning a local war but to deter any military move from the other side that would jeopardise a vital American interest. It is a matter of adequately understood intentions and of political will as well as of military forces and dispositions, but the latter constitute an essential element. The reach of Soviet military power has been steadily increasing with the build-up of air and naval power, and Washington can at least imagine a series of Soviet moves that could threaten the vital oil routes from the Gulf through the Strait of Hormuz and across the Indian Ocean.[4]

Provoked by the invasion of Afghanistan, the United States saw the need for creating a stronger capability for military action in the region. It was to consist of greater naval power in the Indian Ocean, the building up of a 'rapid deployment force' that could be moved to where it was needed in case of crisis, and the use of naval and air facilities in nearby states willing to co-operate.[5] This capability was not yet in being at the time President Carter declared, on 23 January 1980, that the United States would resist with all appropriate means, including military force, any Soviet move (presumably in the direction of the oilfields, the Gulf or the Indian Ocean) representing an assault on the vital interests of the United States. The aim of the declaratory policy was deterrence: figuratively drawing a line on the map and letting the Kremlin know that crossing it would mean conflict with the United States, whether or not the latter was ready to contest every metre of Middle East territory.

The President's declaration, incidentally, bore some resemblance to the statements which both the Soviet Union and the United States had made regarding Iran in the autumn of 1978, as the Shah's rule was disintegrating and neither power was sure what the other might do; so each warned the other of the dangers of military intervention. But so far as the United States was concerned, the Carter statement of January 1980 was a much more measured and portentous announcement of policy.

For the most part the superpowers have created this system of security, based on balance and deterrence, by their own unilateral actions, building up their respective military positions and seeking allies and clients in the Gulf region. Each has posed as defender and protector of the true interests of the local nations against the designs of the other. That was the rationale on the American side, as we have seen, of the Truman Doctrine and all the military dispositions, alliances and aid programmes that followed. On the Soviet side it was the rationale for concentration of forces on the southern frontiers of the USSR, for open threats of force against the 'aggressive' Baghdad Pact and the Central Treaty Organization, for aid to 'national liberation movements' and 'progressive forces' and to states such as Iraq where those forces were in power.

There is another and less dangerous way, however, by which the superpowers might contribute to security in the region, and that is by agreement with one another to control and lower the level of their military confrontation or even to accept the idea of spheres of influence. The 1970s, after all, were the era of *détente* in Europe with a *de facto* mutual acceptance of spheres of influence, creating a situation of greater stability than existed in the time of extreme Cold War. In the Middle East and the Gulf such a stabilisation has not been possible. Neither superpower has recognised the other as entitled to have a preferred position in any Gulf state (even though in fact it might have such a position). The Soviet Union has shown that it is prepared to live for long periods with a situation it regards as basically intolerable. It accepts Turkey's membership in NATO. It conducted normal relations and economic co-operation with the Shah's Iran despite the Shah's close ties with the United States. But the Soviets have not regarded such situations as anything but transitory. While they have shown that they can be extraordinarily patient, and a transitory situation may last a long time, a study of Soviet writing and Soviet policy over the years leaves little doubt that what they seek in the long run in the Gulf region is a position of preponderant influence.[6] Their relative gains in military power, their sense that the 'correlation of forces' is working in their favour, must have strengthened their view that that goal is attainable.

There is no clear line, as there is in Europe, beyond which military ventures by the superpowers are ruled out. The situation in the Middle East and in the Gulf area has no such stability, no equivalent to the Helsinki Agreement. The United States has always thought of the containment line in the Middle East and the Gulf region as running along the southern boundary of the Soviet Union. Now, with the Soviet occupation of Afghanistan, perhaps the line is displaced southward *de facto*, even though the Soviet Union is being pressed verbally to withdraw its forces. The remainder of the region, in the American definition, is to be kept free, i.e. out of Soviet hands. The Soviets, of course, see that interpretation as an attempt to claim the entire region as a sphere of American influence. That is unacceptable to them and actually is not insisted upon by the United States. The Americans have had to deal at one time or another with the reality of preponderant Soviet influence in Afghanistan (well before 1979), Iraq, Syria, Yemen and the PDRY, but they gave no formal recognition of it, just as Moscow accepted no American preponderance in Saudi Arabia, Kuwait, the United Arab Emirates or Iran. Each superpower hopes and works for changes of regime and of alignment in the states which now lean to the other side or which choose strict non-alignment. The result is continuing tension and insecurity in the superpower balance, even as, on the global level, that balance operates to maintain the peace.

The Gulf states, in any case, do not wish to be labelled as being in any power's sphere of influence, formally or *de facto*. If the superpowers can reduce the risks of war by moderating their competition, well and good, but not if it is done at the expense of the states of the region.

If spheres of influence are unacceptable and the present open competition for the alignment or realignment of local states is uncertain and dangerous, there remain two possibilities of achieving greater stability through agreement of the superpowers. One is the recognition by both powers of the non-alignment of the entire group of Gulf states, thus making it unnecessary for either power to seek allies there as a means of denying the area to the other. That is a serious and promising possibility, to which we shall come back later. The other field for negotiation and agreement by the superpowers is that of the limitation of arms levels, their own and those of the local states.

Limiting arms deliveries is a subject much talked about in the United States. Both the Carter Administration and Congress professed to see the need for checking the flow of arms into the Gulf region as it reached flood proportions in the late 1970s. But they found it difficult to do very much about it, since arms sales are an integral part of the complex military and economic relationships the United States has developed with its friends in the region, and those relationships they do not wish to put in jeopardy. It was an extraneous factor, the revolution in Iran, that put an end to the largest of the arms sales programmes, but deliveries to Saudi Arabia continued at a high level, and the Yemen Arab Republic and Oman were added to the list of recipients. Against the strong arguments that the provision of arms is necessary both to enhance security and to keep friendly governments friendly, the more general considerations — that arms races increase the risks of war, that the United States should not have the role of the world's leading 'merchant of death', and that the Gulf countries cannot really use the advanced weapons they are buying and should spend their money more wisely — do not seem weighty enough to bring the United States to adopt severe limits on its own arms deliveries or to make an agreement with other suppliers (including the USSR) to impose such limits. Nor have the Soviets shown much interest, although they may well do so in the future; since most of the arms going in are from the United States, it will be to the Soviet Union's advantage to have limits placed on them.

Agreement with the Soviets to limit or reduce the two powers' own military presence in the region is another matter. Here it is or should be possible to agree on limits or reductions that do not change the existing balance of power and deterrence and at the same time reduce the tension and the costs that go with it. The bilateral negotiations on the naval deployments of the two powers in the Indian Ocean are a case in point. UN resolutions for the denuclearisation of the Indian Ocean or for declaring it a zone of peace have no practical effect. Serious negotiations between Moscow and Washington to freeze or eventually reduce their naval presence, such as took place in 1977 and 1978, could conceivably produce results. But those talks virtually broke down even before the Soviet move into Afghanistan, and after that they could hardly be resurrected, as a build-up of naval power in the Indian Ocean was a central part of the American response.[7] Soviet-American *détente*, since the hopeful days of 1972, has demonstrated its fragility and its limitations. It has not yet been extended to the Middle East or to the Gulf region except in the most elementary sense of recognising the common interest in avoiding a nuclear war.

IV

Considering the awesome power arrayed on both sides of the global balance, the states of the Gulf region might appear to be wholly without influence on the maintenance of security in their area. That is not the case. They have to adjust to the facts of powers, yes, but the balance between the superpowers and the recognised rights of sovereignty give them the opportunity to make choices. Each state's main concern is the preservation of its own independence and security. If it fears attack or pressure from one superpower, it may align itself clearly and openly with the other; it may be more cautious, leaning to one side but avoiding unambiguous alignment with it while seeking reinsurance through agreements and friendly relations with the other; or it may choose a neutral position, depending on the balance, on the absence of a threat to either side, and on an ability to manoeuvre between them. These are not sharply defined alternatives but they give an idea of the range of choice. It can be argued that Iran during the past thirty years has followed one or other of these policies at different stages, and at times has combined elements of all three. The regional states have made their decisions, moreover, not only against the background of relations with the big powers. For them security and national interest is as much involved, perhaps more so, in their relations with each other, and their alignments with outside powers may be useful, or dangerous, to them in that context.

The point is that while the global balance and rivalry of the superpowers may dominate the destiny of the Gulf region, as it does other regions, by virtue of the potential for war and the use of force, neither Soviet expansionism nor Western imperialism dominates the states of that region; and indeed the politics of those states, in the absence of war, has a determining influence on the shape which the superpower competition and balance takes there. The considerations of national security, economic interest or ideology that move Middle East governments and peoples determine whether an outside power secures a military base, a military alliance, a privileged position or a special relationship: or encounters indifference or hostility.

Let us look at some cases. Iraq, in the era of Nuri es-Said, signed the Baghdad Pact and thus aligned itself with the West. Behind that decision were various reasons: the historic ties of the ruling group in Iraq with the United Kingdom, the desire to get arms from the United States; the fact that Iraq did not feel threatened by the West; the fear of radical movements in the Arab world and at home. Nuri saw stability on the international level linked with stability at home. On the Western side the position of the United States and the United Kingdom *vis-á-vis* the USSR was perceptibly strengthened by his decision to join the new regional security pact, and therefore they acquired an interest in his maintaining his position at home. So much were these factors tied together that when revolution came to Iraq in 1958, a combined movement of Arab nationalism and social protest, it brought about almost automatically a *de facto* reversal of alliances, withdrawal from the Baghdad Pact, a turning to the USSR and the Soviet bloc, and a potentially drastic shift in the global balance. From a mood of satisfaction at having contained Soviet expansion by building a wall of Western-allied states across the northern tier, Washington was thrown into a mood of pessimism and fear that Soviet power now extended through Iraq to the shores of the Persian Gulf and would move on further into the Arab world. Iraq by its own actions determined how the two superpowers looked at their own security problem.

Under a succession of radical regimes since 1958 Iraq has been generally at odds with the Western powers and especially with the United States, because of the Palestine question, disputes with Western oil companies and ideological antagonism towards 'the imperialists'. Iraq opened the door to military and other aid from Moscow, and these ties were measurably strengthened after the Ba'th regime took power in 1968. But the road of collaboration was not always smooth. The ideology of anti-imperialism was a factor of solidarity, although the Iraqi Communist Party was often more an obstacle than a help to good relations. The global interests of a superpower did not automatically coincide with the more parochial interests of a regional state. Iraq was more or less isolated in the Gulf and in inter-Arab councils, where its only friend was Libya. It was never able to get full Soviet support for its Arab policies, particularly its hostility to Syria and its extreme stand on Palestine; nor was Moscow able to count on Iraq's support for all its international policies. The role of patron of the Baghdad regime created obstacles for the Soviet Union in its relations with other Gulf states, but since it had so few friends and allies it did not wish to lose its one foothold in Iraq. Iraq, for its part, still felt the need for the Moscow connection but took care to limit the military aspects (reports of a Soviet naval base at the port of Um Qasr were not substantiated) and to look for other ties, both in the region and further afield, that suited its own rather than Moscow's interests.

Iran differed from Iraq in that it had long experience of invasion and pressure from the north. Exposed also to British incursions from the south, it had developed a policy of neutrality to safeguard its independence. But with the disappearance of the British threat after the Second World War the Soviet threat was all the more ominous, and it was natural for Iran to turn to the distant United States as the guarantor of its security. In this case too the ideological factor influenced foreign policy. The government of Iran feared Russia not only as an imperial power but as the propagator of an alien ideology, Communism, with ties to a revolutionary party in Iran, the Tudeh. In the revolutionary situation that developed from the oil nationalisation crisis of the early 1950s, the Tudeh and the anti-Western nationalist forces of Mohammed Mosaddeq were not able effectively to join forces to overthrow the Shah, and the Soviet Union cautiously kept hands off.[8] Thereafter Iran made an advantageous deal with the Western oil companies, joined the Baghdad Pact and relied increasingly on the United States.

For twenty-five years the foreign policy of Iran reflected the outward strength and enhanced confidence of the regime. The Shah retained his concern with the threat from the Soviets, but by the 1960s he felt strong enough to give them a pledge that he would not permit any power (i.e. the United States) to have strategic bases on Iran's territory; he was also ready to establish normal relations with them, and to make large-scale economic deals. He retained his reliance on the United States for ultimate security and for arms supply, but he regulated the military relationship in accordance with his concept of Iran's interest. As his military establishment grew, he envisaged for his country a dominant role in the Gulf and even beyond it; he gave substance to his pretensions by sending Iranian armed forces to Oman to help put down the radical revolt in Dhofar and to safeguard navigation through the Strait of Hormuz. Yet it was not military power but the ability to make its own decisions that gave Iran the capacity to affect the superpower balance and the nature of the security system in the Gulf. Although Washington encouraged the idea of Iran as a pillar of security in the Gulf, the Shah did not consider himself a surrogate of the United States. His goal was a strong and independent role for Iran.

The revolution that brought Ayatollah Khomeini to power changed Iran's domestic scene totally, but its effect on foreign policy was less than appeared on the surface. True, the new regime repudiated the Shah and all his works, including the American connection and the effort to make Iran a leading power in the region. But the revolution did not change the fundamental national interest in the country's sovereignty and integrity. It strengthened the drive for an independent policy, not tied to that of any big power, and for a return to historic traditions in dealing with the outside world. America was the declared enemy, but there was no doubt of the fear of and resistance to Russia, especially after the latter's take-over of Afghanistan. The chaotic state of affairs within the country in the first year of the revolutionary regime raised the question whether Iran could have any effective foreign policy at all. Yet it was clear enough that, barring intervention by force from outside, Iran would make its own decisions.

Saudi Arabia has some similarities to Iran in its geopolitical position, but also significant differences. It has never been under threat of attack from the Soviet Union, but its ruling family has had a fixed ideological aversion to Communism and a tendency to equate it with forces of radical change that were a more immediate threat to the existing system. The special relationship with the United States, which began even before the Second World War when King Abdul

Aziz ibn Saud, distrustful of the British, granted an oil concession to an American company, was a natural one for the Saudis in that it brought real economic benefits as well as security. Saudi Arabia was both a rich and a weak state. It needed an external connection to compensate for its weakness in the face of regional threats (for example from Nasser's Egypt in the 1960s or from radical forces elsewhere in the peninsula in the 1970s), and to help it translate its oil wealth into development. Saudi Arabia never joined any American-sponsored regional security system directed against the USSR, but by its congenital anti-Communism and its special relationship with the United States it played its part in shaping the superpower balance in the Gulf region. Even so, while relying ultimately on America for security, the Saudi rulers sought an independent foreign policy and even a guiding role in inter-Arab relations, using their money as an instrument of political influence.

The three large states — Iran, Saudi Arabia and Iraq — largely determined the international relations of the Gulf. The others were too small to have a significant impact, although Kuwait and the UAE had large quantities of oil and therefore plenty of money. In the realm of high international politics they tended to follow rather than to lead. But some had a potential for trouble, either of their own or of others' making: Kuwait because of its wealth, the volatile Palestinian element in its population, and its vulnerability to aggression by Iraq, which coveted its coastline; Bahrain, the UAE and Oman because of the newness of their independence, possible political instability and the danger of being squeezed by Arab-Iranian rivalry; the PDRY because of the threat of revolution it represented and the danger of its being used by others, the USSR in particular, to undermine other governments in the region.

V

As the Gulf states have chosen what kinds of relations and what degrees of association to have with the two superpowers, there has always been in the background an alternative — non-alignment. This can be a very strong trend because it has historical roots and receives nominal adherence even when it does not wholly square with the facts. Saudi Arabia and Oman are close to the United States in security matters; Iraq has a security relationship with the Soviet Union, as has the PDRY. All of them, however, together with the new Iran, the Yemen Arab Republic and the smaller Gulf States, take part in the world-wide non-aligned movement and attended its latest conference at Havana in 1979.[9] Whatever their ties with the great powers, this is where they feel most at home. They are not and

will not for many years be in the 'first world' of the industrial demo-
cracies and have no desire to join the 'second world' of the Soviet
bloc. China may be a useful counterweight but is too distant,
unknown and unknowable to invite close association; and China
itself in this context assumes the guise of a Third World country. The
major Gulf states are, therefore, in and of the Third World of the
non-aligned, and because of their wealth they aspire to a role of
leadership in that company.

There is hardly a Gulf State which has not declared its aim of
greater independence and freedom from the military presence of
outside powers. Most of them are aware, however, that non-alignment can be more effective if it reflects regional and not purely
national policy. The Shah of Iran broached the idea of a regional
security system in the Gulf to Iraq, Saudi Arabia and others in 1975.
The move proved premature. The Arab states, already members of a
formal multilateral treaty system of their own, the Arab League,
were not ready for it. Past differences and potential Arab-Iranian
rivalry in the Gulf, ideological conflict between Iraq's radical
Ba'athists and the conservative regimes elsewhere in the region and
the struggle then going on in Oman's Dhofar province all combined
to make it more difficult.

The mere fact of the discussions, however, bore witness to a common sense of responsibility and a new way of looking at continuing
ties of individual states with outside powers. Each would keep its
existing ties — Iraq would continue getting arms and other aid from
the Soviets, while others got theirs from America — but the concept
of regional solidarity put some limits on the ways in which those ties
could or would be used, either by regional states or by the outside
powers.

For the near future the great question mark is revolutionary Iran.
Until it has an effective government in control of the country it can
hardly have a regional role, except perhaps in the influence of its
Islamic ideology, which tends to be supportive of Afghan resistance
to the Soviets but disruptive (because it is Shi'a rather than Sunni) of
relations with nearby Arab countries. Nevertheless, the changes in
Iran and Afghanistan have stimulated new thinking and new
exchanges by Gulf states on the subject of the common security,
including consultations between the two leading but ideologically
divergent Arab states, Iraq and Saudi Arabia.

The Soviet invasion of Afghanistan, of course, also provoked the
United States into a more active effort to organise security in the
Gulf region against any further Soviet advance. Yet the degree of
military co-operation forthcoming from states of the area was, to
say the least, uncertain. The fate of CENTO, which had been dealt a
mortal blow by the Iranian Revolution and was formally dissolved

shortly thereafter, was not an encouraging precedent for a new endeavour to create a Western-sponsored regional security system. Iran and Iraq, two key states whose security was threatened from the north, were totally unreceptive to the idea, as was America's good friend, Saudi Arabia.

Any security system in the Gulf region, whether linked to outside powers or limited to local states, must overcome or neutralise the sources of local conflict if it is to be effective. There is probably no way of preventing all conflict among Gulf states, in view of the many historical territorial disputes (*inter alia* Iran-Iraq, Iraq-Kuwait, Iran-Saudi Arabia, Abu Dhabi (UAE)-Saudi Arabia, Oman-Saudi Arabia) which can flare up even though some have been nominally settled by negotiation, to say nothing of unrest and rebellion within states (for example the possible resumption of guerrilla war in Oman's Dhofar province or the outbreak of revolt by ethnic minorities such as the Kurds in Iran or Iraq) which can bring intervention from outside.

The interlocking of regional conflicts with the superpower competition maximises the dangers for all concerned: it encourages local states to look outside the region for support against their neighbours; it encourages outside powers to play on local disputes in order to gain advantage over rival powers; it tends to blow up local conflicts into larger ones by the operation of prior commitments and the fear of losing friends and allies. All those dangers would be reduced if the states of the region could move purposefully and in concert to assert their non-alignment in relation to the superpowers and to organise their own system of security; and if the superpowers, by express agreement or in practice or both, would respect those decisions and would not seek bases or special security ties within the region. Local conflicts would not disappear, but they might have a greater chance of being settled or contained by collective procedures or by the operation of a regional balance of power, with a good chance that outside powers would see their own interests better served by remaining aloof than by intervention.[10]

These possibilities have an air of unreality in the present day and age, for both local states and outside powers have other conceptions of what is required for their interests, their destiny or their security. For those in the Gulf or the West who think of a revived CENTO or for those in Moscow or among the radical groups of the region who see emerging a new socialist order under Soviet leadership, the idea of a non-aligned regional system is not compatible with their own. For the local states the issues are complex and not always presented in clearest form. None wishes to cut outside ties when a reliable regional system does not yet exist. Actually, both these trends, that of interlocking and that of regional non-alignment, are present in the thinking of political leaders and others in the leading Gulf countries, and the two will be contending, probably without sharp and definitive resolution, for some time into the future.

VI

We have dwelt long, perhaps over-long, on the security problems because they are complex, they involve the ultimate questions of peace and war, and because decisions of all parties, local states as well as outside powers, are based so heavily on them. Nevertheless, the real problems of the years ahead, having in mind the global setting of the affairs of the Gulf, are likely to be economic and political. The oil revolution of the early 1970s had important effects other than on military strategy, military ambitions, the balance of power and the security ties of the Gulf states with outside powers.

The main result of the rise in oil prices was to give almost all the Gulf states, large and small, more economic power and more influence on affairs beyond their own region. At home they had large sums available for development. The mere presence of so much money and so much new economic activity tended to take the edge off the appeal of liberation movements and other revolutionary causes. Of course, social change wrought by economic development was bound to generate pressure for change in political institutions as well, and in Iran the combination of conspicuous waste, economic stress, cultural shock and the rigidity and repressions of the political system produced a popular religious-political revolution that overthrew the Shah and brought new elements into contention for power. Although Iran's economy was severely shaken and oil production was at half the pre-revolution level, that production remained crucial to Iran itself, to fellow members of OPEC, and to the oil-importing countries of the world.

The big questions for the future revolved round the positions the Gulf states would find themselves in the world economy, and separately with the developed countries of the West (including Japan), with the Communist countries, and with the Third World. These questions have to do mostly with oil and gas: how much and how rapidly the Gulf states will produce it; to whom they will sell it; what they will do with the money it brings; how long the oil reserves will last; and what situation they will face as the oil age declines. These are indeed big questions, the answers to which do not depend on the Gulf states alone. They depend partly on the main consuming countries, which will be dependent on the oil of the Gulf for the next decade and probably longer. They may depend also on the Soviet Union and Eastern Europe as their demand for oil approaches the point where it will exceed their own supply.

The first thing to note is that oil power is not absolute. OPEC, and especially those of its members in the Gulf region with their very large reserves, have the economic power virtually to dictate the world price of oil, but they cannot do so in total disregard of the damage that may be done to the economies of those states that depend on imported oil, for they would thereby damage their own interests in development and investment and might provoke violent reaction. The surplus oil money certain Gulf states are generating cannot be used indiscriminately; it cannot be wasted (as much of it is now) without heavy cost to the interests of both consumers and producers. By the logic of their complementary economies the Gulf oil producers and the oil-consuming industrial states have come to see that their common interest is a trade-off between oil and development. Co-operation does not always proceed easily and evenly, however, for the terms of the trade-off are by no means agreed, either as to supply or as to price.

Both the Gulf states and the West must look ahead to situations of strain. Their nature and timing are not wholly predictable because the oil supply itself, from the Gulf and from other sources, is not predictable. Yet we can be fairly sure that there will come a time in the 1980s, before the West has developed adequate alternative sources of energy, when its demand for oil will go beyond what OPEC is willing or able to supply, when the strong interest of the consumers will be to get more and more oil from the Gulf and that of the Gulf states will be to raise the price, limit production and keep oil in the ground as an asset for the future. It is at such a point that the hypothetical scenes of dispute and conflict talked about in 1973 and 1974 may become reality.

This is an aspect of the global setting of the future that both consumers and producers would do well to foresee and to guard against. Unless agreements have been reached in advance, within each group as well as between groups, the strain could easily unleash situations of cut-throat rivalry and conflict from which all would suffer. It is not useful to speculate on just what those possibilities would be, but there can be little doubt that Saudi Arabia would be at the centre of them. As the country with the largest oil resources, it would have the most influential position in determining OPEC's decisions on supply and on price or, if OPEC did not hold together, in determining whether the West's economy would face readjustment or disaster. Because of its key position, however, Saudi Arabia might be exposed to pressures, both from within the region and from outside, that its political structure could not withstand.

The present American relationship with Saudi Arabia is a very comprehensive one that seems to satisfy the interests of both parties.

Although uncertainty and mistrust exist on both sides, the 'special relationship' gives both some sense of assurance about the future. It could be a false assurance on the side of the Saudis if they are engulfed in political turmoil at home or in the region, or on the American side if the Saudis find they have a stronger interest in limiting than in expanding oil production. Potential trouble lies also in the thirst of other consuming states for the oil of Saudi Arabia, which some see as having been for too long the near-exclusive preserve of the United States. It will be important for the United States to be in harmony with the other consumers and for Saudi Arabia to be in harmony with the other producers *before* the strains of a supply-demand crisis appear, and that is by no means assured.

The Soviet Union by that time may be much more concerned with the oil of the Gulf than it is today. Now that the Gulf states have virtually completed their take-over of the properties of the Western oil companies and demonstrated their power over the West, the Kremlin can no longer make much of the old theme of unstinting Soviet support for the struggle against the oil monopolies. The Soviet Union is left out of the rapid expansion of development and of foreign trade taking place in the region since it cannot be a major market for Gulf oil and cannot provide the goods those countries want. It may become more involved if its general economic decisions bring it into greater participation in the world economy, but it does not have the hard currency or the advanced equipment to make itself a sought-after partner. The established Soviet pattern, that of bilateral barter deals, is not responsive to the desires of the Gulf states, not even Iraq. But the Soviet Union has a special energy problem of its own that foreshadows new perspectives.

The general phenomenon of shrinking oil supply in relation to demand may affect the Soviet bloc as well as the West. Some Western estimates foresee an inadequacy of Soviet oil to meet domestic demand in the USSR and Eastern Europe as early as 1985.[11] Other estimates put the date later, and the Soviet government itself makes no such prognostication at all. We can be sure that the Soviets will do what they can to avoid a situation of dependence on imported oil. Their entire approach to security and economic policy is to retain control of vital economic decisions. For so critical a resource as oil they do not want to be in the position in which the United States now finds itself. Accordingly, they can be counted on to make great efforts to develop the oil and gas of Siberia, as they are now doing, even at great cost and at the expense of other parts of their overall economic plan. While doing so they may wish to increase imports of oil and gas from Iran, Iraq and certain other Arab states along existing patterns, in order to supply certain areas of their own country and to keep up exports to Eastern and Western Europe, but probably not beyond modest levels.

Questions will arise both for the Gulf states and for the West if the Soviet Union cannot rapidly develop its own energy resources and has to become a net importer of oil. If the Gulf states begin to export more to the Soviet Union, they will have less to export to the West. If they refuse to do so — which is quite likely since the Soviets will be short of hard currency and will want to make their own terms — will they expose themselves to Soviet action more drastic than economic bargaining? The West and Japan will face the question the Soviets have already put to them during past years: whether to help with capital and technology to develop Siberian energy resources, getting a share of the new production to ease their own energy shortage. It would increase total world oil production, presumably to the benefit of all. But this course would raise some questions. If capital is to be poured into development of energy, why not in the Western world rather than in the Soviet Union? Should the West help that country to become stronger and give hostages to it in the process?

If the Soviets should turn their attention to the Gulf as the answer to their energy problem, not to bargain but to use military force, they would have no guarantee of long-term success. They would probably have to cope with sabotage of equipment, non-cooperation, inability to transport the oil and counteraction from the West. Enough risks and problems, perhaps, to rule out military action, but it is useful to take account of 'worst-case' contingencies, for preventive diplomacy as well as for military planning. The oil states of the Gulf have gained tremendously in prestige and in power in the past few years, and they have largely succeeded in keeping their relations with the outside world on the economic plane, where they are strong, rather than on the plane of military power. But in a world of rival superpowers and blocs hungry for oil to keep their economies from running down, the life of nations sitting on the world's largest reserves would not be tranquil. Some time before the mid-1980s the Gulf states and the Western consumers and the Soviets will have to talk about this problem.

In confronting the military giants and their conflicts of interest and ideology that spill over on to other continents, the Gulf oil countries, though now richer than the rich, still have much in common with the poor developing countries of Asia, Africa and Latin America. The relationship is a complex one, not explicable by economic interest alone or any single factor. Historically, the Gulf countries are a part of the Third World. They have had the experience of weak peoples dealing with the strong. They have gone through the anti-colonial revolution and have a feeling of solidarity with others who have done the same. Their assertion of oil power, in turn, was acclaimed all over the Third World as a blow for the common cause, much as Japan's victory over Russia early in this century was widely hailed by coloured and colonial peoples as a great blow struck at the hitherto dominant European powers.

How far have the oil states seen their new role as one of leadership of the developing against the developed countries? Algeria, in its public stance at least, displays no doubt that it is their appointed role to bring about a fundamental change in world economic relations, a 'new international economic order'. Algeria has less oil and less economic power than the rich oil states of the Gulf and has a relish for high-flown rhetoric. Wealthier states like Saudi Arabia do not need a new economic order. They are doing quite well under the present one. Yet the strength of their conviction is not to be taken lightly. They are not cynical but serious in lecturing the industrial countries on their obligation to create a new international economic order based on a more equitable distribution of wealth.

There are two ways in which the oil states can help the Third World to improve its status. The first is by direct use of their own expanded resources to save poor countries from the effects of higher oil prices or to finance their development programme. The second is by using newly gained bargaining power to force the developed countries to make the basic concessions on raw materials, prices, access to markets, development funds and all the other matters that Third World spokesmen had been pushing for at the UN General Assembly, at UNCTAD and elsewhere for a good many years.

The aid which Gulf oil states have given to other countries has been pictured by them as generous and described by critics as inadequate, unfairly distributed, or unduly political. But it has been substantial.[12] Although they have not been willing to sell oil at concessionary prices, they have been willing to help with grants and loans, have created investment agencies, and have contributed to the special facility established by the International Monetary Fund for the purpose of cushioning the effects of the higher price of oil. Except for those monies provided to the IMF, however, the extension of aid has been very much coloured by the national purposes of the donor states and their political relations with the donees. Grants and loans from Saudi Arabia have gone largely to Arab and Islamic countries. The principal lending agencies of Kuwait and Abu Dhabi have limited their loans to the Arab world. Iran under the Shah has paid particular attention to the Indian Ocean region, where he hoped to play a leading political and military role. The Arab states have negotiated aid arrangements with the states of black Africa, but without coming close to satisfying their wants and needs.

Without denigrating the generosity of the oil states of the Gulf or playing down the political importance to them of maintaining goodwill among the developing countries not blessed with oil, it is not to be expected that with their own financial resources they will or can have a major impact on rates of growth or standards of living in the Third World as a whole. Their own needs take priority. The urge for rapid development, concern for investment for their own long-term future and concentration on their own region are so compelling that they alone will not have the resources to pull the rest of the Third World along with them.

It is natural for them to put the monkey on the West's back and join the call for a new international economic order. At the long and inconclusive negotiations at the Conference on International Economic Cooperation in Paris in 1975–7 they made common cause with the other Third World countries, refusing to make direct arrangements with the developed countries on oil matters in the absence of progress on the long set of disputed issues connected with the new economic order. But the deadlock merely illustrated the fact that the only hope for really effective aid to the Third World as a whole over the next two decades lies in a co-operative effort of OPEC and the developed countries of the West to keep a functioning world economy going in which more and more Third World countries can gradually come to play an active part on their own.

The shape of the world economic order, in fact, is being determined not by any negotiations in Paris or at the United Nations, not by the pressure of OPEC on behalf of less fortunate friends in the Third World, but by the actions of the developed countries among themselves and by the growing economic interchange between them and the oil states of the Gulf.

In the global setting of today, both in security matters and in economic prospects, the Gulf region finds itself more and more at the centre of world politics. American officials have ranked it with Europe and the Far East as an area of vital interest, a judgement confirmed by President Carter in his message to Congress on 23 January 1980. The leaders of the Soviet Union have consistently described the region as of primary security importance because of its location on the southern frontiers of the USSR, and the move into Afghanistan was dramatic proof of that conviction. This clash of global interests and, ambitions takes place in an area of endemic instability and fragile political institutions. When there has been apparent calm, it is deceptive, masking problems of internal stress and regional conflict that leave no room for complacency or short-sighted leadership.

The revolution in Iran has created shock waves. Despite the increasing importance of the Gulf nations as independent actors, their future is not entirely in their hands. No region of the world lives in isolation. The superpowers and all the countries in need of Middle East oil have had to learn the lessons of interdependence. The Gulf nations, having gained new power and prestige because of the fact of interdependence, also remain subject to forces generated by it, forces that may be beyond their own will and control.

Notes

1. *United States Foreign Aid Programs in Europe*, Hearings before a Sub-committee of the Senate Committee on Foreign Relations, 82nd Congress, 1st session, 7-23 July 1951 (GPO, Washington, DC, 1951), p. 277.

2. Interview with Secretary of State Kissinger, *Business Week*, 13 January 1975.

3. Oles Smolansky, 'The Soviet Union and the Middle East' in William E. Griffith (ed.), *Critical Choices for Americans: the Soviet Empire, Expansion and Detente* (D.C. Heath, Lexington, Mass., 1976), pp. 269-71.

4. See Geoffrey Kemp, 'Scarcity and Strategy', *Foreign Affairs* (January 1978), pp. 396-414, for contingencies of this nature.

5. Address of Secretary of Defense Harold Brown to the Council on Foreign Relations, 6 March 1980.

6. There is a large body of writing, both Soviet and Western, on this subject. My own summary conclusions on it are contained in two articles: 'Soviet Policy in the Middle East' in Roger E. Kanet and Donna Bahry (eds.), *Soviet Economic and Political Relations with the Developing World* (Praeger, New York, 1975), pp. 85-99; and 'The Soviet Union in the Middle East', *The Middle East Journal* (Winter 1978), pp. 1-12. For a recent detailed and balanced estimate, see Shahram Chubin, *Soviet Policy towards Iran and the Gulf* (Adelphi Paper No. 157, IISS, London, 1980).

7. The two sides held three rounds of talks in 1977. Both said publicly that an agreed limitation on their military presence and activities in the Indian Ocean would be in their own and in the world's interest. However, the United States was unwilling to cut naval forces along the lines the Soviet Union proposed, nor was it willing to ban nuclear-armed ships. The talks lagged and then were discontinued altogether following the Soviet military involvement in Ethiopia in 1978. Then came Afghanistan.

8. See John C. Campbell, 'The Soviet Union and the Middle East, Part I', *The Russian Review* (April 1970), pp. 152-3.

9. It should be noted that the non-alignment stance of the PDRY was patently fictitious. At the Havana conference and elsewhere it was one of those following Cuba's lead in trying to turn the non-aligned movement in pro-Soviet directions.

10. See R. K. Ramazani, 'Security in the Persian Gulf', *Foreign Affairs* (Spring 1979), pp. 821-35; *idem*, *The Persian Gulf and the Strait of Hormuz* (Sijthoff and Nordhoff, Alphen aan den Rijn, 1979).

11. For example, Central Intelligence Agency, *Prospects for Soviet Oil Production* (Washington, DC, April 1977).

12. UNCTAD, *Handbook of International Trade and Development Statistics*, II.D.2 (1979), p. 441; International Bank for Reconstruction and Development, *World Development Report, 1979* (Washington, DC, 1979), p. 157. The latest complete figures, for 1977, indicate aid of more than $5 billion from Middle East oil states in that year.

2 THE STRATEGIC BALANCE AND THE CONTROL OF THE PERSIAN GULF

Geoffrey Kemp

Introduction

For at least the next decade the control of the Persian Gulf will be a key factor in calculations about the relative global balance of power between the Western industrial countries and the Soviet Union. As a result of the revolution in Iran, the Western countries have lost great political, economic and military leverage over the local countries of the Gulf and the adjacent regions. If the Soviet Union, by direct or indirect means, were able to outmanoeuvre the West and gain strategic control of Iran, the impact upon the security of the rest of the Gulf and ultimately the Western alliance system would be extremely grave, in many ways as serious as overt Soviet hostilities in Europe and the Far East.

In this essay it will be argued (a) that the major threat to vital Western interests in the Gulf is the potential for Soviet control; (b) that, while this may be a temporary phenomenon owing to the unique condition of the energy market over the next ten years, the West's vulnerability and lack of consensus on energy policy coincides with a window-of-time during which Soviet military power projection capabilities are growing and its overall military power peaking; (c) that only a coherent and well orchestrated policy by the United States can deter the Soviet Union from adventurism in the region; and (d) that without a coherent Western strategy the temptation to the Soviet Union to interfere in Gulf affairs will grow.

Despite the fact that now it is a truism to say that the Gulf is vital to the West, what does this statement mean? Does it mean that the West will continue to need Persian Gulf oil into the indefinite future and without that oil its industrial furnaces will die down and the Western economic system, as we know it, will collapse? Clearly, the answer is no. Alternative energy supplies, including new oil sources, can be developed and, if the political price is paid, conservation methods can be enacted and economic growth can be slowed down, thereby reducing demand. While a slow-down in growth would have serious political and economic repercussions for Western countries, it should not spell the end of Western civilisation. Gulf oil is important because it is permitted to be important. Unfortunately, the political costs of reducing this dependency have, until recently, been too great for Western, especially American, leaders to pay.

The denial of Persian Gulf oil by local states to the West through revolution, embargo or production cut-backs could cripple the Western economies if *all* the oil flow was reduced for several months. However, to imagine a situation when *all* Persian Gulf countries were prepared to deny oil to the West assumes either that there has been a dramatic change in their policies or that, with the exception of Saudi Arabia, the Gulf countries are prepared to forgo very important revenues for political purposes. Based on their behaviour since 1973, this seems unlikely unless the cut-backs are due to internal problems such as those experienced in Iran during 1979. *In extremis*, the West has the capacity to hurt the oil-producing countries *provided* its leaders are prepared to take risks and ultimately be prepared to stand up to challenges from the Soviet Union. Freezing Persian Gulf oil assets in Western capitals and denying arms and technology could have a serious impact upon development and military programmes in the Gulf. A total embargo might happen in the event of another Arab-Israeli war but that might depend on the role taken by the United States during that war. If the United States did not resupply Israel, the excuses for implementing an embargo would be slender.

In military terms, Persian Gulf oil is not vital to the war-fighting capability of NATO. NATO's requirements for oil in event of a 60-day conflict are small in comparison to the total oil demand for the peacetime domestic economies. By rationing programmes and a reordering of priorities, there is no reason why the NATO countries could not 'oil' a 60-day war. If, however, a general war with the Soviet Union were to be protracted, similar to the Second World War, then the denial of Persian Gulf oil would have a serious impact upon industrial wartime production. However, if one looks at the German and Japanese examples of the Second World War, remarkable things can be done with substitutes under wartime conditions but at an enormous price.

With these caveats in mind, it should be stressed that the strategic importance of Persian Gulf oil stems from its relationship (a) to the peacetime economies of the Western world, especially Europe and Japan, and (b) the possibility that under certain circumstances the oil could fall under Soviet political and military control. If one removes the Soviet Union from the power equation in the Persian Gulf, then the West's security dilemma is more manageable.

The Soviet Threat

There are at least three hypothetical circumstances under which the Soviet Union might threaten Persian Gulf oil: first, in a situation of general war with the West; second, as an outgrowth of conflict in the Gulf if the Soviet Union intervened to protect, help, or hinder one or more local countries; third, in a contingency where neither general war nor local war were under way but where the Soviet Union felt threatened elsewhere and was prepared to disrupt the economic power of the Western world, to redress what it felt were unacceptable threats to its security, for example a major crisis between the Soviet Union and China or a crisis in Eastern Europe.

General War Scenarios

In event of a major non-nuclear war breaking out with the Western allies, there might be advantages to the Soviet Union in threatening Western oil supplies from the Gulf. This could be done in two basic ways: first, by *attacking* the oil supplies themselves either at the source or in transit with nuclear or conventional weapons or by using military power to gain control of all, or part, of the Gulf in order to *threaten* oil supplies. From the Soviet point of view, there are costs and benefits of these options. Attacking oil supplies would be a much easier *military* task than invasion of the Gulf. Yet the risks of escalation would be great. Direct interdiction of the Persian Gulf oil facilities, in particular the Saudi and Iranian terminals at Ras Tanura and Khark Island respectively, would be seen as a deliberate act of war as serious, perhaps, as an attack on Berlin. If nuclear weapons were used, it would be a clear sign that the Soviet Union was prepared to fight a major war with all the weapons in its inventory. This would undoubtedly spur reprisals, if not an all-out conflagration with the West. If conventional weapons were used, the Soviet Union might be able to destroy the oil or put it out of commission for many months but it would also stand a risk of precipitating World War III or major non-nuclear reprisals against Soviet ports and ships on the high seas or even its own highly vulnerable domestic energy system.

On the other hand, a carefully orchestrated non-nuclear invasion could *avoid* direct attacks on oil supplies. However, if such an invasion were taking place in the context of a general war, it can be argued that the West would assume that sooner or later the Soviet Union would either attack or capture the oilfields and, therefore, the risks of escalation, although in the initial stages less severe, would eventually have to be faced. It is possible that a general war with the Soviet Union might be non-nuclear and result in an impasse in NATO and the Far East. In these circumstances, the Soviet Union might have great incentives to capture Persian Gulf real estate in order to have a bargaining chip during eventual negotiations. The assumption here would be that neither the Soviet Union nor the West would want to escalate to nuclear war and would, therefore, be prepared to bargain with whatever territory they held at the 'end' of the conventional general war.

Nevertheless, all general war scenarios involving the Persian Gulf, although interesting and important, would probably take second priority to other tasks that both the Western and Soviet forces would be given. For instance, based on current Soviet doctrine, it is unlikely that they would devote a large portion of their submarine and naval aviation to the interdiction of oil supplies out of the Gulf because they would need these forces for more important tasks in the Atlantic and Pacific. Another major constraint on Soviet interdiction of the sea lines in the Gulf and Indian Ocean relates to constraints on their infrastructure. Until such time as they have adequate basing facilities, their capacity to sustain a naval campaign against the SLOCs would be very limited and they would be vulnerable to Western anti-submarine warfare. If, however, they had a major base facility in the southern seas, for instance in South Africa, this would change the balance of maritime power in the southern seas, at which point oil SLOC interdiction would be a more serious problem.

Similarly, the requirements for an invasion force of the Gulf could be high and very competitive in a general war *provided* the West and the regional countries were prepared to resist and not give the Soviet army a free ride to the Gulf from the Caucasus. The terrain in northern Iran and eastern Turkey is very difficult and a Western defence of these northern and eastern borders is, in theory, possible. However, it would require the co-operation of Iran and the neutralisation of Iraq and the participation of Turkey. Furthermore, until such time as the United States increases the size and lift capabilities of its rapid deployment forces, even in the best circumstances the Western powers might arrive with too little, too late.

Local War Scenarios

The second and more likely case in which Soviet military power might be used in the Gulf relates to local war scenarios. In this case it is assumed that the Soviet Union would have an interest in exploiting opportunities if local conflicts presented it with the chance to win an important victory over the West. A review of the past twenty years in the Gulf region reveals that although there have been a great many *coups d'état* and political assassinations resulting in changes in leadership, and numerous border disputes, some of which remain unresolved, there have been few incidences of inter-state war. This, in part, was due to the fact that until 1971 the UK retained a military presence in the region and, therefore, acted as policeman. It also should be noted that following the British withdrawal the local countries have made serious efforts to resolve outstanding disputes which in the past might have led to conflict: for example in 1975, Iraq and Iran resolved the Shatt-al-'Arab and Kurdish conflicts; Saudi Arabia resolved most of its territorial claims with neighbours; Iran has given up its historic claim to Bahrain; and, although there are still several offshore disputes, especially between Iraq and Kuwait, the track record would indicate that the probability of local countries going to war for territory is not very likely *unless* accompanied by ideological conflict.

There are two basic types of ideological conflict in the Gulf: those that stem from ethnic and religious sources, as have been amply demonstrated in Iran, and those that have their origins in radical-conservative conflicts. Examples of the latter type of conflict have taken place in Oman, where the radical regime in South Yemen has aided radical guerrillas in the Dhofar province of Oman with Soviet arms, and in Afghanistan, where conservative guerrillas have been fighting the Marxist regime.

Although the fear of left-wing radical regimes is a major source of concern throughout the Gulf today, radical threats come from both extreme left *and* extreme right. The revolution in Iran in 1978 and 1979 represented a right-wing religious backlash against the Shah's modernisation programmes. The extremists not only believed that the Shah was 'illegitimate', but that his regime was changing the nature of Iranian society by liberating women, downgrading the power of the religious leaders and introducing decadent Western customs. Iran's present problems highlight the dilemma that all conservative regimes face in adapting to modernisation. The Iranian tragedy is further compounded by a long history of terrorism on the left, ethnic separation and the close proximity of the Soviet Union. Perhaps because the revolution was built upon a coalition between the right and left, internal violence continues to pose a more serious danger to the regime than a *coup d'état* or assassination.

The Soviet Union's capacity for interfering and manipulating the internal Iranian situation is an ever-present factor. Were local ethnic conflict to get out of control in northern cities such as Tabriz or Mahabad, there is the possibility that the Soviet Union could use this as an excuse for intervention. If the Soviets occupied the northern provinces, it would embarrass, perhaps fatally, the Khomeini regime and would not automatically lead to universal condemnation in the West in view of the excesses of the revolutionaries and the ambiguity of the situation.

The question of regime stability in Saudi Arabia poses different problems. There have not been upheavals similar to those experienced in Iran over the years culminating in the 1979 revolution, yet, because the Saudi regime is traditional, it faces potential socio-economic pressures from within the country. If there is to be internal change in Saudi Arabia, it will probably come from within the army, or some faction of the royal family aligned with elements of the armed forces. It is not impossible to conjure up scenarios under which this might occur. For instance, a crisis involving Palestinian terrorism and threats to oil supplies could polarise the elite. More radical junior officers might rebel, especially if the regime were inclined to be ruthless against terrorism. Because of the nature of Saudi society, a change of government could come about very quickly and in those circumstances intervention by external powers, including the Soviet Union, is a possibility, especially if 'invitations' were extended by a radical group that claimed power or which has temporarily ousted the royal family.

As for the other Persian Gulf states, all have strengths and weaknesses. Traditional leaders in Oman, Kuwait and the United Arab Emirates all face potential domestic opposition. This is particularly the case in some of the richer countries where there are very large foreign minorities who are not granted any of the rights normally afforded to people resident in a foreign country. The less rich Gulf countries, including the Yemens, face severe economic problems and, although Iraq has a lot of oil, it needs credits and technology from the West necessary for development. It seems unlikely that the Iraqi regime will work for closer ties with the Soviet Union at this stage, although that possibility should not be ignored.

This overview of the sources of instability in the Gulf region is not meant to be predictive. Although it is not possible to isolate the precise point at which domestic conflict may erupt, domestic upheaval in at least one of these countries will probably occur in the near future. In other words, although the probability of any *particular* violent event occurring is low, the probability of at least one event occurring is very high.

Soviet Intervention and the Global Balance of Power

The third possibility for Soviet intervention would be in circumstances when the Soviet Union was in conflict elsewhere, possibly with China, and was prepared to use its strategic proximity to the Persian Gulf to drive a political wedge between the Western allies, including their own relationships and their relationships with China. For instance, the close co-operation between Japan and China is an anathema to the Soviet Union given its hostilities with China and its own needs for the advanced technology and capital that Japan can provide. In event of a Chinese (or East European) crisis, the Soviet

Union would face great risks in terms of its own future stability as a Communist state unless it could isolate and divide its adversaries with a swift *coup de main*. Threatening direct military intervention against those 'supporting' the enemy would be one obvious route to take but this would have dangers of escalation. Occupying the Gulf or, more specifically, Iran in such circumstances would be a risky operation too, but if it were achieved with maximum surprise and speed the fighting would probably be over before the West could respond. In fact, given the current (November 1979) status of the Iranian armed forces and the US arms embargo against the Khomeini regime imposed during the hostages crisis of that month, it is reasonable to argue that the Soviet army could occupy northern Iran in a matter of days rather than weeks. In these circumstances, the mere presence of the Soviet Union on the Persian Gulf would probably be sufficient to signal to Europe and Japan that support for China was a losing game. The Soviet Union would not need to destroy or control oil supplies; it would be the *implicit* threat of future Soviet control of oil that would have the most powerful impact upon the political leaderships of Europe and Japan.

Security Options for the West

Given the above points, what are the realistic security options for the West in planning for its security in the Persian Gulf region? Because of the importance of the Gulf to the entire Western industrial system, it is difficult to see how the region can continue to be treated as a discrete area decoupled from the military issues of Southern Europe, the Mediterranean and Indian Ocean. The stability of the Gulf is linked to the future stability of Europe and Japan, since threats to one area pose threats to the others. Certainly a major change in the balance of power in Europe would have profound effects upon the Persian Gulf countries themselves; in particular, Saudi Arabia and other 'conservative' regimes. These countries, therefore, have a long-term interest in maintaining a strong Western commitment to a favourable balance of global power. Equally, the Europeans have a major vested interest in the Gulf. These mutually reinforcing interdependencies suggest that a new concept of Western security should be formulated. This should go so far as to extend the mandate of an alliance such as NATO to include the Gulf countries, since this would be politically inappropriate in peacetime despite the fact that from a logical strategic point of view it has a lot of merit.

The relationship between Japan and the Gulf is somewhat more tenuous. A collapse of the Japanese economy would probably not have the same political impact in the Gulf as a collapse of Western

Europe but it would, nevertheless, represent a blow to economic development and the potential loss of a major oil market. In contrast, Japan's dependency on the Gulf is great and, therefore, any change in Gulf policy with respect to oil could have far-reaching domestic repercussions in Japan. Yet Japan has neither the capacity nor the will to consider extending its security perimeter beyond the South China Seas, let alone into the Indian Ocean. However, it does have the capacity and, perhaps, the will to expand its local military capabilities and thereby 'release' elements of the US Eighth Fleet for duties in the Indian Ocean area.

In reconsidering the global map of Western interests to take greater account of the Gulf, the first conclusion to be faced is that a new area of responsibility has been added to Western military commitments at the very time when the overall presence and projection capability of the United States and other allies have been weakened. The immediate impact of this is increased pressure upon the already thinly spread American forces. For the past few years the European commitment has received the greatest attention at the expense, some feel, of the Gulf and Far East. If the new priorities, such as the Gulf, cannot be assumed at the expense of other commitments, then one of two things will have to happen. Either the Western powers will have to increase the overall size of their forces or local powers will have to plan a more active role in joint Western defence efforts. What this might also mean is a new distribution of responsibilities throughout the Western alliance that could include trade-offs, such as a substitution of *some* American presence in the Pacific for a greater Japanese Pacific contribution and, in return, a greater American presence, at least for part of the year, in the Indian Ocean-Persian Gulf region.

Beyond these options, there have been suggestions that NATO should redraw its boundaries to include the Gulf and South Atlantic and Indian Ocean. There are great political difficulties in these suggestions in any peacetime context. Even with NATO's current boundaries, different priorities pertain: the Norwegians have a different view of the importance of the Yugoslavian contingency than the Italians; similarly, it is difficult for Turkey to get too exercised about the problems of Spitzbergen in view of its own immediate territorial proximity to the Soviet Union. Nevertheless, there is, within the NATO hierarchy, a general agreement that certain common goals and force levels must be pursued irrespective of local antagonisms that remain unresolved, such as the Cyprus conflict between Greece and Turkey. In wartime, NATO would obviously redraw its map and extend operations into the Middle East and Indian Ocean if necessary. In peacetime the alliance, as such, can do little other than talk about the need for a more global perspective. However, individual allies, such as France, the United Kingdom and

Turkey, are capable of providing certain military assistance in peace-time to *deter* Soviet adventurism in the Gulf.

Furthermore, it is not out of the question that some local Gulf countries, which have otherwise conflicting views on certain issues such as oil pricing and some territorial claims, might be persuaded to support Western initiatives designed, in part, to help their security needs. The most radical suggestion would be for powerful pro-Western countries, such as Turkey, Israel, Egypt and Saudi Arabia, to formulate some concept of defence co-operation. This is unlikely to happen in the short run given the emotions and history of the region and Saudi antagonism on the issue of the Egyptian-Israeli peace treaty but, if the Soviet threat becomes more serious, then it may be Saudi Arabia rather than Israel that will have to decide whether it is prepared to give up ideological claims for security. The real question is whether the local Gulf countries themselves are prepared to consider more formal military relations with the West. In the case of Iran, this seems unlikely for the foreseeable future. The involvement of Saudi Arabia in any such system is more promising, though proposals for an American military presence in the region, including, for instance, an air base at Dhahran, have made little progress. The Saudi regime wants an American commit-ment but not one that is overtly visible. In peacetime, this means a US maritime presence in the Indian Ocean is more acceptable and more likely than a forward base involving the deployment of American forces in the Gulf itself.

In the absence of any formal treaty arrangements, the alternatives would be to continue current policy, which is for the West to develop strong bilateral relations with pro-Western Gulf states. However, as has been seen in the case of major military programmes in Iran and Saudi Arabia, this can run into serious problems in the United States. For instance, in 1978, the Carter Administration attempted to justify the sale of F-15 Eagles to Saudi Arabia on a broad geo-political threat assessment to the regime over the next ten years. The opposition came primarily from Israel's supporters, who argued that, irrespective of threats posed by hypothetical Russian aero-planes in South Yemen, the most likely use for the F-15s would be in a renewed Arab-Israeli conflict. There can be no doubt that the Israeli argument has to be taken seriously, for the record suggests that, in event of war, weapons will be used irrespective of restraints imposed upon them before the war began. Thus there is likely to be continued controversy over the Saudi Arabia build-up quite apart from questions as to whether the Saudis have the capacity to absorb and operate effectively all this modern equipment.

The absorptive capacity argument is, of course, most relevant in the Iranian case; namely, that although Iran under the Shah made a good case for building up a modern military force, it did not have the infrastructure or technical manpower to operate a modern military force effectively in all dimensions. This seems to have had the overall effect of weakening rather than strengthening its capacity to fight, at least in the short run. It is, after all, the capacity to fight that counts and some have argued it would have been better for Iran to set its sights more lowly for force levels in the first instance before embarking on projects which were unlikely to come into fruition for decades.

What this suggests is that in military terms the contribution of local powers — with the exception of Israel and elements of the Turkish and Egyptian forces — to regional defence is likely to remain small although the participation of countries such as Saudi Arabia is vital in view of their geography.

In conclusion, if Soviet adventurism is to be deterred in the Middle East-Gulf, it will be necessary for the Western powers, especially the United States, to demonstrate the capability to project military forces into the region that *are capable of fighting* Soviet conventional forces and those of its surrogates. This is a difficult task, especially in view of the fall of Iran and the geographical advantages open to the Soviet Union. However, it is not impossible in view of the constraints that the Soviet Union would face in projecting power beyond Iran and the inherent regional advantages the West may have if it carefully orchestrates a strategic policy in the region. What this means in practical terms is that the proposed US 'rapid deployment force' will, indeed, be expensive if it is to be effective. Merely taking forces earmarked for other contingencies will not solve anything. What is therefore required is *additional funding* for this force which, incidentally, is something the United States needs irrespective of its particular interests in the Gulf. This, in turn, suggests that further increases in the European and Japanese budgets will be necessary to preserve some semblance of political equilibrium within the alliance. Unless these steps are made, the Middle East-Gulf will remain a military vacuum and, as such, a highly unstable, dangerous region.

Table 2.1: Gross National Product and Military Expenditure (millions of US dollars)

	Iran		Iraq		Saudi Arabia		Kuwait		Oman		Qatar		Bahrain		UAE	
	GNP	MILEX	GNP	MILEX	GNP	MILEX	GNP	MILEX	GNP	MILEX	GNP	MILEX	GNP	MILEX	GNP	MILEX
1972	16,304	1,189	4,145	473	5,447	941	3,716	106		44		27		4	1,070	18
1973	26,502	2,097	5,235	467	8,130	1,478	5,926	116		77.5		24		5	1,430	26
1974	46,574	3,225	10,591	803	23,197	1,808	10,808	162		169		41		6	172	56
1975	52,835	8,800	13,196	1,191	37,096	6,771	10,934	230	1,595	359						
1976	66,703	9,500	15,400	1,417	44,319	9,938	12,227	320	1,875	768						
1977	75,732	7,894	16,300	1,660	55,400	7,539	12,000	322	2,500	687	1,000		1,700		7,700	100
1978	—	9,942	15,500	1,695	64,200	13,170	—	336		768		61				661

Source: *The Military Balance* (IISS, London, 1979); *OPEC Yearbook 1978.*

Table 2.2: Military Establishments of the Gulf States

	Iran	Saudi Arabia	Iraq	Kuwait	Oman	Qatar	Bahrain	UAE
Total Armed Forces Regular	413 (1978)	44.5	222.0	11.1	19.2	4.7	2.3	25.15
Reservists (000)	300	—	250.0	—	—	—	—	—
Army Personnel (000)	285	35	190.0	9	16.2	4	2.3	23.5
Tanks	1,735 MBT	350 MBT	1,800 MBT	280 MBT	—	12 MBT	—	30 Lt.
Air Force Personnel (000)	100	8	28	1.9	2.1	0.3	—	0.75
Combat aircraft	447	178	339	50	35	4	—	52
Navy Personnel (000)	30	1.5	4	0.2	0.9	0.4	(0.2)	0.9
Major craft	28	4 (+ 120 small craft)	48	28	13	6	9	9

Source: *The Military Balance.*

Table 2.3: Revenue and Expenditure of the Gulf States (millions of local currency)

		1972	1973	1974	1975	1976	1977	1978
Iran (000 mil.)	Revenue	383.3	448.6	1,427.3	1,628.8	1,895.5	2,097.0	1,612.0
	Expenditure	380.3	504.4	1,287.3	1,614.2	1,933.3	2,511.0	2,068.8
Iraq	Revenue	975.5	1,654.9	2,983.5	3,202.6	5,045.0	5,998.4	—
	Expenditure	1,117.9	1,399.9	2,604.9	3,640.6	5,045.0	6,339.1	—
Saudi Arabia	Revenue	13,200	22,810	98,247	110,935	110,935	146,493	—
	Expenditure	13,200	22,810	45,473	110,935	110,935	111,400	—
Kuwait	Revenue	597.7	675.3	2,271.4	3,960.4	3,033.1	2,272.7	—
	Expenditure	396.7	536.7	1,085.2	1,032.6	1,375.3	1,988.0	—
Oman	Revenue	53.0	65.0	303.2	459.4	505.4	613.3	509.0
	Expenditure	69.4	91.7	329.3	495.5	580.7	534.3	560.0
Qatar	Revenue	1,230.4	1,719.7	5,496.6	7,134.7	8,927.2	8,154.5	—
	Expenditure	958.6	1,514.8	1,931.3	5,302.3	5,808.9	7,318.6	—
Bahrain	Revenue	—	—	123,746	137,450	201,862	263,897	280,000
	Expenditure	—	—	77,856	121,768	203,191	256,200	280,000
UAE (Abu Dhabi only)	Revenue	2,180.8	4,001.8	4,211.6	13,083.7	18,401.0	—	—
	Expenditure	1,735.6	3,346.5	3,391.1	12,877.1	18,605.0	—	—

Source: OPEC Yearbook 1979.

Table 2.4: Balance of Trade (millions of current US dollars)

	1972	1973	1974	1975	1976	1977
Qatar						
Exports: total	397	618	2,016	1,808	2,210	2,048
of which oil	382	601	1,979	1,757	2,138	2,031
Oil exports as % of total exports	96.2	97.3	98.2	97.2	96.7	99.1
Imports: total	141	195	271	413	775	—
Trade balance	256	423	1,745	1,395	1,435	—
United Arab Emirates						
Exports: total	1,082	1,801	6,392	6,879	8,543	9,489
of which oil	1,035	1,740	6,306	6,727	8,238	9,135
Oil exports as % of total exports	95.7	96.6	98.7	97.8	96.4	96.3
Imports: total	482	821	1,705	2,669	3,327	—
Trade balance	600	980	4,687	4,210	5,216	—
Iraq						
Exports: total	1,108	1,944	6,600	8,297	9,272	9,664
of which oil	1,022	1,836	6,505	8,177	9,114	9,507
Oil exports as % of total exports	92.2	94.5	98.6	98.6	98.3	98.4
Imports: total	705	894	2,371	4,215	3,470	3,541
Trade balance	403	1,050	4,229	4,082	4,902	6,123
Kuwait						
Exports: total	2,984	3,829	10,964	9,183	9,830	9,832
of which oil	2,833	3,593	10,564	8,593	9,093	8,880
Oil exports as % of total exports	94.9	93.9	96.4	93.6	92.5	90.3
Imports: total	797	1,053	1,552	2,390	3,324	4,460
Trade balance	2,187	2,776	9,112	6,793	6,506	5,372

Table 2.4: continued

Iran						
Exports: total	4,088	6,249	21,516	20,226	23,435	23,974
of which oil	3,637	5,614	20,906	19,634	22,917	23,260
Oil exports as % of total exports	89	89.8	97.2	97.1	97.8	97.0
Imports: total	2,570	3,737	6,616	11,696	12,567	18,394
Trade balance	1,518	2,513	14,900	8,530	10,868	5,580
Saudi Arabia						
Exports: total	4,517	7,630	30,992	27,746	36,125	40,929
of which oil	4,502	7,600	30,955	27,698	36,076	40,881
Oil exports as % of total exports	15	30	37	48	49	48
Imports: total	1,136	1,975	2,859	4,213	8,694	10,770
Trade balance	3,381	5,655	28,133	23,533	27,431	30,159

Source: OPEC Yearbook 1979.

Table 2.5: Area, Population and Population Density of the Gulf States

	Area (Square miles)	Population	Population Density (inhabitants/sq. miles)
Iran	628,000	35,210,000	56
Saudi Arabia	927,000	7,870,000	8.5
Iraq	172,000	12,330,000	71
Kuwait	5,000	4,200,000	216
Oman	82,000	840,000	10
Qatar	4,000	200,000	500
Bahrain	230	350,000	1,521
UAE	32,000	710,000	22

Table 2.6: Volume of Crude Oil Exported 1972–8 (1975 = 100 base year)

	1972	1973	1974	1975	1976	1977	1978
Iran	96.5	112.9	114.9	100.0	111.6	104.4	96.5
Saudi Arabia	82.6	106.3	120.1	100.0	122.0	130.4	116.7
Iraq	69.0	95.0	93.0	100.0	111.0	102.0	116.0
Kuwait	164.0	148.0	123.3	100.0	100.4	90.4	98.5
Oman	82.7	85.7	84.8	100.0	107.7	97.8	92.7
Qatar	112.4	132.7	119.0	100.0	115.9	100.1	112.6
Bahrain (refined)	118.6	124.8	126.3	100.0	108.8	126.5	119.1
UAE	71.0	89.1	97.7	100.0	114.0	116.3	107.3

Source: International Monetary Fund.

3 THE SOVIET UNION AND THE PERSIAN GULF

Shahram Chubin

The persistence of Western debate about Soviet intentions in the Third World has been in some respects overtaken by the general consensus now prevalent that the USSR has, at a minimum and for the first time, achieved military parity with the West. The implications of this too are the subject of debate; some see military power today as too specific to translate into more general influence and see parity and a growing economic interdependence between East and West as a stimulus for conservatism on the part of the USSR. In this view the Soviet Union is becoming a *status quo* power with a stake in the international economic order. An acknowledgement of the USSR's role as a superpower, and a recognition of economics as the primary determinant of its foreign policy[1] would, in this view, contribute to a 'relaxation of tensions'. This school of thought tends to emphasise that Soviet policy is risk-averse, that it is constrained both by the limitations of the USSR in regard to forms of power (other than military) and to the complexities of regional politics and the dynamic nationalism of Third World states inherently resistant to the appeals of Communism and the lures of Moscow. It sees a world of complex interdependence, a *détente* coexisting with competition while the dynamics of regional and national politics stimulate uncertainty and instability in most of the Third World. Recognising the limits of the effectiveness of military power as a solution to these trends this school looks to a Western policy that promotes respect for certain inalienable principles, and to a search for areas of compatibility with local states. It seeks security multilaterally, with proven allies in Europe (and Asia) and by the encouragement of regional co-operation, formal and informal, elsewhere.

A second school of thought exists in the West that differs both in perspective and in emphasis from the preceding one. It cannot be said to be in direct or complete disagreement with much of the thinking of the first, but its focus is sharper, and its concerns more defined. It is more Hobbesian in its view of the international system, less impressed by the limits of military power than by its continued utility (particularly in affecting third parties' judgements) and less disposed to look at the constraints on Soviet power and the alleged paucity of the gains of Soviet foreign policy, than to note the gradual transformation of the strategic environment in a direction adversely affecting Western interests. It is more concerned by the degree of Soviet effort in expanding its influence than by its failure to achieve irreversible breakthroughs. Unremitting Soviet pressure, persistent Soviet opportunism, incrementalism, probing and the setting of precedents have, or could have, in this view, a cumulative effect in transforming regional environments in directions favourable to Soviet influence. Just as the emphasis on 'breakthroughs' or 'setbacks' obscures the long view of history, the focus on regions as discrete entities unrelated or dimly related to the global strategic balance ignores interconnections between regional politics and Western interests. This school of thought, seeing no stable balance of power, is more concerned with its delicacy and with its fluctuations; nuclear deterrence is seen as neither automatic nor comprehensive, other balances are viewed as imperative, especially regional balances, which might include the need for an extra-regional balancer.

These two approaches[2] (admittedly greatly simplified) contend for dominance in US foreign policy and even within the Carter Administration itself. They account for the fluctuations of this administration; for its genuine optimism regarding the US world role in the long run, and the sudden fluctuations and emphasis on military power (which is rediscovered as it were) during crises. This ambivalence is a sign of the contradictions of the times; competition coexists with limited *détente*; public opinion wants limited foreign entanglements and maximum influence; domestic, economic and social issues compete for scarce resources with international demands; leadership is required by domestic needs, yet a troubled and turbulent international order also requires time, effort and patience, with little promise of tangible reward. A complex international system has replaced the more predictable loose bipolar one; hierarchy has vanished, and the capacity of superpowers to manage or 'order' international affairs has correspondingly declined as the agenda of the Cold War has been replaced by a myriad of local issues. Small wonder then that the two approaches outlined should coexist within one administration. Indeed, there are few analysts who do not simultaneously hold elements of both in their thinking. Nevertheless the two approaches and emphases lead to quite different interpretations of Soviet foreign policy and to advocacy of quite different remedies in dealing with it, and the problems of a particular region.

The Persian Gulf and the International System

Although lying outside the two principal blocs and hence constituting a part of the Third World, the Persian Gulf is unusual in several important respects. For the USSR it is an area — through Iran — directly contiguous to it which is assuming greater importance daily both for Soviet (and Eastern bloc) energy needs in the 1980s, and for its growing value to NATO and Japan, which might lend itself to political exploitation. Before assessing the record of Soviet policy in the region it is worth tracing the international context both in terms of the region's importance and of Soviet military power. The vulnerability of the West to interruption of its oil supplies needs little emphasis here.[3] The October 1973 embargo and the revolution in Iran in 1978 demonstrated this in their different ways; cut-offs in oil supplies from even one major producer for several months can damage the health of Western economies, so narrow is the margin of supply and demand. Political pressures within OPEC to reduce production for conservation (or not increase it in the case of Saudi Arabia) have recently increased. So too have the incentives for the manipulation of the 'oil weapon' for political purposes. Quite apart from the purposeful use of oil (prices and production) for political ends, there exist a wide range of factors which threaten the continued supply of oil; prolonged domestic instability; inadequate technical expertise and inter-state war. None of these need be the result of Soviet policy, though presumably some are susceptible to its exploitation.

Whether or not Western dependence on a vulnerable region is exploited by Moscow, the region itself is volatile and subject to sudden and unpredictable change. As a result of mainly domestic transformations, Iran and Pakistan have left the Western camp, while Turkey, dissatisfied with the fruits of its alliance, is only loosely hanging on. The demise of CENTO — formally dissolved in September 1979 — and the threat of disintegration in Iran reflect a transformation of the political environment weakening Western influence. While not attributable to either Soviet power or policy, the effect has been in practice to increase Soviet opportunities for influence. The fact that neither the course nor the direction of change is predictable (or irreversible), and that all Western losses are not clear Soviet gains, does not detract from this. It only underlines the volatility of this region, the evanescence of influence, and the need to see events in both their regional and global contexts.

The growth of Soviet military power, the attainment of strategic parity and a global reach interact with both the fact of Western vulnerability and the instability of politics in various regions. In the Persian Gulf Soviet physical proximity underscores the potential political utility of military power. It need not be a specific tool to be effective. But its value as a specific instrument is undeniable, for example to maintain a friendly regime in power in Afghanistan. And though it need not be immediately transferable into sustained influence across the board in a political relationship, it can as a *new* factor affect the perceptions of local actors. It may be argued that for many states what is worrisome is not the growth of Soviet military power but the decline in Western power and will, and especially the loss of a measure of predictability about US responses. This may indeed be the case but the growth of Soviet military power is, I believe, an independent and concrete source of concern for many littoral states. Soviet naval power and mobility — an ability to shrink the 'effective distance' from the southern USSR to the Gulf — endow the USSR with a new military capability. This makes the USSR a concrete reality for the historically insulated Gulf states, and a new factor which has accordingly to be taken into account. It also endows the USSR with the capacity to use shifts in the regional balance to manipulate these perceptions, and to capitalise on regional discontents by offering its services as ally, protector or arms supplier.

In combination with growing military power the Soviet presence is felt in the Gulf primarily by its establishment of footholds on its peripheries. Soviet friendship treaties have been signed with Afghanistan (December 1978) and the PDRY (October 1979). The Soviet presence in Ethiopia, and in the Red Sea opposite Aden, is also large.

The relentless growth of Soviet military power and its visibility in terms of political commitment to the PDRY and Afghanistan, especially since 1978, may be seen as the acquisition of strategic footholds to exert psychological pressure on governments within the Persian Gulf. They also serve as a reminder to the West of its vulnerability in crises or in wartime. But Soviet interest in South-West Asia, and especially Afghanistan, should also be seen in terms of Sino-Soviet competition. In the event of a war with China the USSR would be hard pressed to supply its navy in the Far East. To escape the geographical constraints which bolster up and contain its navy, and to speed up supplies, there is a certain logic in the acquisition of a strategic infrastructure in this region.[4] Soviet geopolitical investments in Aden and in a port in Baluchistan (Gwadar) on the Indian Ocean, would make sense for this purpose: similarly the north-south Afghan railroad. (Iran with a long Gulf coastline and a long border with the USSR would also be important in such a scenario.)

Whether for 'defensive' reasons *vis-à-vis* China or for leverage *vis-à-vis* the West, Soviet commitments on the periphery of the Gulf have undeniably expanded. It is not yet clear whether military parity has stimulated a propensity for risk-taking. It may be that Western 'restraint' has indeed assured that there would be no risks attendant on this probing. However, in the past year public and repeated emphasis in Washington on the need for interventionary forces, for the assurance of allies, etc., etc., may have ended this policy of indiscriminate abstention. If so, the momentum of Western setbacks may be somewhat arrested. The Soviet Union's willingness to assist in covert and indirect ways — for example through Cubans[5] and East Germans — which has facilitated 'plausible denials' in the past — may be influenced by more concerted Western response.

It seems likely, however, that Soviet military power has had and will continue to have a distinct effect on Soviet policy in the Persian Gulf, first by expanding the definition of her legitimate interests, and second by attempts to convert military power into 'commensurate political influence'.[6] Soviet policy, or rather style, may continue to be blunt and opportunistic; for example, it has not resisted the temptation to exploit setbacks for the West, even if they simultaneously endanger Soviet interests. The expansive definition of 'security' and an over-compensation (or over-insurance) militarily, combined with a prickly *amour propre* contribute to her problems with neighbours whose security and sovereignity are thereby threatened. The result may well be a diplomacy that succeeds only in alienating states who have no illusions that 'equality' in their geopolitical context can mean anything other than Soviet preponderance.

The Persian Gulf: the Local Context

Whereas in almost any other region of the Third World local politics, factionalism and domestic disputes are isolated from world politics, even the smallest tremors in the Gulf potentially impinge on great power interests and raise major issues. For example, the victory of a rejectionist faction in the Saudi leadership, or a shift in Saudi oil policy as a result, say, of a security threat in the PDRY, could have devastating consequences for the West. NATO's cohesion could be undermined by cut-throat competition among oil-consuming states in a tight oil market. Yet the instruments of influence available to outside powers are limited, primarily due to the nature of the threats to Western interests. Many of the 'threats' are in fact inchoate: uncertainty about the nature and direction of social change in societies undergoing rapid and disruptive economic, cultural and social transformation. The case of Iran has shown that rapid economic growth brings with it social and cultural dislocation and that indiscriminate modernisation not only generates demands for political participation but also risks a backlash — a reaction against obtrusive foreign influences and impersonal forms of social order. For all the Gulf states the priorities are local, the remedies structural. Ayatollah Khomeini, for all his appeal in Iran, is a transient figure representing the mystique of charismatic leadership of a bygone era. For most of the Gulf states, be they Iran and Iraq with their fractured societies and minorities, or Kuwait and Bahrain with immigrant populations and diverse religious sects, the pressing concerns are those of national integration and societal cohesion, of meeting the growing demands of ever more restive and expectant peoples. The increased load on governmental structures is matched by a singular asset — cash — but whether it will be a sufficient tool by itself remains doubtful.

The ebb and flow of politics is thus from indigenous sources which do not lend themselves to clear and easy manipulation by outside powers. Indeed it may well be that the greater the involvement of these powers in the development process, the greater the likelihood of xenophobia engendered by them. The stresses of adapting cultures and institutions to meet new demands in novel ways will vary, but the outcome is likely to be both a synthesis (rather than a sterile imitation of any particular model), and a lengthy process characterised by fits and false starts.

In the Arab world, to be sure, there persist conflicts that are exploitable, yet here as in Iran the dominant, transcendent, issue is modernisation.[7] The core of the Arab world has shifted in recent years with this shift in political salience, making the Arabian Peninsula its centre. Iran's revolution underscored this reality of the dominance of local concerns, yet it also unleashed uncontainable social forces throughout the entire region. Quite apart from any policy changes afterwards, the revolution in Iran was itself profoundly destabilising. It provided both a model and an incentive for dissidents throughout the Gulf; for those unhappy with their lot, their political freedom, their religious freedom, the 'pollution' of traditional culture, or whatever. Its reverberations persist particularly in neighbouring states possessing Shi'ite communities (Iraq, Bahrain, Kuwait and Yemen). The revolution also altered the political balance of power in the Middle East, undermining moderate pro-Western governments, giving them the choice between political isolation and a tactful adjustment of policy. Iran's upheaval also demonstrated the intractable problem of containing or 'managing' change for powers outside the region. Quite apart from the palpable defeat for Western (particularly United States) policy, and the inevitable costs for their interests, the revolution provided no simple lessons for handling similar events in other countries. While over-identification with the Shah may have been costly after the revolution, it had provided tangible benefits for several decades. The hasty withdrawal of US support, combined with public equivocation and attempts to accommodate to Iran's new leaders, who despise the West, only succeeded in undermining and alienating Washington's other allies in the region. The upshot was a renewed focus on relations with Saudi Arabia. But is she any more stable and, if not, are there any alternatives to the US cultivation of ties with the House of Saud? It appears doubtful that the West in the next decade can avoid heavy dependence on Saudi oil. So policy choices still need to be made, and Saudi security concerns must be met if there is to be a solid basis for co-operation. The Western response to Iran did much to undermine this vital, though precarious, relationship.

The Soviet response to Iran's revolution is instructive as an example of her more general approach to change in the region. First, there is little evidence of any direct Soviet role in the unrest, although indirectly she assisted the opposition forces through the PLO and the Iranian Communist (Tudeh) Party. Iranian leftist forces, the fedayeen trained by the PLO with Soviet arms, played an important military role in the last stages of the revolution. Second, although adversely affected by the replacement of the Shah by Khomeini (in terms of both economic relations[8] and political predictability), the West was hit harder. Soviet discomfort was thus lessened by the setbacks for the West which Moscow insisted on exploiting and emphasising. The same Soviet ambivalence which arose from the tension between welcoming Western setbacks and accepting similar, if not equivalent, losses characterised Soviet policy in general. Soviet support for the revolution was not publicly articulated until after the Shah's departure in mid-January 1979. On the other hand, Prime Minister Brezhnev's warning to the US against military intervention (of 18 November 1978) in Iran was subsequently used by Moscow as an illustration of the USSR's 'protection of the Iranian revolution'. Once Khomeini was installed, Moscow welcomed him as Iran's leader. Despite the repression of Iranian leftists and Tehran's problems with Soviet friends in the region (Afghanistan and Iraq), despite Iranian allegations of Moscow's suppression of its own Muslims, and despite accusations of Soviet support for Iranian Kurds in their quest for autonomy *vis-a-vis* the central government in Iran, the USSR forbore from any official criticism of Khomeini. Indeed the Tudeh Party in Iran, following Soviet instructions supported Khomeini in *all* his domestic policies, including his demand for an Islamic Republic. Even Tehran's seizure of American diplomats in November 1979, a precedent that could create problems for the USSR, elicited an equivocal Soviet response.

The same ambivalence persisted, and doubts about Khomeini's actions and the future of Iran were more than counterbalanced by the potential benefits to be gained from exploiting anti-US sentiments, particularly if these could be fanned throughout the region.

The Iranian revolution, an upheaval with profound geopolitical repercussions, and a débâcle for Western interests of major proportions, was essentially the result of domestic trends and policies. It set into stark relief the interrelationship between domestic and international politics by underscoring both through its impact the consequences for other states and the limitations on their influence to affect its outcome. The relationship between the strategiç realm and the forces at work in regional politics, though not omni-present, or easy to quantify, is none the less present. Outside great powers, though unable to create trends in particular regions, can modify them; support for moderate states and opposition to revisionist states can affect both the risk-calculus of friend and foe. Soviet persistence, patience and incrementalism can give the impression of an implacable adversary inexorably expanding its influence. If the response to this by the countervailing power is one of timidity and sudden fluctuations, it will diminish the regional states' incentives for identification with it. The United States' performance throughout Iran's crisis and its aftermath succeeded only in narrowing to virtually nil the narrow margin for influence that existed.[9]

Apart from the strategic environment which affects the costs of risk-taking, the regional political context itself is a major conditioner of outside powers' influence. In the Persian Gulf states' foreign policy as often as not is a product of elite orientations. It is seldom buttressed by a deep historical consensus. It is therefore volatile and subject to rapid fluctuations dependent on the perceptions of these elites as to the best course to assure their security. The impression of a militarily strong USSR, self-confident and willing to probe in new regions, if not offset by an equally strong West, is likely to lead to a recalibration of policy to take this into account. One repercussion of Iran's revolution was to accentuate doubts in the Persian Gulf about US willingness to stand by her allies. Saudi Arabia in particular responded by lowering her pro-Western profile and hinting at possible relations with the USSR.

The Soviet Approach to the Region

Three factors stand out in Soviet relations with the Gulf states in the 1980s. First, the proximity of the region to the USSR diminished by technology, accessible to Soviet power by land and sea, and increasingly seen as falling within a zone of 'legitimate' Soviet interest. (Because of her contiguity with both the USSR and the Persian Gulf and Indian Ocean Iran must assume top priority in Soviet planning.) Second, Western dependency on Persian Gulf oil will increase not diminish in the 1980s. As a result the region assumes importance as a point for exercising political (and psychological) pressure against NATO and Japan and perhaps for stimulating inter-alliance feuds. Third, though not as vulnerable as the West, the Eastern bloc as a whole will become increasingly dependent on the region for oil in the next decade.[10] This could result in either commercial competition between the two blocs for oil, or political-military pressure to obtain oil on concessionary terms. In combination the three factors suggest a heightened Soviet interest in a region in which Western interests are vulnerable, and Western influence declining.

The record of Soviet policy, in this as in other regions, is consistent. As a superpower it has sought political parity, a position as co-guarantor with a right to an equal say in the region's affairs. In practice Soviet geographical propinquity would render any notional parity theoretical, giving it a political preponderance analogous to that of the US in the Caribbean. On one level Soviet policies in the region are unimpressive. Persistent interest has not been rewarded by irresistible advances. Growing military power has not seen equal expansion of political influence; Soviet diplomatic assets and liabilities appear equally balanced. An inventory of the former would include proximity and persistence in a turbulent region; a body of doctrine and organisational support; and a revisionist political orientation at least partially in tune with the political opponents of existing regimes in the region. The handicaps, though, are equally impressive; proximity and military power stimulate caution as much as affection among allies; Communism, whatever its theoretical merits, is atheistic and anti-nationalist, unappealing attributes for both Islamic and secular nationalists; and Soviet technical assistance is hardly a currency for influence in a rich region able to buy the best.

On another level Soviet policies appear more threatening, namely the sheer persistence of effort, the hedging of bets, the dominance of the pragmatic over the doctrinaire, and the absence of doubts and guilt feeling which constrain Western policies. For the USSR history is not periodised into four-year cycles, policies do not ebb and flow according to presidential campaigns. While ideologically optimistic, the Soviet leadership has been selective and realistic in its policies. As the Iranian Revolution again demonstrated, the chief criterion for support for a regime is whether it is anti-Western (even if it is also anti-Soviet). This illustrates the Soviet goal of transforming the strategic environment in a direction hostile to the West. Since the USSR's influence in the region has in the past been limited, any reduction of Western influence can benefit it, even if it does not bring with it a direct or conspicuous increase for the USSR immediately. The side-effects of local crises can be exploited to undermine Western alliances and credibility, thereby increasing the Soviet role, at least potentially. As noted, incentives for seeking equidistance between the superpowers increase as the protecting powers' credibility is undermined.

The record of Soviet policy has been uneven. With only two states well disposed towards the Eastern bloc (Iraq and the PDRY), the formal position of the USSR in the Gulf region is unimpressive. Formal diplomatic relations exist with only those states — Iran and Kuwait. Even as footholds in the region, Iraq and the PDRY have been of limited value. The former, politically isolated from Gulf politics until recently, has been, in any case, jealous of its independence. The latter, small and poor, has been on the periphery of Gulf politics politically as well as geographically. Nevertheless progress has been made with both states: in the signing of treaties of friendship; in the encouragement of anti-Western sentiments; and in the utilisation of the anti-Israeli line for a 'strategic alliance'. However, Soviet relations have been impaired by a refusal to take sides with Iraq against Iran (or Syria) or to provide the degree of political support and arms *vis-à-vis* Israel that the Ba'thist leadership in Baghdad has wanted. Cross-cutting regional rivalries, in short, have complicated Soviet choices in the region. The result in Iraq has been a setback for Soviet influence after a high tide in the mid-1970s. In the PDRY exists the only Arab state tightly organised on Marxist lines genuinely bent on regional expansion. This relationship is more promising. The client is poor, weak, dependent and ideologically militant. By providing arms and a sanctuary to the seccessionists in the Dhofar province of Oman it was able to transform a local separatist movement into an ideologically tinged 'national liberation' war. The Soviet Union was willing to assist in this, but not to expand the investment to confront all the Gulf states, including Iran or the US. Since 1978 PDRY pressure on the Yemen Arab Republic and periodic border skirmishes have succeeded in eliciting a strong US commitment of arms to the Sana regime, financed by Saudi Arabia.[11] The PDRY remains a potent instrument for pressure on Saudi Arabia in two ways — first, as a reminder of her continuing military impotence, second, as a threat to her politically. For a united Yemen — whether achieved peacefully or by force — constitutes a major threat to Saudi dominance on the Arabian Peninsula. Thus whether under the leadership of either Sana or Aden, it would be resisted by Saudi Arabia.

Hitherto the Soviet Union has given priority to relations with governments in the region, often at the expense of local Communist parties (for example Iran and Iraq). This policy may well be reversed in the future as relations with governments reach a stalemate and as social strains within their societies give the Communist parties a new lease of life. In the Arabian Peninsula there are no significant Communist parties, although they may become attractive as vehicles for secular opposition to regimes. In the PDRY (as in Afghanistan and Ethiopia) the ideological-organisational element is strong. In the PDRY (as in these other two states) weakness and poverty will combine to make a reduction in the Soviet connection much more difficult.

In sensitive parts of the world, the size or military might of a state is not an accurate gauge of its capacity for disruption. A small injection of force can upset a regional 'balance' and make a difference between success and failure. Externally assisted *coups*, the provision of sanctuary, political assassination and the like make it difficult to discriminate between indigenous and external causes. Surrogate forces and advisers further blur the attribution of responsibility for specific actions which may be plausibly denied.[12] This is not to argue for exclusive attention to delicate regional military balances. Arms and security guarantees can at best provide time, not political solutions. How the time is used depends largely on the regional states, for by timely reforms and attention to demands for political participation many of the roots of instability can be severed before they grow into major security threats which can be harnessed by other states.[13]

Soviet optimism about the prospects for the expansion of her influence derives in large measures from the nature of the political-social forces unleashed by rapid modernisation, and the attendant possibilities for its exploitation. A catalogue of these forces includes:

(1) weak or non-institutionalised means for succession;
(2) increasingly politically mobilised populations with few outlets for self-expression;
(3) heavy and growing demands on weak administrative structures;
(4) societies fractured in differing degrees along religious, ethnic, linguistic lines vulnerable to sectarian feuds, disintegrative tendencies and secessionist movements;
(5) the vulnerability of most states to transnational appeals, be they Ba'athist, Arab nationalist, Pan-Shi'a, or Palestinian nationalist.

In addition to these there persists the Arab-Israeli issue which threatens to polarise the Arab states or to encourage their militance (to assure their security, as in Kuwait). The spill-over effects or chain reaction of instability in this region, demonstrated most recently in the events in Iran and the Arabian Peninsula in 1978–9 illustrate the vulnerability of the region.

How far these indigenous weaknesses are conducive to the extension of Soviet influence is as yet unclear. So far the USSR has managed to convert its attraction as a potential restrainer of Iraq into an arms sales arrangement with Kuwait.[14] That this will translate into influence is not yet proven, although it does provide a precedent. Iran's revolution followed by its move to non-alignment and the fluid political conditions existing in that country have simultaneously undermined stability in the region, constituted a defeat for the West, and opened up the prospect for greater Soviet influence there. A spin-off has been Saudi Arabia's encouragement of informal ties with the USSR, the commencement of Aeroflot visits, and an incipient reluctance to be identified only with the West. The 'revival of Islam', though potentially damaging to the USSR with her forty million Muslims and her avowed atheism, has so far been more damaging to the West. Whether anti-Western feeling can be harnessed to Soviet purposes seems unlikely. Nevertheless to the extent it weakens Western influence and dissolves Western alliances it does benefit the USSR.

The outlook for the USSR in the region is promising. The end of Western primacy in the region closes an era begun by Britain nearly two centuries ago. The expansion of the Soviet diplomatic presence in the Gulf appears likely within the next few years. This will both reflect and accentuate pressures on the littoral states to show greater sensitivity to Soviet interests. Together with a naval presence in the Indian Ocean and quick-reaction interventionary forces positioned in the southern USSR, the Soviet Union will be a major new factor that must consistently be taken into account and even appeased by these states. A willingness to support local allies against their domestic enemies (as in Afghanistan) may indeed make Moscow an attractive partner for regimes worried about internal security. The desire to neutralise such possible interventions in future domestic crises may well constitute a powerful incentive to accommodate Soviet interests by states that are currently lukewarm, if not opposed to it.

Although the prognosis for the region is one of domestic instabilities and turbulence spilling over in some cases into inter-state conflicts, this does not necessarily augur well for external powers. While a breeding-ground for enmities and for outside-power exploitation, these conflicts are unlikely to be clear-cut cases providing them with easy choices. Social and political chaos will not be conducive to systematic exploitation. The balance sheet of Soviet assets and liabilities is as equivocal as the record of Soviet success to date is unimpressive. Nor is the regional environment especially suited to the expansion of Soviet influence. The growth of this influence in time will largely depend on Soviet opportunism, forcefulness and propensity for risk-taking. These may or may not increase as a result of a change in Soviet leadership, a larger Soviet bloc stake in the region's oil, or a new reading (or misreading) of Western powers' responses.

Nowhere in the world is *détente* likely to be tested as keenly as in the Persian Gulf in the 1980s. Whether tacit agreement on a code of conduct of mutual restraint (of reciprocal access) emerges, or whether *détente* is limited only to Europe, the West will not be able to escape a dilemma. In an era of growing political and economic demands for priorities *within* the industrialised world there remains a very strong requirement for an active foreign and security policy in the Persian Gulf region. And while many local forces are converging to undermine stability in that area, the military dimension of security policies remains a powerful instrument to assure interests. Soviet policy will be powerfully affected by Western policies; timidity, guilt feelings, scapegoating and wishful thinking about the utility of military power will continue only to narrow its utility — asymmetrically at that. Security in the Persian Gulf and access to oil will surely not be achieved only by military means, but equally surely they cannot be buttressed without them. Above all, Soviet policies which encourage if they do not instigate disruptive forces can be deterred and a more cautious and moderate policy instilled only through an adequate policy that includes a military counterpoise, combined with a reputation for its judicious use.

Notes

1. Marshall Shulman, 'Toward a Western Philosophy of Co-existence', *Foreign Affairs*, vol. LII, no. 1 (October 1973).

2. Admittedly highly stylised here, few individuals would subscribe to either fully, and most would agree with elements in each; nevertheless this summary is intended to highlight the differing emphases of two approaches.

3. The US depends on Saudi Arabia for 19% of her imports, roughly 10% of total consumption, on Iran for 4% of total consumption. This dependence on Gulf oil is much higher for continental Europe and Japan, ranging from 50% to 70%. For the Western alliance as a whole dependence on the Gulf region will continue to grow throughout the 1980s at least. For a detailed discussion of Soviet policy towards the Persian Gulf, see the author's *Soviet Policy towards Iran and the Gulf*, Adelphi Papers, no. 157 (IISS, London, 1980).

4. See Michael McGwire, 'Naval Power and Soviet Global Strategy', *International Security*, vol. 3, no. 4 (Spring 1979), pp. 134–89.

5. There are 500 Cubans in South Yemen, according to official US sources, and 150 in Iraq (*IHT*, 22 October 1979).

6. See Helmut Sonnenfeldt and William Hyland, *Soviet Perspectives in Security*, Adelphi Papers, no. 150 (IISS, London, 1979), p. 21.

7. This includes its pace, scope and direction, especially the reconciliation of modernisation, with what Patrick Seale calls the 'moral basis of society', a consensus in the roles of church and state.

8. Especially in the cut-back of gas sold on concessionary terms to the USSR and

the cancellation of a larger project involving a three-way swap of gas in the 1980s, 1GAT-II.

9. See my 'The Strategic Repercussions of Iran's Upheaval', *Survival* (May/June 1979); apparent US acquiescence in Soviet definitions of the 'permissible' in relation to assisting allies starkly contrasts with the failure of US protests to make any impression on Soviet intentions.

10. The USSR holds 11% of the world's oil reserves. Space precludes a detailed discussion of this here but the assumptions are that Soviet oil production will decline, that the USSR will then face a choice between cutting exports (which provided 50% of her foreign exchange in 1977 of $6.7 billion) accepting a cut in economic growth, or limiting subsidised oil exports to East Europe. The last two have serious domestic political and alliance-weakening implications. Even if all three measures are followed, however, Soviet interest in foreign oil will increase; the natural area of interest will be the Persian Gulf.

11. But this was followed by an equal $300 million commitment of arms by the USSR to Sana in late 1979. Soviet arms are likely to be more effective because they have been the principal supplier and therefore can count on some knowledge among the Yemenis.

12. For example, is foreknowledge or acquiescence in a *coup* part of abetting it?

13. I have Oman in mind here.

14. The arms sold in 1976 were SAM-7 missiles. Soviet advisers did not come with them.

4   THE UNITED STATES-IRANIAN RELATIONSHIP 1948–1978: A STUDY IN REVERSE INFLUENCE

C.D. Carr

The conventional view of US-Iranian relations during the reign of the Shah is that of Iran as the dutiful pro-Western ally of the United States under the aegis of a ruler who owed his position to direct US intervention in 1953 and who remained a US 'puppet' throughout his tenure of office. To support this view, factors such as the acceptance of US intelligence gathering facilities on Iranian soil and the unwavering support of the Shah for US actions in South-East Asia are proferred as evidence. Indeed, the major reason given for the Shah's fall from power is that he was closely identified with the policies and politic-economic philosophy of the United States, with the inference that the United States exercised control over the Shah's actions and dictated policy from Washington. However, available data from primary sources now indicate that far from taking a lead from the United States and being controlled by the US executive, the Shah himself influenced and often controlled the US policy-making process in pursuit of the goal that dominated his philosophy throughout his reign; the pursuit of the total physical security of the state through the expansion and equipment of the Iranian armed forces to the highest qualitative level.

Variously described as his 'personal quirk', obsession or pre-occupation, the Shah's interest in the development of the Iranian armed forces and especially in the acquisition of advanced weaponry caused to create an environment of coercive diplomacy between himself and successive US administrations that occasionally lapsed into evident crises, with US-Soviet competition being forced into a confrontation by the deliberate actions of the Shah. The trauma induced by such crises, coupled with a carefully constructed campaign of diplomatic attrition on US-Iranian security matters emanating from the Shah, so effectively narrowed US options in regard to Iran that by 1972, when President Nixon allowed the Shah unprecedented *carte blanche* on arms procurement from the United States, this was simply the recognition of the *status quo*. The Iranian tail had been wagging the US dog for nearly two decades before that date and the control of US-Iranian relations, especially on security matters, had been held in Tehran and not in Washington.

The Iranian Control System

Richard Cottam, in his analysis of competitive interference, identifies two basic types of leverage available to states indulging in coercive diplomacy: active and manipulatable and passive and less manipulatable.[1] The latter is aimed at creating and maintaining a bilateral relationship whose environment is generally conducive to a beneficial, to the applier of the leverage, alliance. The former lever is used specifically to achieve a fixed and obvious goal through the exertion of threats and pressures against the antagonist. The Shah used both forms of leverage throughout his rule and, despite the manifest crudity of many of his actions, succeeded in reducing the constraints imposed upon him by the US foreign policy-making process.

At an early stage the Shah was forced to realise that his own perceptions as to the strategic importance of Iran to the United States and to the West and the means of safeguarding this 'shield of the Middle East' were at odds with US policy.[2] Even in 1947, barely a year after the Soviet 'puppet' regime had been driven out of Azerbaijan, the US Department of State had considered that, for military assistance purposes, Iran could not be considered amongst those states that were vital to US security or 'under direct and immediate danger'.[3] Under the original legislation on the US military assistance programme, the Mutual Defense Assistance Programme of 1949, Iran was lumped together with the Philippines and Korea under Title 3 status, to share a total of $27 million, whilst Greece and Turkey, with Title 2 status, were to receive more than $211 million. This disparity especially in regard to US military assistance to Turkey, was to prove the major bone of contention for the next decade and was to be the basis of the crisis in US-Iranian relations that emerged in January 1959.

The realisation that even a thousand-mile border with the Soviet Union and a history of Soviet interest and interference in Persia/Iran was not enough to persuade the United States to treat Iran as a special case caused the Shah to construct the passive leverage system that he hoped would persuade the United States to underwrite his security programme. Primarily designed to inhibit pragmatic, nuts-and-bolts issues, such as the ability of the Iranian armed forces to absorb large amounts of sophisticated weaponry or for the economy to support excessive defence expenditure, the system concentrated upon a campaign of continuous advertisement of the vulnerability of Iran and of the danger that such vulnerability posed to US security.

The Shah needed to achieve certain goals in relation to the US foreign policy-making body: he had to establish the importance of

Iran to the United States; the importance of himself to Iran; and the importance of Iranian security, in terms of numbers of armed forces personnel and the quality of their equipment, to himself. To achieve this he took every opportunity to stress the instability of Iran in relation to external threat and to promote his own plan to reduce that threat. By personalising his demands, the Shah ensured that his requests for US assistance reached the highest levels of the US executive, often to the President himself. Thus, US-Iranian relations are often a direct insight into the mind and functioning of the President of the day and as such provide valuable knowledge of the presidential management of foreign affairs.

Two letters from the Shah to Presidents Eisenhower and Kennedy respectively illustrate the Shah's technique of applied leverage. Both were ostensibly to congratulate the President on an election success (Eisenhower's re-election in 1956 and Kennedy's election in 1960), but each used the pretext to press the Iranian case for a special relationship with the United States, especially on military assistance matters.[4] The Eisenhower letter begins with hyperbolic flattery, as does the letter to President Kennedy (to the latter the Shah writes: 'We all rejoice at the prospect of a young and vigorous personality taking in his hands the reins of government at a crucial juncture in the affairs of a troubled world.') The letter to Eisenhower continues with the Shah particularising current regional and global problems (the Hungarian uprising and the Suez crisis) to the situation in regard to Iran, stressing that 'regional armed conflicts with conventional weapons are not to be ruled out as a thing of the past'. Taking the argument further, the Shah postulates that 'aggression can be forestalled, if countries occupying key positions are well prepared and their military as well as financial and economic needs supplied'. He asserted that Iran was such a key state and that 'the present military weakness of Iran would. . .constitute a danger not only to herself, but also to the Middle East region and as a corollary to the whole free world'. Re-emphasising Iran's 'unique position', the Shah requests the personal intervention of the president on his requests for military assistance and signs the letter: 'Believe me, my dear Mr. President'.

The letter to President Kennedy is almost identical in tone and content. The Shah stresses Iran's role as oil supplier to the West and as the 'key to Asia. . .and the key to Africa in the near future' (remarks tailored to fit events in Laos and the Congo). The Shah then proclaims the physical insecurity of Iran 'in these troubled times' and notes that Iran is in need of assistance that 'only America can furnish'. The letter finishes with a reminder to the president that the Iranian budget had to be prepared by March 1961 and therefore could the President inform the Shah of how much Iran could expect in the way of military and economic assistance for the coming year?

The letters are simply illustrations of a process that was continually present within US-Iranian relations, particularly during the Eisenhower, Kennedy and Johnson administrations. The effect was to create an acquiescent response from the US executive through attrition; it was easier to conform to the Shah's perceptions as to the security of Iran than to attempt to stem the torrent of requests through argument or counter-proposals. However, occasionally the Shah's demands for assurances and *matériel* from the United States could not be met, and it was on these occasions that the Shah utilised the active leverage device.

Prior to 1953 the United States had not committed itself wholeheartedly to the Shah as the most propitious leader for Iran. Their initial support for him was based upon the 'least worst' thesis; in October 1949, US ambassador John Wiley wrote to President Truman: 'We must perforce hope for much from the Shah since we may expect so very little from others in [Iran].'[5] A year later, Secretary of State Dean Acheson ventured: 'was this not a case of corrupt and incompetent government [in Iran] which no matter how much equipment or money [the US] put in it would be doomed to fail?'[6] Clearly the United States was less than committed to the Shah at the time and therefore he was not in a position to apply leverage. But after the United States assisted him in regaining control of Iran in 1953 he recognised an important corollary of their action that was to form the essential basis of his leverage system.

After the return of the Shah in 1953 his opponents, both within and outside Iran, proclaimed him to be a puppet of the United States and that he would be forever in their debt. But the Shah recognised that the United States, through their support for him personally, had signalled that they regarded both the stability of Iran and his continued presence as ruler important enough to undertake politically risky active intervention on his behalf. Through their actions the United States policy-makers had 'crossed the Rubicon' in their relations with Iran and had handed the initiative to the Shah. As a by-product of this commitment the Shah also learned the important lesson of never allowing any likely candidate to emerge that the United States might possibly be inclined to support in preference to himself. As a result, when the Shah finally fell from power there did not exist any group or individual with the experience, training and unblemished record capable of representing the middle ground in Iranian politics.[7]

In the years following the counter-revolution in Iran the United States found that it had hitched its wagon to an uncertain and volatile star. The Shah's 'appetite for soldiers and military hardware was unrealistically unlimited' and the pressure on the US exchequer for assistance on a global scale precluded accession to all of the

Shah's demands. Even after the 1958 *coup* in Iraq had persuaded the United States to promise more support for the Shah, this did not satisfy the Iranian leader and as a result he made use of the active lever for the first time.

The active lever was comprised of a 'controlled crisis', with the Shah choosing the issue, the time scale and the options. The controlled crisis itself required a number of factors to be present: the Soviet Union had to be visibly prepared to play a catspaw role; the issue had to be clearly defined and simple to implement; the US target had to be isolated (in the 1959 case it was President Eisenhower and Secretary of State Dulles) and capable of unilateral policy-making if pressed to do so; the Shah had to be convincing in his threats to turn to the Soviet Union if the United States did not acquiesce to Iranian demands.

Threatening to turn to the Soviet Union for aid if such *matériel* is not forthcoming from the United States was (and is) a fairly standard tool in developing state diplomacy. This threat, however, tends to lose much of its potency when uttered by a conservative autocrat whose political philosophy is the very antithesis of Soviet socialism. The Shah recognised this impediment and overcame it in two ways. First, he never threatened to ally himself distinctly with the Soviet Union but rather threatened to 'go neutral'. In the bloc-building atmosphere of the 1950s and 1960s to lose an ally to neutrality was tantamount to a 'win' by the competing ideology and this the Shah realised. He therefore sought to make it quite clear that he was capable of going 'neutral'; the Department of State opined in 1961 'that the Shah is capable of making such a switch [to neutrality] — one of our Ambassador's main tasks has been to dissuade him, to soothe him, and to reassure him of US support'.[8] The other device that he used to ensure that the United States was convinced of his earnestness when negotiating with the Soviet Union was through the projection of himself as a 'non-rational actor' on matters concerned with Iranian security. With the US executive convinced that the Iranian armed forces and military security were an 'obsession' resulting in an 'insatiable appetite', the Shah destroyed any rationalist approach to a controlled crisis by robbing the US policy planners of any attempt to construct lines of logic that might defeat his objective.[9]

The controlled crisis also relied upon the imposition of a time-urgency factor to further confuse and constrict the US policy-makers. In respect to President Eisenhower, who was a man who relied upon a broad spectrum of canvassed opinion before making decisions, this was particularly important, and the Shah ensured that the crisis of January 1959 had to be resolved extremely quickly (within twenty-four hours), with the resolution being handled by the

President, Secretary of State John Foster Dulles (who was ill) and the US ambassador in Iran. As a result, the President took the line of least resistance and acquiesced to the principal demands of the Iranian leader.

The controlled crisis device is an element of coercive diplomacy. The United States termed it 'blackmail' and the Soviet Union, recognising that they had been used for political purposes, accused the Shah of being a 'liar and a tool of the US'.[10] The Shah considered it to be a legitimate process, capitalising on the 'power of the weak' to overcome the interference of a major power in the maintenance of security of a sovereign state. Whether viewed from Washington, Moscow or Tehran, however, the willingness to use such a device illustrated that Iran was far from being the pliant, unquestioning ally of the United States that formed the official public image of Iran. Indeed, so successful was the Shah in applying leverage against the Eisenhower Administration that he became a victim of this success, for when the Kennedy Administration required a state upon which to practice its own more tightly controlled foreign assistance philosophy and programme, Iran became the natural choice.

Like many propositions of dubious validity, the Shah's assertion that Iran deserved special treatment from the United States was plausible if taken at surface value. Iran did have a long border with the Soviet Union and that country had traditionally coveted Iran as an outlet to the Indian Ocean. The Iranian armed forces were not of the size nor well enough equipped to overcome a Soviet attack. And Iranian oil was becoming increasingly important to Western economies, including the United States. But whilst these arguments obviously carried some weight with the US foreign policy-makers it was the scale of the Shah's demands and the manner in which he conducted his bilateral relationship with the United States that placed him in dispute with successive administrations. In 1949, he requested US support for a 300,000-man army, with at least 150 tanks and three wings of jet aircraft.[11] In 1958, he requested that the United States furnish equipment for five extra divisions, even though the twelve divisions already present in the Iranian Army averaged less than 40 per cent in strength.[12] He also requested F-100 aircraft, even though the Imperial Iranian Air Force had trouble maintaining the F-84s in its inventory, and further demanded NIKE and HONEST JOHN missiles.[13] This illustrates the 'most of the best' ethos that was to pervade the Shah's weapons procurement programme from the start and which was to culminate in six years of acquisition, from 1973 to 1978, when the Shah ordered more than 10 billion dollars' worth of arms from the United States alone.

Apart from being the largest purchaser of US arms under the Foreign Military Sales (FMS) programme, Iran achieved a number of other 'firsts' in relation to US foreign assistance. Iran received more, in dollar terms, under the Military Assistance Programme (MAP) than any other country not in formal alliance with the United States. Under the transitional FMS credit scheme, Iran received more than twice as much as any other state, including more than $200 million under the US Export-Import bank's 'Country X' scheme. In qualitative terms, Iran was the first state to receive a number of sophisticated weapon systems; the F-5 aircraft, the F-4D and the F-I4 being just three.[14]

It was to attempt to constrain this invasion of Iranian funds from the civil to the military sector that the United States, up until the Nixon presidency, attempted to influence the Shah's policies. Only the Kennedy Administration succeeded in overcoming the restrictions imposed by the Iranian control system and the premature termination of that presidency allows there to be some doubt as to the long-term success of the administration's countermeasures.

In order fully to assess the extent to which US-Iranian policy was controlled by the Iranian leader it is necessary to review certain events during the period 1953–78 and to establish certain facts. By following the train of circumstances it is possible to understand why the United States allowed itself to fall victim to the 'king's new clothes' delusion in regard to Iranian stability and why it was so unprepared for the revolution of 1979.

The Eisenhower Administration

The period of the Mossadegh government had two important effects upon US attitudes towards Iran. Apart from forcing the United States to recognise the Shah as the only Iranian capable of maintaining the pro-Western orientation of the country, the confrontation between Mossadegh and the British government over the nationalisation of British oil interests in Iran saw the beginning of the eclipse of British power in the Gulf region which was finally to come to pass with the decision, in 1968, to withdraw the British military presence from the area. The United States, in supporting the Iranian stance on the issue, assumed the mantle of guarantor for the security of the Gulf and thus Iran passed from the UK sphere of influence to that of the United States.

When the United States ensured the Shah's return to power in August 1953 it did so with the knowledge that Mossadegh had been a popular leader backed by the 'vast majority' of the Iranian people.[15] The Shah, therefore, would need tangible support from the United States, in terms of both economic and military assistance, if he was to build a power base within the bureaucracy and the armed forces.

As a result, US military assistance to Iran increased nearly fivefold from 1952 to 1953, with a similar rise in non-military aid. Much of the aid was in the form of grants under the various provisions of the Mutual Defense Assistance Programme (MDAP) and the Mutual Security Act of 1954. But one category of funds, the defence support grant, existed in an appropriations limbo that allowed it to be used with some flexibility by the US executive.

The defence support grant allowed the budget of the recipient government to be balanced by directly injecting US funds into the military appropriations sector of the budget. In the two years 1956–7, Iran received more than $60 million in defence support funds from the United States and this enabled the Shah to pursue his security goals whilst ensuring that the civil sector received enough funds to continue for a further year. Even with this support, however, the Iranian government announced a budget deficit of $80 million in June 1957 and the United States was made aware that Iran expected the US to 'pick up the tab'.[16]

This seeming ingratitude by the Iranians stemmed, in part, from what the Shah and many others of his countrymen felt was an implicit promise by President Eisenhower fully to support the Iranian armed forces development programme if Iran joined the Baghdad Pact.

During the Eisenhower years the philosophy of collective regional security agreements as a bulwark against Communism was zealously promoted by both the President and his Secretary of State, John Foster Dulles. For the Northern Tier states, of which Iran was one, the United States promoted the Baghdad Pact, a formal military alliance with the United Kingdom as a full member but with the United States only maintaining an associate membership. Iran joined the Pact in 1955 and thenceforth claimed that the United States had lured Iran into abandoning her traditional neutrality with promises of increased military assistance that was not forthcoming. As was reported by the US ambassador in 1959: 'The Baghdad Pact has meant nothing to the people or government of Iran other than the strong hope of massive aid and/or territorial guarantees from the US in return for Iranian adherence to the Pact.'[17]

On a number of occasions the US government had attempted to convince the Shah that it was economic madness to attempt to build up the Iranian forces to a level whereby they might hope to hold off the Soviet Union.[18] Iran could not hope to conduct a *tous azimuts* defence policy and therefore the best guarantee of Iranian sovereignty lay in 'the deterrent strength of the United States'.[19] This was somewhat undermined by the unwillingness of the United States to commit itself to full membership of the Pact but, in compensation, President Eisenhower proposed to equip the armed forces of Iran to a level that he considered to be advanced, in terms of quality of equipment if not in numbers of personnel.[20]

President Eisenhower's generosity was overtaken by events when, in July 1958, the government of Iraq was overthrown by a group of radical army officers. In an attempt to counter unease amongst the other Pact members, Dulles and Eisenhower proposed an 'executive agreement' between each of the Pact members (apart from Iraq) and the United States, on a bilateral basis, which guaranteed the security of each state in the event of external threat.[21] For the Shah this was not good enough. He desired a firmer commitment by the United States, which he wished to be partially in the form of an immediate increase in US budgetary support and partially in the form of assistance for the formation of an additional five divisions for the Iranian Army. The United States felt itself unable to conform to this demand and the situation developed rapidly into a confrontation.

In the second week of January 1959 the Shah contacted the Soviet Union and indicated that he was willing to enter into negotiations with the Russians over a non-aggression treaty. The Soviet ambassador and his immediate superiors in the Soviet Foreign Ministry were aware of the Shah's motives and were extremely wary in their response. It was Khrushchev who personally decided to send a negotiating team to Iran and who decided to 'give the Shah almost anything he might want'.[22] The Shah began negotiations by stating that Iran would remain within the Baghdad Pact and although the Soviet team were later to agree to this point, their deliberations delayed matters long enough for the United States to initiate counter-moves.

The US ambassador, reporting directly to Secretary Dulles and the President by airgram, interpreted the Shah's move as 'blackmail' for more US security support and proposed a number of options:

(1) the substitution of a territorial guarantee or treaty for the proposed bilateral executive agreement;
(2) provide sufficient budgetary aid to satisfy the Shah, to be 'topped off with a showy offer of rockets, destroyers or other hardware';
(3) hope that the Shah will take fright at the last moment or that the Soviet negotiators would 'overplay their hand'.[23]

In the event, a compromise was reached through which President Eisenhower, in a personal letter to the Shah, pledged to reduce the Iranian budget through an increase in the US defence support fund, to increase the level of military assistance to Iran and covered all with a warning as to the dangers of negotiating with the Soviets.[24] The Shah received the letter and shortly thereafter became diplomatically indisposed and the Soviet negotiating team dispersed with some rancour. Upset at having been misused in so visible a manner, the

Russians began an anti-Shah propaganda campaign that was to last for more than three years and which, when the Shah found it necessary to use the Soviet Union for leverage purposes in 1966, made a sufficient impression on the Iranian leader as to encourage him to compensate them with a small order for Soviet military equipment.

Despite the warning from the US ambassador that 'repeated experiences with such appeasement show that its adoption and execution would foreordain another, and probably more serious, crisis within one year at the most', the Shah did succeed in his immediate aim of levering more budgetary support from the United States. His knowledge of the US policy-making process and of fiscal arrangements within the executive had made him aware that if the President was sufficiently pressed he could, through judicious manipulation of certain funds, find additional monies. With the controlled crisis providing the incentive, President Eisenhower diverted $13 million from the Presidential Contingency Fund and thus met half the cost of the Iranian budget deficit.[25]

Whether the Shah received promises of extra hardware is unclear. The lead-time on such items as NIKE missiles would have precluded their arriving in Iran before the end of Eisenhower's term of office and the assumption of President Kennedy to the position of chief executive ushered in a completely different attitude towards Iran. The armed forces were, however, expanded during the period 1959/60 and US military assistance to Iran also peaked during these years, to an average of $90 million per year. The Shah had manifestly succeeded in applying both passive and active leverage during the Eisenhower years and this served further to fuel both his grandiose military plans and his own belief in his ability to manage the US policy-making process. Unfortunately for the Shah, President Kennedy and his advisers also believed in their own capacity to manage and to dictate and the Shah and Iran were chosen as a primary target for a re-emphasis on the aims of US foreign assistance policy.

The Kennedy Administration

In March 1961, President Kennedy announced his foreign assistance policy in the form of a special message to Congress.[26] After announcing changes in the administration of the US foreign aid programme, the President outlined a philosophy that centred upon long-range planning for the economic development of the recipient states and upon the implicit right of the United States fully to involve itself in all matters pertaining to utilisation of American aid. For the recipients, and especially for the Shah, this augured the beginning of the most active period of US interventionism, a time in which 'you [the US] tried to impose your type of regime on other people'.[27] For the supplier, the United States, the Kennedy initiative, as laid down in the Foreign Assistance Act of 1961, sanctioned the right of the donor to participate in 'social engineering' on the grounds that grant aid represented US public money and should be administered and accounted for as such.

President Kennedy personally ordered a review of the US aid programme to Iran in early 1961 and a presidential task force was forced to formulate a long-term programme for Iran.[28] After reporting upon the immediate internal political problems within Iran during the first months of 1961, President Kennedy charged the task force with investigating the possibility of the US providing further support for the Iranian armed forces for counterinsurgency purposes (this being at the onset of the 'counterinsurgency era') and also to report on the size and composition of MAP aid to Iran.[29] To achieve the latter the task force canvassed the opinions of those agencies most connected with military aid to Iran: the Joint Chiefs of Staff, the Department of State, Bureau of the Budget, Department of Defense and the Central Intelligence Agency. The replies of each of these agencies provide an interesting mosaic of bureaucratic response to contemporary attitudes on US-Iranian relations.

The State Department report was an amalgam of 'facts to be faced', arguments based upon the advantages of the *status quo*, and insubstantial proposals for development.[30] After admitting that the Iranian elections of early 1961 were 'largely rigged', the position paper painted a bleak picture of mob-ruled, xenophobic conditions if the United States was to withdraw its support from the Shah. Adopting a pragmatic stance, the paper then concluded that the United States had little or no control over the actions of the Shah:

> It is often suggested that the United States, using its aid programs as leverage, could issue orders to the Shah which would, by their implementation, result in political tranquility. It has been suggested that some of these reform measures would include the ending of corruption, the establishment of genuine democratic institutions, the downgrading of the military. . . These suggestions presuppose that the Shah is a creature of the United States. . .,a common misperception in Iran. Any United States ultimatums or even heavy-handed hints would be regarded by the Shah as an intolerable interference in his affairs and would probably result in corresponding moves on his part toward the USSR and neutralism.[31]

On this basis, the Department of State recommended to 'continue its present policy of reassurance to the Shah. . .along with delicate inferences by our Ambassador to the effect that the Shah should devote his attention to his internal political problems rather than to foreign and military affairs'.[32]

The Joint Chiefs of Staff, somewhat predictably, supported an increase in US assistance to the Shah, couched in military terms that included full US membership in the Central Treaty Organization (CENTO), the replacement for the Baghdad Pact, and the stationing of 'atomic weapons' in Iran.[33] Also predictably, the Bureau of the Budget report accused the US bureaucracy of 'procrastina-tion. . .irresolution. . .and the apparent inability of the country mission to project an impression of competence'.[34]

The Bureau of the Budget report was important, since it called into question the impartiality of the US mission in Iran, and claims that it had lost its objectivity resulted in the necessity of the President having to send his own representative, Chester Bowles, to Iran in early 1962. The BoB contended that:

> the preoccupation of the Shah with military forces appears to have influenced US policy posture to such a degree that support of the government has been equated with efforts to satisfy the demands of the Shah for military assistance activity.[35]

The CIA report hedged its bets, identifying the principal US problem as being 'how to give the Shah sufficient support to preserve his present pro-Western policy without encouraging excessive demands for aid'.[36] It also warned that if the Shah was 'convinced that the US was withdrawing or significantly reducing its support for him, the chances of his working out an accomodation with the USSR would be much greater'.[37] Thus the consensus opinion within the bureau-cracy was to continue to support the Shah at least at the level that had been achieved during the Eisenhower Administration.

In June 1961, President Kennedy met Premier Khrushchev in Vienna and the subject of Iran was raised. As a result of the Soviet leader's interest in Iran and because of the doom-laden nature of Khrushchev's comments, Kennedy returned to the United States determined to investigate further the stability of the Shah and his country. The result was a determination to redirect Iranian efforts away from military matters and towards the socio-economic development of the state.

The bureaucratic input into the task force analysis of 1961 had demonstrated that the President required a more detached and objective judgement on the situation in Iran if he was to formulate a feasible long-term programme that he could present to the Shah. He therefore sent Chester Bowles to Iran in February 1962 to assess for himself the nature and extent of the social, economic, political and military problems and to report back directly to the President. Bowles met the Shah and other Iranian leaders and, despite fierce opposition from the US ambassador, recommended that the military element of the US aid programme should be downgraded and supported the proposal made by the task force entirely to eliminate the budgetary support programme.[38]

By March 1962 President Kennedy and his staff had prepared a proposed approach to the Shah on the question of reducing his armed forces to 150,000 men (down from 170,000 and 90,000 less than the projected level that had resulted from the January 1959 crisis).[39] Stressing the interrelationship between military, economic and political factors, the proposal took the form of classic 'carrot and stick' approach to the problem. In return for accepting the cut in forces and the termination of defence support funds, the Shah was offered a military assistance package that stressed the qualitative aspect of procurement that the Shah held so dear. At a cost of some $330 million, the MAP proposal included two squadrons of advanced aircraft, a squadron of medium transport aircraft, the complete replacement of all the soft-skinned vehicles in the Iranian inventory and the completion of a military airfield.[40] But the Shah was unimpressed and for more than six months 'difficult and delicate negotiations which involved the President, the Secretary of State, the Secretary of Defense and the Joint Chiefs of Staff' were conducted between Washington and Tehran.[41] Finally, in September 1962, the Shah accepted the inevitable and signed the agreement.

The question must be asked as to why the Shah did not invoke the controlled crisis leverage system in order to modify the US programme in his favour. It is possible that he did in fact endeavour to do so but was foiled by the resolution of President Kennedy and his advisers. Evidence, albeit much of it circumstantial, indicates that on hearing of the US proposals the Shah began to inject uncertainty into the US-Iranian relationship through such devices as publicly implying that he would abdicate if the United States would not make concessions and warning the United States that 'if America laid down the foreign assistance burden, he was sure that the communists were willing to assume it'.[42] But these statements were simply precursors to his central coercive argument.

Since the events of January 1959 the Soviet Union had been conducting a vigorous propaganda campaign against the Shah and this had disturbed him greatly.[43] Any gesture that he might make to appease the Soviet government would have been welcome and therefore the Shah entered into negotiations on a matter which, in the climate of 1962, was as potentially injurious to US foreign policy objectives as the non-aggression treaty had been in 1959. Aware that Iran was considered by the Soviet Union to be 'analogous to United

States relations with Cuba', the Shah reacted favourably to a Soviet proposal to reach an understanding which would ban all 'foreign rocket bases' from Iranian soil.[44]

The Shah ensured that the United States was made cognisant of his negotiations during his visit to Washington in April 1962 and that he was continuing his dialogue with the Soviets after his return.[45] He was forced to realise the intransigence of the Kennedy Administration during the visit of Vice-President Lyndon Johnson to Tehran in August 1962, and with the termination of supporting assistance he appeared to capitulate. But on 16 September 1962, as foreign missile bases were beginning to take on a deep significance, the Soviet Union announced that Iran had pledged not to have foreign missiles within its borders and that it would 'never become the instrument of aggression against the territory of the Soviet Union'.[46]

Whether the Shah's actions were the result of pique or whether he found it necessary to underline his independence at this particular juncture is unclear. Relations with the Soviet Union did improve after this agreement, so it did have the desired effect upon Iranian-Soviet relations. But it failed to impress the Kennedy Administration, which pressed ahead with the oversight of the Iranian reduction of forces and reorganisation of budgetary priorities.

The premature ending of the Kennedy Administration leaves a number of questions unanswered. Would the Iranians have accepted the run-down in their forces or was the Shah preparing to exert more pressure in order to lever more assistance from the US? Would the resolve of the United States have continued at a high level to resist the hostility of its own bureaucracy to a plan formulated and largely implemented by the President's personal staff?

Whatever may have been the case, the Kennedy Administration was able to prove that with sufficient political will and with a viable, long-term proposal it was possible to impose restraint upon the Shah without Iran 'going neutral'. Since it was the only period in more than thirty years that the United States ever attempted to modify the Shah's ambitions and priorities, this ensures that the Kennedy proposal is somewhat of a milestone in US-Iranian relations. Whether or not one agrees with the contemporary assertion that the United States had not only a right but an obligation to intervene in the internal affairs of sovereign states in order to safeguard its own security, the important fact is that whilst all US administrations from Truman to Johnson believed in this right, only the Kennedy Administration attempted to apply it to Iran.

The Johnson Administration

If the Kennedy Administration represented the period of greatest presidential involvement in US-Iranian relations, then the Johnson Administration represents the period of least presidential interest. Important decisions were made in respect to the development of US-Iranian relations during this period, but it was the traditionally administrative sections of the US bureaucracy that took charge of this development, rather than the upper echelons of the executive.

President Johnson remained preoccupied with affairs in South-East Asia and with the formulation of his own domestic social programmes throughout his time in office. Only when events reached crisis proportions, as they did in respect to US-Iranian relations during 1966, did the President personally take an interest. For the most part, policy remained in the hands of 'middle-level officials', with the all-important task of co-ordinating US arms sales being orchestrated from the small office for International Logistics Negotiations (ILN) within the Department of Defense.[47]

One of the major decisions in which the President did take a personal interest was the conclusion that, with oil revenues increasing, Iran could afford to purchase the defence *matériel* that it required. Against apparent Iranian opposition, the United States and Iran signed a Memorandum of Understanding on 4 July 1964 which committed Iran to purchasing military equipment for cash, through credits provided by the United States.[48] As a result of this agreement, Iran was to receive $504 million in credits to purchase US military services and equipment during the years 1965–9, of which more than $200 million came from the Export-Import Bank (ExImbank) through the 'Country X' loan scheme.[49] This was a device whereby the Department of Defense could utilise ExImbank funds without that agency knowing what was to be purchased or even which country would be using the credit. The availability of these funds and of other sources of cash and credit enabled the ILN to control an arms purchase from 'the cradle to the grave', without the necessity of having to involve superiors in the department or in other bureaux. In this way, during the formative years of US arms sales policy the control of both formulation and implementation rested with a small group of bureaucrats within the State and Defense Departments, whose chief motivation was to increase the dollar value of US arms sales for parochial reasons.[50]

Even with the Iranian parliament prepared to sanction the Shah's regular requests for funds to support military credits, the cost of the most modern weaponry mitigated against the purchase of such systems as the most advanced combat aircraft, of which, in the mid-1960s, the F-4 represented the apotheosis. Nevertheless, even with procurement cost of more than $2 million (1965) per unit, the Shah determined to obtain at least two squadrons of the aircraft and in early 1966 succeeded in having a team from the Joint Chiefs' staff go to Iran to investigate the legitimacy of the Shah's claim on the aircraft.[51]

The Joint Chiefs' mission returned to Washington in March 1966 and reported that there was military justification, in the light of the threat posed by the Iraqis to the Iranian oil installations, for the acquisition of two squadrons of F-4D aircraft. But not everybody within the US executive was able to concur with this decision (Secretary of Defense Robert McNamara and the Agency for International Development both objected to the drain that the purchase, which would total $200 million, would place upon the Iranian economy).[52] The Shah was pressed to acquire more F-5 aircraft (a design specifically related to the needs and purchasing power of developing states) which had been in the Iranian inventory, under MAP, since January 1965. The Shah remained adamant on the F-4s, however, and the impasse began to develop into another controlled crisis confrontation.

Since the *rapprochement* with the Soviet Union that had begun with the missile bases agreement of April 1962, Iran had made demonstrable moves towards a closer relation with the Soviet Union and its Eastern European allies. Trade agreements had been signed with Poland, Czechoslovakia, Hungary and Romania. Most significantly, the Shah had signed an agreement for Soviet assistance in the construction of a steel mill near Isfahan, with payment to be made in natural gas, which up until that time had been flared off by the Iranians.[53] In essence, the Iranians were receiving the plant as a gift from the Soviet Union.

With this new background of cordiality between Iran and the USSR, the credibility of an Iranian threat to turn to the Soviets for advanced weaponry, which began to emerge in early 1966, was enhanced. After the standard preliminary warnings (in a speech to the Iranian parliament, the Shah stated: 'We take orders from no-one. . . We shall now see what our oil revenues will be and what will be the terms of sale of. . .military commodities. We shall then act according to Iran's best interests'[54]), the Iranians let it be known that they were considering a purchase of Soviet missiles and aircraft if credits for the F-4s were not forthcoming from the United States.

Aware that the decision on the financing of the F-4s was to take place in Washington in mid-July, the Shah injected his own time-urgency factor through the device of a publicly stated, if somewhat veiled, threat. In a newspaper interview on 14 July 1966, the Shah stated: 'We don't have the money to pay cash [for the F4s] and we will know in a week to ten days whether the United States understands our problem.'[55] With the United States aware of the distinct possibility of Iran purchasing advanced weaponry from the Soviet Union, with the political and strategic implications that such a move would have upon the regional balance, there began a week of intensive consultation. The President, the National Security Council and the US ambassador were all involved in the discussions which resulted in acquiescence to the Shah's demands.[56] In September 1966, Iran contracted for a squadron of F-4s, with training and support, for $160 million, with options (subsequently taken up) on a second squadron for $40 million.

Apart from being another instance in which the controlled crisis was used with evident success, the sale of the F-4s was to have wider implications for US foreign policy. The Shah, fully cognisant of the extreme reaction within the Soviet Union engendered by his use of the USSR as a bargaining tool in the January 1959 negotiations, sought to militate against such a reaction in 1966 by offering the Russians a consolation prize. In February 1967, the Iranians announced the low-technology defence *matériel*, to the value of $110 million, was to be purchased on credit from the Soviet Union.[57] By this move, the Shah not only appeased the Soviet Union but also signalled to the United States that his threat of July 1966 was not completely hollow.

As an unfortunate by-product of the announcement of the agreement with the Soviet Union, the press and public within the United States were made aware of certain inconsistencies in policy-making and management surrounding arms transfers. Congress, which had been kept in a deliberately unenlightened state on arms sales matters, became angered that it had not been informed of the sale of the F-4 to Iran until a press announcement in December 1966 and instituted hearings into arms transfer policy, which resulted in the ending of the Country X loan scheme, the curbing of the power of the ILN and, through the Foreign Military Sales Act of 1968, legislation aimed at bringing arms sales within the realm of accountability to Congress.[58] But all this was to have little effect upon Iranian arms procurement ambitions, for by 1969 the Shah was beginning to pay for most of his arms from the United States in cash and the constraints imposed upon him by credit purchase were no longer present.

Although stymied in the early stages of the Johnson Administration by the hostility that was made evident by the termination of grant aid in 1964, the Shah was able to establish his autonomy very successfully during this period. He emerged out of the interventionist shadow of the Kennedy era and, by the time of the election of Nixon in 1968, had begun to symbolise a permanency and power that was not only extremely rare amongst developing states but was becoming increasingly rare amongst all of America's allies.

The Nixon Administration

Prior to 1969 the Shah of Iran had been forced to contend with a US foreign policy philosophy which was basically at odds with his own ambitions for the development of Iranian security programmes. The US belief in the necessity of interventionist policy, coupled with what it considered to be the right and obligation to play an active role in the formulation of Iranian foreign and domestic policy given to it through the extensive civil and military assistance programmes, imposed severe constraints upon the Shah's plans for a militarily and politically strong and autonomous Iran. As outlined in the Shah's 'independent national policy', the Iranian leader, dubious as to the continued willingness and ability of the United States to guarantee the security of Iran (and of himself as the ruler of Iran), decided upon a course of action that, whilst still exploiting the benefits to be gained from Western technology, aspired towards a military and economic strength that precluded external interference, especially from the United States.

Iran was greatly assisted in its desire for recognition as a regional power through the announcement by the British, in 1968, that their military presence in the Gulf was to be terminated. The Shah immediately promoted Iran as the new 'gendarme' to fill the vacuum and to stop the Soviet Union, together with the Iraqis, from turning the Gulf into a 'Russian lake'. It was to this problem to which President Nixon addressed himself in the early months of 1969 and which, in May 1972, was to lead to the end of all attempts by the United States to influence the plans and ambitions of the Shah for a 'Great Iranian Civilization', founded upon a physically secure state underwritten by large amounts of sophisticated military hardware.

In July 1969, Nixon's security adviser, Henry Kissinger, had ordered a review of the Gulf situation by the staff of the US National Security Council (coded NSSM-66).[59] In the previous month President Nixon had outlined his own security policy in the Guam Doctrine, which stressed heavily the requirement for 'self-help' amongst the allies of the United States. As a result, the NSC study reached the conclusion that Iran, together in partnership with Saudi Arabia (fulfilling a minor military role), should be fully supported in its desire to fill the vacuum left by the British withdrawal.[60] With Iran and Saudi Arabia acting as the 'twin pillars' of Western interests in the area, the threat of Soviet interventionism could be minimised without the need for direct US involvement. But if Iran was to act as a proxy of the US, it required that it be given the proper tools to do the job.

The United States, in concert with the British, pledged to underwrite the Iranian arms procurement programme in an effort to build

Iran into the undisputed military power in the Gulf and this gave the Shah the freedom of movement and action that he had pursued, through the use of the control system, since 1948. With credits supplied by the US government and with increased oil revenue resulting from successful negotiations with the international oil companies, the Shah began to order military equipment of a qualitative and quantitative nature that hitherto had been unimaginable. Between 1969 and 1971, orders for US equipment included 30 C-130 transport aircraft, more than 200 helicopters (US-designed but produced under licence in Italy) and hundreds of US armoured vehicles. But, despite the support given to him by President Nixon and Henry Kissinger, the Shah still felt constrained by the process of control through which all arms requests were forced to pass through within the US bureaucracy. These controls, especially in regard to the state-of-the-art aircraft that the Shah desired to procure for his air force, appeared to be thwarting him in his grand design for Iranian security, and he appealed to the President to be allowed to submit his own list of requirements without the necessity of each request having to pass through the standard review process.

In May 1972, President Nixon and Dr Kissinger visited Tehran. During that visit the Shah was told that henceforth all Iranian arms requirements would be allowed to be formulated by the Iranians themselves and that the United States would act simply as an implementational agency.[61] This decision was transmitted as a memorandum to the US bureaucracy in July 1972, instructing them to allow the Shah to have virtually any conventional weapons that he desired and for which he could pay.

Not every agency within the United States had supported the President's decision. Prior to the May 1972 trip, the Department of Defense had 'specifically advised the president in writing' not to commit the United States to a *carte blanche* policy on arms sales to Iran.[62] The President and Dr Kissinger, however, chose to disregard this advice and indeed evidence suggests that prior to this 'unprecedented step for a non-industrial country' there was no 'major interagency review' of US arms sales policy to Iran before the decision was made.[63]

Both the President and his security adviser may have been relying upon the financial constraints imposed on the Shah through the high cost of sophisticated weaponry to moderate the Iranian demand for arms. However, even by November 1972, the Shah was accelerating his arms procurement programme to previously unimagined limits (he ordered 400 helicopters from the United States in that month alone, bringing to 700 the number of such aircraft on order by that date).[64] The quantum jump in oil revenues brought about by the October 1973 crisis did not itself engender the Shah's $12,000 million 'shopping spree' for arms. The process had begun decades before, had been accelerated by the decision to sell the F-4D to Iran in 1966, and sanctioned by the presidential decision of May 1972. The revenue from the October 1973 crisis simply allowed the Shah to place orders from his list of optimal requirements.

Although by the onset of the Nixon Administration the Iranian control system had been made redundant, the Shah continued to make the US policy-makers aware of its latent threat through periodic references to the option of turning to the Soviet Union for military and non-military trade.[65] Apart from keeping the US 'honest', these utterances were aimed at overcoming any questioning of a relationship that the Shah now considered to be one of a dialogue between equals. Challenge to his right to indulge in what an increasing number of observers considered to be a frivolous waste of Iranian resources on unnecessary weaponry was answered with paternalistic hyperbole and allusion as to the power of the oil weapon. In this manner, as in the past through allusions to the East-West balance of power, the Shah was able to inhibit debate and co-opt disbelievers.

To argue whether the Iranian adoption of an aggressive stance on oil price rises was the result of the Shah's predilection for advanced weaponry or whether the increase in revenue stimulated that desire is a 'chicken and egg' debate of dubious value. But nevertheless, the Shah, the supposed staunch ally of the United States and the West, was a prime mover in the OPEC campaign for higher oil prices that brought about considerable hardship to that group of nations to which the Shah had always proclaimed a special bond, the developing states, and which sent the developed states into economic recession. This factor tended to be ignored within the United States when Iranian orders for US goods and services (especially the $15 billion bilateral trade agreement signed in March 1975) appeared to be 'sopping up' the petrodollars that had been accumulated as a result of the 1973 oil price rise. Even the *New York Times*, often a forceful critic of the Shah and his policies, proclaimed, in 1975, that Iranian orders for arms and other US products was 'a stepladder out of the recessionary cellar', forgetting that it was Iran that had helped place the United States in that cellar.[66] But, as with many other aspects of US-Iranian relations, the argument that the United States was actively benefiting from Iranian oil wealth was an illusion. In the period 1972–8, US imports from Iran, almost wholly of oil, rose from a current dollar value of just over $2 billion to nearly $29 billion. In the same period, US exports to Iran, also at the $2 billion level in 1972, rose to just under $18 billion, leaving a deficit of $11 billion in the favour of Iran.[67] Even the great capacity of US industry could not absorb the damage done by the increase in oil prices.

The Nixon and Ford administrations' unquestioning support for the Shah did not constitute aberrant behaviour in regard to US-Iranian relations but was merely the logical extension of the way that those relations had been developing since 1948. Worn down by decades of conflict with the Shah's regime, the US bureaucracy had been forced to rationalise its acquiescence to Iranian *diktat* in the same inflated terms that the Shah himself had used to justify increased aid to Iran in the early stages of the relationship. What had been unacceptable then had been made acceptable by the attrition of decades of applied leverage, assisted by what has been termed the inertia quality of the 'curator mentality' within the US Department of State and by the presidential seal of approval that was the Nixon Doctrine. What had been the 'Iranian problem' during the Truman, Eisenhower and Kennedy administrations had, by 1969, been transformed into an 'alliance and partnership' which precluded even constructive criticism.

Although the question of US support for the Shah's national security programme was not the only issue between the United States and Iran in the post-war period, it so dominated the relationship as to force all other issues into insignificance. In its simplicity, the clash of perceptions and philosophy over the Shah's concept of what constituted a reasonable outlay on defence should have resulted in a reasonable compromise being found at some juncture during the thirty years of the Shah's rule. The imposition of the will of either side, attained by the United States during the Kennedy Administration and by the Shah after May 1972, was not a matter of compromise but of victory and defeat, and the medium-term effects of both of these confrontations was to inhibit the free exchange of ideas and criticisms that a genuine alliance and friendship should foster.

After the Fall: Where did the US Go Wrong? A Post-mortem

In January 1979, when it became obvious that the Shah's regime was close to the finish, the United States began to question why it had been so unprepared for the Iranian Revolution. The US intelligence community was blamed for not warning the President and the executive of the impending chaos and investigations were instituted.[68] The reality, of course, lay far deeper and was far more fundamental than a failure of intelligence. The years of appeasement that the US ambassador had complained of in 1959 had robbed the United States of the ability to deal honestly with Iran and its problems. More important than its inability to conduct an honest dialogue with the Shah, however, was the inability to conduct an honest appraisal of US-Iranian relations within the policy-making and implementational process of the United States. Years of what was seen to be necessary and expedient acquiescence to Iranian demands became an exercise in justification and self-propagandisation that was to result in the facade of US-Iranian friendship and symbiosis becoming the accepted reality.

With pragmatic economic and political arguments providing support for an unquestioning US attitude towards the Shah, the 'king's new clothes' ethos that dominated US-Iranian relations in the last decade almost inevitably contributed to the build-up of pressure within Iran. With the United States championing human rights as a cornerstone of US foreign policy but ignoring the history of abuse of such rights within Iran for pragmatic reasons, the result was to ensure a general and violent dislike of the United States as a hypocritical nation without which the Shah would have been unable to remain in power. This build-up of pressure, which because of its seeming dormancy but cataclysmic results might be termed the 'Krakatoa effect', had vented on a number of occasions (in 1953, 1961 and 1963), but had been capped through aggressive action by the Shah and by the United States. But to suppress such a force is not necessarily to defeat it, but may simply ensure that when it does finally 'blow', the result is an explosion of undirected, destructive energy.

In justifying his support for the Shah's demands on defence matters during the debate in 1962, US ambassador Holmes stated:

Because of the Shah. . .we have [in Iran] a government aiming. . .at the betterment of the people without having to resort to demagoguery, hysterical xenophobia or foreign adventures of the sort of thing that plagues us in many other underdeveloped countries. It is the Shah's authority which has saved Iran from being so plagued. . .I agree that the Shah is obsessed with the question of military security but believe that by alleviating these worries and increasing his confidence. . .we will more readily obtain full cooperation on other matters of great importance to us.[69]

A year earlier, before President Kennedy was to meet with Khrushchev in Vienna, an anonymous State Department official was charged with preparing, on a 'devil's advocacy' basis, the likely views of the Soviet Union on the Shah and his regime. Two such likely views were:

(1) if the Iranian government does not heed the voice of the people and alter its policies, the people will take matters in their own hands and make such changes themselves;

(2) irrespective of the changes in foreign policy by the present government, it is inevitable that the people of Iran will replace it with a government truly responsive to their desperate needs and demands, because the Shah cannot carry out the reforms demanded by the people without destroying himself — something he will never do.[70]

From both of the above can be divined, in the light of hindsight, a large measure of irony. The ambassador's plea for appeasement takes on the attributes of a self-fulfilling prophecy, whilst the anonymous State Department official, if he had been reporting, in early 1978, in his own guise, rather than that of a Soviet counterpart, might have been credited with oracular powers. But both, and most particularly the ambassador's communication, touched upon the essential error of US policy towards Iran: the belief that *ad hoc* responses could be substituted forever in place of a thoughtful, long-term plan for the mutually beneficial development of US-Iranian security interests. In the face of a single-minded monarch with fixed ambitions, the looseness and inconsistencies that form many of the safeguards of a democratic state became, for the Shah, exploitable foibles.

Perhaps if anything is to be learned from the US-Iranian experience it is to be found in the comment made by Lincoln Bloomfield, in testimony before a subcommittee of the US Senate's Foreign Relations Committee during hearings into US arms sales policy in 1976. Speaking specifically in regard to US arms sales policy towards Iran, he stated: 'But we now also know that few. . .countries remain either United States or Communist allies. Like all countries, they have no permanent friends or permanent enemies, only permanent interests.'[71] The question to be posed on the matter of US-Iranian relations during the tenure of the Shah is this: was thirty years of appeasement that achieved, in security terms, relative stability during that period, worth the 'inevitable' result? It is a question that has wider implications than those simply relating to the US-Iranian experience.

The Iranian Revolution has served to break the continuity of US-Iranian relations not simply because the Shah has departed, but because the revolution is a rejection of the value system that the United States represents and which the Shah used as a yardstick of Iranian development. Whatever the disputation that had emerged between the United States and the Shah over the priorities for that development, the Shah's admiration for Western technology and the symbols of the advanced industrial society remained an unwavering constant throughout his rule. When conflict arose between Iran and the United States it was on matters of time-frame and applicability of such symbols rather than the advisability of applying essentially alien values upon a traditional culture. Under the Shah, progress was equated with numbers of miles of multi-lane highway under construction, visible public works on a grandiose scale and, most importantly, with armed forces developed to the limits of defence technology. It is these representative icons of Western interference that have borne the brunt of the revolutionary fervour and such is the force behind the rejection of these symbols that any Western attempt to explain or justify their presence in Iran will, for the foreseeable future, meet with suspicion, hostility and repudiation.

During the Shah's rule the United States craved for the public identification of Iran with US ideological and foreign policy programmes and goals. So successfully had the facade of amity and symbiosis been maintained that with the departure of the Shah the wrath that the revolutionaries vented upon the deposed leader inevitably overflowed to include the United States. All revolutions need readily identifiable enemies as well as manifest heroes and the twin 'evils' of the Shah and the United States provided that convenience within the Iranian Revolution. With no colonial heritage or experience of an independence struggle, it is perhaps understandable that the target of the Iranian revolutionaries should be what many in the developing world consider to be the arch-promoter of neo-colonialism and the purveyor of illusions of prosperity, the United States. But the fervour will diminish in time, the United States will be forced into reaching an accommodation with Iran and there will be obvious pressures to return to nostalgic policies.

Keeping Iran from 'going neutral' or 'going Communist' will inevitably dominate future US policy in Iran as it has done in the past. How the United States might actively or passively ensure that such an eventuality does not take place will require the United States not only to forget the slights, real and imagined, that have been directed towards it during the revolution but also to rid itself of all vestiges of the old, paternalistic order within the US policy-making and implementational process. Advice from elements within the US government departments that dwell upon the 'success' of the *coup* of 1953 and of the 'stability' imposed by the Shah upon Iran can only be of disservice in the formulation of any renewed US-Iranian relationship. Honest counsel from flexible minds uncluttered by embitterment or by past loyalties will be at a premium when the situation stabilises to the degree whereby normal diplomacy prevails. After thirty years of self-indoctrination such minds will be difficult to find, but must be a prerequisite to a mature and balanced attitude towards post-revolutionary Iran.

If Iran is as important to the United States as the actions of successive US administrations have indicated, then a fundamental adjust-

ment in the way that the United States should approach and negotiate with any future Iranian government should not be an
unacceptable price to pay. It is an adjustment that the great colonial
powers had to make on the dissolution of their empires and if it is
made correctly it does not necessarily mean a diminution in the
global status of the United States. Indeed, by adopting a less
obviously cynical approach to relations between the developed and
the developing states the United States could steal a march upon its
rival, the Soviet Union. Above all, the United States must demonstrate that involvement does not have to be synonymous with intervention. The temptation to manipulate and dictate must be avoided.

The sour after-taste of the Iranian Revolution will linger for some
time in both Iran itself and in the United States, and it will feed off a
distillate composed of the thirty-year rule of the Shah. It is, therefore, extremely important that in an environment that encourages
instant mythology and diatribal hyperbole that the factual evidence
should be approached and utilised with as much candour as possible.
The history of post-war US-Iranian relations has a validity for post-
revolutionary relations if it is used to highlight pitfalls, rather than to
score political points. It may not be able to tell the United States how
to conduct future diplomacy with future Iranian governments, but it
might be able to save the United States from making some mistakes
for a second time.

Notes

1. Richard Cottam, *Competitive Interference and Twentieth Century
Diplomacy* (University of Pittsburgh Press, Pittsburgh, 1967), pp. 82–3.
2. The Shah to President Eisenhower, letter dated 20 November 1956, Dwight D.
Eisenhower Library (hereafter DDE Lib.).
3. Memorandum of Conversation on Iranian Purchase of Military Supplies,
from Edwin Wright, Assistant to the Director of the Office of Near East and African
Affairs, dated 14 April 1947, in *Foreign Relations of the United States 1947*, Vol. V
(GPO, Washington, DC, 1971), p. 905.
4. Shah to DDE, letter 20 November 1956. Also letter from the Shah to President
Kennedy, dated 26 January 1961, John F. Kennedy Library (hereafter JFK Lib.).
5. Letter: US Ambassador in Iran to President Truman, dated 25 October 1949,
President's Secretary's File, Truman Library (hereafter Truman Lib.).
6. Summary of daily meeting with the Secretary of State (Dean Acheson), dated 1
March 1950, in *Foreign Relations of the United States, 1950*, Vol. V (GPO,
Washington, DC, 1978), pp. 482–3.
7. 'We should of course be on the alert for the rise of competent and creative
alternate leadership [to the Shah], in or out of the military, which might allow a reconstruction of alternatives. . .[though] this latter is very difficult in Iran. . .since all
such contacts run the risk of alienating the Shah', from 'The Current Internal Political Situation in Iran', Department of State Position Paper, dated 11 February 1961,
JFK Lib.
8. Ibid.

9. 'I agree with Ambassador Bowles that the Shah is obsessed with military security,' US Ambassador in Iran in letter to the Secretary of State, dated 19 February 1962, JFK Lib.

10. Telegram, US Ambassador in Iran to the Secretary of State, dated 30 January 1959, DDE Lib., and Telegram, US Ambassador to Secretary of State, dated 16 February 1959, DDE Lib.

11. *Foreign Relations of the United States 1949*, Vol. VI (GPO, Washington, DC, 1978), pp. 471 and 488.

12. Memorandum from the Joint Chiefs of Staff, dated 3 February 1959, DDE Lib.

13. Ibid.

14. 'Foreign Military Sales and Military Assistance Facts, 1975 and 1978', (Defense Security Assistance Agency, US Department of Defense, Washington, DC).

15. Briefing Memorandum for the President re meeting with Premier Mosadeq [*sic*], dated 22 October 1951, signed by Dean Acheson, Truman Lib.

16. *New York Times* (hereafter *NYT*), 8 June 1957.

17. Telegram, Ambassador to President, 30 January 1959.

18. 'If we attempted to build up our military establishments to a level comparable to that of the Soviet Union, we would wreck our economies and leave ourselves so weakened that we would collapse without even being subjected to military attack': Secretary of State Dean Acheson, in Memorandum of Conversation, dated 18 November 1949, Truman Lib.

19. Background Information on the Visit of the Shah of Iran, dated 28 June 1958, John Foster Dulles to the President, DDE Lib.

20. 'The President said he felt strongly that we should assign first priority to increased military and economic aid for Turkey and Iran. They should have all the assistance they can absorb. The Secretary said we had trouble with Defense about going further than 10 divisions for Iran and the President replied that we should get those 10 decisions fixed up fine [*sic*]'; Telephone Log, dated 16 July 1958, DDE Lib.

21. President Eisenhower was worried that the Baghdad Pact states might misinterpret the term 'special agreement' proposed by Dulles at a meeting of the Pact in London in July 1958 as being in the form of a treaty, which would have had to be ratified by the Congress. Dulles informed him that he told all of the Baghdad Pact states that the United States would *not* sign treaties with them, only make the less binding 'executive agreement'; Telephone Calls, the President to J.F. Dulles, dated 28 July 1958, DDE Lib.

22. Telegram, US Ambassador in Iran to Secretary of State, 16 February 1959, DDE Lib.

23. Telegram, Ambassador to Secretary of State, 30 January 1959.

24. Ibid., also Telegram, J.F. Dulles to US Ambassador in Iran, 30 January 1959, DDE Lib.

25. Summary of Obligations and Expenditures, Assistance Program for Iran, International Cooperation Administration, undated report (1962), JFK Lib.

26. Special Message to the Congress on Foreign Aid, 22 March 1961, *Public Papers of the Presidents*, John F. Kennedy, 1961 volume (GPO, Washington, DC), pp. 205–13.

27. *US News and World Report*, 27 January 1969.

28. Arthur M. Schlesinger, *A Thousand Days* (André Deutsch, London, 1965), p. 380.

29. Memorandum: Robert Komer to McGeorge Bundy, dated 22 May 1961, JFK Lib.

30. Position Paper, 'The Current Internal Situation in Iran', dated 11 February 1961, JFK Lib.

31. Ibid., p. 7.

32. Ibid., p. 9.

33. Ibid., p. 10.

34. 'Some Notes on the Situation in Iran', Bureau of the Budget, dated 20 March 1961, JFK Lib.

35. Ibid.

36. National Intelligence Estimate NIE 34–61, Central Intelligence Agency, 1961, JFK Lib.

37. Ibid.

38. 'US Ambassador Holmes proceeded to take a series of positions that were directly opposed to my own. I was trying very hard to push the Shah to move ahead with a land reform program and other long-overdue reforms. But [the Ambassador] wanted to bring all these planes in all the time to please the Shah. So we were on opposite sides'; Chester Bowles, Oral History Transcript, JFK Lib., p. 92.

39. Memorandum: National Security Council, Subject: NSC Action 2447, Proposed Approach to the Shah of Iran, dated 8 March 1962, JFK Lib.

40. Schedule of Alternative Categories for the Modernisation of Iranian Armed Forces, Possibilities for FY 1962–67, Department of Defense, JFK Lib.

41. US Military Assistance to Iran — Position Paper, Department of Defense, dated 22 April 1963, JFK Lib.

42. *NYT*, 13 and 14 April 1962.

43. CIA, NIE 34–61.

44. The President's Meeting with Khrushchev: Department of State Position Paper, dated 25 May 1961, JFK Lib.

45. *NYT*, 16 September 1962.

46. Ibid.

47. 'There is evidence to suggest that the type and destination of American military equipment is determined by middle-level officials in the Department of Defense'; statement by Senator Symington, *NYT*, 24 July 1967.

48. In a statement in 1967, Lieutenant-General Khatami, Commander of the Imperial Iranian Air Force, stated, when asked about the US policy of changing from grant aid to arms sales to Iran, 'I think it is a mistake. I am really sorry to see it. Once you make a mistake like that you pay and pay a lot more to make up for it,' *Aviation Week and Space Technology*, 7 August 1967.

49. *Foreign Military Sales Facts 1975*, p. 19.

50. In a letter to the National Security Council, Jeffrey Kitchen, a State Department official responsible for the integration of US arms sales with foreign policy objectives, complained strongly about the heavy-handedness of the ILN: 'the roughness of ILN pressure tactics is leaving a legacy damaging to the long-term local contacts [of the US embassies in countries to which the ILN had sent representatives] and that it is denigrating the role of the local US representation because the real decisions are being made by the ILN/Treasury team from Washington,' Memorandum from Jeffrey Kitchen to Alexis Johnson, National Security File, dated 24 March 1964, Lyndon Johnson Library.

51. Henry Kuss (Deputy Assistant Secretary of Defense for International Logistics Negotiations), in a statement before the Subcommittee of Near East and South Asian Affairs of the Senate Foreign Relations Committee, Hearings on Arms Sales to the Near East and South Asia, 90th Congress, 1st Session, 1967 (GPO, Washington, DC), p. 12.

52. US Armament and Disarmament Problems: Hearings before the Subcommittee on Disarmament, Senate Foreign Relations Committee, 90th Congress, 1st Session, 1967 (GPO, Washington, DC), p. 76.

53. *Keyhan International*, 6 June 1966.

54. *Keyhan International*, 2 March 1966.

55. *NYT*, 14 July 1966.

56. 'In 1966. . .I negotiated on behalf of my government with Iran to determine whether it could possibly afford to borrow 50 million dollars from the United

States. . . It took a week to negotiate that and we finally concluded; yes, Iran could barely handle a 50 million dollar loan'; Testimony of Leonard Alne, before the Special Subcommittee on Investigations, of the House International Relations Committee: *Hearings on The Persian Gulf, 1975: The Continuing Debate on Arms Sales*, 94th Congress, 1st Session, July 1975 (GPO, Washington, DC, 1976), p. 176.

57. In mid-1966, Senator Fulbright, Chairman of the Senate Foreign Relations Committee, heard that the Shah was negotiating for F-4 aircraft and sent a member of his staff to Iran, under the cover of an Interparliamentary Union group, to assess the need for such an aircraft for Iran. The staff member reported that he could see no such need and the resulting staff study, *Arms Sales and Foreign Policy*, served to start the controversy that ended with intensive investigation of US arms sales policy and the entering of the Foreign Military Sales Act on to the statute books — interview with Dr William Bader, Washington, 3 November 1978.

58. Ibid.

59. Tad Szulc, *The Illusion of Peace* (Viking Press, New York, 1978), p. 167.

60. Ibid.

61. *US Military Sales to Iran*, A Staff Report to the Subcommittee on Foreign Assistance of the Committee on Foreign Relations, US Senate, July 1976 (GPO, Washington, DC), p. VIII.

62. Multinational Corporations and United States Foreign Policy: Hearings before the Subcommittee on Multinational Corporations, Senate Foreign Relations Committee, Part 17, 94th Congress, 2nd Session (GPO, Washington, DC, 1977), p. 176.

63. *US Military Sales to Iran*, p. 41.

64. *Aviation Week and Space Technology*, 13 November 1972 and *International Herald Tribune*, 14 May 1973.

65. See the remarks of the Shah in an interview in *Business Week*, 24 September 1977: 'if the US were to cut off arms supplies. . .so hurt for hurt, if we have no other alternative, we could buy arms from the Soviet Union.'

66. C.L. Sulzberger, 'The Biggest Deal of All', *NYT*, 15 March 1975.

67. *International Monetary Fund Directory of Trade Yearbook* (IMF, 1979), p. 22.

68. Hearings on the Performance of US Intelligence in Iran, House of Representatives Subcommittee on Intelligence (GPO, Washington, DC, January 1979).

69. Telegram: US Ambassador in Iran to Secretary of State, 19 February 1962, JFK Lib.

70. President's Meeting with Khrushchev, Position Paper.

71. Lincoln Bloomfield, Testimony before the Subcommittee on Foreign Assistance, Senate Foreign Relations Committee, 94th Congress, 2nd Session, *Hearings on US Arms Sales Policy*, September 1976 (GPO, Washington, DC, 1977), p. 98.

5 PERSIAN GULF NUCLEARISATION: PROSPECTS AND IMPLICATIONS

Lewis A. Dunn

The overthrow of the Shah of Iran has not fundamentally changed the prospects for the spread of nuclear weapons to the Persian Gulf. By the mid-1980s, many countries of that region, including the Iran of Ayatollah Khomeini or his successors, will have available the technology for acquiring at least a rudimentary nuclear weapon capability. More important, the change of regime has removed only one possible political impetus to widespread proliferation in the Gulf: an Iranian nuclear weapon programme driven by the Shah's pursuit of regional hegemony and global prestige. Two other triggers — an expanding nuclear arms race between India and Pakistan and Iraqi acquisition of nuclear weapons in an attempt to upset the Middle East *status quo* — remain. The not improbable result well could be the dangerous entry of nuclear weapons into some or even many Gulf countries' arsenals by the late 1980s.

Eroding Technical Barriers

During the next decade, the technical barriers to nuclear proliferation in the Persian Gulf will gradually erode. A growing number of the countries there will acquire the rudiments of a civilian nuclear infrastructure — and with that knowledge begin to ascend the nuclear ladder towards the technical capability to acquire nuclear weapons. In addition, the probability of expanding nuclear grey marketeering will further erode those technical barriers and allow countries to compensate for the gaps of indigenous technologies.

Up the Nuclear Ladder

Of the Persian Gulf countries, Iran until the overthrow of the Shah clearly had the most ambitious civilian nuclear energy programme. Building on the modest nuclear infrastructure of the early 1970s — which consisted solely of the operation of a small research reactor; the availability of only a limited pool of trained Iranian nuclear technicians, engineers and physicists; and a semi-moribund National Iranian Atomic Energy Commission established in 1958[1] — Iranian plans had called for the rapid and ambitious development of an indigenous civilian nuclear industry. To achieve that goal, the former regime began construction of two West German reactors,[2] initiated negotiations with the French firm Framatome to purchase additional nuclear power plants,[3] began sending students and others abroad for training,[4] undertook to build with assistance from the French Commissariat l'Energie Atomique a nuclear research centre at Isfahan,[5] and purchased a 10% share in the French-sponsored Eurodif uranium enrichment plant.[6]

These nuclear energy development plans have been drastically curtailed under the Khomeini regime. With the exception of possibly finishing the two West German facilities at some future date, there are no plans for building additional nuclear power plants.[7] Nonetheless, the still existent even if weakened domestic nuclear research establishment, students still training abroad, and those near-completed plants provide a basis for later resumption of Iran's ascent of the nuclear ladder.

By contrast, Iraqi nuclear energy activities have accelerated. Organised in 1957, Iraq's Atomic Energy Commission since 1968 has operated a small 2 MWe Soviet-supplied research reactor. Successful negotiations have been completed for French assistance in the creation of a new Iraqi research centre outside Baghdad, with its centerpiece to be a French 70 MWe research reactor.[8] It appeared initially that that reactor would be fuelled with a material directly usable for bombs; but in fact such a reactor destined for shipment to Iraq was sabotaged mysteriously in April 1979.[9] France has agreed to replace the reactor but apparently hopes to use the available time to redesign the core to permit use of other than high enriched uranium.[10] Finally, Iraq is negotiating to purchase a 600 MWe nuclear power plant from France.[11]

Elsewhere in the Gulf, the Kuwaiti government also has indicated that it has plans for developing civilian nuclear technology. British, French and German companies have been requested to bid on helping Kuwait set up a nuclear research and training centre including a 40–50 MWe research reactor and desalination facility. In addition, statements by Kuwaiti officials indicate a longer-term interest in acquiring several dual-purpose power-generating/water-desalinating plants in the 1980s and 1990s.[12]

Similarly, Saudi Arabia has decided to set up an atomic research centre and has evinced an interest in using nuclear reactors for desalination.[13] Nor should Saudi Arabian financial support for Pakistan's aborted purchase of a French reprocessing plant be overlooked in considering its interest in nuclear technology. And though its future civilian nuclear programme goals remain vague, there are reports that Saudi Arabia may send some of its future engineers and physicists to Pakistan for training.[14]

Thus, the dissemination of civilian nuclear technology in the Persian Gulf, though still limited, will continue in the next decade. Even in Iran's case, the one example of diminished activities, some students trained abroad will return home and some limited ongoing nuclear research programme will remain. And as that process of mastering nuclear know-how and technology continues, these countries will move closer to the capability of producing rudimentary nuclear weapons, whether by misusing civilian nuclear research or power facilities or by seeking to build small semi-indigenous facilities dedicated to production of nuclear explosive material. Their gradual ascent of the nuclear ladder — as well as that of key countries in neighbouring regions — is depicted by Table 5.1.

Grey Market Assistance

The emergence of more extensive nuclear grey marketeering in the early 1980s would accelerate the erosion of technical barriers by compensating for the gaps in indigenous nuclear capabilities. Although reasons of space preclude a detailed discussion of this threat,[15] several aspects of this phenomenon should be noted.

First, following Pakistan's recent example, discussed more fully below, a country might circumvent the controls on the major suppliers' nuclear exports by purchasing 'grey area' components or materials — items that have legitimate civilian uses as well as being necessary for acquiring a nuclear weapon capability. Reliance on purchasing agents and various similar covers in order to hide the ultimate destination of the purchases also could be a part — as they were in Pakistan's efforts to acquire centrifuge technology — of these grey area transactions.[16]

In addition to such purchases of grey area components and materials not fully covered by existing nuclear exports controls, a Gulf country could use its financial resources to hire nuclear mercenaries. Especially if the domestic market for nuclear power in advanced countries continues to shrink, there may be a growing number of out-of-work nuclear engineers, technicians, scientists and administrators whose backgrounds would run the gamut from reactor design and operation to plutonium reprocessing and handling. They could provide aspirant Persian Gulf or Middle East proliferators with useful technical know-how and practical experience as well as needed organisational skills for setting up and running a nuclear weapon programme. Further, others among them might well have had experience with nuclear weapon design itself. Depending on the state of the indigenous technology and the particular incentives of the recipient, the assistance of nuclear mercenaries might speed up completion of a semi-indigenous nuclear weapon programme not dependent on misuse of the fuel cycle,

Table 5.1: Growing Technical Capabilities

		[as of] 1980	1985	1990
6.	Capability to build enrichment facility	Israel	Israel	Israel
5.	Capability to build small plutonium production reactor (2–5 bombs/year)	Egypt (?); Iran (?); Iraq (?); Israel	Egypt; Iran; Iraq; Libya (?); Saudi Arabia (?); Syria (?)	Egypt; Iran; Iraq; Libya; Saudi Arabia; Syria
4.	Effective access to significant quantities of divertible fissile material from civilian nuclear fuel cycle		Iraq	Egypt (?); Iran; Kuwait; Syria
3.	Operation of nuclear power plant(s) and start of nascent nuclear infrastructure		Iran (?): Saudi Arabia	Egypt (?); Iran; Kuwait; Syria
2.	Nuclear power plants under construction or planned	Egypt; Iran, Iraq; Kuwait; Saudi Arabia Libya; Syria	Egypt; Kuwait; Libya; Syria	Libya
1.	Assimilating basic theoretical knowledge			

Sources: See 'World List of Nuclear Power Plants', *Nuclear News* (August 1977); *Nucleonics Week*; John R. Lamarsh, 'Dedicated Facilities for the Production of Nuclear Weapons in Small and/or Developing Nations' and 'Level II Dedicated Facilities' in *Nuclear Proliferation and Safeguards*, Appendix Volume II, Part Two, Appendix VI-A and Appendix VI-B (US Congress, Office of Technology Assessment, Washington, DC, 1977); Albert Wohlstetter *et al.*, *Moving Towards Life in a Nuclear Armed Crowd?* (Pan Heuristics, 22 April 1976); and Ted Greenwood, George W. Rathjens and Jack Ruina, *Nuclear Power and Weapons Proliferation*, Adelphi Paper no. 130 (International Institute for Strategic Studies, London, 1977).

permit a more ambitious indigenous programme, or facilitate illegal diversion from those civilian nuclear fuel cycle facilities. Nor is talk of nuclear mercenaries simply speculation: Pakistan's efforts to build a centrifuge enrichment plant were greatly aided by the return of a Pakistani national who had had access to sensitive centrifuge design information at the URENCO plant in the Netherlands, and according to a recent report several Dutch scientists pessimistic about the prospects for nuclear energy in the Netherlands are considering leaving for jobs in other countries.[17]

Grey market nuclear collaboration with another country is a further means by which a Persian Gulf country could acquire a nuclear weapon capability. Whether involving the barter of oil for technical assistance or a joint venture in which each partner supplied a component or material that the other lacked, such collaboration could readily compensate for technical weaknesses. From this perspective, Saudi Arabian ties with South Korea and Taiwan could take on added significance if political pressures on the Saudis to move towards a nuclear weapon option intensified in the 1980s.[18]

Thus, in a variety of ways grey market transactions could supplement the capabilities of prospective proliferators in the Persian Gulf, further reinforcing the conclusion that the technical barriers to proliferation in that region are likely to erode in the next years.[19] But that erosion is a necessary but not sufficient reason for envisaging the spread of nuclear weapons to the Gulf. More important are the political dynamics that could drive some of those countries to 'go nuclear'.

The Political Dynamics of Persian Gulf Proliferation

Before the fall of the Shah, most speculation about proliferation in the Persian Gulf centred on Iran's incentives and disincentives for 'going nuclear'. An Iranian nuclear weapon programme motivated by the Shah's idiosyncratic pursuit of regional hegemony, global status and Iranian grandeur was regarded as the most likely trigger to proliferation in the Gulf. The Shah's overthrow — and the turn of Iran in the direction of the more circumscribed goals of its traditional foreign and security policy consensus[20] — has removed, therefore, that impetus to the spread of nuclear weapons in this region. None the less, forces already gaining momentum in both South Asia and the Middle East could set in motion expanding proliferation chains eventually spilling over into the Persian Gulf.

An India, Pakistan, Iran, . . . Proliferation Chain: Late 1980s Persian Gulf Proliferation

Building on nearly two decades of atomic energy-related research and development, India detonated a nuclear explosive device in May 1974. The longer-run precipitates of that device may include successively a matching Pakistani test, a fully fledged Indian nuclear weapon programme, nuclear arms racing in South Asia, heightened pressures for a matching Iranian decision to acquire nuclear weapons, and proliferation elsewhere in the Gulf.

In the aftermath of India's 1974 test — claimed to be that of a 'peaceful nuclear explosive' — there was considerable pressure from Indian scientists to test additional nuclear devices. Partly responding to hostile foreign reaction, the then Prime Minister Indira Gandhi resisted those urgings. Then, in 1977, Mrs Gandhi's government was ousted in parliamentary elections and Morarji Desai became Prime Minister. Desai reiterated his earlier opposition to an Indian nuclear weapon programme and made that opposition government policy.[21] However, Desai's forced resignation as Prime Minister in July 1979 removed that constraint and once again restored a measure of fluidity to Indian nuclear weapon policy. Of greater importance, there are several pressures that could result in a fully fledged Indian nuclear weapon programme by the mid-1980s.

Evidence is increasingly available that soon after that Indian test the Pakistani government of the then Prime Minister, Zulfikar Ali Bhutto, initiated a two-pronged attempt to acquire a nuclear explosive capability. The most publicly visible part of that attempt was Pakistan's effort to purchase a spent-fuel reprocessing plant from France, a deal which ultimately fell through. That plant would have permitted Pakistan to separate plutonium from spent fuel taken from its one operating nuclear power reactor; and, as Bhutto admitted in 1978 during his trial by the military government that replaced him, Pakistan intended to use illegally that separated plutonium for a nuclear weapon test.[22] However, even while it was attempting to complete the purchase of that reprocessing plant, Pakistan was also pursuing another route to nuclear explosive material. It became clear in 1978 that the Pakistani government had been engaged in building a centrifuge enrichment facility to supply nuclear weapon-grade uranium. Much of that activity, as noted earlier, relied heavily on nuclear grey market transactions to avoid nuclear exports controls. As a result, though many uncertainties remain, by 1980–1 Pakistan may have sufficient weapon-grade uranium for a nuclear test.[23]

As these Pakistani efforts became increasingly more visible in the late 1970s, pressures on the Indian government to reactivate its by then shelved nuclear research intensified. At first Desai and then his interim successors took a moderate line of response, stating only that India was closely watching developments in Pakistan but as yet had found no reason to change its current nuclear weapon policy.[24] Thus if Pakistan's nuclear activities stop short of actually testing a nuclear explosive device, it may yet be possible to head off an Indian response and reactivation of its nuclear programme. However, should Pakistan go ahead and test, the chances of prevailing on the Indian government not to move towards a fully fledged nuclear weapon programme would be minimal. Indian security and status as well as domestic political considerations would supply the motivations for answering what could be seen in Delhi as Pakistan's challenge, if not affront. That is, in the early 1980s a spiral may emerge in which Pakistan's responses to the initial Indian nuclear test will trigger new Indian actions and further Pakistani responses.

Even setting aside Indian concern about Pakistan nuclear activities, there are other factors that could contribute to an Indian decision to proceed with a fully fledged nuclear weapon programme in the mid-1980s. One such factor — India's continuing quest for international recognition and the concomitant desire of her leaders to assert Indian political independence — partly motivated the decision to test in 1974 and could re-emerge as an incentive for resumed activities. That deeply ingrained demand to be more than a 'pawn on the global chessboard',[25] to use Mrs Gandhi's phrase, is likely to continue influencing Indian policy. Moreover, those who contend that 'going nuclear' constitutes a necessary symbolic assertion of both India's unwillingness to be 'pushed around' and her claim to due respect cite the American recognition of the People's Republic of China as an apt example of nuclear weapons' political utility. Further, just as the 1971 decision to manufacture a nuclear device stemmed partly from adverse reaction to the United States' decision to sail the aircraft carrier *Enterprise* into the Bay of Bengal in that year during the Indo-Pakistani war, a future decision to resume nuclear weapon activities might be encouraged by a bitter clash with the United States in the early 1980s over India's unwillingness to accept full-scope nuclear safeguards.[26]

India's relations with the People's Republic of China in the mid-1980s also could increase the status and security-related incentives for nuclear weapon acquisition. Some within India had hoped that the May 1974 test would produce Chinese acceptance of India's political equality. The exchange of ambassadors and resumption of diplomatic relations may have been a step in that direction. But to the extent that in the future that recognition of what is considered full and proper Indian status is perceived to be incomplete, incentives for nuclear weapons as a political symbol *vis-á-vis* China could intensify. Similarly, more security-related incentives entangled with Indo-Chinese relations also increase pressures for an Indian weapon programme. One objection of the Indian leadership to proposals to establish a South Asian nuclear-free zone is that the zone would exclude China, the major nuclear threat to India. And even though until now they alone have proved an insufficient trigger, growing Chinese nuclear capabilities could reinforce the other Indian nuclear weapon incentives. In fact, increased Chinese conventional military capabilities, including the purchase of advanced combat aircraft from the United States, could also heighten Indian incentives in the 1980s to acquire nuclear weapons. In particular, erosion of the conventional balance with the People's Republic could partly weaken the Indian military's current scepticism about nuclear weapon acquisition and foster a 'more bang bang for the rupee' approach.[27]

In addition, scientific momentum and domestic politics also could enhance the build-up of support for an Indian nuclear weapon programme in the mid-1980s. The urgings of Dr Homi Bhabha, the first Chairman of the Indian Atomic Energy Commission, greatly contributed to the incremental Indian development of a nuclear weapon option; while during the period from the Chinese test of 1964 to the 1971 Indian decision to test, as well as since the 1974 test, key Indian scientists pushed for a nuclear weapon programme and had to be restrained by the political leadership. There is no reason to believe that pressure from these scientists will relent in the 1980s — at a time, moreover, when the technical options would be all the more available.[28] Alternatively, if Mrs Gandhi or her supporters emerge in strengthened positions from the current political turmoil, that, too, could affect the balance of forces on this issue. Thus, the fall of Prime Minister Desai removed the one key domestic impediment to a resumption of Indian nuclear weapon activities.

Therefore, a range of status and influence-related, security-related and domestic institutional factors could readily lead India to resume its shelved nuclear weapon programme. What partial constraints that would exist, for example concern about outside sanctions, cost, domestic opposition and presently if temporarily limited technological capabilities, appear likely to be discounted or at most to influence only the programme's timing. Consequently, an Indian nuclear weapon programme in the mid-1980s is far from unlikely.

Turning to the next link in this South Asian proliferation chain, it is difficult to believe that India's emergence as a fully fledged nuclear weapon state in the mid-1980s would not place irresistible pressures on Pakistan to intensify its own nuclear weapon programme. Even a crude nuclear force could be estimated as essential for resisting Indian nuclear blackmail or unilateral Indian nuclear weapon use in a future conflict between the two countries. After Pakistan's experience in both the 1965 and 1971 Indo-Pakistani wars, reliance on an American or other countries' security guarantee — the main alternative to nuclear weapons — in all probability would be rejected. At the same time, these security-related pressures are likely to be reinforced by domestic elite and military pressures for an 'in-the-business bang' if that had yet to take place or, more likely, for the deployment of a crude nuclear force. Without a bomb, the leadership may fear a marked deterioration of military and bureaucratic morale. And, if civilian rule had yet to be restored in Pakistan, the ruling military faction might think that its failure to take those necessary steps to acquire Pakistani nuclear weapons would enhance the likelihood of its overthrow or at least greatly erode its internal position. Thus, notwithstanding the possible costs, failure to respond to India's bomb by seeking its own nuclear force would probably be estimated by Pakistan to entail too high domestic costs and external political risks.[29]

The emergence in the mid-1980s of nuclear arms racing between India and Pakistan, in turn, would generate both security and status-related pressures in Iran to resume earlier nuclear activities and to move to acquire a nuclear weapon capability. And, as is not improbable, had the Khomeini regime since been replaced, perhaps by a military-civilian government, these pressures would be all the greater.

Notwithstanding the current compatibility of many aspects of their security interests, the Iranian government of that day might conclude that once Pakistan had even a rudimentary nuclear weapon capability, Iran would have to match it. Simple balance of power calculations would be the most critical driving force. That is, prudence would be seen to suggest the rejection of a militarily weaker position in an anarchic international environment in which security and survival depended on self-help. Uncertainty about possible changes in the unstable Pakistani political situation would reinforce those dictates of prudence, for a future upheaval, it easily could be argued, might bring to power a government hostile to Iran. Though these motivations may appear insubstantial now, similar calculations have more than sufficed to support increased military spending and programmes in other situations.

Depending on the make-up of any future Iranian regime, status and prestige incentives for 'going nuclear' in the wake of Indian and Pakistani acquisition of nuclear weapons would also intensify. Though no longer committed to becoming the 'fifth great power', as was the Shah, a future Iranian government may still be reluctant to see India, let alone Pakistan, and not itself among the ranks of the nuclear powers. Such prestige considerations have already been a key factor in other countries' pursuit of nuclear weapons.

Though less acknowledged now than in the past, Pakistan's territorial integrity will continue to be important to Iran's security. Not only would Pakistan's dismemberment and the creation of an independent Pakistani Baluchistan increase unrest within Iranian Baluchistan, but the break-up of Pakistan would provide possible openings for greater Soviet involvement in the Gulf. In this context, India's emergence as a fully fledged nuclear weapon state could increase Iranian security incentives to follow suit. For a matching Iranian nuclear weapon capability could well be viewed in Tehran as a necessary precondition for exerting a restraining influence on a nuclearised India in its dealings with Pakistan. Similarly, such a matching capability could come to be regarded as necessary insurance and a bargaining buttress should events in Pakistan erupt into an Indian-Iranian confrontation.[30]

Taken together, if not sufficient separately, the preceding set of incentives could result in an Iranian decision to move closer towards a nuclear weapon capability. As a party to the Non Proliferation Treaty, Iran would probably withdraw from that treaty under Article X, citing a threat to its supreme national interests. Such a formal withdrawal, it would be hoped, would reduce the risk of a hostile external reaction. In addition, the regime might believe that Western dependence on Iranian oil exports could be used to bargain for a reduction of the scope of any sanctions. And paradoxically, the curtailment of the Iranian nuclear energy programme since the Shah as well as the diminished purchasing of advanced American conventional arms will have reduced Iranian vulnerability to these measures. In that sense, at least, and with a volatile and militant regime in Tehran, events since the fall of the Shah have adversely affected non-proliferation prospects by lessening potential Iranian disincentives to acquiring nuclear weapons.

Further, the possible fall-out of an Indian nuclear weapon programme in the mid-1980s would in all probability extend even beyond Iran. Specifically, Iran's decision to follow Pakistan and India into the nuclear age or to take steps in that direction could be expected to add to Iraqi incentives for 'going nuclear', as well as to reinforce greatly those of Saudi Arabia.

On the one hand, the long-standing rivalry between Iran and Iraq would provide a fertile climate for arguments that Iraq had to match Iran's nuclear weaponisation. These motives with their balance of power logic would be reinforced by domestic pressure, especially from military opinion within Iraq. Coming on top of those Israel-oriented incentives discussed below, the result is likely to be an Iraqi decision to acquire nuclear weapons.

On the other hand, given nascent Iranian and Iraqi nuclear weapon programmes, it is difficult to believe that Saudi Arabia would not seek to follow suit, although its technological weakness would probably force it either to purchase grey market nuclear mercenaries or assistance or to engage in grey market nuclear collaboration with another prospective proliferator to buttress its ambitions. To recall, the latter collaboration could range from creation of a joint nuclear weapon programme with a politically compatible but more technically advanced prospective proliferator to a direct one-time purchase from a new proliferator of critical materials, know-how, expertise or other components. Particularly in light of Saudi financial support for Pakistan's purchase of a spent-fuel reprocessing plant, Pakistan could be one possible direct source of such supplies or even of a joint programme partner. Alternatively, Saudi Arabia could seek to purchase key nuclear weapon components and expertise from India whose leaders might be tempted to do so for financial reasons and pressured to do so by fear that Pakistan would complete the sale if they did not. Or, to reiterate, Saudi ties with South Korea and Taiwan could provide a framework for covert nuclear co-operation.

Thus, through a proliferation multiplier effect, the initial Indian decision to detonate a nuclear device could set in motion a chain reaction that might well lead during the 1980s to overt proliferation in the Persian Gulf. Of particular concern, moreover, is the fact that the initial elements of this proliferation chain are already unfolding. But even if events in South Asia take a different turn and the key linkages of this chain are severed, there is yet another route to Persian Gulf proliferation. This entails an Israeli-triggered proliferation chain encompassing Iraq, Iran and then others within the Persian Gulf. And here, too, the first links are already being joined.

The Middle East Path to Gulf Proliferation

Many observers have concluded that Israel already has covertly acquired one or more nuclear weapons, so-called 'bombs in the basement'. Even if that estimate is exaggerated, few doubt that since initiating its ascent of the nuclear ladder in the 1950s Israel has continually refined its nuclear weapon option to the point of now being within days of fully assembled nuclear weapons.[31] In the chain of reactions of several Arab states to Israel's status as a proto-nuclear weapon state are the seeds of more proliferation in the Middle East and beyond.

To begin, since the early 1970s Libya's Colonel Qadaffi has been attempting without success to acquire nuclear weapons. In 1973 he tried to purchase a nuclear weapon from the Chinese.[32] More recently he offered financial aid to Pakistan's nuclear programme in return for nuclear explosive material but apparently was turned down — if some Pakistani sources are to be believed.[33] These Libyan aspirations could be fulfilled in the 1980s, most likely either by ascent of the nuclear ladder or possibly by some type of nuclear grey marketeering.

There are reports that Iraq and Syria are also seeking nuclear weapon capabilities.[34] Had that French-supplied research reactor not been sabotaged, its fuel (with reloads) would have provided sufficient weapon-grade uranium for several Iraqi bombs. Though under safeguards to deter misuse, Iraq well might have thought the cost of a hostile foreign reaction worth paying. Without that reactor fuel, Iraq will now have to seek to build up an indigenous programme for producing nuclear explosive material or grey market support to satisfy its nuclear weapon ambitions. And rumours of Iraqi interest in any plutonium separated by Brazil may be illustrative of how Iraq will proceed.[35] As for possible motivation, acquisition of a nuclear weapon would be a symbolic way to upset a Middle East *status quo* which already appears to have become increasingly hostile to Iraqi interests. Syria's recent efforts to acquire nuclear technology and reported assessment of the nuclear weapon option have been motivated partly out of concern with such recent Iraqi as well as Israeli activities.[36] But once again the apparent diplomatic utility of 'going nuclear' could also be playing a role as well.

Should any of these countries acquire nuclear weapons in the 1980s, others would probably intensify their efforts to follow suit. Particularly, either the prospect at that point of Iraqi acquisition of even a crude nuclear weapon capability or its actuality could readily trigger a matching Iranian effort. Past rivalries and disputes evaluated against the framework of an unstable Iraqi political system within which a sudden domestic change could bring back to power more radical anti-Iranian leaders would be sufficient incentive. Even for his successors the Shah's balance of power reasoning, that 'if ever a country [of this region] comes out and wants to acquire atomic weapons, Iran must also possess atomic weapons,'[37] may prove a surprisingly convincing guide to policy. Iraq's and Iran's emergence as nuclear weapon states would be likely then to trigger or greatly reinforce the incentives of others within the Persian Gulf.

Prospects for Stability in a Nuclearised Persian Gulf

Both greater regional instability and conflict are likely to follow the nuclearisation of the Persian Gulf. Mutual suspicion on the part of Iran, Iraq, Saudi Arabia and others within the Gulf about each other's nuclear weapon programme intentions would supply a new source of disputes. Moreover, to the extent that the key countries sought more than a simple, non-operational 'in the business bang', this effect would be exacerbated. In addition, the risk of local nuclear war could increase significantly. Much is likely to depend on the technical characteristics of these nuclear forces. At least initially, some — for instance those of Iran, Iraq and Saudi Arabia — may justifiably be labelled 'serious but technically deficient' forces. In particular, these forces well might be characterised by a serious risk of unauthorised access to nuclear weapons by military factions or domestic dissidents, inadequate command and control systems and procedures, vulnerability to an opponent's first strike and so on. Given these deficiencies, these forces could have a high propensity to catalyse a nuclear war. Should a conflict or crisis arise, whether or not involving disputants solely within the Persian Gulf, the risk of inadvertent, miscalculated or unauthorised nuclear exchange due to these 'pre-emptive instabilities' may increase significantly.

Of equal, if not greater, importance, Persian Gulf nuclearisation may result in increased internal conflict within these new nuclear weapon states punctuated by incidences of the 'nuclear *coup d'etat*'.[38] That is, with faulty protection against unauthorised access to the nuclear arsenal, nuclear weapons may be seized by an internal military faction or domestic group and used as bargaining levers during domestic upheavals or *coups*. Moreover, though there probably would be no intention to employ these weapons, such use cannot be precluded. Events might get out of hand or someone could act out of desperation. Further, in light of its past political instability, Iraq would appear especially vulnerable to such nuclear *coups* and upheavals. And now with the fall of the Shah, continuing domestic instability in Iran also appears a likely pattern; thus a struggle for succession to the Khomeini regime in the 1980s could pit against one another domestic forces which the Shah's strategy purposefully had kept divided and competitive. In that political environment control of the nascent nuclear arsenal could provide or be seen as likely to provide diffuse bargaining advantages.

Nor should the potential spill-over effects of such Persian Gulf nuclear *coups d'etat* be missed. For example, assuming a domestic upheaval in a nuclear-armed Iraq which threatened to bring to power a far more radical leadership, Iran, Syria or even Israel might think it had no course but to intervene. Otherwise its failure either to destroy or remove the Iraqi nuclear arsenal or to support the more moderate leadership could result in nuclear weapons falling into 'the wrong hands'. Similar spill-over scenarios for other regional nuclear weapon states, as well as for those countries bordering the Persian Gulf in the Middle East and South Asia, could be delineated. Thus, the risk of nuclear *coups d'etat* is of concern not only because it most typifies the possible increase of internal conflict within a nuclearised Persian Gulf but because the final result of such *coups* could well be regional intervention and conflict.

The change of regime in Iran thus appears likely to have had a smaller impact on the prospects for proliferation in the Persian Gulf than might be thought at first glance. Rather, those prospects are most dependent on events emanating from outside the Gulf itself, events unconnected to the upheaval in Iran. To wit, if it proves impossible to head off a nuclear arms race in South Asia or to prevent Arab acquisition of nuclear weapons in response to Israel, a proliferation multiplier effect spilling over into this neighbouring region is not unlikely. The ultimate result could easily be greater internal conflict, local rivalry, and even the use of nuclear weapons.

Notes

1. Personal communication to author.

2. *Nuclear News* (Mid-February 1976), p. 55.

3. *Nucleonics Week*, 20 October 1977, pp. 13–14.

4. *New York Times*, 27 April 1975.

5. Personal communication to author.

6. *New York Times*, 6 January 1975; Paul Jabber, *A Nuclear Middle East: Infrastructure, Likely Military Postures and Prospects for Strategic Stability* (Center for Arms Control and International Security, University of California, Los Angeles, 1977), pp. 8–9.

7. *Financial Times* (London), 11 August 1979.

8. *Nuclear News*, October 1975; *Wall Street Journal*, 16 November 1976.

9. *New York Times*, 9 May 1979.

10. *Nuclear Engineering International* (July 1979).

11. Ibid.

12. Jabber, *Nuclear Middle East*, pp. 13–14.

13. *New York Times*, 9 April 1979.

14. *Nucleonics Week*, 16 June 1977, p. 2.

15. See Lewis A. Dunn, 'Nuclear Gray Marketeering', *International Security*, vol. 1, no. 3 (Winter 1977).

16. *Washington Post*, 2 May 1979.

17. *NRC Handelsblad* (New Rotterdam, Holland), 16 June 1979.

18. The ties with South Korea are typified by the presence of tens of thousands of South Korean construction workers in Saudi Arabia. And, apparently impressed by Taiwan's brand of anti-Communism, the Saudis have guaranteed low-priced oil shipments to that country since 1973. *New York Times*, 19 June 1978; *Washington Post*, 28 May 1979.

19. These countries already have access to some form of nuclear-capable delivery system, especially aircraft, so that as well is not a serious constraint on their ability to 'go nuclear'.

20. Shahram Chubin, 'Repercussions of the Crisis in Iran', *Survival* (May/June 1979), pp. 98–9.

21. See Paul F. Power, 'The Indo-American Nuclear Controversy', *Asian Survey*, vol. XIX, no. 6 (June 1979).

22. *Washington Post*, 8 December 1978.

23. *Washington Post*, 2 May 1979; *New York Times*, 12 August 1979.

24. *New York Times*, 20 April 1979 and 3 May 1979; *International Herald Tribune* (London), 21–22 April 1979.

25. Indira Gandhi, 'India and the World', *Foreign Affairs*, vol. 51, no. 1 (October 1972), pp. 65–78, p. 75.

26. For a well stated explanation which is equally an articulation of this quest for recognition, see Baldev Raj Nayar, 'Treat India Seriously', *Foreign Policy*, no. 18 (Spring 1975), pp. 133–54.

27. This was suggested to me by Onkar Marwah.

28. Ashok Kapur, 'India and the Atom', *Bulletin of the Atomic Scientists* (September 1974), p. 27; Onkar Marwah, 'India's Nuclear and Space Programs: Intent and Policy', *International Security*, vol. 2, no. 2 (Fall 1977), pp. 98–9.

29. Pakistani perceptions are reviewed in Anwar H. Syed, 'Pakistan's Security Program: a Bill of Constraints', *ORBIS*, vol. XIV, no. 4 (Winter 1973), pp. 952–74, esp. pp. 952–63. See also Alvin J. Cottrell, 'Pakistan: Internal Unrest and Military Weakness' in R.M. Burrell and Alvin J. Cottrell, *Iran, Afghanistan, Pakistan: Tensions and Dilemmas*, The Washington Papers, vol. 11, no. 20 (Sage Publications, Beverley Hills and London, 1974), pp. 53–68.

30. On Iran's interest in a Pakistani buffer state, see especially Shahram Chubin, 'Iran: Between the Arab West and the Asian East', *Survival* (July/August 1974), pp. 172–82, pp. 175–9; Cottrell, 'Pakistan', pp. 57–8; Sepehr Zabih, 'Iran Today', *Current History* (February 1974), pp. 66–9, p. 68.

31. See Robert E. Harkavy, *Spectre of a Middle East Holocaust: the Strategic and Diplomatic Implications of the Israeli Nuclear Weapons Program* Monograph Series in World Affairs, Volume Fourteen, Book Four (University of Denver, Graduate School of International Studies, Denver, 1977), pp. 3–19.

32. *New York Times*, 30 July 1977.

33. *New York Times*, 9 April 1979; *Washington Post*, 9 April 1979.

34. *New York Times*, 30 July 1977; *Financial Times* (London), 18 April 1978.

35. *The Middle East* (July 1979), p. 93.

36. *Nucleonics Week*, 23 February 1978, p. 2.

37. *Teheran Journal*, 16 September 1975.

38. See Lewis A. Dunn, 'The Nuclear Coup d'Etat', *The Journal of Strategic Studies*, vol. 1, no. 1 (May 1978).

6 THE IRANIAN MILITARY: POLITICAL SYMBOLISM VERSUS MILITARY USEFULNESS

Steven L. Canby

The fourfold increase in OPEC mandated oil prices in 1973 created the unusual situation whereby Iran could design and purchase a radically different military establishment than previously. Such a shift raises three questions: (1) the military's 'back-end' ability to absorb the new equipment and force increases; (2) the competitive 'sidewards' impact on the civil economy; and (3) 'front-end' military appropriateness.

Western countries have experienced and accommodated back-end and sidewards effects during periods of abrupt rearmament and mobilisation. However, few countries (including Meiji Japan) have ever attempted radical adoption of military structures that their own populace cannot produce, operate and maintain. The Shah attempted this. In addition his country was in the midst of a demanding social and industrial modernisation process. The back-end deficiencies in the Iranian military were well known.[1] The sidewards effect snowballed under the dual impact of over-ambitious economic planning and faltering oil revenues.[2] The third front-end question of military appropriateness has generally not been recognised, though it is a phenomenon that has historically debilitated many militaries, as for instance the French (and many others) in 1940. It is a question in the domain of general staffs and the interplay of tactical, operational and strategic factors.

There is a tendency throughout the world to equate sophistication in weapons with military usefulness and from there to military and political power. In point of fact, however, little relationship may exist between sophistication and usefulness and power may be more apparent than real. Except for the major powers who are fighting in a very special context (and it can be argued that even they sometimes unwittingly trap themselves into over-sophistication), it can be shown that weapons sophistication, while having a certain micro attractiveness, can in general be counter-productive.[3] Technological sophistication often substitutes for military thinking. Nowhere was this more apparent than in the Shah's armed forces. They were ill suited for all but one of their intended tasks: political symbolism.

Iranian Security: Problems and Solutions

Any Iranian government faces diverse military concerns such as military loyalty, internal security, suppression of separatism, border integrity, hegemony in the Persian Gulf, coastal protection, maritime presence, regional balance, air space protection and defence against Soviet intimidation and invasion. The Shah's solution was textbook American: armoured and mechanised divisions, an air force more sophisticated than any in Europe, and a pocket navy. This implies the Shah's military was not designed to cope with his specific concerns; and even more important, no attempt was made to address the special features of the Iranian context.

In particular, small powers such as Iran cannot fight the Soviets on their own terms. Instead, they must learn the peculiarities of the stronger opponent, identify weaknesses, and learn to take advantage of them. A 'relational' approach of this kind implies strategy and tactics which are shaped by the doctrine and character of the main enemy, the quality of his leadership and high command, the tactical skill of his field commanders and soldiers, his rigidities and flexibilities, his capacity to react under pressure, and so on. The aim is to apply specialised or localised strengths (for example terrain) against the identified weaknesses of the enemy in order to prevail by avoiding the direct clash of symmetrical capabilities. Iran violated these relational guidelines. The Shah could have learned much from the Israeli experience:

Israel has realized that it cannot adopt foreign doctrines of the bigger powers which are incompatible with its material capabilities, political situation, and cultural milieu. It had to find its own solutions for its [own] problems. The reserve system, the weapons-acquisition and procurement processes, the logistical structure, and all other elements. . .had to be tailored to Israeli needs, and on occasion, had to be developed from scratch.[4]

The Former Strategy of Iran: Technological Superfluity

Although the goal of the Shah's strategy was to make Iran the leading military power of a region extending from the Levant to India and including the whole of Arabia, Iran's ground force deployments had an almost purely defensive and internal security character. In fact, three-fifths of its army was deployed near the Iraqi border, and half of the remainder was stationed in Tehran itself. Nearly all the armour was oriented towards the Iraqi border but the Shah's plans called for mechanising the remaining regular infantry (three divisions and one independent brigade) including those forward deployed near the Soviet border (three brigades). The desolate eastern border facing Afghanistan was garrisoned by a single infantry brigade also to be mechanised. Only a single airborne and a Special Forces brigade were available for rapid reinforcement within Iran and also for use in the Gulf region. Except for the demonstration effect of his air and naval forces, the Shah actually would have had but a limited capability to intervene in areas not contiguous to his own borders.

The concentration of forces near the Iraqi frontier was consistent not only with the obvious need to face the Iraqi threat, but also with long-standing American notions on the containment of the Soviet threat. It was always believed that countries such as Iran could at best delay a Soviet invasion, until the arrival of large-scale US reinforcements. Accordingly, the decisive battle would then be fought on the central Iranian plateau, and Iranian forces deployed facing the Iraqi border would be readily available to fight there. In any case, it was believed that Iranian forces (and particularly armour) placed well forward on the Soviet frontier itself would only be lost early on, and could also be provocative in peacetime.

Strategically, this plan had a major flaw from the point of view of regional balance and hegemony. By implicitly leaving the entire northern rim open to Soviet occupation, the plan made it unlikely that Iran could really be an effective counterweight to Soviet-sponsored pressures like Iraqi incursions against Kuwait and the other Gulf states. A threatening Soviet posture on the common border would ensure the paralysis of the forces nominally deployed against Iraq and the two brigades of non-mechanised infantry which would have been the only Iranian forces capable of effectively delaying and defending in the mountains rimming northern Iran. Obviously some degree of Soviet coercion would be feasible with any pattern of deployment, but the dual-purpose deployment actually adopted by Iran provided the Russians with an almost mechanical tool for leverage. This of course, negated much of the Shah's purpose in building Iran into a major military power in its region.

The deployment plan was in any case based on two dubious assumptions: first, that Iranian armoured forces could actually wage war in the armour-mobile manner against Soviet forces, skilled as the latter are in true armoured manoeuvre, certainly as compared to Iranian forces. Second, the plan assumed timely and sufficient US reinforcements, in spite of the obvious difficulty of airlifting US forces (and particularly heavy units) to Iran.

But a defence of Iran cannot be based on armoured forces. Iranian armour cannot possibly match the general technological sophistication of Soviet forces,[5] nor their troop quality. Iranian armour can be used to good effect in an attack *into* the Iraqi flatlands. In this mode, however, the Iranians do not require a homogeneous armour/mechanised force. As the Germans did in the Second World War and the Soviets do today with their Category III divisions, only the spearhead forces need be armoured and of high quality. The remainder can be a simpler infantry for consolidating the gains of the tank spearhead. But Iranian armour can *not* be used *defensively* against Iraqi mountain infantry invading into the Iranian mountains. A defence or delay in mountains cannot be mounted by armoured forces. It is too easily flanked and its line of retreat and sustenance cut by infantry, moving by foot or by helicopter.

An armoured defence in mountains is necessarily positional. Its positions may be strong, but the offensive actually has the advantage. To be sure, an attacker moving against a well entrenched defensive position is generally at a severe disadvantage; hence the well known 3:1 rule of thumb. But this is only true for *frontal* attacks against *alerted* defenders. The essence of tactics and of the operational art of warfare, however, is to subvert the defender's potential advantage, by two general means: stratagems and outflanking. The first depends upon deception and (then) surprise, the second upon opportune manoeuvre. The problem of a defender relying upon the firepower of fixed positions is typified by the dilemma he faces in countering outflanking moves. If he relies on well defended but isolated outposts, these will be vulnerable to turning movements across their line of retreat;[6] and the attacker need not attack them at all. To impose a disadvantageous frontal attack upon the enemy, the defender must therefore extend his lines; but in doing so, even a much more numerous defence force can then become over-extended. This then allows a competent attacker to develop stratagems to penetrate and separate the defender's extended line which can then be defeated in detail.

Because of the pervasive assumption that unassisted Iranian forces could not cope with the Soviet Union, the Shah placed very few of his troops near the Soviet border. Only small forces were readily available for forward defence and delay operations. It may be argued that the Shah could always have redeployed his forces from elsewhere for delay operations against the Soviet Army. But given the structure of forces, this was not in fact possible. Any attempt to use armour well forward would have led to the early loss of the expensive armoured/mechanised forces, and possibly also to the rapid disintegration of the entire army from induced panic. Armoured units cannot be used to defend or delay in mountains; they can only be deployed *behind them* to seal the exits. In mountain valleys their positions can be readily turned; and once cut off, armour cannot be extricated. Since armoured troops are psychologically unprepared for non-armoured combat, the result is inevitably defeat in detail and infectious panic.

For an armoured defence of the plateau to be workable, the Iranians would have had to delay significantly a Soviet advance across the northern mountains in order to gain time for the redeployment of their own armoured divisions arrayed on the Iraqi border and for US reinforcement to make up for a shortfall in forces. A delay in the mountains would have required light infantry. But subsequently the Iranians would have had to fight on the plateau and this would have required armour and not infantry, let alone of the light variety. The delay phase and defence of the central plateau would thus have required two very different force structures. Before the Shah's overthrow, Iran had four armoured divisions and was in the process of mechanising its four infantry divisions; this would have left only two non-armoured brigades. The problem thus arose that even if the Iranians could have fought in an armoured manner, they lacked the light forces necessary to gain the time to do so.

Assuming that the Iranians could have mounted the required delay operations by acquiring mountain infantry and by a correspondingly reduced emphasis on mechanisation, the outcome would then have depended on their ability to use tanks in combined-arms teams. It is questionable whether the Iranian Army had this capability; very few armies do. Many armies have tanks but few have the ability to co-ordinate tolerably well the branches of the combined-arms team. Even fewer have the mindset, tactics and communications needed to use armour in *fluid* manoeuvre, as opposed to semi-static setpiece movements. These capabilities would have been very difficult to acquire for the Shah's army. Aside from cultural factors, it was the Shah's practice to compartmentalise the branches of his armed forces, and to centralise control in his own hands. This, of course, reduced the chance of a military *coup d'état*, but it also militated against the joint training and co-ordination needed for true armoured warfare.

Accordingly, it is reasonable to assume that Iranian armoured forces would have been no match for Soviet armour once the latter reached the plateau. Iranian forces would probably have been deployed piecemeal, in separated blocking positions; consequently, they would have been quickly outflanked and defeated even by quantitatively inferior Soviet armoured forces. The situation could only have been stabilised by a rapid and large-scale US reinforcement. But until enough American forces arrived to form a significant share of the total allied force, any American units in the field would also have been jeopardised by the collapse of Iranian units on their flanks.

Finally, the conduct of a large-scale armoured defence on the

Iranian plateau would have been dependent upon Iraqi benevolence. Whether fluid or FEBA-like, a defence of the Iranian 'waist' would uncover the Iraqi border. This in turn would have created the possibility of Soviet passage through Iraq directly to the Gulf; the only rail LOC and the main road LOC from the outside to the plateau would thereby have been threatened.

In short, an armoured defence on the central plateau was not in fact militarily feasible. For the Iranians, American reinforcements were too uncertain, if only because of the NATO contingency. For the US, on the other hand, the option amounted to a foolish reinforcement race with the USSR. The time factor was not an independent variable; under the circumstances it was largely dependent on the quality of Soviet planning and the size of their forces committed. There was thus very little likelihood that the defence could have held long enough for significant US reinforcements to arrive. In the interim, US units in place would have been in great jeopardy. If the situation *did* stabilise because of US reinforcements, the United States would have been saddled with an unattractive protracted conflict in circumstances apt to favour Soviet rather than American persistence.

It can thus be concluded that for tactical, operational and strategic reasons, a defence based on expensive armoured forces is inappropriate for Iran. Armoured forces are suitable for attacking into the Iraqi flatlands, but not for defending against Iraq within Iran's own (mountainous) borders. But most important, a defence based on tank forces is not viable against the Soviets and leaves northern Iran hostage; the ensuing weakness vitiates the Iranian role in the regional power balance. Outside alliances do not materially offset this deficiency. For Iran's lesser military concerns, the armoured force structure is constricting. Armoured forces cannot be moved about readily and they lack the infantry content necessary for internal security, suppression of separatism, defence of the rough and thinly populated eastern border, and intervention among the Gulf states.

Similarly, it can be argued that Iran had no real need for a sophisticated navy and air force. Iran's vital importance as an oil exporter eliminates its need for an expensive 'blue-water' fleet, or an expensive air defence. And the shift from an armoured force to a defence based on agile mountain infantry eliminates much of the need for air defence of, and ground support for, ground forces. Thus strong political connections with the West simplify and even eliminate the most expensive and demanding (for Iran) military concerns. For the Western connection made it unnecessary for Iran to develop naval forces capable of coping with Soviet interference with Iranian seagoing commerce. Instead of trying to cope with this threat directly as it did, Iran actually needed only to control its own coastal waters and to *circumvent* a Soviet naval blockade by transferring the burden of securing maritime access to the major Western powers — a task which the latter could not avoid, given their dependence on Persian Gulf oil. In this case, the linkage between Iran and the West would clearly work to the benefit of the Iranians.

The Western connection could also have been valuable in the other arena of high-cost technology — air defence, where the main purpose (other than the assertion of sovereignty over the air space) would have been to contain Soviet military intimidation by over-flights and intrusions and to limit terror bombing. The Soviet Union could not exercise the upper range of intimidation (the threat of nuclear attack) for fear of the US reaction and the long-run effect upon world-wide nuclear proliferation. Nor could the Soviets have exercised the option of (non-nuclear) strategic bombing against Iranian cities without risking similar reactions. In any case, Soviet strategic bombing capability remains limited: Soviet fighter-bombers are still too restricted in payload and range to do more than mere terror bombing. A strategic bombing campaign would require Soviet use of vulnerable heavy bombers of 1950s vintage.

The Western connection was thus most important and most useful to Iran in dealing with those threats that required a high-technology military response,[7] while a shift to a relational military structure further reduced the need for sophisticated weaponry.

Relational Defence: More Defence for Less Money

It is apparent that Iran's lesser military concerns can only be satisfied by an infantry-oriented force structure. The question to be established in this section is whether such forces could satisfy the more demanding military concerns, the most demanding being a Soviet invasion. This can be of two forms: a whirlwind *coup de main* and the more traditional in-strength invasion. If Iran could design its defence to resist both a surprise attack and the more deliberate invasion, northern Iran would no longer be hostage to the Soviets, Soviet intimidation would have little credibility, and Iran could play a more meaningful role in a regional balance. It also follows that if the Iranians could defend in the mountains against the Soviets, a similar capability would exist against lesser opponents, even if they were more appropriately structured for mountain warfare. Nor in the postulated design would Iran lose the capability to attack into the Iraqi flatlands with armour.

In designing a defence strategy against a conventional ground invasion by the Soviet Union, Iran cannot possibly expect to match such an enemy in terms of numbers, technology or troop quality.

Any Iranian solution presupposing a contest of material resources,
firepower and Lanchesterian-type attrition models is doomed to
failure. Soviet reinforcement capabilities are simply too overwhelming. To be sure, the ground transport net leading to the
Iranian plateau from the USSR is constraining and is also potentially
vulnerable; but other outside lines of sustenance on to the Iranian
plateau are even more constrained. In a direct clash of armour and
firepower, the Soviet Union is bound to prevail. Only a *relational*
defence, designed very specifically to exploit both terrain advantages
and the particular weaknesses of the Soviet force structure can offer
hope for success. For example, Soviet armour-mechanised forces are
plainly unsuited for combat in high-mountain terrain, while Iranian
forces could be specifically so designed. To be sure, mountain
terrain will not favour a *positional* defence against a more fluid
offence; but mountain barriers do allow scope for a combined
defence featuring light infantry blocking and counter-stroke tactics,
complemented by positional elements, and by armour in the rear, to
cover exit routes from the mountains. While the Shah's planned all-
armoured force structure could not have implemented a relational
defence (and was not meant to do so), the latter remains a feasible
(and much cheaper) alternative and it calls for a force structure
largely made up of mountain-oriented infantry.

In addition to providing for a defence against an invasion in the
conventional manner, Iran, as other countries directly threatened by
the Soviet Union, must also cope with *coup de main* operations.
Among other things, this calls for some armoured cavalry for
deployment in the deep interior, near the nerve-centres that would be
the primary targets of Soviet air-landed operations. In what follows,
it is argued that a relational defence strategy for Iran would have to
be based on the barrier on the northern mountains; no effective
defence can be achieved by armoured combat in the plateau, or by an
enclave strategy focused on the Zagros mountains: nor is a territorial
('people's war') defence a realistic proposition given Iran's separatist tendencies.

A Neglected Aspect of the Threat: Coup de Main *Operations*

In conventional assessments, a Soviet *coup de main* against Iran is
sometimes dismissed as a piece of worst-case analysis, not worthy of
serious consideration. Yet from the Soviet perspective a rapid, low-
casualty *fait accompli* is obviously desirable. Soviet planners do not
believe in the measured and constrained allocation of forces in their
offensives. Their model is likely to be that of the Manchurian operation. This becomes apparent when it is realised that strategic surprise
is not in itself a critical requirement.[8] All that is necessary is that a
sufficient uncertainty of intentions be maintained to inhibit the

victim from taking necessary precautions for fear of provocation. The critical factor is the ability to mount a high tempo *coup de main*. This calls for tactical surprise as to the *location* and *manner* of attack.[9]

A *coup de main* can take many forms. While the separate techniques are known, or discernible, their combination is not. The aim of the *coup de main* is to create an overwhelming sense of helplessness by combining confusion measures in the interior with the image of irresistible military forces soon to arrive. While no contingency plan for the defence can be foolproof, it must at a minimum contain the following elements:

(1) media arrangements to dispel disruptive rumours;
(2) a police/gendarme network to protect key installations and personalities, and to contain saboteurs and small air-delivered enemy raiding parties;
(3) an air-defence system capable of inhibiting movement by air at least *after* the initial surprise (the denial of the first air penetrations is not a realistic goal);
(4) ground forces capable of pocketing and then destroying large air-delivered groupings; and
(5) a capability to delay the *movement* of the main follow-up forces, invading across the border.

The characteristic instrument of *coup de main* operations is not force *per se*, but rather the *illusion* of force contrived by the attacker, which can lead to a paralysis in the defender's ability and will to resist. The classic German Blitzkrieg of 1939–41 was based on such effects, and even a full mobilisation is not a sufficient response to the phenomenon. But whereas in Europe a *coup de main* is easy to mount due to the small distances involved and the dense transport net, Iran as a relatively large country with few good roads does have some natural protection. The northern rim of rugged mountains can be a military asset for Iran, *vis-à-vis* this threat. Notably the geography could make airborne assaults into the deep interior of Iran a risky proposition *if* a credible delay capability were at hand against the land invasion threat. The Soviets are unlikely to accept such a risk to their elite airborne-assault forces (it must always be remembered that Iran is only of secondary strategic importance to the USSR).

In the logical sequence of a defence against a *coup de main*, Iran's first requirement is to deal with airborne assaults intended to create disarray in the interior. This task is made easier by a good air defence. But air defence is *not* a prerequisite. An over-emphasis on air defence — as in Iran's case — can be counter-productive and weaken overall defensive capabilities.

The effective counter to airborne assault then is not a foolproof air defence system but rather quick-reaction *armoured cavalry* forces on the ground, and the effective use of the rural gendarmerie system. The task of Soviet airborne assault forces would not just be to seize and defend their air LOC for subsequent reinforcement: the air-head would only be a means with which to launch immediate raiding operations — operations that cannot be launched directly from Soviet territory due to the distances involved. In other words, the air-landed force would immediately send out small raiding groups to disrupt the Iranian reaction to the whole Soviet offensive. A few helicopters and some light-armour vehicles would be available to the air-landed force; but motor-cycle troops might also play a role. (Used as the lead, disruptive elements of the (1939–42) German *Panzer* divisions, motor-cycle troops are now being increased in the divisional reconnaissance battalions of the Soviet Army.)

The value of light elements are often discounted, since they do not rate highly by the twin attrition criteria of firepower and survivability. But light elements would act as 'dragoons' relying on prompt manoeuvre rather than firepower. Their purpose would be to move quickly to points of logistic and tactical importance, in order to seize them before the defender begins to react. This would create the impression of omnipresence, spread confusion and demoralisation among the population and in the military command system, and would force the defender to attempt to dislodge the attackers, who would then enjoy the advantages of the tactical defensive.

Against such raids and seizing parties emanating from an air-head, gendarmes and armoured cavalry units are the most effective antidotes. The gendarme system offers the possibility of intercepting the smaller Soviet 'desant' groupings *en route*, as well as of guarding key installations (and personalities) before their arrival. Armoured cavalry would provide an integrated combat team ready to deal quickly with larger 'desant' groupings. Cavalry units can be moved rapidly, they have both heavy elements for 'fixing' and light elements for 'working in' and — most important for a quick response — their battle team is already organically integrated. This avoids the time-consuming preparation that would be required to organise a co-ordinated response from distinct tank and infantry formations, oriented as these are for more formal methods of combat.

If the tentacles emanating from the air-head can be defeated, the air-head itself loses much of its purpose. In fact, because of the enemy's obvious need to achieve a ground-force link-up and do so quickly, the air-head then becomes an enemy liability. For reasons of prestige and morale, the attacker must strive to sustain it, but if the ground link-up is prevented, and its tentacles destroyed, the air-head can no longer consolidate the initial gains — even if the necessary reinforcements can be delivered. The air-head thus becomes a trap and resource-sink for the attacker, which in due course can be annihilated.

Even though an air-head can be made useless by destroying its tentacles, it would still be necessary to contain it. In the case of Iran, Soviet air-heads would have to appear in the proximity of one of the crucial nerve-centres, and perhaps only Tehran itself is truly critical. An airfield is obviously a desirable target which would facilitate subsequent operations, but it is *not* critical. An airfield is only essential for the deployment of large forces and to sustain their prolonged combat and that of course would be the very negation of the purpose of the operation. Nevertheless it is obvious that one or more airfields could be one of the many initial objectives of the air-delivered element of a *coup de main*.

In combating the air-head force itself, the two important ingredients are rapid containment and air defence. At least for the initial sealing off and containment of the air-delivered force, armoured cavalry again offers the best prospects. It has two advantages over regular line formations. First, it is more suited to sealing off the approaches from the air-head because its combat teams are organic. Second, it is designed in part for the security role, which would be important since air-delivered forces would seek to 'flow' around containing blocking positions. Thereafter, and particularly if it is deemed desirable to destroy the airhead by close combat, regular line formations would be more suitable.

Air defence is an important element in containing and then eventually destroying an air-head. But neither fighters nor sophisticated SAM missiles are likely to be as important as automatic cannon in close proximity. These weapons could also serve as a major element in the containment and destruction of the air-delivered forces in ground combat. The aim of air defence against the air-head is obviously to prevent reinforcement and sustainment. In practice, this would be accomplished by making air landing and parachuting prohibitively expensive. This is a task for low-level air defences, still the recognised domain of the gun. Enemy aircraft flying above the gun envelope at 10,000 feet or so cannot reinforce the air-head and neither could they provide close support. Fighter-bombers flying in from their USSR bases would necessarily be payload limited; nor would 'smart' ordnance solve Soviet problems since seeker devices would not work well against the low-contrast containment forces (including optically directed AAA).

It can of course be argued that a good air defence alone could be sufficient to deter and/or prevent a *coup de main* through the destruction of Soviet aircraft *en route* to the objective. This argument, however, overlooks the implications of surprise: (1) sophisticated air defences are not robust against one-time countermeasures; (2) air defence is a 'sieve' system, which takes time to tighten; and (3) the loss of surprise as far as the air-defence control centre is concerned does not automatically translate into a loss of surprise on the ground. The time lost in identifying the threat and disseminating warnings depends on command linkages between the ground and the air forces (in the Shah's time, *he* was the link), on the readiness of the ground forces concerned, and on the ability of the ground formations to form and deploy responsive battle groups. In the case of Iran, an air defence warning would not have translated into a prompt and effective warning on the ground, except during special periods of alert (which of course would themselves be cause for the postponement of a *coup de main*). Thus even if the air defence system worked well from the first, a *coup de main* could still succeed. On the other hand, it must be recognised that sophisticated air defences would set a higher 'entry' price for the Soviet Union, and they add important risk factors for them.

The worth of Iran's sophisticated air defences against the *coup de main* threat thus depends on two unknowns: the 'entry' price necessary to deter a Soviet attack, and the robustness (= degraded effectiveness) of the system itself, once the Soviets use all the countermeasures available to them. The combat effectiveness of highly centralised and electronically sophisticated air defence systems remains an open question. The US Air Force pins high hopes on such systems, but it is noteworthy that the RAF and Luftwaffe do not, at least in the cluttered conditions of European warfare.[10] An air conflict in Iran would of course be much less cluttered, but on the other hand much less scientific expertise has been devoted to the special problems of electronic-wave propagation in Iran. It is of course well known that the Soviets themselves are very active in electronic warfare while the Iranians are merely the recipients of electronic packages produced by others. Hence in a conflict against the Soviets, there is a very high possibility that Iran's air defence system would be temporarily neutralised.

The final aspect of a defence against a *coup de main* is the delay of the main invasion forces advancing to link up with the airborne 'desant' elements. Against this threat, Iran has a distinct geographical advantage as compared to most other neighbours of the Soviet Union. The Iranian plateau is protected by a high mountain barrier (on the Iranian side of the border) which cannot be outflanked, and must therefore be penetrated. While there is legitimate argument over the merits of a mountain-based defence in protracted war, it is nevertheless clear that such a system is unambiguously advantageous as far as delaying actions are concerned. In mountains, defensive forces can significantly delay much larger and heavier forces through demolitions and direct combat.

Across the 1,000 miles of the Iranian-USSR border as the crow flies, there are only ten routes suitable for vehicular passage (including the Herat route from Afghanistan). The immediate Soviet aim in a *coup de main* offensive would be to reach and reinforce the air-heads before they are destroyed by the Iranians. Since they are not short of units, and since they would seek to maximise the appearance of strength, as well as to exploit allocation errors by the defenders (virtually inevitable in the confusion of a surprise attack), the Soviets would undoubtedly send forces into most if not all the approaches. Some of these forces may be small, but all will be of sufficient strength to push through (and secure) thinly guarded routes until exploitation reinforcements can be brought up.

The Soviet problem is to devise an approach that would allow them to get one or more land columns into position to relieve quickly the pressure on their air-heads in the Tehran region. The normal Soviet procedure for the advance would have two shortcomings: (1) their standard formation of march columns with advance guards and recce well forward is likely to act as a triggering mechanism for Iranian demolitions guards; and (2) the land routes from the USSR itself are too long, and worse, they converge into only three approaches while still at some distance from Tehran. The Soviet advance is therefore more likely to be opened by light precursor forces which would try to seize key points along several of the major routes. Lead columns aimed at Tehran might originate on the Caspian Sea, for example by amphibious landings at Chalus and Babol Sar. While most of the land approaches from the USSR converge most unfavourably from the Soviet point of view, a landing at Babol Sar would offer the prospect of divergent paths. This of course means that reinforcement echelons could be swiftly assigned to the routes that become open, thus multiplying the effectiveness of the invasion force as a whole. This consideration, plus the fact that the initial link-up column has as much symbolic as substantive military importance, enhances the attractiveness of the Chalus and Babol Sar approaches, even though this implies that the initial relief forces would be relatively small. As in any surprise operation, the safety of these columns would not derive from their own capabilities, but rather from the confusion generated by the offensive as a whole.

In this scheme, the light precursor elements would seize bridges, tunnels, passes and the like, in a variety of exercised 'special operations'. The key is obviously to secure critical locations before local gendarmes and army forces can react. In many situations, this would merely mean overcoming unsupported guards; in some cases, it might simply mean posting Soviet guards before the gendarmes can move into their designated guard-posts.

While precursor forces can take various forms, the most obvious possibility is the use of helicopter-borne infantry. Helicopters are of course ideal for landing small 'desant' parties and flat-deck ships in the Caspian Sea could serve as platforms for helicopters. Helicopters based in the USSR itself would not have the range and carrying capacity to support the necessary surprise operations in the mountains bordering the Caspian Sea. Flat-decked ships (which could be provided without loss of technical surprise) would solve this problem and would also be of use to support main forces moving along the coastal routes before turning into the mountains. Helicopter-delivered motor-cycle troops[11] could also be landed with 'desant' teams to move quickly by road, thus adding another dimension to surprise.

The basic elements of the envisaged 'precursor' units are already present in the reconnaissance companies of the tank and rifle regiments, and in the reconnaissance battalions of the Soviet tank and motorised rifle divisions. The reconnaissance battalion TO&E includes a motor-cycle platoon and also a long-range recce company composed of small teams. The recce company of the regiments has a small motor-cycle scout section. In each unit, additional personnel are available to use motor cycles in scout-like operations. Thus in the standard formations engaged in an offensive against Iran, a considerable 'desant' force would be organic in any case and would be available for precursor duties even if all airborne and air-assault divisions and brigades would be assigned their primary role, and would thus be unavailable. Out of the 24 divisions in the three military districts adjacent to Iran, Soviet TO&Es would call for as many as 1,700 motor-cycle troops and 120 long-range reconnaissance teams. Even if divided among the ten routes into Iran, this force alone could be seriously disruptive. And, of course, there is no reason why this 'base' could not be enlarged by the temporary assignment of recce units from the remaining 137 Soviet tank/MR divisions.[12]

In addition to heli-borne elements, more old-fashioned means could also be used to seize and secure the entry points of the road net. A subversive network of Soviet sympathisers could be created to be activated when needed. Dissident ethnic groups could be exploited on a similar basis. Even commercial trucking (and tourism) from the USSR could be used for 'Trojan Horse' operations. Those means already provide ample opportunities for peacetime route reconnaissance. The techniques these groups would use would be quite similar to those of the 'desant' groups. The difference is mainly in the means used to arrive on location; one uses visible transport; the other covert means.

There is a tendency to think that the solution to surprise lies in high technology, such as sophisticated early warning radars and remote surveillance techniques. It is obvious, however, that these would only be effective against high-signature modes of transport. Such technology is certainly not effective against approach and seizure techniques which rely on cover and deception. It would therefore be unwise to spend large sums on sophisticated technology. Moreover, there is also reason to doubt the effectiveness of high-technology systems in countering heli-borne penetrations. These systems can provide warning, but it is doubtful if such warning can be used in a meaningful military way, except to alert guards already in place. High-performance aircraft are not suitable for intercepting low-flying helicopters, and the early warning likely to be available (assuming Soviet deception to mask the operation until the launch of the aircraft) would not be sufficient to deploy ground air defences suitable for use against low-flying helicopters. One hardware solution of possible relevance in this case would be the anti-helicopter helicopter, such as the Soviet Union appears to have developed.

While a Hind-like anti-helicopter aircraft and early warning systems would be useful, the only robust solution to the problem remains a force of guards capable of rising to the demands of the situation. Certainly, only guards can cope with 'desant' operations based upon cover and deception. A system capable of coping with these threats is also capable of dealing with clandestine penetrations of the border areas. There would be some merit in dealing with the highly visible, high-technology end of the spectrum, but the real focus must be on organisational solutions, which are both cheap (as far as the hardware goes) and also militarily robust and versatile.

The solution to the precursor problem must be found in the *gendarmerie* system of internal security, which Iran has (or will at least have again, when order is restored). Iran's 74,000 gendarmes are now distributed in many platoon company and battalion size outposts. Their primary duty is the maintenance of law and order. But their dispersion also gives the central government (1) a useful means of keeping remote localities under observation, (2) a quick-reaction guard capability, and (3) a means of rapid alert and mobilisation. The gendarme system thus offers a ready-made framework for disrupting desant-type operations. Their numbers in the mountain belt would have to be augmented, and they would also require prompt reinforcement with army units. Assuming manpower of tolerable quality, given automatic weapons and suitable training, gendarmes could make the quick seizure of bridges, tunnels and passes rather difficult for the Soviets. Equally important, the gendarmes have an inherent interception capability: to detect suspicious activity, to ambush the smaller 'desant' groupings in transit, and even to use REDEYE-type missiles as well as automatic weapons against over-flying helicopters.

Forward Defence and the Northern Mountain Barrier

It is widely believed that as between defence and offence, the defence is the stronger of the two. It would therefore follow that if the barrier strength of mountains is added, a mountain defence must become stronger still. This conclusion is often confirmed by eclectic examples drawn from history, such as the German success in containing the allies on the Italian Front in the Second World War. In point of fact, however, while the defence generally has had the advantage in *open* terrain, the reverse is true in a mountain defence. The Italian example is atypical for several reasons: the German command, and notably Field Marshal Kesselring, was exceptionally gifted; the Allied command, for its part, was cautious and schematic.[13] But most important — the Germans practised *fluid* tactics behind screening entrenchments rather than positional warfare, and most armies are quite incapable of fluid tactics in the compartmentalised terrain typical of mountain environments.

Clausewitz wrote that the defence is in general stronger than the offence, but not in the case of positional mountain warfare in which the attacker was strongly favoured. Clausewitz's line of argument is particularly important because it also contains a seminal outline of German Blitzkrieg theory.[14] Clausewitz recognised that in open terrain the defence has the emplacement advantage of static blocking positions and, more important, it has the advantage of the second move against an attacker's flanking attempts. In mountain warfare, the defender does have a greater static-position advantage *but the compartmentalisation of terrain forecloses the more important second advantage.* The attacker can therefore turn even strong positions, cut off their line of sustenance and retreat, and thus induce a general collapse unless the defence is distinctly more agile. In Clausewitz's thinking, the use of reserves and the relative tempo of manoeuvre are the keys to both the defence and offence. The firepower criterion is only germane to the defence of static positions, but in mountain warfare especially the attacker's objective is to outflank while the defender's proper reaction is to counter-flank. It is therefore wrong to size the forces required by means of firepower scores, or by the capacities that avenues of approach could support. It is not the *lead* echelons of the attacking force that the defender must worry about, but rather the follow-up echelons, ready to peel off in order to turn blocking positions.

It is thus to be concluded that the key to victory in mountain warfare offensive or defensive is the same as in armoured manoeuvre: echeloned reserves, fluidity and an advantage in the relative tempo of action. It is clear that such a defence cannot possibly be based upon a combination of armoured formations and static entrenchments. Armoured formations can have no role in the mountain barrier itself. A light-armour cavalry screen and even some armour may be needed *forward* of the Northern Mountain barrier for peacetime presence functions. But these forces would almost certainly be unable to extricate themselves through the barrier and they would add little to the defence of the barrier itself. The more important role of armour would be to close the exits from the barrier to the central plateau, as well as in countering *coup de main* airborne landings.

On the other hand, a fluid and agile defence of the mountain barrier can be highly effective. This would still need some positional elements. Indeed fortifications are the indispensable anchor of the defence and they are critical to prevent surprise seizures of the road net. *What has to be avoided is the notion that positional defences in themselves can provide a meaningful defence.* Even major fortifications provide only a temporary check of the attacker's advance. The only *permanent* solution is a mobile reserve which can rapidly counter the attacker's flanking movements and attack his rear echelons. But this is by definition difficult to achieve in the compartmentalised terrain typical of mountains, though helicopter transport offers an apparent solution. On the other hand, if the defence is seduced into a cordon deployment by the apparent advantages of positional defences, it will lack the wherewithal to form sufficient reserves, and the troops will become not only too sedentary but also too dependent upon roads.

As in armoured warfare, positional defences should be viewed as no more than pivot points for the manoeuvre of fluid offensive forces. There are, however, four distinct differences.

First, the troops of the pivot positions must mentally condition themselves for eventual exfiltration, with the abandonment of whatever heavy weapons are used in the fortified position themselves. Only light weapons can be saved in each move; the attempt to bring back more will simply lead to the loss of the garrison and perhaps also to the spread of infectious panic. In today's world, the mortars and automatic weapons and light cannon which should be the mainstay of positional defences are relatively cheap. For the price of a single high-performance aircraft, one can buy hundreds of automatic weapons or mortars. Guns and such no longer have their former symbolic significance; they should now be viewed as expendable and their replacements can be pre-stored in successive fall-back positions. But garrisons cannot be sacrificed so easily, if only because of the effect on the morale of the remaining troops.

Second, flanking counter-attacks do not obtain their effect from their size or firepower. Attacks may be co-ordinated with artillery, but platoon and company-size operations will be the norm. Their usefulness springs from the manner in which they attack: they must materialise out of the mountains to launch hit-and-run attacks. What protects them, and also magnifies their morale impact, is deception and surprise. Against enemy infantry attempting to out-flank pivot positions, their task would be to turn the enemy's own flank. This can serve to lengthen the life of the defensive position, but their main task is to attack the attacker's own deep flanks — in the area where the enemy's soft supporting forces are to be found. In mountain warfare, particularly against an opponent attempting to push armoured columns through, successful attacks against the supply units in the rear can quickly lead to the demise of the (heavy) main forces.

Third, if fluid forces are to obtain the requisite degree of deception and surprise in mountain warfare, they require logistical autonomy. Only this can allow them to 'spring' from the mountains, to acquire an aura of destructive evanescence. To the Western military mind, keyed to the heavy tonnage requirements of front-line troops, it seems that such autonomy cannot be achieved. It is, however, a virtue of genuine mountain infantry forces that they are inherently adaptable to logistical stringency. Theirs is not the world of mechanisation with its attendant demands on fuel, spare parts and maintenance. Stealth and the exploitation of terrain compart-mentalisation substitute for heavy firepower support. Thus their main logistical requirements are for the human body, for small arms and grenades, and for a limited amount of mortar support. These are all cheap, *long-life*, small-tonnage items. Most usefully, they could be cached throughout the mountains in peacetime. This would allow mountain troops to move about freely and it would reduce enemy efforts in coping with them to mere shadow-boxing.

Fourth, and finally, there is the wide opportunity for demolitions, a dimension to warfare that is not so important in the flat lands. The unusually large numbers of bridges and tunnels which can be demolished obviously enhances the defence and adds to its delay potential. Particularly important for the long-term defence is that demolitions could exhaust an enemy's engineering capacity, particu-larly if the obstacle gaps are well defended, and the enemy's engineers are made top-priority targets. Attacks against the enemy engineering troops are particularly effective given the unusually heavy demand of armoured forces for engineer support in mountain terrain, and the relative scarcity of engineers in the overall Soviet force-structure. For the Iranians this would have favourable implications: either a Soviet underestimation of their engineering requirements, possibly leading to a Soviet inability to advance; or an increment to deterrence should the Soviets fully appreciate the heavy burden that would be placed on their scarce engineering units.

The complication of a Soviet advance is one goal of demolitions, but the latter could also contribute to the direct destruction of Soviet formations; in fact they could lead to demoralising Soviet defeats *if combined with fluid counter-attacks*. Troops advancing in mountain terrain, whether they are attacking positional defences or moving administratively in columns, are vulnerable to all the special stratagems of mountain warfare: induced rockfalls, contrived landslides and avalanches, and the like. These are not only deadly, but also terrifying to the survivors. Demolitions are also useful in congesting enemy units whose advance is temporarily blocked and in isolating them from assistance (by demolitions on their rear) while they are attacked suddenly and unexpectedly even by relatively small units. Non-combat supporting units are particularly vulnerable to such moves. The only protection against this tactic would be unpalatable for the Russians: the widespread dissipation, and stringing out of the relatively scarce Soviet infantry strength along the routes of march. The first weakens the Soviet thrust; the second presents an opportunity for the Iranians to focus their attacks on the Soviet infantry in the knowledge that once this component is destroyed, the remainder of the Soviet force becomes particularly vulnerable.

The *operational goals* of a mountain strategy are similar to those of a fluid armoured defence: to induce exhaustion and over-extension so as to set the stage for annihilation. The enemy should be allowed to exhaust himself by pursuing apparent success; he is to be enticed into attacking and flanking successive road blocks in depth, the final block being the defender's own armoured force covering the exits from the northern mountains. During this mountain phase, the defender's priority targets would be the Soviet engineers and infantry and *not* the armour. The main task of the position elements would be to prevent the breaching of obstacles, with a priority of effort against engineering equipment. It should also attempt to target as much of the enemy infantry as possible, ideally while still mounted or in the process of dismounting from its vehicles. But this obviously requires tactical surprise which is hardly possible if the attacker is properly preceded by light reconnaissance elements. The enemy response preferred by the defence would obviously be the frontal assault; it must be prepared for this eventuality, but much more likely the attacks will be flanking moves on the ground or by helicopter. Such attacks are vulnerable during the movement phase; it is the task of the fluid component of the defence to catch the enemy in disadvantageous positions while his forces are still *en route.*

The exhaustion and over-extension of the enemy, desirable goals in their own right, also fit into the larger scheme of manoeuvre warfare by being the pre-conditions for decisive counter-strokes. Soviet tank and artillery — the prime targets in flatland warfare — should *not* in general be primary targets at this stage. These components are not well suited to mountain combat, and their destruction will come about anyway if the overall operation is successful. So long as these elements are intact, the enemy command will be impelled to press on. *Hence a narrow-minded focus upon tank-destruction would misdirect the efforts of the defending force.*

The critical decisions for the defence are to choose the timing and form of the counter-stroke. Should it be early and in the form of many repetitive attacks against the enemy column as it inches forward? Or should the defence content itself with pinpricking the columns by stand-off fire and demolitions until the invading formation is over-extended? From the purely military viewpoint, the latter course is more decisive. On the other hand, the political leadership may want to report early victories both for its own prestige and to bolster public morale.

For Iranians against Russians, it is important that successive blocking positions be able to hold for significant periods. It may therefore be necessary to initiate smaller counter-strokes from the beginning. The risk is that the defence will also be exhausting itself, by having to attack into (or in the proximity of) the armoured vanguard itself instead of softer targets. If the blocking positions are effective, the defence is much better served by biding its time. If the Iranian units prove of high mettle, the same overall strategy can be unfolded more rapidly and to more effect. In this case the positional element need mount little more than a delay, withdraws on to the flanks, and allows the mechanised column to move into a large-scale trap. In both cases the counter-strokes then aim at the isolation and destruction of the soft element in the enemy supply columns and of his logistical support in general. Thereafter, the columns could be progressively split up, and defeated in detail.

In counter-stroke operations, the over-extension of the enemy is an intermediate goal whose aim is to force the vanguard to out-run its logistical support (or suspend the advance) and also to stretch out the combat units beyond their range of mutual support. In mountain warfare, over-extension accomplishes three purposes. *First* (and most important), it allows the defender to cut off the hard mechanised elements by attacking soft spots in an extended chain of communications. If this line of supply is not quickly restored, the logistically demanding armoured elements may find themselves immobilised, or even forced to abandon their equipment. *Second,* the enemy's *effective* frontage becomes 'U' shaped. His efforts are focused upon moving through the blocking positions but in doing so, his flanks become progressively weaker and more vulnerable to counter-attack. Time is then tactically on the side of the defenders.

The *third* reason why it is advantageous to aim for over-extension is because it allows the defender to launch remote and distracting attacks by fire prior to the counter-stroke. In particular, stand-off tactics can then be used to snipe at the attacker's infantry and engineers and generally wear down his strength. Demolitions can be repeatedly set, bringing down landslides and the like upon the attacker's columns. PGMs could also add a new dimension by picking off the enemy's vehicles at long range, in particular engineer and infantry-laden vehicles. One possibility would be to form amorphous observation and firing parties which would control and designate terminally guided rockets in an indirect fire mode. This system is based on the ability of the observation and firing parties to remain masked at some distance from the target area. If discovered, they would fade into the terrain, if possible ambushing the pursuing enemy infantry. A variant could consist of line-of-sight laser-designator parties a kilometre or so from the target with firing parties three to five kilometres from the target. Each laser spotter could target three or four vehicles per minute until the column's vehicles masked themselves with smoke or moved off the road to seek cover — if available. Low-powered radios and M-10 (mortar) plotting boards would be quite sufficient for command and control.[15] Another variant would consist of spotting parties with high-powered radios for communication to firing parties far away on the flanks, or well behind the line.[16]

It should by now be apparent that in mountain warfare the determining factor is the relative *fluidity* of the forces, i.e. *the very antithesis of the presumed advantages of positional defences as measured in relative firepower scores*. In flatland warfare, Clausewitz assumed equal fluidity; in the mountains he presumed an asymmetry in favour of the attacker. But assuming that the temptation of adopting a positional defence with the resulting operational passivity is avoided, the defender can then obtain two distinct advantages from his prior possession of the terrain.

First, he can cache supplies and thereby increase the logistical autonomy and fluidity of his mountain infantry. *Second*, by prior study of the terrain and skilful use of adjoining positional defences, the defender can shape in his favour the framework in which military operations will take place.

A small country arrayed against a large one can have a third advantage. It can design its military forces for the specific circumstances in which it would have to fight while large countries cannot.

Their forces and thinking are usually shaped to meet their own more dangerous adversaries. The Soviet Army has a force structure completely unsuited for combat in mountains. Soviet 'motorised rifle' divisions are not infantry at all, but in fact heavy armoured forces, a reality not much affected by the apparent training of parts of some of these units in mountain warfare. *It is unlikely that the Soviet Army would re-shape its standardised forces to match an Iranian shift to an agile mountain defence.* The Russians tend to be contemptuous of their smaller neighbours and expect them to oblige their might by a swift collapse. Further, Soviet planners tend to think in terms of handling smaller countries by *coup de main* operations. (The present Soviet force structure is very well suited for such operations). Additionally, even if Soviet planners were aware of a possible problem, it would be difficult for them to change their force structure. An Iranian change in force structure would be unlikely to generate a sufficient impulse for responsive Soviet change until a moment of crisis, when structural change would no longer be feasible.

Finally, structural change to accommodate local conditions is incompatible with the Soviet mobilisation system. The Soviet Army is oriented towards combat in open terrain against NATO and the Chinese. The cutting edge of their forces are the Category I divisions while their Category II and III divisions are follow-up and space-consolidation forces. Specialising a force for Iran would disrupt this scheme. Special Category I (and back-up Category II and III) divisions would have to be organised for Iranian (and similar) contingencies. This increases costs while reducing reserves suitable for NATO and Chinese contingencies. From the Soviet viewpoint, the latter two can threaten the security of the state while a certain degree of force inefficiency in a secondary theatre such as Iran does not.

It is for these reasons that there is the possibility that even a small power such as Iran could defend itself alone against the Soviet giant. But this is only possible if Iran can specifically organise its defence to take advantage of specific Soviet weaknesses, and of the contextual conditions. It should also be noted that a mountain-defence orientation is compatible with Iran's remaining security requirements. A force structure oriented for mountain warfare is cheaper, more easily redeployed and more effective in *defending* Iran's borders with Iraq and Afghanistan than the present flatland force structure. Iran would still need some armoured forces to implement this option and thus it would still retain a capability to launch punitive expeditions into the Iraqi flatlands.

There is finally the issue of internal security. A modern army with sophisticated weapons is much less suited for population control than a force consisting primarily of light infantry. In armoured forces too much of the structure is support-oriented while the combat forces themselves are far too heavy in firepower and far too destructive for effective population control. (For the Shah, there was the special factor that the more sophisticated the force, the larger the proportion of potentially disaffected urban recruits within it, and the smaller the proportion of potentially more loyal rural recruits.) Most governments in politically unstable countries find it necessary to fractionalise their military forces and this makes it very difficult, as noted earlier, to exercise armoured forces in the proper combined-arms manner. However, a structure oriented towards mountain warfare is compatible with command compartmentalisation.

How Much for Tactical Air Power?

Iran will always require some air defence to affirm sovereignty, to protect its air space, and to inhibit intimidating terror- and counter-value bombing. Deterrence against countries like Iraq require Iran to have similar counter-value capabilities. But capabilities of this order do not require an air force of the size and sophistication of a RAF or Luftwaffe. A 'Belgian' or 'Dutch' air force would suffice for these purposes. If an even larger air force is nevertheless desired, consideration should be given to updated versions of such *strafing* aircraft as A-1s and Mustangs. These aircraft are cheap, easy to maintain, and could be particularly effective in Iranian conditions. They can assist the army in the lesser military concerns and in mountains where sophisticated high performance aircraft would not be effective. If dispersed on small strips on the deep flanks of likely Soviet approaches, they could also be effectively used against rearward supply columns and the precursor elements which precede and broaden a Soviet advance.

Above this minimum, the amount and type of air power is very much a function of the strategy and type of ground force. For example, an armoured defence on the central plateau allows full play for tactical air power. The armour must be protected and the enemy's own armour and resupply made vulnerable to air attack. A defence of the Zagros Mountains would reduce the need for friendly air defence while increasing the scope for offensive air against an invader stretched across poorly netted mountains and plateaus. On the other hand, defence of the Zagros also entails abandonment of more than half of the supporting air base structure. A territorial defence by definition requires no air support at all. But, as already suggested, these are not interesting strategies. What needs to be investigated is the requirement for tactical air power in support of the postulated strategy of forward defence in the northern mountain barrier with agile mountain infantry.

The Role of Offensive Air in Mountain Warfare

It is widely believed that offensive air power is very effective in mountains. This thinking is derived from the belief that offensive air is a powerful instrument of interdiction and that its effect can be enhanced by the restrictive nature of mountainous terrain. But as is so often the case in conventional warfare, what is apparently true tactically is often not true operationally.

The problem with offensive air is that it does not relate well to the needs of a fluid mountain defence against a predominantly mechanised Soviet attacker. The object of the attacker is to push his columns through the barrier on to the plateau. The object of *delay* — in which offensive air could indeed be useful — is to cause the enemy to expend time and effort against relatively small forces by placing repeated blocks against the head of the columns. The tasks of air power are then to reinforce by fire the blocking positions, and more important, to provide its own delay by interdicting the road-bound columns. On the other hand, since even small forces can delay very large forces in mountains, it is also apparent there is a trade-off between prior preparation and offensive air. Prior preparation is obviously the more cost-effective; on the other hand, it is also to be recognised that unanticipated situations will arise even in the best case and that tactical air can be instrumental in coping with such situations until ground forces can be suitably deployed.

Delay in mountains by the nature of its dependence on static blocking positions falls into the category of a passive defence. This is a correct use for small forces, for only by relying on positional defences (and demolitions) can such a force impose a significant delay. The defender's main problem is the timing of his withdrawal to successive positions. Early withdrawal undercuts the purpose of the delay; late withdrawal leads to the possible loss of the forward forces to flanking movements by the enemy. But a defence in mountains should not be passive at all, and its purpose is no longer delay but rather the annihilation of the enemy's entire force. The focus is now no longer on the attacker's spearheading lead units but on the force as a *whole*, as explained above.

Offensive air can provide close air support and battlefield and supply interdiction. Close air support can be used to complement positional blocking defences; but it is not essential. The attacker is best stopped by an obstacle covered by fire. The tasks of firepower are to prevent the enemy from repairing or bypassing the breach and from flanking the defending force. Tactical air power is ill suited for these tasks. Its firepower lacks the continuity of a force on the ground for covering an obstacle and for countering local flanking efforts. It can also be circumvented by night movement. Even with good visibility, spotting and targeting the enemy's flanking infantry requires a forward air controller, while weapons delivery and weapon effectiveness are degraded by the steep slopes and cover provided by the terrain.

In mountain warfare interdiction loses its normal content. In flatlands warfare, the purpose of supply interdiction is to reduce the *size* of the force that can be *sustained* in combat. Air power cannot be expected to completely stop the movement of supplies, but rather to impede and cut the supply tonnage to some fraction of full capacity. In practical terms, since even a thin transport grid can support army groups (for example the Eastern Front in the Second World War) and a modest road an army (for example Africa Corps and British Eighth Army), supply interdiction reduces supportable forces from 'armies' to 'corps'. Once the Soviet attacker has broken on to the plateau (or is attacking into the Zagros), this reduction is an important consideration, particularly given the 'reinforcement race' with US deployments. But in the mountains itself, road capacity is not a constraining factor. The force being fought in the latter case is only that at the very tip of the column — basically a battalion-sized task force. It is only this 'battalion' tip that will be demanding the full array of supporting services. In breaking through the mountains, the entire force stretched in 'administrative' column behind the tip battalion can be no more than 1–2 divisions. This means that the force itself will be operating well within the full tonnage capacity of the communication line. Thus supply interdiction is not likely to have a meaningful impact until *after* the break-out on to the central plateau when larger forces must be assembled for sustained combat.

Battlefield interdiction is also unlikely to be very useful in a mountain defence, given a fluid infantry defence against a predominantly mechanised Soviet attacker. Battlefield interdiction against an attacker has two functions: disruption and isolation while the attrition of enemy elements is a by-product. For a positional defender, the purpose of battlefield interdiction is to disrupt the attacker's planning and co-ordination and the flow of reinforcements necessary to exploit any success. The two subordinate aims are to reduce the effectiveness of enemy forces and to prevent the enemy from transforming tactical into operational success, thus in effect easing the front-line demands on friendly ground forces and providing time for positioning them advantageously. As in flatlands combat, tactical air power can be a useful complement for this. The difference is in scale: in flatlands, large forces are involved; there is thus not only a large pay-off in disrupting co-ordination and the flow of reinforcements, but considerable firepower must be mounted and this can generally be done *only* by air power. In the mountains, however, the forces involved are smaller, co-ordination is accordingly simpler and presents less opportunity for disruption, while on the other hand even small groups of defenders can prevent the conversion of tactical into operational success.

For counter-attacks, the purpose of battlefield interdiction is again disruption and isolation, but with the emphasis upon isolation of the battlefield, physically and psychologically. The mountainous terrain reduces this task to the creation of blocks on the road so that column segments can be isolated from mutual support and attacked in detail. Tactical air power is suitable for this task; but it is done better by ground roadblocks and demolitions to provide continuity in the block and to create the impression for the offence that his forces are surrounded and attacked by overwhelming force. Tactical air cannot be used in direct support of the counter-attack itself, because of the difficulty of co-ordination and the proximity of the defender's attacking troops themselves to the effects of the air-delivered munitions.

In short, as long as there is an asymmetry between a fluid (infantry) defence and an attacker basically structured for armoured combat, there is little need for offensive air in support of the mountain infantry. The ground forces do not really need the supplemental firepower it provides. The problem of the ground forces is to cope with stratagems and the flanking movements — and for these tactical air offers little help. Similarly the disruption power of tactical air yields little that the ground forces cannot provide themselves.

Disruption itself is also less meaningful. It is to be recalled that its two benefits are to reduce the effectiveness of assaults and to impede the flow of exploiting reinforcements. In mountains, defending (as opposed to delaying) positional forces are not significantly helped by reducing the effectiveness of frontal assaults against them, while small units can be positioned in depth to block successful penetrations along the road axis.

It should be emphasised, however, that this conclusion is dependent upon an asymmetry, whereby the defence is designed for its special conditions while the attacker is not. If the attacker were to modify his forces, reducing their armour content to acquire mountain infantry, tactical air power (and helicopters) would then assume more importance due to the resulting compartmentalisation of the defending forces now compelled to distribute themselves across the mountain frontage. But it has also to be reiterated that the Soviets are unlikely to convert their forces in this manner. If they were to restructure, it would follow that while a better and more lengthy resistance could still be offered in the mountains, Iran would be eventually overwhelmed by the weight of Soviet superiority. In that case, the best that Iran could expect would be a *conditional* defence, i.e. a defence based on *relative* performance in the hope that the offensive would become too costly and slow for the Soviet Union. A conditional defence implies a protracted capability, and this too rules out the possibility of meaningful role for Iranian tactical airpower. Against the Soviet Air Force, the IIAF would most likely be too fragile and would be lost early, thereby compromising a defence dependent upon tactical air power. American air power could of course fill the void, but it should be noted that active US participation would undercut a conditional defence since the Soviet Union would not be dissuaded by the embarrassment and cost of becoming bogged down in a secondary theatre against a putatively third-rate opponent.

Weapon Effectiveness in High Mountains

The discussion above was based on the general nature of mountain warfare and the role of tactical air power in the overall scheme of battle; in other words, air power was treated as more than just air-delivered firepower. In contradiction to the above is the view that air power is so destructive that its firepower alone justifies its existence. This raises the question of the destructiveness of air power in mountains. Targets can be classified on a spectrum of difficulty: the most difficult are small and dispersed infantry groups infiltrating in mountain terrain; the easiest targets are high-contrast positional defences. In between the two are bridges and vehicles on the roadnet. It is obvious that tactical air cannot cope with the first set of targets. It is equally obvious that tactical air can readily target high-contrast positional defences. The critical target category, however, is the roadnet. It is against this category of targets that tactical air is generally claimed to be highly effective.

There is some question, however, whether tactical air can in fact attack effectively vehicles or 'bridges' in highly mountainous terrain. In this type of terrain the roadnet and vehicles assume high contrast. But their location is generally masked by the terrain itself, thus seriously complicating target acquisition and weapons delivery. Where the road twists and turns, there is a problem of intervisibility in targeting vehicles. But the more general problem is that a road running inside the folds of the mountains can readily be masked by wafting smoke from generators or pots, without affecting visibility on the road itself. Even light masking can defeat target acquisition from high-flying aircraft which seek to deliver optically guided PGMs. (Similarly IR-guided PGMs can be defeated by decoy hot spots set along the road.).

Low-flying aircraft can, of course, fly right into the haze and acquire their targets. But it is obvious that jet aircraft can only do this at considerable peril in reduced visibility. As it is, 'F-4s' are not manoeuvrable enough to fly in close mountains; and 'A-10s' lack the thrust to 'stand-on-tail'. In addition to flying into the mountainside, pilots must also be cautious of flying into a cross-fire from automatic guns and heat-seeking missiles shooting *down* from the ridges along the flight approaches to the more obvious targets.

Finally, there is the question of munitions for low-flying aircraft. As against tanks, only the A-10 has a suitable weapon with its 30mm GAU-8 cannon. Tanks and other armoured vehicles can be protected against cluster submunitions by 'chicken-wire' detonating rigs on top. Conventional 'iron bombs' have CEPs too large to be useful against armoured vehicles, but they can be useful for starting rockslides and the like.

In combination, these factors complicate the usefulness of offensive air. In particular, against heavy combat formations with considerable organic air defence, tactical air power may be effectively neutralised. Offensive air would be most effective against the attacker's softer logistic formations which generally lack escorting air defences. This, however, amounts to supply interdiction and implies that the Soviets would already have crossed the mountain barrier to reach the central plateau.

Air Defence in Mountain Warfare

While offensive air may not be of particular value for a defender, it is nevertheless true that air defence is of paramount importance. This follows from two differences between the attacker and the fluid defender: the defender's need to base his blocks on readily targetable positional defences and the attacker's need for helicopters to mount flanking movements and to cope with the defender's fluid counter-attacks (nourished by pre-positioned caches). This, however, is primarily a *ground* air-defence requirement. A fighter air defence provides a psychological uplift to ground troops and is sometimes instrumental in maintaining their resolve. Fighters, however, cannot cope with terrain-hugging helicopters and an Iranian fighter defence would in time be worn down by the superior weight of Soviet air power. It is therefore fortunate that the air defence requirement can be handled with light automatic cannon and with missiles of the REDEYE variety. For the positional defender the main task of air defence (as always) is to enforce stand-off distances in order to degrade further delivery accuracy (already degraded by terrain conditions). Large numbers of randomly dispersed small patrols with machine-guns and REDEYE missiles could make helicopter operations impractical given the degraded performance of the helicopter at high mountain altitudes and their inability to overfly the light missile and light gun weapons envelope.

Unlike the positional elements, the defender's fluid infantry groupings are not vulnerable to tactical air power. The major threat to these groupings is from enemy infantry delivered by helicopter after their presence or intent has been discovered or disclosed.

There is, finally, a limited air defence requirement for the LOCs. This requirement is alleviated by the general difficulty of targeting where roads run within deep folds of the terrain, and also by the attacker's desire to capture the road more or less intact. In an agile mountain defence, dependence on the roadnet is minimised to begin with by the prior caching of supplies and by the prior readiness to withdraw cross-country, when the position becomes flanked and made militarily untenable (the main enemy tactic). In general, the defender will be more interested in allowing the LOC to deteriorate. His strategy calls for allowing the attacker to push into the depth of the mountains, absorbing his engineering capability and troop labour effort on a partially destroyed LOC, while withdrawing on to the flanks in preparation for later counter-attacks against the flanks and rear of an over-extended mechanised force.

In Conclusion: The Theory of the Relational Force Structure

While not widely recognised, the demand for large, complex and advanced high-technology weapons is a choice derived from that country's method of warfare. Even with identical estimates of the magnitude, composition and immediacy of the threat, sharply different weapon requirements may arise, depending on the place of the chosen operational method in the attrition/manoeuvre spectrum.

In attrition methods of warfare, the enemy is treated as a mere array of targets; the goal is then progressively to reduce this enemy by administering upon him firepower of sufficient volume and accuracy. While tactics are undemanding and the results quite reliable — so long as the enemy chooses to operate in conveniently targetable mass formations — attrition methods generate a demand for combat aircraft with large payloads, battle tanks and much artillery. Above all, this method of warfare absolutely requires either superior technology or a net *matériel* advantage overall, hence the much alluded trade-off between force quantity and technological quality.

The attrition approach is familiar, for it is the style of warfare adopted by the Western Allies in the First and Second World Wars and taught and spread in their military asssitance and weapons-selling programmes. In fact, it may not always be realised that there is an alternative in the relational/manoeuvre approach. Associated primarily with the German Army at various times and more recently with the Israeli armed forces as well as with irregular guerrilla forces, the starting-point of relational/manoeuvre methods is the assumption of material inferiority. Therefore the aim must be to exploit identified shortcomings in the enemy array and any locale advantages in order to win by manoeuvre; instead of applying strength to main strength as in attrition methods, localised and specialised strengths are to be applied to the identified weak points of an enemy array which may be greatly superior overall, in an inventory sense and even in troop quality. (Hence the paradox that the best regiments are British but the best armies are German.)

While attrition methods tend to be standardised and homogeneous, relational/manoeuvre must be place-specific, responsive to the cultural milieu, and highly attuned to terrain factors. As a result, a relational/manoeuvre response to any given threat generally results in a greatly reduced demand for large, complex, advanced high-technology weapons, as compared to an attrition response to the identical threat. For example, a relational/manoeuvre defence of Iran *vis-a-vis* the Soviet Union can be based on the use of agile mountain infantry to hold the northern barrier of mountains, instead of armour-mechanised forces held back to fight it out on the plateau. And given the first choice, thin air defences can suffice, since mountain infantry would not present many lucrative targets to enemy air attack; by contrast, once primary reliance is placed on armour-mechanised forces, a thick and sophisticated air defence is essential, since such forces present high-contrast targets of high individual value.

Needless to say, territorial defence against the Soviet Union is by no means the only perceived security need in Iran's defence planning. But it is the most demanding in terms of size, technology and cost, and it illustrates the potential of relational/manoeuvre methods in making possible a defence just as effective — and often much more resilient — even while generating a greatly reduced demand for expensive and provocative high-technology weapons.

Notes

1. See for instance *US Military Sales to Iran*, a Staff Report to the Subcommittee on Foreign Assistance of the Committee on Foreign Relations, US Senate, July 1976.

2. For a discussion, see Theodore Moran, 'Iranian Defense Expenditures and the Social Crisis', *International Security* (Winter 1978), pp. 178-92.

3. See for instance, Jack N. Merritt and Pierre Sprey, 'Negative Marginal Returns in Weapons Acquisition' in R. Head and E. Rokke, *American Defense Policy* (Johns Hopkins University Press, Baltimore and London, 1976); and Steven Canby, 'American Defense Policy: the Problem is Not More Money', *AEI Foreign Policy and Defense Review* (American Enterprise Institute for Public Policy Research,

Washington, DC, April 1979).

4. Michael Handel, *Israeli's Political-Military Doctrine*, Occasional Papers in International Affairs, Number 30 (Harvard University, July 1973), p. ii.

5. The Shah's forces were acquiring many highly visible items of sophisticated weaponry, but specific items do not equate to across-the-board sophistication in fire-power, control, electronic warfare, etc. It is to be particularly noted that some of Iran's sophisticated weaponry would have been quite ineffective against the Soviets without the immediate reprogramming aid of American EW specialists.

6. The very poor showing of the Indians against the (outnumbered) Chinese in the Himalayan War can be explained by this phenomenon. The Indians nominally held the advantage of entrenched positions, but their overall defence was static while the Chinese operation was fluid.

7. In regard to other threats from the USSR, it was much less useful. For example, the best long-term insurance against the threat of direct Soviet support of insurgency would be a diplomatic balance and such economic linkages as the Soviet importation of Iranian gas and, later, oil.

8. Historically true strategic surprise is a rare phenomenon. The Soviets were well aware of German preparations in Spring 1941, as were the Japanese of the Russian in the summer of 1945. For an excellent discussion of the broader implications of the Manchurian model, see J. Despres *et al.*, *Timely Lessons of History: the Manchurian Model for Soviet Strategy* (RAND, July 1976).

9. For instance, the Belgians knew in 1914, and in 1940, that the Germans had to capture the Liege fortresses quickly; yet in both cases the Germans successfully executed *coup de main* operations.

10. For an elaboration, see Steven L. Canby, 'Tactical Airpower in Armored Warfare'.

11. As much as one-third of the infantry element of German Panzer divisions in 1939–41 were motor-cycle troops. It is to be noted that these troops were mainly used to seek paths around points of resistance: they usually fought mounted but on occasion dismounted, as in the turning of the British positions on Mount Olympus in 1941.

12. *The Military Balance 1978–1979* (The International Institute for Strategic Studies, London, 1978).

13. For a polite but lucid critique of Allied performance, see Field Marshal Kesselring and General of Cavalry Westphal, *Questions Regarding the German Strategy During the Italian Campaign* (US Army Historical Series, MS. B-270, undated).

14. It is interesting to note that Austro-German mountain tactics in the First World War closely resembled the future 'Hutier' and subsequent German armour tactics. The parallel is most vivid in E. Rommel's *Infanterie Greift an*. As early as 1915 Lt. Rommel of the Wurttemberg Mountain Battalion was using tactics that would later be called 'Hutier' tactics. The similarity of mountain tactics with what later came to be known as Blitzkrieg tactics can also be seen in Clausewitz's discussion of the defence in mountains; *On War*, Book Six, Chapters 15–17, pp. 417–33 in the Howard/Paret edition (Princeton University Press, Princeton, 1972).

15. Components for such systems are already available. Since US military services have no requirement for this approach, its potential has been ignored, and the US RDT&E community has been unwilling to invest in component integration. For example, the anti-tank rocket could be a standard 2.75-inch rocket with an anti-tank warhead and a terminal seeker. Rocket and warhead make up the system's bulk and weight. Large numbers of the rockets/warheads could be economically cached in the mountains; the high-cost seekers would be kept by the firing party.

16. With the use of the US Navy's SMARTROC, a 500 lb warhead could be fired from simple guide rails or commercial trucks at a distance of 26 kms for modest cost. Time lags would not allow this system to be fired at moving columns, but SMARTROCs could be fired against fixed targets to block roads at weak links (passes, culverts etc.). A second SMARTROC with an APAM warhead could then be fired at vehicles queuing up at the block.

7 ARMS TRANSFERS, INDIGENOUS DEFENCE PRODUCTION AND DEPENDENCY: THE CASE OF IRAN

Stephanie G. Neuman

Introduction

Manufacturing defence items is not a cost-effective enterprise for most countries. Few countries in the world, whether more or less developed, can produce military technology as economically as can the United States and a few European states. Why then are more and more governments clamouring for licensing rights to produce arms indigenously rather than buying arms directly from major suppliers?

This chapter analyses the relationship between the military industrial capabilities of Third World countries and their dependency on the states which supply them with arms. It focuses on the tension between the foreign policy goal of independence, which leads many governments to establish a domestic military industry, and the internal constraints which prevent them from achieving their goal. It discusses the kinds of trade-offs Third World defence planners must make between economic factors and perceived security needs.

Two main hypotheses serve as the organisational framework for this chapter.

(1) Arms transfers to less industrialised countries (LICs) initiate an evolutionary progression toward the indigenous production of military technology.
(2) Dependency for Third World states is no less a product of indigenous defence production than of arms transfers.

Although these hypotheses are formulated in general terms to apply to all Third World states, the Iranian Air Force (IIAF) in particular is used for the purpose of illustration. Iran was chosen for several reasons. First, during the 1960s and 1970s the Iranian military acquired a large number of arms which spanned the spectrum of sophistication, from simple to advanced. This is particularly true for the Iranian Air Force.

Second, Iran received arms transfers for a relatively long period of time, from a variety of suppliers, under a number of different financial agreements. Thus Iran, because of its relatively long and diversified history of arms transfers, provides a unique research opportunity to study the relationship between economics and defence within the military sector over time. If there are common elements in the defence planning of Third World leaders, this chapter assumes they are most likely to appear in the policies of those countries which have had extensive procurement experience.

The Escalator of Development

Hypothesis 1: *arms transfers to less industrialised countries initiate an evolutionary progression towards the indigenous production of military technology.*

It is hypothesised here that arms transfers and the indigenous production[1] of military equipment are part of the same development continuum. As the first shipment of military equipment arrives, an 'escalator of development'[2] begins with the *support of* imported technology and ends with the *production of* components and/or total weapons systems. The stages of this developmental process, although varying widely in time intervals across countries, are so intimately connected to the arms transfer process that the dividing line between indigenous production and arms transfers is often indistinguishable.

Beginning with the delivery of the first weapon system, the sequence follows a predictable, although not necessarily orderly, pattern. It is characterised at each stage by increasing recipient participation:

(1) servicing and repair of imported weapons systems;
(2) overhaul of imported weapons systems;
(3) weapon system assembly under licence;
(4) fabrication of simple components under licence;
(5) co-production of weapon systems under licence;
(6) indigenous design and development.

The first two maintenance phases of the developmental sequence are generally the most difficult and time-consuming to achieve in any service. The US Air Force had identified three different levels of technical expertise necessary for the operation and maintenance of defence equipment.[3]

(1) *Base or Organisational Level Maintenance.* This, the most elementary kind of maintenance, is essentially a servicing operation (such as gassing, lubrication, etc.) which includes making minor repairs by removing and replacing spare parts. Work is performed

on, or in direct support of, an aircraft on the flight line or in the inspection dock.

(2) *Intermediate Level Maintenance*. At this level, work is performed on aircraft systems, subsystems and components which have been removed from the aircraft and brought to a shop (generally on the base). This is synonymous with 'off aircraft' maintenance and is often referred to as the 'shop' or 'field shop' part of 'base maintenance'. Mechanics at this level are trained to do minor internal repairs of components (for example hydraulic cylinders) which can be pulled apart if necessary, certain parts replaced, and then reassembled.

(3) *Depot Level Maintenance*. The most complicated repairs are done at this level, generally off base at a designated military or commercial facility where components are sent for complete teardown and reassembly. This kind of maintenance encompasses the major inspection and repair as necessary (IRAN) maintenance functions which include overhaul and modification of the airframe, the aircraft system, subsystem and components. It involves the repair of equipment that cannot be done at the base level and requires a higher technological skill than either of the other two forms of maintenance. As one industry employee commented: 'Once you learn how to tear down and reassemble an aircraft, the capability for domestic production of aerospace components is relatively easy to acquire.'

This ascending order of fundamental maintenance tasks suggests a close connection between support and production, and the kinds of basic skills necessary to master these capabilities. The limits to growth of the military sector in any particular country are clearly dictated by the number of complexity of systems to be supported or produced, and the technical skill level of the population. But the size of a country and its level of industrial development are equally important factors. In all military services, the decision to establish a depot-level facility is determined not only by the skilled manpower resources available, but by economies of scale. In many smaller countries, the force structure of the military cannot sustain a depot-level industry. In the air force, for example, there are often not enough planes to keep a depot busy, so it is more economical to have major repairs done elsewhere. For most developing countries, major repairs are sent to depot-level shops in either the US or Europe. Only Israel and Taiwan are known to have depots of their own.

To comprehend any country's technical ability and its potential for indigenous military production, one would need information about the level of competency in many skills throughout the military sector, and some concept of the existing industrial infrastructure.

The simple 6 × 6 matrix below includes only some of the data categories needed to estimate domestic military-industrial capabilities.[4] The 'escalator of development' can be thought of as operating across weapons systems, services, time and countries. Thus the aircraft industry in country X can be at one level of development while naval production is at another. The reverse kind of production capability may be characteristic of country Y. The discussion of Iran (below) will elaborate on the number of human and material resources necessary to acquire an indigenous production capability in one military service. The matrix included here is designed to help the reader graphically imagine the vast resources required for an 'across the board' capability in the other military services as well. Little wonder so few countries have been able to attain it.

The Iranian Air Force

The Iranian Air Force, between 1964 and 1978 was confronted with the task of modernising rapidly. Although the large number of arms transferred to Iran, their degree of sophistication and the short time span within which the deliveries were made is not typical for most less industrialised countries, the fact that so much happened so quickly affords us a condensed, or telescoped, glimpse of the stages of development within the military.

For all practical purposes, the modernisation of the Iranian Air Force began with the delivery of 106 F-5A/B supersonic jet fighters in 1964. Between 1968 and 1970, 39 more F-5s arrived — a total of 145 F-5s to be absorbed within seven years.[5] In addition to these transfers, 10 C-130 transports were delivered between 1968 and 1970[6] and 36 US F-4 fighter jets (the workhorse of the USAF in Vietnam and the state-of-the-art air system at that time).[7] By 1978, there were 64 C-130s in Iran's inventory, and 20 Boeing 707 and 747 to supplement the transport force. Iran had received over 200 F-4s;[8] 169 of the latest model F-5E/F; and 78 F-14A fighter jets,[9] the latter one of the most sophisticated aircraft in the US inventory, which the US Navy was still having problems absorbing. Thus, collapsed into a fourteen-year period, and not counting training planes, helicopters and other smaller air force programmes, the IIAF was tasked with the maintenance and operation of seven major weapons systems approximating 500 aircraft (see Figure 7.1).

To accommodate this equipment, the IIAF had grown to a strength of 100,000 men, with operational units which included 10 fighter-bomber squadrons, 10 ground attack squadrons, 1 reconnaissance squadron, 1 tanker squadron, 4 medium and 4 light transport squadrons and 5 surface-to-air squadrons.[10] By 1978, arms transfers from the US had made the IIAF inventory one of the most modern in the world.

Table 7.1: The Escalator of Development. Matrix of Technical Skills in Ascending Order of Sophistication across Weapon Systems

	Aircraft	Missiles	Ships	Armoured Vehicles	Small Arms Ammo	Electronics
Servicing and Repair						
Overhaul						
Assembly (Licence)						
Fabrication of Simple Components (Licence)						
Co-production (Licence)						
Indigenous Design and Production						

Figure 7.1: 11AF Aircraft History

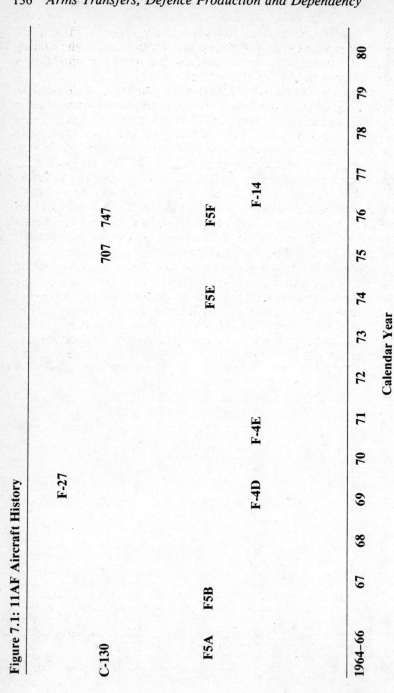

In order to utilise these systems effectively, however, the Iranians were faced with the overwhelming job of training enough technical and managerial personnel to perform the necessary operational, maintenance and logistical functions.

It is estimated that over 10,000 trained managers and technicians were required (excluding depot manning personnel) to maintain in operable condition just the F-5, F-4 and F-14 systems in Iran's inventory in 1978 (see Table 7.2).[11] Of this 10,000, approximately a quarter needed managerial and technical skills (see Table 7.3) requiring 5–10 years of training and 'hands-on' experience.[12]

A large training programme was instituted in the US and Iran to meet this and other IIAF technical needs. Between 1964 and 1972, 4,609 Iranians were trained (under MAP and FMS[13]) in US Air Force (USAF) technical schools. By 1977, 5,954 more had been trained, a total of 10,563 men.[14] Thousands more were learning maintenance functions in on-the-job training (OJT) in Iran with hundreds of US contractor and air force technical training teams instructing them.

As plans for acquiring a large modern air force took shape within the Iranian military, the Shah and his advisers decided in 1968 to begin developing a depot-level maintenance capability in-country. By 1968, large numbers of F-5s and C-130s were in inventory and F-4s had just begun to arrive. Many more planes were expected in the future. To the Shah, the speed with which the aircraft were delivered

Table 7.2: Maintenance Manpower Requirements

	F-5E/F (181)[e]	F-4E (225)[e]	F-14 (78)[e]
Direct[b]	116	226	292
Indirect[c]	111	152	159
Overhead[d]	23	38	45
	250[a]	416[a]	496[a]
Number of planes in inventory/18	10	13	4

Notes:
a. Number of personnel determined for 18 aircraft; 25 flying hours/aircraft/month (FH/MO); 85.2 maintenance manhours/man/month.
b. Direct maintenance refers to base and intermediate level maintenance.
c. Indirect maintenance refers to fixed numbers of technicians needed to support maintenance and operations (e.g. support, precision measurement and laboratory equipment, weapons loading, weapons release, gun services, munitions maintenance, storage and handling).
d. Overhead maintenance includes management, staff and administration.
e. Total number of aircraft in the Iranian inventory (1978) (computed from the *DMS Market Intelligence Report*, 1979).

Table 7.3: Distribution of Maintenance Technical Skill Level

	F-5 E/F		F-4 E		F-14		Total Manpower Requirement
	per 18 ac	per 181 ac[a]	per 18 ac	per 225 ac[a]	per 18 ac	per 48 ac[a]	
Superintendent[b] (9 level)	8	80	12	156	14	56	292
Technician[c] (7 level)	50	500	83	1079	99	396	1975
Specialist[d] (5 level)	138	1380	228	2964	272	1088	5432
Semi-Skilled[e] Specialist (3 level)	54	540	93	1209	111	444	2193
							9892

Notes: a. Total number of aircraft in the Iranian inventory (1978) (computed from the *DMS Market Intelligence Report*, 1979).
b. Chief administrator — responsible for overall administration (similar to a licensed doctor who does not practise but administers a hospital). 8-years of experience on the job.
c. Administration with some 'hands-on'. Responsible for keeping a specific operation going. 5–10 years of experience.
d. Expert technician with 1–5 years of experience.
e. Trained technician with no on-the-job experience. Finished speciality course, just beginning on-the-job training.

and their numbers indicated that unless Iran established an independent maintenance and overhaul capability its dependence on the US for technical expertise and spare parts would become permanent. Iran's geopolitical position and long experience with foreign intervention in its affairs only served to reinforce the Shah's desire for self-sufficiency.[15]

The depot was an ideal vehicle with which to realise his foreign policy and strategic goals: (1) self-sufficiency: the Shah's short-term goal was to establish an indigenous capability to perform enough maintenance and fabrication of spare parts to service the IIAF's strategic needs without outside assistance. His long-term objective was to develop a research and manufacturing capability similar to that of Israel Aircraft Industries, with the ultimate aim the production of an aircraft suited to Iran's particular defence needs; (2) establishing Iran as the major military power in the Middle East. In the short term Iran's role in the Middle East would be enhanced by servicing, maintaining and overhauling aircraft for the entire region. Doing so would also enlarge the scale of the depot's activities, turning it into a more economically viable venture. Long-range plans included the production of aircraft to fill regional needs.[16]

In September 1970, Iranian Aircraft Industries (IACI) was formed as a joint venture between the Northrop Corporation and the Iranian Military Industrial Organization (MIO) to train middle-management technicians.[17] The middle-term objectives were maintenance and logistics support for the IIAF and perhaps for Iran Air. Long-term goals included licence production for fasteners and spare parts; overhaul work on some components for the whole Middle East; assembly and some fabrication on remotely piloted vehicles (RPV), light civilian and transport planes, and the F-18 jet fighter (in ascending order), with eventual research and development of an F-X fighter and other aircraft. The time frame for this progression of events was estimated to be 20 years.[18]

By 1975 Northrop had sold its interest in IACI to the Iranian government and in 1977 IACI contracted with Lockheed Aircraft Service Co. to expand its aircraft overhaul and maintenance capabilities. When completed in the early 1980s the facility at Mehrabad Airport, Tehran, was to be the most modern and one of the largest aircraft and engine service facilities in the world. The facility was designed to handle all Iranian military and civil aircraft and would support aircraft and engine overhaul requirements throughout the Middle East.[19]

By early 1978 an infant manufacturing capability was in fact in the process of being developed in Iran to support, for the most part, the Iranian aerospace programme. The *DMS Market Intelligence Report* stated:

The Imperial government negotiated contracts with several aerospace companies that created significant co-production agreements. By early 1979 agreements had been concluded that would have eventually enabled Iranian industry to produce aircraft, helicopters, advanced computer terminal products, electro-optical products and surface-to-air missiles. [20]

In all, seven co-production contracts had been signed by early 1979:

(1) *Helicopter production and maintenance*: in 1975 Bell Helicopter was contracted to establish two capabilities, one a depot-level maintenance and logistic centre which would also supply training and support services for the Bell helicopters acquired from the US, and the second, construction and operation of an Iranian helicopter industry. Initial production was scheduled to start in 1979 to build 400 advance model helicopters. Included was a training programme to instruct Iranian personnel to assemble, produce, operate and manage the industry, which would eventually be turned over to the Iranian government. [21]

(2) *Co-production of the Rapier ground-to-air missile*: in 1976 Iran Electronics Industries (IEI) (a subsidiary of the Iranian Military Organization (MIO), which had been established to form an electronics manufacturing capability in Iran) formed a joint company with British Aerospace Corporation (BAC) (65 per cent financed by IEI and 35 per cent by BAC), [22] to manage a programme leading to co-production of the Rapier. As an interim measure Iran was to procure the missiles directly from BAC and install them. [23]

(3) *TOW missile*: in 1976 Iran concluded an agreement with Emerson Electronics and Hughes for co-production of the TOW anti-tank missile and launcher. [24]

(4) *Switch Manufacturing Capability*: in early 1975, IEI joined with GTE in a joint venture to supply Iran with electronic switching equipment for telecommunications and to establish a switch manufacturing plant.

(5) *Computer Terminal Products*: IEI and Control Data Corporation established a jointly owned company to design, develop and manufacture advanced computer terminal products. [25]

(6) *Maverick Missile*: in spring 1978 IEI and Hughes contracted to co-produce Maverick air-to-ground missiles. A factory was being built at the time of the revolution. [26] The future of the programme has not been determined. [27]

(7) *Small arms and ammunition*: relatively little is known about this MIO industry which supplies the Iranian ground forces (IIGF) with small arms and ammunition. It is one of the oldest military industries in Iran, dating back to 1924 and almost always under

licence to German contractors. During the late 1960s it developed its capabilities considerably and is now, according to Iranian sources, self-sufficient in small arms and some categories of ammunition. The factory has also reverse-engineered and produced a Soviet rocket.[28] The role of the German firm on contract to MIO and the number of third country nationals (TCNs) employed is unknown.

It is not the intent of this chapter to evaluate the actual capabilities of the Iranian military or industry but to demonstrate the sequential pull towards co-production. That there were severe constraints on progress because of a limited pool of skilled labour, insufficient construction facilities and inadequate infrastructure is a well known story. What is unknown is whether with time a viable military industrial complex could have been sustained, and whether the large amounts of equipment could have been absorbed to create a force as potent in war as it was on paper.

Prior to the events of 1978–9, there were signs that an 'escalator of development' within the Iranian military sector was operating. According to several US military observers, although the IIAF was experiencing difficulties in absorbing the newer systems, those that had had ten years or more to mature had achieved significant maintenance and operational success. In the F-5, F-4 and C-130 programmes, all were reported to be manned by Iranian crews, with maintenance support provided mainly by Iranian technicians.[29] (One MAAG informant reported that in all three programmes organisational and intermediate level maintenance had been substantially achieved and that some depot-level support was in progress.) Only minimal direct US or third-country involvement was necessary.[30] Both the F-4 and F-5 programmes were cited by State Department and DOD officials as examples of the absorptive capacity of the IIAF.

Similar progress was noted for IACI. Significant achievements were reported in the IACI Executive Briefing Progress Report of September 1975. Airframe tasks had become greater and more complicated. For example, modification of the F-4 and F-5E to incorporate the leading-edge wing slat had been accomplished. Engine maintenance and overhaul performance had also progressed. By 1975 IACI was providing maintenance and overhaul for two types of engines, the J-79 and the T-59, processing 200 engines a year. At the beginning of 1974 all J-79 engine components had been sent abroad for repair and overhaul. By the end of that year, 90 per cent of all J-79 components were being overhauled and by mid-1975 all components were repairable in-house. According to the IACI Report's evaluation, by 1975 IACI was moving towards self-sufficiency.[31] Iranian managers occupied 53 per cent of the management positions, an increase of 130 per cent over 1974. By 1977 manning figures showed approximately 2,000 Iranians, 600 third-country nationals and 50 US expatriates in the employ of IACI.[32] During 1974 training programmes had increased the number of skills certified to employees from about 50 in 1973 to 680, although a breakdown of skills by nationality was not available.

The fates of the other industries listed above, as well as the expansion of IACI, are now either undetermined or cancelled. Although the seeds of a large military-industrial complex had been planted, socio-political events turned back the industrial clock for Iran. It will be difficult to assess whether an indigenous arms manufacturing capability could in fact have taken root.

In conclusion, the Iranian experience suggests that an 'escalator of development' leading to some form of indigenous production is the end product of the arms transfer process.[33] If these stages can be detected within the Iranian military sector struggling to absorb massive shipments of weapons in a compressed time frame, this sequence may be even more typical for those LDCs with more modest and less dramatic arms transfer programmes.

Make versus Buy: the Bureaucrats' Dilemma

Hypothesis 2: *dependency for Third World states is no less a product of indigenous defence production than of arms transfers.*

It is postulated here that decisions to 'make or buy' military technology do not affect the short- or long-term dependency of recipients on suppliers. States opting for an indigenous military-industrial capability are unable to produce all their required weapon systems. Instead they are forced by socio-economic constraints to choose between *what* to make and *what* to buy. Arms transfers, therefore, do not terminate with the decision to develop a production capacity. Although a decision to produce may reduce the number of complete weapon systems imported, other kinds of technology (components, machinery, manufacturing equipment and know-how) are transferred instead.

Freedom from foreign influence is sought by most states. One of the most obvious expressions of this desire is government support for indigenous arms production.[34] For the industrialising countries, goals of 'sovereignty' or 'self-sufficiency' stand in constant tension with the necessity of using Western know-how to foster development in military and civilian sectors.[35] Even LDCs blessed with substantial resources have found self-sufficiency in the military sector to be an unattainable goal. Listed below are some of the constraints limiting the indigenous arms production options of industrialising elites.

(1) *Human Resources.* In Iran we have seen how shortages of managerial and technical manpower forced the Iranian government to rely on third-country nationals and supplier expertise for maintaining tasks. Manpower shortages also delayed aircraft co-production plans.[36]

(2) *Size of the Military Market.* Unless a large number of a particular weapons system or component is required by the armed service, or substantial export sales are anticipated, certain military items are too costly to manufacture. Economies of scale are as vital for military industries as they are for civilian.[37]

(3) *Time Frame.* Estimates of when a weapon is needed for projected force structure requirements and the adequacy of the lead time also affect the outcome of a 'make or buy' decision.

(4) *Complexity of the Weapon System.* Closely related to the time frame is the technological complexity of the system to be produced. It determines whether the lead time is sufficient or not.

(5) *Cost Differential.* In deciding whether to 'make or buy' a weapon system, governments in all LICs consider the cost differential between options. In general, the differential favours buying directly off the supplier's shelf. One reason is the cost of establishing a new factory, which is a major (non-recurring) expenditure.[38] Unless large numbers of the weapon system, or its components, are to be produced in-country over which non-recurring expenses can be pro-rated, the unit cost of the system remains too high to justify domestic production. Cost differentials vary among systems. Smaller military items, such as weapons and ammunition, break even earlier than larger systems. But for those LICs interested in producing planes, according to one industry spokesman, even the smallest American tactical aircraft, such as the F-5, requires 'a buy of over 200 to achieve a slight reduction in unit cost'.[39]

(6) *Supporting Industrial Infrastructure.* Creating an indigenous arms production capability also requires the support of many secondary industries and facilities. Building an aerospace industry, for example, entails the production of castings and forgings, fabricating sheet metal, machining, plating, as well as the manufacture of electrical and electronic equipment, gears, bearings and plastics. In order to design and develop aircraft, there is a need for certain specialised laboratory and test facilities as well (for example engineering test laboratories, wind tunnels, flight simulators, etc.). The decision to 'make' often means developing these secondary facilities, a task that may be beyond the technical and economic capabilities of a less industrialised country.

How these considerations affect 'make or buy' options in the LICs is illustrated by the Iranian decision not to attempt co-production of the F-5 jet in the early 1970s and a more sophisticated fighter in the 1990s. Time was an important factor in the Iranian decision. Acquiring an indigenous capability for fighter production is a lengthy and complex process. (India had twenty years of experience with the Marut before the government and industry experimented with a more sophisticated aircraft.[40]) Although the F-5 was and is considered to be an 'intermediate' technology,[41] projected strategic requirements were expected to outpace the Iranian manufacturing capability. They chose not to invest years learning how to produce an aircraft which would be unsuited to their future defence needs. Instead the Iranians opted to buy F-5s until acceptable levels of maintenance and logistics management were attained for the IIAF inventory. Their goal was to achieve intermediate-level maintenance capacity for high-technology planes and depot level for the F-5. In 1975, plans to co-produce (assemble, with some fabrication) other aircraft, including ultimately an indigenously designed and developed F-X,[42] were also deferred. This time technical manpower shortages and the size of the projected capital investment[43] (to train men and build supporting facilities) moved the Shah to declare it was 'too much, too soon'.[44]

Even after the basic decision to 'make or buy' a system has been taken, other second- and third-level choices are necessary. For example, when it is decided to *produce* rather than purchase, a determination must be made as to which of the supporting technologies, equipment, skills and other capacities will be developed internally or acquired abroad. If, on the other hand, the decision has been made to *buy* equipment, the infrastructure necessary to accommodate the technologies must be obtained. Whether to use foreign or domestic capital for investment raises still a third layer of economic and political trade-off questions for policy-makers.

For example, IACI developed a matrix for the government of Iran which estimated that no less than 80 different kinds of resources and equipment were needed to support a decision to 'make' rather than 'buy' an advanced fighter jet by 1990. Of these resources, fourteen were available only in the US or Europe, and others, although obtainable in-country, were less expensive to purchase from Western sources. However, as the study pointed out, 'make or buy' decisions are fluid and change over time. A decision to procure all items outside of Iran can be phased into all-made in Iran, given a long enough time frame using licence arrangements. Time in which to develop capabilities changes the long-term cost-effectiveness picture considerably.

Decisions to 'make or buy' are part of an ongoing process of trade-offs between self-sufficiency and development in the less industrial countries. The implications of these decisions reach beyond individual country borders into the larger international system.

Conclusion

Because conventional arms transfer relations involve dependency for the recipient, building an indigenous arms production capability represents an attempt on the part of less industrialised states to reduce supplier leverage. But self-sufficiency in weapons production is beyond the reach of less developed countries. Domestic production creates other dependencies.

It can be argued that in an interdependent environment, sovereignty is unattainable for even the most industrialised states. But in the real world of inequality, where resources are inequitably distributed, dependence and independence are relative, not absolute, values. Well endowed states have more leverage than other states. For the smaller, poorer countries, the choice between arms production and arms transfers implies only greater or lesser dependency.

Glossary of Abbreviations

BAC	British Aerospace Company
DOD	Department of Defense (US)
FMS	Foreign Military Sales (US)
F-X	Fighter Experimental
IACI	Iran Aircraft Industries
IEI	Iran Electronics Industries
IIAF	Imperial Iranian Air Force
IIGF	Imperial Iranian Ground Forces
LICs	Less Industrialised Countries
MAAG	Military Assistance Advisory Group (US)
MAP	Military Assistance Program (US)
MIO	Military Industrial Organization (Iran)
SFRC	Senate Foreign Relations Committee (US)
SIPRI	Stockholm International Peace Research Institute
TCNs	Third Country Nationals
USAF	United States Air Force

Notes

1. The term 'production' is used here in the generic sense to include all phases of the maintenance and/or manufacture of defence items. This usage conforms to the US Department of Defense definition of co-production which encompasses any programme which 'enables an eligible foreign government, international organization or designated commercial producer to acquire the "know-how" to manufacture or assemble, repair, maintain and operate, in whole or in part, a specific weapon, communication or support system, or an individual military item'. (US Department of Defense Directive 2000.9 (ASD-I and L), International Co-production Projects and Agreements Between the United States and Other Countries or International Organizations, 23 Jan. 1974).

2. Daniel L. Spencer, 'An External Military Presence, Technological Transfer, and Structural Change', *Kyklos*, vol. 19 (1965), pp. 451–73.

3. Operational skills (such as flying and weapons operations) are omitted from this discussion since they are less related to 'the escalator of development' towards indigenous production than maintenance skills.

4. To describe more fully a particular country's defence industrial capability, a matrix would have to indicate the kind of military items being 'produced' and their level of sophistication. For example, country X with a capability to *overhaul* a J-79 engine has acquired more sophisticated skills than country Y which *assembles* rifles. This same kind of differential may apply to different services within the same country, too.

5. *DMS Market Intelligence Report,* 1979, 'Iran Force Structure, Aircraft'.

6. Ibid. According to other sources, some C-130s arrived as early as 1964–5. Figure 7.1 uses the earlier date.

7. The F-5E/Fs were purchased to replace the F-5A/Bs. During the early 1970s, an undetermined number of the F-5A/Bs were transferred to Pakistan, South Vietnam, Jordon and Greece, according to the *DMS Market Intelligence Report*, 1979.

8. Ibid.

9. Ibid.

10. *DMS Market Intelligence Report*, 1979.

11. The 10,000 plus manpower requirement is estimated by dividing the number of F-5s, F-4s, and F-14s in the Iranian inventory (1978) by 18 (into US squadrons) and then multiplying the total maintenance manpower requirement for each jet type (see Table 7.2) by number of squadrons. Thus, in 1978 the IIAF had 181 F-5s, 225 F-4s and 78 F-14s; translated into squadrons this becomes approximately 10 F-5 squadrons, 13 F-4 squadrons and 4 F-14 squadrons.

12. Interview with a US Army colonel who served in Iran with the US Military Assistance Advisory Group (MAAG) as an administrator of the US Foreign Military Sales Programme (FMS) to Iran.

13. MAP = Military Assistance Program (US); see note above for FMS definition.

14. These figures were supplied by the US Defense Security Assistance Agency (DSAA) and unfortunately do not break out operations from maintenance. The 10,563 figure includes pilots and weapons operators.

15. Interview with General Toufanian, Tehran, Iran, January 1978.

16. Interview with Iran Aircraft Industries (IACI) personnel, Tehran, Iran, December 1977.

17. The Company's charter stated:

1. The Government of Iran has determined that IACI is vital to the national interest and will:
Establish and expand military and commercial aircraft repair, maintenance and overhaul capability; satisfy a critical need with respect to national defense

and commercial aircraft requirements; provide management and technical expertise through on-the-job and other IACI training programs.

2. IACI will also as directed:

Manufacture, through license, coproduction, or internal design and development, air vehicles and air vehicles systems either governmental or commercial; provide a basis for the planning and development of a self-sufficient aerospace industry.

It is the intention of the Government of Iran that IACI be a vital link in the development of self-sufficiency, and that it serve not only as the major overhaul, modification, manufacturing, and repair center for all Iranian aircraft but serve also as the base for developing a self-sufficient Aerospace Industry. IACI Management and Shareholders are dedicated to this task (Preface to Iran Aircraft Industries; *Executive Briefing Progress Report*, September 1975).

18. Interviews with Northrop personnel, February 1979.

19. *DMS*, 'Iran Summary', p. 6, and interviews with MAAG personnel (July 1979).

20. *DMS*, 'Iran Summary', p. 4.

21. Bell suspended work in 1978 and the contract was subsequently cancelled. *DMS*, 'Iran Summary', p. 5.

22. *SIPRI Yearbook*, 1979, p. 165.

23. In late 1978 the Iranian government cancelled plans to build the system in Iran. *DMS*, 'Iran Summary', p. 5.

24. *SIPRI Yearbook*, 1979, p. 165, and Institute for Policy Studies, *Arms Trade Data*, 'U.S. Arms Transfer to the Third World, 1973–78' (n.d.)

25. *DMS*, p. 5.

26. A MAAG informant, 25 July 1979.

27. *SIPRI Yearbook*, 1979, p. 165.

28. Interview with General Nemati in Parchin, Iran, January 1978.

29. It was estimated by one US Department of Defense (DOD) official that in the F-5E/F programme all units were operational and flyable at a rate close to 90 per cent. By 1977 over 500 pilots and 1,500 maintenance personnel had been trained. A similar success was reported for the F-4 programme. All F-4 units were operational and flyable at rates in the 80 per cent range. Over 1,500 operators and 5,300 maintenance personnel had been trained (interview, August 1979).

30. The story was very different for the newer systems. From the beginning even on the less complex systems, Iranian operational capability exceeded its support abilities. It was estimated by both DOD and State Department officials that in 1977 a technical manpower shortage of about 7,500 personnel in the air force would make it difficult for Iran to support their most complex equipment. Large numbers of Americans (6,900 at the end of 1977) and third-country nationals were necessary to keep them going. It was estimated that US and third-country technicians (for base functions of civil engineering and vehicle maintenance) would remain an important part of the Iranian defence programme until 1990. Although progress was being made, time and continued foreign assistance would be necessary for the foreseeable future. In 1978, other informants suggested that there had been a significant deterioration in maintenance capability of both the F-4 and F-5 programmes. The F-14 was pulling the most experienced technicians away from these earlier systems, causing an across-the-board shortfall of technical manpower. A US Senate report has documented the IIAF's absoption problem with the F-14. The personnel figures supplied to me by DOD and State Department officials differ from those contained in the US Senate study (United States Senate. Comittee on Foreign Relations. 'U.S. Military Sales to Iran', A Staff Report to the Subcommittee on Foreign Assistance (July 1976), pp. 30 and 32).

31. It was reported by various informants that IACI employees had also built a glider by themselves, of which they were justly proud. It was considered by the

Iranians as the first step towards the manufacture of airframes.

32. Data supplied by the Manager of Foreign Employment for the Northrop Corporation, November 1978.

33. Although part of the 'escalator of development' is dependent on spin-offs from maintenance functions, it is also dependent on leaders' motivation. The motivation to establish an indigenous arms production capability derives from such pragmatic considerations as reducing dependency on foreign powers (discussed below, p. 142 ff) and balance of payments incentives, particularly in those countries with negative trade balances. New technologies have also impacted on the motivation of Third World leaders to establish a domestic arms industry. As one Third World defence analyst has noted, the proliferation of Precision Guided Munitions (PGMs) and the attendant large weapons attrition rate will make resupply a critical factor on the battlefield, further fuelling the perceived necessity for an autonomous supply (Shai Feldman, 'Some Observations on Indigenous Arms Production', a commentary prepared for the ACA/IISS Conference on Conventional Arms Transfers, Bellagio, Italy, May 1979, p. 5). Ultimately, however, available resources, human and material, determine each country's success in achieving a military-industrial capability.

34. See Robert R. Ropelewski, 'Arabs Seek Arms Sufficiency', *Aviation Week and Space Technology*, 15 May 1978, pp. 14–16; Donald E. Fink, 'Nationalists Update Fighter Force', *AWST*, 5 June 1978, pp. 14–16; and [Taiwan] Center Designs Two Aircraft', *AWST*, 29 May 1978, pp. 14–16; Philip J. Klass, 'New Capabilities Building Rapidly (Israel)', *AWST*, 10 April 1978, pp. 32–7; 'South Korea's Industry: Boom-Boom', *The Economist*, 2 December 1978. See also Hugo Sada, 'Arms Transfers: Dependence, Influence, and Regional Stability: Indigenous Weapons Production Capabilities', unpublished paper prepared for the ACA/IISS Conference on Conventional Arms Transfers, Bellagio, Italy, May 1979.

In this connection, Shai Feldman observes: 'The greater the political costs involved in dependence, the greater the incentive to go indigenous. . . Possibly the greatest accelerators of the development of indigenous arms production capabilities in Israel have been France's efforts to affect Israel's defense and policy by imposing an arms embargo in 1967, and U.S. efforts to achieve the same by delaying shipments of supplies during the initial stages of the 1973 war' ('Indigenous Arms Production', p. 2).

35. The interrelatedness of military and civilian development for the Shah is discussed by S. Neuman, 'Security, Military Expenditures and Socioeconomic Development: Reflections on Iran', *Orbis*, vol. 22, no. 3 (Fall 1978), pp. 569–94. See also Shahram Chubin, 'Iran's Security in the 1980s', paper presented at the International Studies Association Annual Meeting, St Louis, Missouri, March 1977.

36. The number of trained people necessary to build a co-production capability for sophisticated technology is suggested in the IACI expansion plan report. In order to achieve a self-sufficient maintenance and overhaul capability for the IIAF, in addition to a design and manufacturing capacity, the study estimated IACI would require 39,000 people, including 3,850 managers, 3,250 engineers, 6,000 technicians and 24,000 other employees.

To perform just the maintenance and overhaul mission for Iran's commercial aircraft, with some second-country capability, would require 9,000 employees, including 850 managers, 250 engineers, 4,000 technicians and 4,000 other personnel. Given the context of this plan, these figures are probably conservative (IACI Conceptual Plan, 1975).

37. For example, the IACI Report outlining a plan to establish an aerospace manufacturing industry in Iran by 1990 cautioned the Iranian government to start with light aircraft which could provide a self-supporting market without need for export. The plan called for manufacturing variants of a military trainer which would fill an internal strategic requirement, with the possibility of sales in the region as well.

The plan also pointed out that it makes little technological or economic sense to design and build aircraft already being produced by multiple sources elsewhere. Using the jumbo jet for illustration, the study showed that other sources were manufacturing enough to satisfy long-term world needs and the market demand within Iran was too small to justify a cost-effective programme. Since jumbo jets provided no more advanced technology than light aircraft (such as a military trainer or short-haul transport), the report argued that buying rather than producing made more economic sense. It might be added that it also made political sense, since the availability of multiple sources of supply limited the leverage of suppliers — which was the primary reason for production in the first place. Why manufacture if the product can be bought economically elsewhere without political penalty?

Furthermore, the IACI report warned that without a steady market of some scale the Iranian aerospace industry would be unable to avoid the peaks and valleys of employment which have impacted so negatively on the economies of other arms-producing states.

38. Building a new factory for co-production of an American weapon system for example, means buying all the tooling machinery from American firms. The real expense is associated with achieving commonality — procuring the same equipment (e.g. jigs, milling machinery), training the personnel, acquiring a duplicate set of *translated* plans, etc.

39. In some instances industrialising elites are willing to pay a 'tuition fee' to gain know-how. Taiwan, for example, in 1973 decided to pay a cost differential of $25 million to co-produce 250 F-5E jets. Even then Taiwan was scheduled for only about 10 per cent of the production, most of which was limited to final assembly and flight testing. Domestically manufactured parts were for the nose sections only. What made even this limited co-production plan economically feasible was the size of the procurement package. Taiwan, according to one industry informant, was the only LIC to buy over 200 of any major weapon system on a co-production basis. Brazil's decision to 'buy' *not* 'make' further illustrates the problems of scale and cost differential. In 1974, Brazil planned to acquire 42 F-5E fighter jets. The smaller number of planes to be procured, however, meant spreading the non-recurring 'start-up' expenses over fewer items which escalated the cost of each plane considerably. Brazil opted to buy off-the-line rather than co-produce.

Switzerland, although not a Third World country, was confronted with similar options because of its size. The Swiss decision to acquire 72 F-5Es meant that if they decided on a large co-production programme, the unit cost of each plane would rise. Yet for domestic political reasons, the Swiss opted for final assembly in Switzerland. Even though they would have to pay a cost differential it would be a relatively small one and the political trade-off was worth it. Besides, an additional (government-to-government) agreement had been negotiated whereby Northrop and General Electric (which builds engines for the F-5) consented to 'offset' the cost differential by marketing the equivalent value of Swiss industrial products abroad (information gathered from interview with industry executive, October 1979, and Captain R. Kenneth Bowers, USAF, 'Coproduction: the U.S. F-5E in Taiwan and Switzerland', *Defense Systems Management Review*, vol. 2, no. 2 (Spring 1979), pp. 34–45.

40. The newer Ajeet is a Mach II version of the licence-built British Gnat. See Gregory Copley, 'Third World Arms Production', *Defense and Foreign Affairs Digest* (September 1978), pp. 24–41, for a description of India's military industry.

41. The term 'intermediate technology' is a relative one. The most advanced defence technology extant determines the relative sophistication of other military items. Therefore the meaning of 'intermediate', or for that matter other descriptors of military hardware such as 'advanced', 'critical', 'lead-edge' or 'vintage' is constantly changing. In a recent interview, a US government official defined 'intermediate' weapon systems as subsonic jet aircraft, transport aircraft, medium and light armoured vehicles, missile patrol boats, frigates, patrol submarines, tactical missile

systems, radars and battlefield electronics. He noted, however, that, in the Third World, for many countries these are 'advanced' systems. Only a few of the LICs can produce a few of them. None can produce all of them (interview with US Department of State official, November 1979).

Nevertheless, over time, there is a steady upgrading of the level of weaponry throughout the world. Today's 'advanced' technology is tomorrow's 'intermediate'-level weapon system. Third world countries are constantly modernising older military items with new components. One example is Korea's effort to increase its military capabilities. With US assistance, South Korea has improved Western Electric Nike Hercules missiles previously furnished to Korea by the US. These modifications include 'upgrading some electronics to solid state for improved reliability, improved conventional warhead munitions, and the capability to operate the missiles in a ground-to-ground mode'. (See Bruce A. Smith, 'Koreans Seek New Military Air Capacity', *Aviation Week and Space Technology*, 22 October 1979, pp. 62–3.)

42. Acronym for an 'experimental fighter'.

43. The OPEC price increase during 1973–4 precipitated a world-wide economic recession. Iranian oil sales began to decline. By 1975 they had dropped 12.5 per cent. See Michael T. Klare, 'Arms and the Shah', *The Progressive* (August 1979), p. 20.

44. Interview with Northrop Corporation Manager of Support Services, 20 August 1979.

8 SAUDI ARABIA AND IRAN: THE TWIN PILLARS IN REVOLUTIONARY TIMES

Richard Haass

A large body of literature has demonstrated that the foreign and defence policies of modern nation-states are not determined simply by some monolithic decision-making entity rationally assessing interests, capabilities and options. Rather, policies are also the product of procedures and processes involving leaders, organisational structures and bureaucratic forces. Put succinctly, form and function affect substance.

This is not to say that major differences do not exist among states and the ways in which they go about making policy. Where political institutions are developed and enjoy a large degree of popular support, a considerable continuity in policy tends to exist from one year to another. Individuals and parties exercising power may change, but policy usually remains within the bounds of widely accepted parameters. Alternatively, in states characterised by relatively shallow political institutions lacking strong historical and constitutional underpinnings, policy is far more vulnerable to radical shifts in direction brought about by changes of leadership in which contending coalitions share little regarding outlook or intentions.

This latter model is commonly (but not exclusively) found in developing countries whose 'political culture' is often as weak as their economic structures. Leadership tends to be elitist and isolated, the degree of popular participation in political processes minimal, and mechanisms for orderly succession or political transition almost totally absent. Moreover, the traumatic experience intrinsic to the process of economic development by definition taking place in these countries further exacerbates the strains of political development. Not only does rapid modernisation create severe dislocations in traditional life-styles, but new sources of wealth and patterns of economic interaction can alter the basic interests and capabilities of these states. In short, amidst conditions of such dynamic economic and political change, there are few constants on which to base any policy, foreign or otherwise.

Much of the above description pertains to the 'Twin Pillars' of the Persian Gulf, Iran and Saudi Arabia. Receipts from the production and export of oil and gas have transformed the economies and socie-

ties of both states within a span of only several years. Iran's vulnerability to revolutionary upheaval has been made obvious, and new
uncertainties must be added to any estimation of Saudi Arabia's
prospects for domestic stability. But despite all the implications,
actual or potential, of political and economic change, internal
factors comprise but one source of nation-state instability. The more
traditional agenda of inter-state competition and even conflict continues to influence the stability and autonomy of states. The futures
of Iran and Saudi Arabia cannot be divorced from either regional or
global developments. Perhaps the only mistake worse than ignoring
the so-called lessons of Iran would be to learn the wrong ones;
domestic determinants of stability in developing countries must
count for more, but inter-state sources of instability must not count
for less.[1]

It is within this context of multiple threats to stability, or multiple
sources of instability, that the relationship between Iran and Saudi
Arabia must be viewed. In the past, a large number of observers
debated whether the co-operative or competitive elements of the
relationship would prevail. With Iran's revolution effectively
marking the end of an era, it is now possible to reach some conclusions regarding relations between the pillars 'after the British'.
More difficult but no less important is the need to attempt to build
on these conclusions and reach some tentative understanding about
the possible or even probable course of relations 'after the Shah'. To
return to an earlier theme, what degree of continuity can one expect
to encounter in relations between these two key states of the Persian
Gulf? Asked another way, will revolution in one of the pillars
revolutionise either the other or the relationship between them? It is
to these and related questions that this chapter is directed.

Co-operation and Competition

The importance of the Saudi-Iranian relationship was a fact
explicitly recognised by US policy towards the region after the 1968
announcement by the United Kingdom that it would complete its
withdrawal from the Gulf by 1971. As articulated some years later by
a senior American official:

> In the spirit of the Nixon Doctrine, we are willing to assist the
> Gulf states but we look to them to bear the main responsibility for
> their own defense and to cooperate among themselves to insure
> regional peace and stability. We especially look to the leading
> states of the area, Iran and Saudi Arabia, to cooperate for this
> purpose.[2]

Over the next few years, the Nixon Doctrine was applied to these states as nowhere else. A host of diplomatic, economic and military initiatives, ranging from frequent top-level meetings and development commissions to military transfers and naval presence, were instituted by the United States to further its objectives at a reduced direct cost to itself.

This policy notwithstanding — indeed, one can almost say because of it — a number of individuals both inside and outside government in the United States and elsewhere challenged the wisdom of placing so much emphasis on the relationship between Iran and Saudi Arabia. What was argued was that the entire 'twin pillar' concept was a flawed one; to continue the imagery, that it provided a weak foundation upon which to build an enduring foreign policy. Two separate but related themes characterised this perspective. On one hand, it was maintained that it was unreasonable to expect Saudi-Iranian co-operation in light of their many historical, cultural, political, religious and linguistic differences. Instead, it was predicted that as the two most powerful and influential states in the region the two would be unable to resist competing for local primacy once the moderating factor of British presence had been removed. Secondly, it was argued that the very direction and nature of American and Western policy, and the military transfer aspect in particular, would have the inevitable effect of exacerbating this inherent rivalry. Thus, while few observers disagreed with the premiss that Saudi-Iranian co-operation would be desirable, a considerable number concluded it unlikely in any event and especially so in light of US policy.[3]

Even a quick appraisal of their relationship yields evidence to support this point of view. Although they are the two largest states of the region, their different locations produce different outlooks. Saudi Arabia is on the Arabian peninsula itself, bordering directly on the other states of the peninsula and those of the Middle East, with those of the Horn of Africa nearby. Iran, while bordering Iraq and separated from the peninsula by only a narrow stretch of water, is none the less partially removed from the Arab world by geography. It shares a thousand-mile border with the Soviet Union to the north and touches Turkey in the West as well as Pakistan and Afghanistan in the East. Saudi Arabia's environment is thus one of the peninsula it dominates and the lands to its west; Iran has also to contend with developments in southern Asia.

There are a number of other basic differences as well. Population varies greatly not only in numbers — Iran's 35 million people as contrasted with Saudi Arabia's approximate 5 million — but in density and the degree of urbanisation. Population thus has very distinct effects in each of the countries. In Saudi Arabia, the low level of population limits the ability of the country to absorb its oil-produced revenues, and acts as a brake on the pace of, and demands for, economic development. Iran, while also lacking sufficient indigenous human resources, has had no such 'problem'; on the contrary, funds have been unable to keep up with ambitious development plans.

There are as well the historical and cultural differences. Saudi Arabia is an Arab country, whose people are predominantly Sunni Muslim and Arabic speaking. Iran is largely Shi'ite, and culturally and linguistically Persian. Examples of competition and strife sprinkle accounts of their history. Indeed, it is this tradition which is best symbolised in modern times by the controversy over whether the region should be termed the Persian Gulf or the Arabian Sea/Peninsula.

Yet these obvious dissimilarities do not reflect the totality of the Saudi-Iranian relationship. Despite considerable differences in social stratification, both are societies with large, active traditionalist-religious forces suspicious of modernism, Westernism and secularism. Modernisation and attempts at rapid economic development are common to the two, as are many of the by-products — inflation, corruption, a large number of foreigners, social resistance and dislocation — of these same processes. Both remain essentially 'cash-crop' economies depending almost totally upon receipts from oil and gas production for government revenue and foreign exchange. Politically, and the recent changes in Iran notwithstanding, the two are ruled by authoritarian governments whose tolerance for democratic institutions and dissent is severely limited.

What clearly exists between Iran and Saudi Arabia, as it does between other key regional pairs such as Brazil and Argentina, India and Pakistan, and perhaps Greece and Turkey, is a spectrum of relations potentially ranging from conflict to co-operation, or from rivalry to concert. In the case of the Gulf, the differences and their implications are significant for the region and the world as a whole. Actual military confrontation between the two, even if managed so additional states did not become directly involved, would disrupt and possibly destroy energy production for months or years. In light of the basic importance of energy revenues to both, it is difficult to underestimate the political and economic consequences of such a development.[4]

Yet actual physical confrontation is not the only possible adverse relationship. A period of high tension and resulting military readiness would distract attention and drain resources from pressing domestic concerns in each. Neither would enjoy much latitude in regional affairs, as any initiative would be likely to elicit a countervailing response from the other. The viability of OPEC could also be placed in jeopardy, as Saudi Arabia, in its capacity as 'swing' producer, would have a new incentive either to increase output or lower price so as to hurt the more vulnerable Iran. In addition, a more competitive relationship between the two key Gulf states would create new opportunities for outside states to manipulate their relationship, thereby raising the spectre of an enhanced role for the Soviet Union in the region.

By contrast, a relationship between Iran and Saudi Arabia characterised by co-ordination and trust would have equally profound consequences. Almost by definition, the possibility of military confrontation and its potential for ruin would be eliminated. Diplomatic and even military arrangements for regional and possibly extra-regional security initiatives could be established, thereby deterring potential instabilities and limiting actual ones. Common foreign policy postures towards the Gulf, the Middle East and South Asia would have a significant impact on these regions and on the interests of outside states in these regions. At the same time, an atmosphere of co-operation would enhance the political and economic stability of both countries. OPEC would be far better placed to withstand fluctuations in demand if Saudi Arabia were willing to adjust its own production levels so as to enable the cartel to avoid the difficult process of pro-rationing production. Equally, economic development programmes could be co-ordinated to enable both states to benefit from economies of scale and preferential access to markets.[5]

The Past as Prelude?

What should be apparent from the above is that Saudi Arabia and Iran, as the two key states of the Gulf, possess the potential for a significantly varied relationship in the future, the nature of which will have repercussions that far transcend the immediate region. Amidst the continued volatility of current political events, as well as the always present uncertainties in regard to the future, however, any predictions about the evolution of the Saudi-Iranian relationship must be tentative and heavily qualified. At the same time, and as was stated at the outset of this chapter, there are also likely to be some limits to the range of options facing each country owing to basic economic, political and social realities that will constrain virtually any regime. As such, the past relations between the two countries, especially in the four critical areas of oil, arms, regional security and approaches to the (Arab-Israeli) Middle East conflict, offer a guide to future developments in these areas and to the overall relationship between the two countries.

Just as one can cite elements of co-operation and disagreement in the general relations between Saudi Arabia and Iran, so too it is possible to point to both elements in the more narrow framework of relations concerning energy. Thus, while the production and export of petroleum and gas have been essential to the well-being of each, basic differences exist. These are borne out by statistics. Saudi Arabian reserves of oil are far greater. Figures reflecting 'proved and probable' reserves of crude oil show Saudi Arabia possessing amounts several times that of Iran, an advantage only partially offset by Iran's greater gas reserves. In addition, given the fact that exploration has been more complete and intense in Iran, it is likely that over time this proportion will shift further to Saudi Arabia's advantage. Moreover, this relative abundance has permitted Saudi Arabia to sustain a far higher level of production of oil than Iran. Beginning in 1972, Saudi production outstripped that of Iran, and between 1972 and 1977 Saudi production increased at an annual rate of 9.8 per cent as compared with only 2.4 per cent for Iran.[6]

These disparities take on greater significance when seen in the larger context of population and the resulting capacity to absorb revenues. Iran, with its far larger population and ambitious plans for revenue use, was in a position of maximising output (and therefore revenue) and spending whatever proceeds became available. Indeed, at times demand was so high that additional financing became necessary to support programmes. In contrast, Saudi Arabia, despite being able to absorb income and spend at a rate greater than that which was anticipated by many observers, has all the same accumulated a sizeable surplus of funds. Moreover, this pool of wealth could have been increased had Saudi leaders elected either to support higher prices for energy or expand production at a faster rate.

These factors contributed to differences between the two key members of OPEC on matters of supply and price alike. Iran, dependent upon a continuous source of income to meet the domestic demands, was unwilling to interrupt sales. It thus became a 'conservative' on matters of supply, willing to supply oil to all countries and not willing to enter into supply restrictions or embargoes for political purposes. As a result, Iran stood aloof from the Organization of Arab Exporting Countries (OAPEC) embargo of 1973/4, and until late 1978 continued to export oil to both Israel and South Africa.

Saudi Arabia, however, was and remains far better situated to reduce or terminate supply for prolonged periods. The Saudis have exercised this ability politically, both during the 1973/4 embargo, and more generally against Israel. This same Saudi ability to reduce supply for extended periods without suffering serious economic or internal political problems has permitted it to adjust its own production levels, and indirectly that of OPEC's, during periods of excess supply or 'glut'. By so doing, Saudi Arabia reduced market pressures which could have ruptured OPEC solidarity and ultimately reduced the price of oil. Indeed, it was Saudi willingness to do exactly this that enabled OPEC to weather the temporary glut of 1976–8.

But if Saudi Arabia was willing to be 'radical' in the context of supply, it was conservative in the context of price, arguing consistently for modest rather than severe increases in oil prices. Behind this Saudi posture was a realistic assessment of its own ultimate dependence upon the political and economic health of the industrialised West, and the United States in particular. Iran, however, was less able to afford this perspective, as its immediate demand for revenue and long-term supply questions created the need to maximise revenues in the short-term.

Despite these structural and political differences, the two states were for the most part able to harmonise their energy policies, and particularly those regarding price, until the revolution in Iran. With Iran often among those states taking the initiative, Saudi Arabia consented to the major price increases of 1973 and 1974. At the OPEC meeting of December 1976, however, and amidst much 'off-stage' criticisms of personalities and policies, a split emerged between the two, and more generally between Saudi Arabia and the rest of OPEC, over price increases. Iran, anxious at the time over the decline in the real price of oil owing to the decline in the relative value of the dollar, and equally concerned about the decline in the purchasing power of its revenues arising from inflation and the increased costs of imported goods and services, argued for a significant increase in the posted price of oil. In the face of Saudi opposition, Iran compromised, proposing an immediate price increase of 10 per cent to be followed by an additional 5 per cent increase in six months. The Saudis, more sensitive to American requests to hold the line on price increases and to the more general Western problems associated with the recovery from the economic recession of the early 1970s, argued for a more limited increase of 5 per cent. When compromise proved impossible, a formal two-tiered OPEC price structure emerged for the first time.

Within six months, however, the rift was healed. In June 1977, Saudi Arabia increased the price of its crude by a further 5 per cent, thereby bringing it in line with the rest of OPEC; in return, the other members agreed to forgo the planned further increase in their own price. Behind this compromise was not simply a desire to maintain the cohesion of the organisation, but also a recognition of Saudi Arabia's unique potential to affect the fortunes of all other members by a unilateralist policy. This potential was again underlined in 1978, as Saudi Arabia reduced its production by nearly 2 million barrels a day from 1977 levels in an effort to place supply more nearly in line with demand.

Some observers have viewed this six-month split, and more generally the series of disagreements between Iran and Saudi Arabia over pricing, as evidence of a basic divergence in energy policy. Yet when viewed in the larger context of oil pricing since 1973, and OPEC's success, the disagreement fades in significance when compared to the large degree of commonality in aims and practices. Iran, like the other members of OPEC, was forced to accept Saudi Arabian primacy within the organisation as the price for its co-operation — a co-operation essential to the functioning of the cartel.

If oil leaving the Persian Gulf is the item which has attracted most of the world's attention, it is the flow of arms into the region that has attracted comparable concern among outsiders. By virtually any yardstick — defence expenditure, actual imports or deliveries, cumulative inventories, orders — the attention appears to be justified. Not surprisingly, this rapid and massive influx of military might has given rise to the claim that the major arms-supplying countries, and the United States in particular, is fuelling an arms race in the region, and more specifically between the twin pillars of Iran and Saudi Arabia.[7]

But military increases, however measured, are not sufficient grounds in themselves to conclude that an arms race is either taking place or is imminent. As Samuel Huntington wrote years ago, an arms race is a 'form of reciprocal interaction between two states or coalitions. A race cannot exist without an increase in arms, quantitatively or qualitatively, but every peacetime increase in arms is not necessarily the result of an arms race.'[8] To this perspective can be added an additional point, namely that not every influx of arms, whether in the context of an arms race or not, is inherently destabilising or undesirable; to the contrary, the flow of arms can add to the security and stability of regions, depending upon the circumstances.[9]

In the case of Iran and Saudi Arabia, there is little difficulty in demonstrating that a dramatic change in the defence postures of the two states has come about because of arms transfers. Defence spending in each has risen sharply: in Iran's case, from US$500 million in 1968/9 to $2.01 billion in 1973, and to nearly $10 billion in 1978/9. For Saudi Arabia, the increase came later, as defence spending was only $380 million in 1970/1, but nearly $7 billion in 1976/7 and nearly $10 billion in 1978/9.[10]

Inventories changed with similar rapidity and scale. Whereas in

1968/9 Iran possessed only several hundred medium tanks, a handful of small ships and some 200 combat aircraft, a decade later her inventories included nearly 1,900 light, medium and heavy tanks, 11 surface ships as well as hovercraft and patrol boats, and more than 450 combat aircraft. Saudi Arabia's increase was also significant, as it developed from a minimal force to a country with two armoured brigades, a small navy, and some 170 combat aircraft by 1978/9. In all cases, increases in quantity were associated with equally sharp increases in quality of *matériel*.

Yet while statistics do demonstrate a mutual enhancement of military capabilities, it is far less clear that the data imply an arms race. To some extent, the sharp percentage increases reflect the very low starting or basing point for both countries. Similarly, spending is also a reflection of the escalating cost of modern military hardware, and in both cases again reflects equally the ability to afford such purchases in the wake of the 1973/4 increases in the price of energy products.

The arms race model of Saudi-Iranian relations during the past decade fails to convince on other grounds as well. One basic shortcoming in the arms race notion is that it fails to account adequately for the discrepancy in the direction and scope of the efforts of the two countries. Although actual spending figures approximated one to another, a far greater percentage of the Saudi effort went towards the infrastructure needs — the roads, ports, airfields, communications, logistics, training and so on — basic to civil as well as military development. Iran, a relatively developed society, was in a position to devote a far greater proportion of its resources to actual equipment and personnel. By 1978/9, for example, Iran's army outnumbered that of Saudi Arabia by a factor of 6, its navy by 19, and its air force by more than 8. Lesser but still significant orders of difference result from comparing the systems of the two countries. Although comparing like with like is often a misleading way of calculating military balances, the sheer asymmetry in this instance suggests that the two establishments were not solely reacting to the other.

Indeed, what is suggested here is that the efforts of Iran and Saudi Arabia in the military sphere reflected more the internal concerns of each and a different assessment of the external environment. Iran, reflecting the ambitions and perceptions of the Shah, began to acquire a highly capable military force in line with its regional ambitions and its 'tous azimuts' sense of threat. By contrast, Saudi Arabia's more modest effort reflected less a desire to project force or even deal with a significant threat from land than an attempt to lay the foundation for a modern military and produce a serious if not decisive capability to defend itself from airborne attack.

In short, patterns of military spending and hardware acquisition cannot be divorced from the larger political context. Iran's build-up can thus be best understood as an effort to gain independence from Soviet pressures, to assert a regional role, and perhaps most specifically, to counter the more parallel capability of Iraq. In the process, it may have contributed to the general Saudi view that the widespread militarisation of the region necessitated a military response of its own. But the factors mentioned above, together with deployment patterns and the geographical relationship between Iran and Saudi Arabia, cast doubt upon any explicit arms race competition between the two. Moreover, to the extent any such doubt remains, the generally friendly political relationship between the two pro-Western pillars over the last decade should largely settle the matter.

Further evidence to support this contention of general Iranian-Saudi co-operation over the past decade can be gleaned from examining the issue of Gulf security. At the time of the 1968 announcement by the United Kingdom of its intention to accelerate its withdrawal from East of Suez and from the Persian Gulf in particular, the future of regional security was very much an open question. Fear was widespread that the British decision would render the area a political-military vacuum easily exploited by the Soviet Union, which was soon to extend the forward deployment of its navy into the Indian Ocean. The United States was still preoccupied with South East Asia, and other than upgrading its small naval presence in the area was unwilling to assume a major, direct role in the security of the Gulf or the wider domain. At the same time, the local states lacked the military capacity to police their own area, much less defend it from outsiders; in any case, a host of political controversies, territorial disputes and traditional rivalries made any talk of local collaboration premature.

More than a decade later, the record of stability in the Gulf looked far brighter than virtually anyone had imagined. One can attribute this to several factors. The local states managed to settle peacefully a number of major disputes. Iran gave up its claim to Bahrain, while Iraq was dissuaded from pressing its claim against Kuwait. Of major importance as well was the Irani-Iraqi *rapprochement* of March 1975, in which the border question was settled to the satisfaction of both. The degree of superpower involvement has been kept indirect and relatively muted; there have been no replays of the post-Second World War Soviet intervention in the region. Lastly, although more difficult to prove, stability might have resulted in part from Iran's demonstration of its willingness to act on behalf of its interests in the peninsula. On two occasions — in its take-over of the three small islands at the critical mouth of the Gulf in November 1971, and in its military role in Oman on behalf of the Sultan's regime against the

Dhofar rebels, Iran depended on military force to further its interests. These actions, as well as the more general build-up of Iran's military, could well have had a deterrent effect on other potential challengers to the *status quo* in the Gulf.

Any explanation of the source of this stability must in large part reflect Irani-Saudi co-operation, which in turn resulted from a basic coincidence of regional aims. Whatever anxiety Saudi leaders felt about Iran's ambitions and strength was allayed by the recognition that the two states shared many sources of security. Both opposed a major Soviet role in the region, and both were wary of any signs of radicalism regardless of source. Armed conflict in the region was to be avoided if possible, and oil production and sea lanes protected against interference or interruption.

At the same time, the strengths of the two states tended to complement rather than compete. Iran, for all its military might, was never able to challenge Saudi legitimacy and leadership among Arab states, while Saudi Arabia, for all its economic and political influence, lacked the ultimate arbiter of military power. The intervention in Oman marked the clearest example of this diplomatic 'division of labour' — Saudi diplomatic and economic support was matched by Iran's despatch of troops and equipment. Years later (in 1977), the two were also able to co-ordinate their reactions in response to instability on Africa's Horn.

This is not to say that approaches to the matter of Gulf security were seen identically in Tehran and Riyadh. Iran's frequent calls for the non-involvement of all external states and the two superpowers in particular in regional affairs found little echo amongst Saudi leaders who made a clear distinction between American and Soviet diplomacy. More importantly, and despite collaboration in Oman and the Horn, Iran and Saudi Arabia, along with the other states of the region, were unable to make significant progress towards the creation of a formal Gulf security system or structure.

The actual record of such efforts is not a large one. The July 1975 Islamic Foreign Ministers meeting in Jeddah, while the venue of discussions regarding such matters as the exclusion of foreign powers from the Gulf, the territorial integrity of existing states, a non-aggression pact, settlement of outstanding offshore sovereignty claims, military co-operation and guidelines for mutual assistance against subversion, failed to produce any agreement on specific measures. The meeting a year later, in Muscat in November 1976, was if anything a step backwards.

In part, this failure was a direct result of Arab suspicion and anxiety over Iran's power and regional ambitions — a theme reflected in Kuwait's initiative after the Muscat session that several of the Arab states of the region first arrive at a set of common principles. Yet more fundamental to the failure of local initiatives aimed at establishing a comprehensive security system for the Gulf was the basic reality that the entire notion was premature. No common definition of threat existed among radicals and conservatives who held very different ideas about the desirability of the *status quo* and what constituted an improvement. Similarly, there were differences of opinion about the role of outside states and the legitimacy of change by force. Small states quite naturally feared the isolation of the region could promote the hegemony of the most powerful local states, while the local powers viewed one another more as competitors than allies. Lastly, there were precious few economic and political precedents to build on. Yet this inability to construct a formal structure encompassing all the states of the region should not be allowed to obscure the fact that a large degree of informal and tacit co-operation existed between Iran and Saudi Arabia, reflecting a similarity in aims and a complementarity of means.

The last of the four major arenas of Saudi-Iranian interaction, the Middle East, appears to have been somewhat less central than those of oil, arms and regional security. Israel's existence, as well as its territorial reach and control of Jerusalem, has been a more salient issue for Saudi Arabia. For several reasons this should not be a surprise. To the extent the Middle East crisis can be described as an Arab-Israeli one, it does not involve Iran directly; indeed, one might even go so far as to say that Iran and Israel share the fate of being part of a non-Arab minority in this part of the world. Owing to its location, Saudi Arabia cannot remain unconcerned with Israel's military capability; it is vulnerable both to Israeli naval forces operating in the Red Sea and to the Israeli Air Force. This said, Saudi Arabia, unlike the immediate front-line states, still retains a good deal of flexibility as to how and how much it allows itself to be drawn into Middle Eastern disputes. The chief constraint here is a political one, as Saudi Arabia remains vulnerable to radical forces that could choose to see the road to Tel Aviv passing through Riyadh if Saudi Arabia were seen to abandon the Arab cause.

In the 1960s, tensions between Iran and Saudi Arabia resulting from the Middle East reflected a mixture of Iran's unilateralism and Saudi inflexibility. As early as 1960 Iran extended *de facto* recognition of Israel. A regular source of oil for Israel, Iran refused as well to participate in the 1973/4 oil embargo designed to pressure the West, and indirectly the Israelis, to compromise. A number of commercial and technical exchanges between the two countries were carried out. Yet Iran balanced these policies with a certain sensitivity to the Arab and Saudi position. *De jure* recognition of Israel was withheld, while Iran argued for the return of the occupied territories (within the context of UN 242) and the return of Jerusalem.

At the same time, the evolution of the Saudi stance on the Middle East question brought the policies of the two Gulf states more nearly into line with one another. Increasingly concerned with Soviet and radical influence in the larger region and aware of the dangers of continued war, Saudi Arabia abandoned its often unconditional anti-Zionism. In the wake of Nasser's death and Sadat's emergence as the key political figure in the Arab world, Saudi leaders strengthened their ties with Egypt, supported Sadat's ouster of the Soviet Union, worked to bring about the 1973 *rapprochement* between Egypt and Syria, financed Arab military efforts, and allowed oil to be used as a political weapon to influence American and other Western policies towards Israel and the area more generally. As such, by the mid-1970s both Iran and Saudi Arabia found themselves working for a Middle East settlement largely in league with efforts sponsored by the United States and the moderate wing of the Arab world.

Revolutionary Change?

In all four of the areas discussed above, it is the large degree of commonality of interests and purpose between Iran and Saudi Arabia throughout much of the past decade that impresses the observer. Despite differences over the price and availability of oil, the two were instrumental to OPEC's ability to both survive and thrive during a period of fundamental change in the international political economy of oil. Massive importation of arms and mutual military development did not bring about deep hostility or conflict between the two countries, while the absence of formal machinery for the promotion of regional security did not preclude co-ordination and tacit co-operation. Lastly, differences between approaches to the Arab-Israeli Middle East question narrowed rather than widened over time. Although it would be wrong to deny that elements of anxiety and rivalry existed, it would be far more incorrect to deny that the overriding pattern was one of a mutual identification of interests between the pair.

Any doubts that this was the case should have been erased by Saudi Arabian reaction to the Iranian crisis and ultimately revolution of 1978.[11] Statements by Saudi leaders throughout the crisis indicated their clear preference for the continuation of rule under the Shah; what was feared in Riyadh was not simply change *per se*, but also its ramifications. The twin pillars concept may have been flawed, but not owing to relations between the pillars themselves.

But what of the future? Can one pillar survive without the existence of the other? More to the point, what are the likely effects of

Iran's revolution on Iranian policy, on Saudi policy, and ultimately on relations between the two? To answer these and related questions, one must return to the theme introduced at the start of this essay; that is, to the effect of revolutionary change in the domestic format of modernising countries on their foreign policies.

Any such attempt at analysis or even prediction must at least begin with a catalogue of the unknowns and uncertainties. The situation in Iran continues to unfold and unravel, and there is little evidence that the country is about to become united and centralised once again. The anti-Shah coalition, no longer united in purpose after it had realised its one common objective, has disintegrated as its various and varied components compete for influence in what can only be seen as the second phase of the revolution. Confrontation will ultimately escalate between factions representing left and right, religious and secular, and Persian and minorities. To what extent order and consensus will be restored, and what form this process takes, remains impossible to predict; the only thing that is certain is that Iran will remain a weaker, more divided and more inward-looking country for the foreseeable future.

Equally, any consideration of the future course of Saudi policy must take into account new uncertainties. Indeed, it is impossible to examine Saudi Arabia in the aftermath of Iran's upheaval without asking whether the same thing can happen there. Although there is no definite response to such a question, there are a number of points which deserve emphasis. Important distinctions can be drawn between pre-revolutionary Iran and present-day Saudi Arabia. Strong familial and tribal ties have created there a relatively large and close-knit ruling class with a vested interest in a political continuity that ensures its own survival and dominance. This extended royal family is scattered throughout the country, and in general is both more numerous and less isolated than was Iran's former ruling elite. Events following the assassination of King Faisal in 1975 demonstrated the resilience of this network as the problem of succession was dealt with speedily. There are no large urban concentrations, no real middle class pushing for economic and political power, and few religious leaders who resemble the alienated Shi'ite figures in pre-revolutionary Iran. The ratio of wealth to population is far more favourable in Saudi Arabia than was the case in Iran, with absorptive capacity rather than revenue the real constraint on the rate of development and modernisation. Lastly, it is impossible to imagine that Iran's example has not made its impression on Saudi leaders, who must be more sensitised to the dangers of social discontent of any type or from any source.

This is not to imply that it is impossible to draw parallels between the Shah's Iran and Saudi Arabia, nor that Saudi Arabia is free of additional sources of potential domestic unrest. The political leader-ship is still clearly isolated from the bulk of the population, corrup-tion is widespread, and inequalities of wealth and privilege manifest. There is mounting frustration and sophistication among the increas-ingly large military, student and professional elites, and growing dis-sidence among the Shi'ite population in the Eastern province. Factions within the House of Saud exist, reflecting not simply rival ambitions for leadership but more fundamental disagreements over domestic and more recently foreign policy. The possibility of a mili-tary *coup* can never be discounted. More than anything else, there is the impact of what happened in Iran; if, as was noted before, it has helped alert present leaders to potential sources of discontent, it has also removed a psychological barrier to radical change by having shown that such change can take place. This potential for radical change was in turn heightened by the November 1979 Grand Mosque incident, which had the additional effect of weakening the regime's claim to represent (and satisfy) the forces of religious orthodoxy in the kingdom. Thus, while on balance the existence of such factors as the larger ruling elite, the integration of religious forces into society and above all the safety valve provided by the fantastic wealth of the country should allow Saudi Arabia a stable future, there are too many additional factors that give cause for caution and thereby preclude confident prediction.

These uncertainties notwithstanding, it is still possible to reach some conclusions as to the likely course of relations between Iran and Saudi Arabia within the four critical areas of policy examined earlier.[12] In the energy context, the immediate impact of Iran's revolution, with its initial interruption in oil production and its later partial recovery, has been to bring to an end the temporary period of supply surplus that had provided a respite to consumers everywhere. The volatile 'spot market' of early 1979 demonstrated the new demand-supply ratio all too clearly as prices surged; the OPEC meeting in June only confirmed what the market had already revealed.

Ironically, the behaviour of Iran's new government resembled that of the Shah's between 1973 and 1976. Both sought maximum price increases. The differences, however, was one of motive; whereas the Shah sought revenues to fund his ambitious develop-ment and military programmes, the heirs to the Peacock Throne required higher receipts per barrel to compensate for the loss in output. In the process, Saudi Arabia became more isolated than ever within the organisation on the subject of price.

At the same time, Iran has terminated its shipments of oil to Israel, and is clearly prepared to participate in supply manipulations intended to achieve political aims. This is not necessarily a sign of a new consonance of policy, as it is possible to imagine Iran and other states using the 'oil weapon' at times and for purposes quite different from those Saudi Arabia might choose. Taken together with the manifest signs of divergence over pricing policy, it is apparent that relations between the two producers will be less easy than in the past. Yet Iran's lowered production also reduces its bargaining strength; Saudi Arabia may be more exposed than was the case in the past, but its importance as swing producer has been reinforced.[13]

The military relationship between the two states will also be affected by the political changes in Iran. General political relations between the countries are still such that any outbreak of fighting remains virtually unthinkable; in any case, the high vulnerability of oil economies to modern warfare has conditioned states of the region to limit their competition. Yet if one accepts the argument that no arms race existed before Iran's revolution, the continued acceptance of this thesis will have to rest on changed conditions.

Among the first acts of the new government, like the short-lived interim government before it, was to cancel outstanding orders for military equipment. In light of the continued economic disarray and the desire to dissociate the new government from the ways of the Shah, it is highly unlikely that any major resumption of military modernisation will take place. Moreover, what was already in Iran has begun to deteriorate seriously. With organisation, leadership and discipline almost totally absent, equipment has gone without maintenance and use; over time, Iran's paper inventory will bear less and less relation to its actual military capability. The exodus of the mostly Western technicians and advisers has only exacerbated the situation.

Whatever military capacity that can be salvaged will most likely be committed to civil and regional challenges to the government's authority. The ability to project force around the region, or even mobilise force to defend the state, will decline markedly. On one hand, this will bring about a sharp reduction in Iranian influence outside its own borders; on the other, it will have a major impact on Saudi policy. Without its conservative and once-powerful ally, and faced with a far more unstable situation in the region in large part resulting from the change in Iran, Saudi Arabia is likely to accelerate its military development. Interestingly, today's weak Iran is more likely to stimulate Saudi defence efforts than was yesterday's strong Iran.

The impact of Iran's upheaval on the region will be similarly important. A number of religious and nationalist revivals will challenge existing boundaries and more generally the authority of existing governments. The demonstration effect of its revolution may contribute to such changes elsewhere. Perhaps most important, a weakened and internally preoccupied Iran will be in no position to exert direct influence outside its borders; although Iraq will achieve a degree of local primacy, the post-Shah vacuum in the Gulf is and will be far more noticeable than the post-British one.

Saudi Arabia, despite its economic and diplomatic weight and its growing military strength, is an unlikely heir. Some peace-keeping is within its capacity on the scale of its contribution in 1979 to Oman; anything more, however, is unrealistic to expect. Improved political relations with the Soviet Union and local radical states might ease the burden which has come to rest on the Saudis, but the wide range of policy differences and the lack of any formal regional security structure suggest a future less stable than the recent past.

Lastly, Iran's revolution will only make the quest for a Middle East settlement more difficult, and in the process again increase the pressures and burdens on the Saudi leaders. Iran's support for the rejectionist cause, its more religious nature and its cut-off of oil to Israel are not likely to increase Israeli willingness to compromise. In addition, revolution in Iran has only worked to justify Israel's contention that peace agreements with Middle Eastern states are inherently precarious owing to the lack of strong democratic institutions and mechanisms for orderly succession and policy continuity. For Saudi Arabia, already walking a tightrope between supporting Egyptian efforts while keeping a foot in the rejectionist camp should Sadat's initiative fail to yield a comprehensive settlement, Iran's revolution has made compromise more difficult in the Arab World and flexibility less forthcoming from Israel.

The Saudi Inheritance

As many appreciated at the time, it has been impossible to contain the impact and implications of the fall of the Shah. Supplies of oil have fallen, prices have risen to new levels unimaginable less than a few years ago. The direct and indirect effects of Iran's new weakness and militancy will frustrate the search for stability, both in the immediate region and the larger one. In the process, relations between Iran and Saudi Arabia have predictably suffered. They are once again at loggerheads in OPEC and are pursuing very different lines towards both local and global problems.

Yet the real importance of Iran's revolution is less for its effect on Iran's relationship with Saudi Arabia than it is on the role of the latter. In every context, Saudi Arabia finds itself with greater influence and responsibilities, but also facing greater threats and challenges. While progress in reducing world-wide energy consumption, in reaching a Middle East settlement, and in moderating external power competition will lessen the pressures on Saudi leaders, they cannot erase the picture of a country alone and beleaguered. Moreover, such progress is not probable. What is most significant about Iran is not so much what it is as what it is no longer. As a result, and as any architect would point out, the stress on the remaining pillar is much greater, and stability all the more difficult to maintain.

Notes

1. Early post-mortems of Iran's revolution and its causes include Walter Laqueur, 'Why the Shah Fell', *Commentary*, vol. 67, no. 3 (March 1979), pp. 47–55; the Round Table, 'The United States and Iran's Revolution', *Foreign Policy*, no. 34 (Spring 1979), and *Strategic Survey 1978* (IISS, London, 1979), pp. 50–7.

2. James Noyes in *New Perspectives on the Persian Gulf*, Hearings before the Subcommittee on the Near East and South Asia of the Committee on Foreign Affairs, House of Representatives (USGPO, Washington, DC, 1973), p. 39.

3. Besides the source just cited above, see the debates and varying views included in other volumes of hearings produced by the same congressional committee. These include *U.S. Interests in and Policy Toward the Persian Gulf* (1972), *The Persian Gulf, 1974: Money, Politics, Arms, and Power* (1975), *The Persian Gulf, 1975: the Continuing Debate on Arms Sales* (1976), and *United States Arms Policies in the Persian Gulf and Red Sea Areas: Past, Present, and Future* (1977). For a non-governmental view, see Ali Banuazizi, 'Iran: The Making of a Regional Power' in A.L. Udovitch (ed.), *The Middle East: Oil, Conflict and Hope* (D.C. Heath, Lexington, Mass., 1976). (This is vol. X of the Critical Choices for Americans series.)

4. For considerations of the usefulness of force in oil producing areas see *Oil Fields as Military Objectives: a Feasibility Study* (prepared for the Special Subcommittee on Investigations of the Committee on International Relations by the Congressional Research Service of the Library of Congress and published in Washington by the USGPO in 1975) and the 1979 study by John M. Collins and Clyde R. Mark, also of the Congressional Research Service, entitled *Petroleum Imports From the Persian Gulf: Use of U.S. Armed Force to Ensure Supplies*.

5. See Louis Turner and James Bedore, 'Saudi and Iranian Petrochemicals and Oil Refining: Trade Warfare in the 1980s?', *International Affairs* (London), vol. 53, no. 4 (October 1977).

6. Oil statistics have been obtained from various editions of the annual publication by British Petroleum Company Ltd, *BP Statistical Review of the World Oil Industry*.

7. In addition to perspectives expressed in the sources cited in notes 2 and 3 above, see Dale R. Tahtinen, *Arms in the Persian Gulf* (American Enterprise Institute, Washington, DC, 1974) and Edward Kennedy, 'The Persian Gulf: Arms Race or Arms Control?', *Foreign Affairs* (October 1975).

8. Samuel P. Huntington, 'Arms Races: Prerequisites and Results' in Robert J. Art and Kenneth N. Waltz (eds.), *The Use of Force: International Politics and Foreign Policy* (Little, Brown and Company, Boston, 1971), p. 366.

9. On this point, *Strategic Survey 1973* stated the following: 'As arms become more widespread, so political violence is made easier, and any conflict that results more bloody. The current willingness to supply arms [to the Gulf] may therefore be creating the danger that potential disputes will be fuelled. On the other hand, however, Iran's growing strength, and that of Saudi Arabia, may have exactly the

opposite effect: that of helping to bring about stability in an area that is geopolitically very attractive and vastly important to the world at large' (IISS, London, 1974), p. 45. It should perhaps also be pointed out that it is not at all clear that arms, either in themselves or as a drain on resources, contributed to the domestic instability in Iran.

10. Statistics on defence spending and arms have been derived from various editions of *The Military Balance* (IISS, London) and US Arms Control and Disarmament Agency, *World Military Expenditures and Arms Transfers 1967–1976* (US ACDA, Washington, DC, 1978).

11. See, for example, 'L'Arabia Saoudite apporte son soutien au chah d'Iran', *Le Monde*, 25 August 1978.

12. For another such assessment, see Shahram Chubin, 'The Crisis in Iran and its Repercussions', *Survival*, vol. XXI, no. 3 (May-June 1979).

13. For views of the long-term implications of Iran's revolution for the world energy market, see *The Future of Saudi Arabian Oil Production*, a Staff Report to the Subcommittee on International Economic Policy of the Committee on Foreign Relations, US Senate (USGPO, Washington, DC, 1979) and *Iran and World Oil Supply*, Hearing before the Committee on Energy and Natural Resources, US Senate (USGPO, Washington, DC, 1979), Parts 1 and 2.

9 THE PERSIAN GULF IN REGIONAL AND INTERNATIONAL POLITICS: THE ARAB SIDE OF THE GULF

John Duke Anthony

Public commentary in the past decade about expanding great power interest and involvement in the Persian Gulf has often laid greater emphasis on the regional role of Iran than on the other littoral states. One of the most far-reaching consequences of the October 1973 War and its aftermath, and particularly after Iran's revolution, has been a fundamental shift in focus away from Iran towards other factors in the area. The Arab oil embargo and subsequent steep rise in petroleum prices, the rapid accumulation of monetary wealth by several Arab states and the expansion and deepening of Western and especially American-Arabian Peninsula ties have resulted, in effect, in greater attention being paid to the Arab states in the Gulf. The reasons are not surprising: 6 of the 7 littoral states are Arab (counting the 7 members of the United Arab Emirates as a single state) and these polities, not Iran, are responsible for most of the area's oil production, possess the overwhelming majority of its petroleum reserves, and control the bulk of its impressive financial holdings.

An understanding of the regional dynamics among these countries is essential to any assessment of their future roles in Gulf and international politics, let alone of what contributions they might be expected to make to the cause of regional security. This chapter examines three questions that bear on the local and regional aims and interests of these governments and the way that these shape relations both among themselves and between them and outside powers. The first concerns the nature of political interaction among these states. The second focuses on the contest between conservative and radical regimes in the area, and the third — the question of overriding importance in view of the world-wide energy situation — deals with the connection between these states and the Arab-Israeli conflict.

Political Interaction among the Arab Persian Gulf States

In general, political interaction among these states has historically been a complex mixture of economic and political rivalries, under-girded by long-standing dynastic, national and territorial conflicts with distinct ethnic, religious and tribal overtones. With the arrival of the British in the Gulf, these conflicts subsided but did not disappear. Both throughout and since the long period of British domination in the emirates, such tensions have remained major factors in the political processes of the area.

At the root of much of the conflict has been a quest for control of the region's limited economic resources. Prior to the discovery of petroleum, the tribes of the region struggled with one another incessantly over such issues as control of maritime and overland trade, fishing and pearling rights, access to grazing lands for their flocks and control over strategic water holes. Simultaneously, there were innumerable struggles within and among the ruling familes of these states over questions of territory, commercial pre-eminence and dynastic leadership.

The discovery of oil, and the realisation that millions (and subsequently billions) of dollars were at stake, while not completely superseding these traditional forms of rivalry, nonetheless added a new and vastly different dimension to them. It was largely in this manner that the disputes among these states took on increased significance both inside the area itself and in the eyes of the outside world. The significance is one whose validity is likely to persist as long as the issues contested remain unsettled or unsatisfactorily ameliorated in the eyes of the parties concerned.

A major component of the regional dynamics of these states remains the interplay between their territorial and (excluding Iraq) their dynastic rivalries. The more important territorial disputes outstanding — most of which have involved outside powers in support of one or more of the parties to the conflict — remain those of:

(1) Iraq and Kuwait over their common frontier and the question of control over Warbah and Bubiyan, two strategic islands lying in their offshore waters;

(2) of Bahrain and Qatar over the Hawar Islands group located in their offshore waters and over the village of Zabarah on the west coast of the Qatar Peninsula;

(3) of Sharjah, 'Ajman, Umm al-Qaywayn and Iran over offshore waters in which petroleum was discovered in 1972 near Abu Musa Island';

(4) of Sharjah and Fujayrah over their respective land boundaries, a dispute which re-erupted in June 1972 and resulted in the death of some two dozen Sharjan and Fujayran tribesmen and in the late 1970s still necessitated the mediating presence of a United Arab Emirates Defense Force battalion;

(5) of Dubai and Sharjah over territory being commercially developed on the border between them;

(6) of Ra's al-Khaimah and Sharjah over a valley area believed to contain potentially lucrative deposits of phosphate;

(7) of Oman and Saudi Arabia over Umm Zamul — a waterhole and surrounding territory in the area of their undemarcated border at the northernmost reaches of the Rub' al-Khali desert; and

(8) of Ra's al-Khaymah and Oman over their respective land and offshore boundaries on the Musandam Peninsula.

In addition, there are other territorial disputes less well known which could become prominent in the future.

Territorial disputes, formerly more frequent over issues of land usage in and between states with sizeable Bedouin populations, even nowadays, as indicated in the foregoing account, centred largely on questions of sovereignty over strategic islands and border areas. The pattern of petroleum discoveries has undoubtedly been a factor in this shift in focus. In the 1950s, the United Kingdom attempted to resolve the boundary disputes then impeding the granting of oil concessions and drilling operations in the area of the seven member states of the present United Arab Emirates. A final resolution was proposed to some two dozen of the nearly three dozen live cases at the time, and most of the recommendations were accepted by the parties involved. Nevertheless a dozen or more conflicting claims to land boundaries in this area remain outstanding. The Dubai-Sharjah dispute, noted above, was a principal reason behind a crisis in leadership that confronted the UAE in the summer of 1976. In addition, nearly a dozen offshore boundaries among these states, and between some of them and Iran, have yet to be demarcated.

On the other hand, it is important to note that substantial progress has been achieved in the past decade in close to a dozen offshore disputes, most of which were resolved in conformity with the principle of the median line. In some of the disputes settled, as for example in establishing the maritime boundaries and the consequent sharing of offshore oil revenues between Bahrain and Saudi Arabia and between Abu Dhabi and Qatar, it was relatively easy for the states concerned to arrive at agreement. By contrast, the issue of sovereignty over Abu Musa Island, which involved a number of similar legal issues, produced a quite different result. Half a decade later that long-standing dispute — the handling of which contributed directly to the assassination of the Ruler of Sharjah in 1972 — was no nearer to *de jure* resolution than when the United Kingdom and other countries attempted to resolve it in the late 1960s. Unlike most of the other disputes, however, the additionally complicating factors of ethnicity, religion and rival nationalisms were present in this case.

A second category of political interaction occurs exclusively among the conservative Arab Gulf states and centres on their dynastic rivalries. These occur both *within* and *among* the area's twelve ruling families. The most recent intra-dynastic challenge took place within the Al Qasimi ruling family of Sharjah. In February 1972 a former Ruler of that state, who was deposed in 1965, returned to Sharjah and, capitalising on public resentment of the Ruler's handling of the Abu Musa affair with Iran, attempted to overthrow his successor. Although he and his followers failed to regain the rulership, they managed to murder the incumbent before they were captured and arrested.

In another case, scarcely a month before the assassination of the Ruler of Sharjah, the Ruler of Qatar, of the Al Thani dynasty, was overthrown. In that incident, Qatar's then Deputy Ruler and Heir Apparent ousted his cousin and seized the throne for himself. In July 1970 Sultan Qabus, thirteenth member of the Abu Sa'id dynasty to serve as Ruler of Oman, participated in a palace *coup* which forcibly replaced his father, Sultan Sa'id bin Taymur. And in Abu Dhabi in 1966, Sheikh Zayid bin Sultan, of the proud Al Nahyan family, over-threw his brother.

Throughout much of the 1970s a different kind of intra-dynastic competition among leading ruling family members for the post of Heir Apparent has figured prominently in the political dynamics of Saudi Arabia, Kuwait, Qatar, Oman and most of the seven UAE states. In the late 1970s the first three states appeared to have resolved this issue — in 1975, 1977 and 1978 respectively. There was much less certainty, however, as to whether and, if so, when and indeed how these matters would be decided in Oman and several of the UAE states, where several Heirs Apparent had yet to be named.

Dynastic rivalries *between* these states occur with similar frequency, but often have an irredentist or secessionist motive or have arisen out of competition between particular rulers for individual prestige; in some cases both factors have been involved. An example of competition of the latter variety has been the rivalry, often appearing to be muted and good-natured, between Kuwait and Saudi Arabia. This kind of inter-dynastic competition, moreover, played an important role in the manner in which Bahrain, Qatar and the UAE attained their independence in 1971. More than many outside observers are aware, such competition can at times influence, to a greater degree than any other factor, the way and the extent to which the conservative states on the Arab side of the Gulf are prepared to co-operate with one another in matters of mutual concern.

The basis of the dynastic rivalry between Abu Dhabi and Dubai encompasses several factors. The rivalry is historically rooted in the fact that a branch of the ruling tribe in the former state seceded from Abu Dhabi in the early nineteenth century and settled in Dubai. In more modern times the rivalry between the heads of these two states has at times been personally antagonistic in view of that thirty years ago they collaborated with opposite sides in armed clashes between their respective emirates. Nowadays, Sheikh Zayid of Abu Dhabi and Sheikh Rashid of Dubai, the two most important rulers among the former Trucial States, compete with each other for influence in the only federation in the area — the United Arab Emirates — in which they hold the posts of President and Vice-President respectively.

The rivalry between Qatar and Bahrain is rooted in the outstanding claim of the ruling family of Bahrain to sovereignty over portions of Qatar, territory it once controlled, and, more recently, in their jockeying for influence and position in the Gulf as a whole. The dynasties of many of the lesser states have had and continue to have similar, though less dramatic, disputes and contests among themselves and with the rulers of Iran and Oman.

An additional aspect of the inter-dynastic rivalries between these states centres on ancestral lineage. The ruling families of Sharjah, Ra's al-Khaimah and Bahrain, for example, consider themselves of more noble ancestry than some of their comparatively affluent and powerful neighbours. In the case of the Al Khalifa ruling family of Bahrain, this aristocratic self-perception contributed to Bahrain's persistent reluctance, and ultimately its refusal, to enter into an equal relationship with the Al Thani dynasty of Qatar during the negotiations for a nine-state federation between 1968 and 1971. Dynastic rivalries between Bahrain and Qatar diminish the likelihood that these two states will combine in any meaningful form of political union in the near future. Similarly, Ra's al-Khaimah's Ruler, of the proud Qasimi family, is still bitter at having to assume a subordinate status to the ruling families of Abu Dhabi and Dubai. These dynasties proposed, as a precondition for membership in the United Arab Emirates, that Ra's al-Khaimah be allotted only six seats in the federal assembly, while Abu Dhabi and Dubai received eight each and their rulers were given veto powers — powers denied the Ruler of Ra's al-Khaimah and the rulers of the other emirates.

The foregoing examples of the manner in which these states relate to one another — quite apart from how they relate both as a group, and as individual states, to Iran — underscore the point that this particular subregion of the Gulf is one in which an uneasy equilibrium persists between competing forces. These forces — whether in the form of territorial rivalries between all of them, or of dynastic rivalries between the ruling families of the traditional regimes, underscore the complexity of this area in terms of regional and international politics and serve as a foundation conditioning how these states relate to one another politically.

The Radical-Conservative Contest

The impact on regional security questions of territorial and dynastic competition among the Arab states of the Gulf would undoubtedly be far less were it not for the additional, often exacerbating, factor of cleavage between differing belief systems and ideologies espoused by the various parties concerned. The most pronounced of these kinds of differences are those that arise periodically under the rubric of conservatives ('reactionaries') on one hand, pitted against radicals ('revolutionaries') on the other. Although much has been written of this feature of inter-state relationships in the area, perhaps no subject remains more shrouded in misconception and myth in terms of its relevance to questions pertaining to Gulf security.

Perhaps the first fact to underscore in speaking of the radical *versus* conservative contest among these states is the fact that competition thus far has been grossly unequal. To begin with, only one state — Iraq — can be classified as 'radical' in terms of its political values and orientation *vis-à-vis* the rest. The other six are conservative states, ruled by dynasts whose foreign policies and official attitudes have by and large been quite friendly not only to the West, but, perhaps of even greater importance, to the so-called 'moderate' forces of political and socio-economic change in the Middle East and elsewhere. The domestic policies of the Gulf's conservative Arab states are heavily weighted against the small minority of their citizens and non-national residents who harbour revolutionary sentiments, and every indication points to the determination of these rulers to prevent radical groups from gaining a foothold in the area.

The striking imbalance in the ratio of conservative to radical states in the area is a fact so basic and for that reason perhaps too obvious to warrant serious consideration by policy-makers of its implications. Yet in practice, it is the factor that poses more formidable obstacles than any other to the area's actual and would-be dissidents. In the case of Iraq, geographical and ideological factors combine to isolate that country politically and to limit its capacity for fomenting internal unrest among the Arab states of the Gulf that are not its neighbours. There are, moreover, relatively few 'overseas Iraqis'. And among those who are living and working in the emirates and elsewhere, for example, most observers concede that the number capable of mounting a serious operation of subversive activities aimed at toppling the traditional regimes would be very small.

However, Kuwait, Iran and Saudi Arabia all have lengthy borders with Iraq which in part afford that country little more than an exceptionally limited opportunity to foment internal dissidence in the states mentioned or even to contribute substantially to forces seeking to foster instability in the border regions.

In the case of Iran, Iraqi subversive activities can be and often have been offset by Iran's capacity for creating a wide range of problems for Iraq. It was the superiority of Iran's military might, for example, that in 1969 permitted the Shah unilaterally to abrogate the treaty between Iraq and Iran regulating navigation rights in the Shatt-al-'Arab, the river which separates their two countries. This abrogation permitted the Shah's naval forces to traverse those waters at will until a final boundary settlement between Iraq and Iran was reached on 13 June 1975.

In the case of Kuwait, the deterrence is not so much military. It is doubtful whether Kuwait by itself could successfully resist an Iraqi invasion. Rather, the deterrence is mainly political and diplomatic. In short, not a single Arab dynastic state could be expected to extend a meaningful level of support to any serious Iraqi attempt to violate Kuwaiti territory. When Iraqi forces in 1973 occupied Kuwaiti border outposts and demanded control over the Kuwaiti islands of Warbah and Bubiyan in exchange for recognising Kuwait's sovereign status, the Baghdad regime was unable to persuade any of the other Gulf states of the validity of its claims. Of even greater significance in this connection is the fact that Kuwait, by contrast, has received both official and private assurances of support not only from nearby Arab states but also from Iran, the one state which has had until recently the means, the will and the tacit support of all the other states in the area to do whatever might be necessary to contain possible Iraqi expansionism.

As for Saudi Arabia, the fact that Iraq shares a long boundary with that country does not seem to have affected any territorial ambitions *vis-à-vis* the Kingdom or to have played a major role in the Baghdad regime's calculations thus far. Furthermore, possible Iraqi desires to subvert the regime of King Khalid are limited to the Ba'thist government's ability to instigate and/or influence political and social disequilibriums inside the Kingdom. Elements of domestic dissatisfaction in Saudi Arabia, as in the case of neighbouring traditional states, cut across the social and political spectrum. These include portions of the newly educated, the military, the tribes, regional ('national') groups such as the Front for the Liberation of the Hijaz and, according to some reports, even members of the numerous ruling house of Sa'ud. The extent of Iraqi manipulation of these groups is difficult to ascertain and its success or failure may rest primarily on the dynasty's ability to accommodate or otherwise ameliorate satisfactorily the demands of its domestic critics.

Iraq, in short, despite its position as the bastion of revolutionary socialism in the Gulf, is far more isolated, both militarily and politically, than many writers, especially Americans, have been prone to acknowledge. Compounding its isolation is the fact that the radical ideology espoused by the Ba'thist leadership in Baghdad has been rejected *in toto* from the beginning by all the other Gulf states. By contrast, Iraqi attempts to fashion a 'Gulf policy' acceptable to the Gulf states, based on *realpolitik* considerations of coexistence with the existing regimes, can be expected to encounter bitter opposition from ideologues within the Iraqi Ba'th Party. Iraqi foreign policy in the Gulf is further inhibited by the distraction of the recurrent ideological cleavage with the Ba'thists in Syria. On more than one occasion this dispute, in effect, has been exported to the emirates, causing substantial embarrassment. This was the case in October 1977 when UAE Minister of State for Foreign Affairs Sayf Ghubash — one of the brightest and most talented government officials in the area — was accidentally assassinated at Abu Dhabi International Airport while seeing off Syrian Foreign Minister Abd al-Halim Khaddam, who was the intended victim.

Iraq's role, thus severely circumscribed and in practice much more cautious and conservative than many are aware, is largely limited to its traditional position as a cultural pole for many Arab students in the area; to its commercial ties, mainly with Kuwait and Bahrain; and to the training and other forms of covert support it has extended over the years to radical groups operating in the Gulf. To the extent that these links afford it opportunities to encourage subversion in the area, Iraq's regional role is unquestionably a matter of concern to the heads of all the Gulf's conservative states, both Arab and Iranian. This conceded, the revolutionary potential of Iraq is not a pressing issue with which either the rulers or the key administrative elites in Saudi Arabia, Oman and the nine emirates are daily preoccupied. On the contrary, most of these leaders are encouraged by the fact that Iraq, despite its past involvement in subversive activities in the area, managed to have very little influence on the political dynamics of their states. In general, the decision-makers in most of these states are further encouraged by the ongoing close monitoring of former Iraqi-sponsored radicals by their armed forces, intelligence and internal security personnel. For all these reasons, they see, on balance, little indication of a likely revolutionary threat from Iraq increasing substantially.

It is appropriate to ask whether there are any other radical states in the general area that have recently, are presently, or might in the near future be seeking to undermine the political *status quo* in the Gulf. If the focus is on individual countries, the answer is that none come to light. Looking on the northern side beyond the mouth of the Gulf to Pakistan and India, neither of these states has at any point up to now had designs on the area that could be construed as destabilising. On the contrary, Pakistan and India have both played an active, if indirect, role in supporting the regional *status quo* through those among their citizens who serve in the armies and internal security forces of the conservative Arab regimes. In addition, both India and Pakistan have acquired significant economic interests in these states in the form of worker remittances and foreign aid, which their governments wish to protect.

Only if one travels a considerable distance southward — to the far side of the Arabian Peninsula — to Southern Yemen, will one find another state which stands opposed to the conservative governments in the region. The radical socialist regime there was bitterly opposed to the manner in which nine of the twelve Arab states under examination achieved their independence in 1971, and not until the mid-1970s did it undertake to extend them diplomatic recognition. Since 1975 it has established diplomatic relations with Bahrain, Qatar and the UAE and since May 1976 with Saudi Arabia. Although congresses of the ruling party in Aden, the United Political Organization, regularly used to issue declarations calling for the overthrow of the Gulf's conservative regimes, the country's practical support for revolutionary movements in the region was limited mainly to Oman, where they assisted Marxist guerrillas who sought to overthrow the Sultan and institute a socialist government.

Although this assistance was extended without interruption from 1968 onwards, it is significant that, nearly a decade later, the guerrillas controlled even less territory than they did when the aid programme was begun. Although undoubtedly one of the most protracted and fiercely fought of any Arabian insurgency in this century, the rebellion, in short, remained confined largely to Oman's southernmost province of Dhofar, 500 miles from the emirates with the vast al-Rub' al-Khali Desert, which in this instance helped protect Saudi Arabia as well, in between. The most telling limitation to the role of South Yemeni aid to the rebels, however, was that it was never extended in sufficient amounts to pose a credible prospect of effectively fighting to a standstill, let alone defeating, the British-officered and, of even greater importance as time moved on, the Iranian-bolstered forces of the Sultan. In December 1975 the last of the rebel forces were officially reported to have been crushed and the Dhofari Revolution pronounced dead by the Omani Sultan Qabus.

With the Dhofari guerrillas suppressed, the potential for insurgency to erupt elsewhere in Oman seems remote. The Sultan's position was strengthened substantially by increased financial and military support from Saudi Arabia, Iran, Jordan and the UAE; by the ability of the government to integrate Dhofar more fully into the state, and by widespread arrests in 1973 of a number of the insurgents' sympathisers and fellow members in the emirates, where the guerrillas had hoped to open a second front. The combination of these factors dealt an immense setback not only to dissidents in Dhofar but to elements in the emirates and elsewhere who have sought to undermine political stability and internal security in the conservative Arab states beyond Oman.

What has been said thus far in terms of the two categories of Arab intra-regional dynamics affecting questions relating to stability in the area could easily be construed as suggesting that a greater degree of cleavage than co-operation exists among the states concerned. Although accurate and applicable to the categories of interaction examined, the analysis would be incomplete were it to fail to include an account of the interests these states have in common which, despite their differences, tend to promote their collaboration.

First, among the dynasties, there are at least four categories of shared interests which transcend their rivalries and competition for influence in the area. Briefly, their interests are in: (1) the perpetuation of their respective conservative monarchical regimes; (2) the prevention of radical groups from gaining a foothold in the area; (3) the continuation of an uninterrupted flow of the Gulf's oil resources to markets outside the region; and (4) the procurement of the maximum revenue in exchange for their oil. Each of the dozen Arab dynasties in the area shares these four interests not only among themselves but also with Iran, although the definition of the 'highest price possible' for oil may and often does differ among these states, as was made clear at the OPEC meeting in Doha in December 1976.

Moreover, despite the ideological polarisation between a dozen dynasties on the one hand, and a single republic on the other, common interests exist between both groups. For example, doctrinal differences apart, the interests of conservative and radical states alike coalesce in the third and fourth categories, cited above, which relate to regional security questions bearing on maritime strategies and increasing their oil incomes, respectively. Finally, two other interests — the preservation and enhancement of Arabism and orthodox Islam — have the potential to help them surmount their ideological differences. In this context, for example, it has not been uncommon for Iraq and the conservative Arab regimes to stand in unison against Iran whenever they have perceived Iranian policies or practices as posing a threat to Arab interests. This kind of solidarity notwithstanding, the conservative *versus* radical contest between them occurred in reaction to Iran's past claims to Bahrain prior to

1970 and in 1971 when Iran seized the Greater and Lesser Tunbs Islands from Ra's al-Khaimah.

In the realm of religion, although theological considerations in general serve as somewhat less of a unifying force among these states nowadays than in years past, the Muslim faith none the less does tend to distinguish the Arab states, both the dynasties and republican Iraq, all of which are *officially* Sunni, from Shi'ite Iran, the citadel of heterodox Islam. Both factors, the national-ethnic as well as the religious, tend to forge even great solidarity among the Arab states in the Gulf on the third question, namely the linkage between these states and the Arab-Israeli conflict.

Linkage between the Arab-Israeli Conflict and the Persian Gulf

The regional linkage between the Gulf states and the Fertile Crescent ('confrontation') states involved in the Arab-Israeli dispute occurs essentially within three different contexts. One of these is in the realm of specific events that occasionally occur in one of the areas, such as the sabotage of an oil installation in Syria or Lebanon, that have a direct impact on developments in the other area. The second is in the context of interrelationships between particular states with interests in both areas, as for example between Jordan and Saudi Arabia, Jordan and Iran, or Israel and Iran. The third context is the extent to which the countries most directly involved in the Arab-Israeli conflict perceive the mineral and monetary might of the Arab oil-producing states in the Gulf to be a political and economic arm of the conflict.

The linkage between the two areas in the context of specific events pre-dates the 1973 war. Early in 1973, for example, a pro-Palestinian group set fire to Aramco's storage tanks in Lebanon, directly impairing the shipment of Saudi oil to Mediterranean terminals. Previously, pro-Palestinian guerrillas had on several occasions blown up sections of Tapline, the then American-owned pipeline through which nearly half a million barrels of Saudi oil were conveyed to the Levant every day. Pre-civil war fighting in Lebanon between Palestinian guerrillas and the Lebanese Army on more than one occasion forced oil tankers in the Mediterranean to stay at sea rather than risk coming close to shore to load while the conflict was raging, thereby reducing substantially the amount of Saudi petroleum that could be sent to Aramco's Nahar Zahran terminal. Although a price dispute with Lebanon and the competition of supertankers resulting in a loss of $100 million were the main reasons for Saudi Arabia's closure of Tapline in April 1975, the collapse of the 10 August 1975 agreement to re-open the pipeline was laid in part to the increasing intensity of the Lebanese fighting. Furthermore, on 9 July 1976 the Sidon refinery was shelled and set on fire. Finally re-opened in 1978, the operation of Tapline remained tenuous because of the fragile nature of 'peace' in Lebanon. Fear of the vulnerability of oil installations in the Gulf states to sabotage has also come into play as a result of the Arab-Israel problem. Increasingly widespread awareness of the legitimacy of this concern has been a contributive factor in the preference of some of these states, especially Saudi Arabia, to lessen their dependence on the Persian Gulf. The Kingdom seeks to utilise the Red Sea as the alternative route in the future, thereby diminishing, at one and the same time, the possibility of a disruption of their exports in the event of a clash with Iran or a threat to regional security posed by one or more of the emirates.

Many frustrated Palestinians have long perceived the Gulf states' policies *vis-à-vis* the Arab-Israeli conflict as overly moderate. Among their more militant elements are those who have advocated sabotage of the oil facilities as a means of demonstrating disenchant-ment. Others argue in favour of undermining these regimes and their sources of wealth as a means of indirectly striking the Western and other powers which support Israel. Incidents such as the explosion at the Umm Sa'id gas plant in Qatar in April 1977 and the pipeline ruptures and fires in Saudi Arabia near Dharan in May 1977 and at the Abqa'iq gas pipeline in June 1977 heighten the fears of those con-cerned with security and highlight the exceptional volatility and vulnerability to sabotage of the petroleum industry.

Beyond events such as these that have repercussions in both areas, there is a second category in which the connection between the Arab-Israeli conflict and the Gulf states occurs in a more institutionalised fashion, as for example in the relationship between particular states with interests in both regions. At this level, one set of linkages is that between Egypt and Jordan on the one hand, and Saudi Arabia and Kuwait on the other. In 1967, some three months after the Six Day War, Egypt and Jordan became the chief beneficiaries of the Khartoum Agreement whereby Libya (then still under the monarchy) and the two largest Arab producers in the Gulf — Saudi Arabia and Kuwait — agreed to provide them with substantial financial assistance in the form of regular payments. Since then both countries have continued to receive considerable financial aid under this arrangement, despite the termination of funds from Libya following Jordan's crack-down on the fedayeen in September 1970, and despite a brief interruption in the flow of funds from Kuwait to Jordan for the same reason. In addition to direct financial transfers, Egypt has been assured of Saudi financial assistance in its planned purchases of arms and is also involved in the Arab Military Indus-tries Organization (AMIO) with Saudi Arabia, Qatar and the UAE.

AMIO, established in 1975, with an investment of slightly over a billion dollars, is designed to examine and plan for the defence interests of the members. Although the security needs of the member states differ, if this organisation proves successful it will increase even further the growing nexus between the Arab states in the Gulf and the Arab 'confrontation states' on a wide range of issues pertaining to the Palestine problem. On economic and military planning grounds alone, both Egypt and Jordan therefore have important interests in the Gulf.

In addition to their economic and defence concerns, Jordan and Egypt have related political interests in the area. Of the two, Jordan has been particularly active in contributing to the maintenance of the political *status quo* in the Gulf. Towards this end, individual Jordanians are engaged in many of the emirates' military and internal security forces — the principal pillars of support for the dynastic regimes in the area. Jordanian army officers and police and intelligence personnel on secondment and private contract, for example, hold key positions in the defence and internal security forces of Bahrain, Qatar, the United Arab Emirates and the Sultanate of Oman. These Jordanians are generally acknowledged by the conservative Arab regimes as among the most respected and trusted of the various expatriate groups working in the area. In return for the Hashemite Kingdom's multi-faceted role in enhancing the security and development of the emirates, Jordan receives important political and diplomatic support from these states in inter-Arab councils.

Linking the Arab states of the Gulf to the confrontation states in the Arab-Israeli conflict directly are Iranian-Israeli ties. These two countries enjoyed a close political relationship and collaborated in military and economic matters as well. After the June 1967 War, for example, military equipment bearing Soviet markings found in the Kurdish areas of Iraq bordering Iran was discovered to have come to Iraq not from the USSR but from Iran *via* the Sinai, where Israel had recovered considerable amounts of abandoned Soviet-made weaponry in June 1967.

Iraq, moreover, long bristled over the fact that Iran, with Israeli support, sent arms and money to Iraq's Kurdish population as part of an ongoing programme of subversion directed against the Baghdad regime. This point of friction was removed as a result of the 'Algiers Accord' between Iran and Iraq in March 1975, but having served the interests of Iran and Israel once before, changed circumstances could re-introduce it into the relationship. Iran, in short, shared with Israel a common strategic-military interest in containing Iraq and the forces of Arab radicalism in general.

The relationship between Iran and Israel in the field of petroleum was also close until 1979. Israel continued to receive substantial quantities of oil from Iran during and after the 1973 war and the Iranian Navy provided protection for Israel-bound tankers going to and from Iran to purchase and deliver the oil. After the October War the close relationship between the two countries in matters pertaining to petroleum increased dramatically. Whereas before and after the war Israel relied on Iran for two-thirds of her energy requirements, following Israel's return of the Abu Rudeiss oilfields to Egypt, pursuant to the terms of the 'Sinai II' Agreement signed in September 1975, the degree of Israel's dependence on Iran as a source for her oil increased dramatically to nearly 90 per cent. With the overthrow of the Shah these ties were severed in January 1979.

Lastly, it remains as clear as ever that the countries directly involved in the Arab-Israel conflict consider the oil of the Arab states in the Gulf as an important political and economic arm of that dispute. This perception persists despite growing Arab financial and economic interests in the West which could be jeopardised if another oil embargo were imposed. Before the 1973 war the Kuwaiti parliament passed a resolution calling on the Emir to stop the flow of oil the moment hostilities between the Arab states and Israel resumed. This action was followed shortly thereafter with a declaration by the Minister of Petroleum of Saudi Arabia stating that his Kingdom was willing to increase its oil production to help the US solve its energy problems but implied that such measures might be contingent upon the willingness of the US to alter its Middle Eastern policy, with the clear implication being US policy towards Israel and the question of finding a just and lasting settlement of the Palestinian problem. These policy positions were taken in part in response to considerable prodding of the Arab regimes in the Gulf by states outside the region, notably Syria and Egypt.

The possibility of another Arab oil embargo and the associated alarms that accompany its plausibility serve only to heighten the concerns of importing countries about threats to the security of their oil supplies. In order to understand better the credibility of such a scenario, it is instructive if one examines what happened during the three previous instances — in 1956, 1967 and 1973 — in which the tactic of oil stoppages was actually adopted. In 1956, following the Suez Crisis and the tripartite invasion of Egypt by Israel, the United Kingdom and France, the Arab states of the Gulf applied an embargo, and an 'oil crisis' of sorts did occur — for France and the United Kingdom, and to some extent the US. Yet that crisis turned out to be rather short-lived, because the US, Venezuela and, among the Persian Gulf states most significantly Iran, helped to meet the needs of that day.

The second occasion when the oil producing states on the Arab side of the Gulf participated in an embargo followed on the heels of the Six Day War. In June 1967, the Ministers of Petroleum of Iraq, Syria, Bahrain, Abu Dhabi and Qatar attended a meeting in Baghdad which ended with a resolution that these states should cut off oil shipments to the states charged with having rendered assistance to Israel in the war. It will be recalled that shortly thereafter Libya, together with the three biggest producers among the Arab Gulf states, Saudi Arabia, Kuwait and Iraq, also stopped their oil exports to the US and the United Kingdom, both of which had been charged with aiding Israel during that conflict. Within a week, however, Saudi Arabia had resumed its shipments to the West and by late July all but Iraq had returned to the normal production patterns which existed before the war broke out.

The following month, when the Arab heads of state convened at Khartoum, Sudan, to assess the general situation arising from the June defeat, Iraq stood alone in its call for a continuation of the embargo. In consideration of the embargo's effectiveness up to that time, the consensus of most of those who attended was that the results were inconclusive. If anything, the evidence seemed to indicate that the consuming countries were not unduly disadvantaged by the embargo. In response to the Arab oil exporters applying the embargo only to specific countries, the multinational oil companies managed to reroute their shipments and draw greater supplies than usual from Iran, Indonesia and Venezuela. In this way they were able to replace the shortfall loss of Arab oil and to lessen the impact of what, in any case, was never more than a temporary inconvenience for certain consumers.

The situation in 1973, however, was fundamentally different. After 1971, the relationship between the companies and the producing countries had changed irrevocably in favour of the countries. This was especially the case not only with respect to such matters as price and levels of production but, also, with respect to questions of equity and majority ownership. Of equal, if not greater, significance was the absence of adequate shut-in supplies from the non-Arab states that had helped the consuming countries to circumvent the 1967 embargo. The latter factor proved crucial to the considerations of the producers at their meeting in Kuwait in October in the midst of the war and buttressed their decision to adopt an approach of phased production cutbacks. By managing to contract supply, which they had neglected to do in 1967, the impact was immediate in terms of demand, price and, over time, inconvenience to the importing countries.

What is less well known about the 1973 embargo is the manner in which it was proclaimd and the objectives of the participants. Among many foreign observers the perception persists, for example, that the action was undertaken, implemented and controlled collectively by OAPEC; that the OAPEC member states acted more or less in concert; and that the prime instigator was Saudi Arabia. The reality was quite different, however. Responsibility for implementing the embargo decision, as distinct from the decision of production cut-backs, devolved on the individual oil states, not on OAPEC; there was, moreover, much difference of opinion within OAPEC on the efficacy of the oil weapon; and the prime movers in favour of production cutbacks were not the Saudis but, rather, the Kuwaitis, the Libyans and the Egyptians; and in the matter of which Gulf states moved to embargo the US and the Netherlands, those who led the way were Iraq, Kuwait and Abu Dhabi, not Saudi Arabia.

Recalling the chronology and some of the forces and variables that led to the 1973 embargo is instructive in other ways as well. In retrospect, for example, it is clear that actions and attitudes attributed to certain states and organisations representing the Gulf governments were, in reality, more the outgrowth of intra-regional dynamics, such as the rivalries and tensions in the Iraqi-Kuwaiti relationship and specific calls by Libya and subsequently Egypt for the politicisation of oil.

The most significant initiative in this direction came on 10 October from Kuwait when 37 out of the 50 deputies in the then existing Kuwait National Assembly issued a statement condemning the 'continued US backing of Israel' and proposing a 'reconsideration of the export of Kuwaiti oil to the US and the withdrawal of Kuwaiti funds from the USA'. On the same day, the Kuwait government, in response to mounting pressure both from within Kuwait and from Iraq, Libya and Egypt, contacted other members of OAPEC with a view to holding an urgent meeting to discuss the role of oil in light of the new Arab-Israeli war. In this context, it is important to note that Kuwait was in 1973 the only working parliamentary democracy in the region. As such, the Iraqi presence and influence in Kuwait notwithstanding, the Kuwaiti government was arguably more sensitive than any other OAPEC government to local public opinion and the views of the Kuwait deputies.

It is also clear that the Kuwaiti initiative, the first step along the road to the oil cut-backs and the embargo, occurred at least partly in response to repeated Iraqi calls for Kuwait and others to use every means to stop the flow of oil and to take over US interests in the Arab world. These calls were coming from a state that had only four months previously renewed its claim to sovereignty over portions of Kuwait and had actually seized control of a Kuwaiti border post.

The massive military aid which the US began to send to Israel in the course of the war — from 13 October until the end of the war on

25 October the US made more than 500 military supplies flights to Israel — was regarded by many as direct US intervention on behalf of the occupying power, Israel. This aid served only to hasten the Arab resolve to use the oil weapon. The decision seems to have been dictated more by the turn of the war against the Arab armies — for example, it was on 17 October, when the Israelis consolidated their position and presence on the West Bank and the Suez Canal, that the OAPEC member states moved to impose restrictions on their oil exports to the Western world. Yamani himself has been quoted as saying that 'the pressure for curtailment came mainly from the Libyans and the Iraqis but that the effort was also being pushed by the Kuwaitis and would therefore be very difficult to turn around'.

Even so, there were problems of conceptualisation and implementation. The problem was to devise a formula which would damage the enemy and encourage friends. Of the three options considered — expropriation, consumer country embargoes and production cut-backs — the first option was rejected as poorly suited to a carefully orchestrated approach of the reward and punishment variety. Instead the delegates opted for a combination of consumer country embargoes and graduated production cut-backs. This policy proved especially suitable owing to the ease with which it could be directly administered and monitored by the OAPEC members. An embargo alone, for example, would have posed immense difficulties of implementation and control. The reason: responsibility for carrying out these functions would devolve not on OAPEC but, rather, on the multinational oil companies which produced, exported and refined OAPEC oil.

The ten OAPEC members — of whom six were from the Gulf (Saudi Arabia, Kuwait, Iraq, Abu Dhabi, Bahrain and Qatar) agreed on 17 October to reduce their oil production by at least 5 per cent using the September 1973 level as a base and thereafter by a similar percentage each month. Of significance, however, is that this decision held each country to only the 5 per cent minimum monthly cut-back formula: otherwise, each OAPEC member was free to adopt its own individual approach to the embargo question — itself an indication that the policy did not reflect unanimity of viewpoint. In short, the OAPEC members' inability to adopt a comprehensive and binding oil policy demonstrated not only the absence of a common strategy but equally the limited utility of OAPEC as a means of administering an embargo. Among the Gulf states, Abu Dhabi — quite possibly feeling threats from radical quarters similar to those that were pressuring Kuwait, which had experienced a close call with radical revolutionaries the preceding spring — proclaimed the embargo almost immediately. Not until 20 October did Saudi Arabia follow suit and declare its own embargo of the US, citing the 'increase in American military aid to Israel'. Algeria joined on the same day, and Qatar and Kuwait did likewise on 21 October, and, by the end of the month, so had Oman, Bahrain and Dubai. Iraq, however, cited the likelihood of adverse reactions in Europe from any serious interruption in oil supplies. Noting that most European states had begun to move closer to the Arab position since 1967, Iraq refused to endorse the production cut-backs.

If a common strategy was not developed among these states, it was equally clear that the lack of response to UN Resolution 338 and the cease-fire initiative was governed by their respective national needs and concerns, not the collective interests of the region at large. Indeed, few if any of the Gulf states under examination perceived the October War as 'their war'.

Was the 1973 embargo a success from the Arab point of view? Obviously the conditions established for lifting the embargo at its inception — i.e. Israeli withdrawal from all the Arab lands occupied in 1967, including East Jerusalem, and restoration of Palestinian rights — were not realised. Nevertheless, the technique demonstrated an ability on the part of the Arab states to act collectively and decisively, and it had stimulated heightened recognition and knowledge of the Arab cause against Israel. The embargo was lifted in March 1974 primarily because OAPEC considered that, on balance, the tactic had derived its probable maximum political benefits. To have continued the embargo beyond that time could have been counter-productive in those countries which by then had already been sensitised to the Arab point of view. Moreover, the tactic was proving to be costly to most of the states involved in its implementation, for, from a domestic development and planning perspective, the fourfold increase in oil prices militated in favour of resuming earlier production and export levels.

On balance, use of oil as a pressure mechanism yielded certain political benefits to the Gulf dynasties. This was especially so with respect to King Faisal, who ascended to a stature of greater statesmanship and regional leadership than ever before, and with respect to the force of his voice and that of other Gulf leaders in favour of moderation and the promotion of evolutionary change in the area as a whole.

Iranian Hegemony

An equal if not greater factor than the Arab-Israeli dispute in affecting prospects for regional security is the basis for Arab concern about ultimate Iranian intentions in the area. The apprehension is rooted not so much in the ethnic, linguistic, sectarian and other cleavages of old as in the steady and, to date, comparatively massive build-up over the past decade of Iranian military might. In the face of this build-up and in the absence of an effective counter-force, Arab fears have grown proportionately about the past and potential uses of such power.

Much of the nationalist literature in Arabic refers repeatedly to this escalation in highly lethal and sophisticated arms. Such a build-up is frequently linked to an alleged Iranian goal of acquiring, presumably at some unspecified point in the future, 'additional' Arab territory or of exercising, if necessary by diktat, a preponderance of influence over matters in which Arab interests might not always be in agreement with those of Iran. With varying degrees of accuracy, relevance and plausibility, the focus is usually on one or more of the following phenomena:

(1) the highly emotional and frequently quite militant tone of Iran's long-standing claim to Bahrain, relinquished only in 1970;

(2) the controversial take-over from Sharjah in 1971 of half of Abu Musa Island and a corresponding portion of the revenues from a nearby offshore oilfield that had been developed by a Sharjan concessionaire. Although Iran had secured written authorisation from the Ruler of Sharjah, the agreement was signed under circumstances equivalent to coercion and the Ruler was assassinated for this act sixty days later.

(3) the violent seizure from Ra's al-Khaimah, also in 1971, of the Greater and Lesser Tunbs islands. Particularly offensive in Arab eyes was the heavy-handed manner in which the operation was carried out (the warship that was despatched to seize uninhabited Little Tunbs was reportedly longer than the island captured);

(4) the continuing Iranian military presence in Oman's southern province of Dhofar, where Iranian forces played a major role in quelling a local rebellion, although the war was officially ended nearly three years ago;

(5) a tacit agreement between the heads of state of Iran and Oman to patrol 'jointly' — meaning, in practice, mainly by Iran — the Straits of Hormuz, a strategically important waterway that oil tankers continue to traverse (the principal shipping lane falls in the territorial sea of Arab Oman), at the rate of one every twelve minutes; and

(6) Iran's extensive intelligence network in the area and the widespread Arab belief that much of the intelligence collected has long been shared with Israel.

To be sure, references in the Arab media and in other forms of public and private expression to these specific points often make little or no distinction between past and present. Nor is causality always considered. The problem of emotional and ethno-nationalist bias on the subject notwithstanding, Arabs have reason to be apprehensive about Iranian interests in and policies towards the area. Their concern, however, is not so much with any Iranian desire, actual or potential, to acquire additional Arab territory. Rather, in the context of day-to-day decision-making among Arab elites in the area, the concern is over the multi-faceted character of ongoing Iranian involvement in their affairs.

In recent years the more controversial side of Iranian involvement in Arabia has occurred through actual armed intervention; through the provision of financial and other kinds of aid to acquire influence; through encouragement of the positions of certain rulers versus those of others in the United Arab Emirates; and through support for the border claims of one Arab head of state against those of another in the Musandam Peninsula, the most strategically important of any territory in the Gulf. Unfortunately for the goals of Iranian strategists and policy-makers, the cumulative effect of these intrusions has frequently been to decrease the prospects of co-operation between Iran and these states on regional security questions and other issues of mutual interest.

Although Iranian involvement in Arab affairs is usually undertaken in the name of enhancing security, the efficacy of such an approach, as revealed by the record to date, has clearly been mixed. Arab willingness to accept a pre-eminent Iranian role in regional security matters seemed possible in 1970 when Tehran relinquished its age-old claim to sovereignty over Bahrain. The image of an Iran capable of pursuing and implementing an area-wide policy on issues involving Arab pride that could be realistic and practical, if not magnanimous, reached its zenith following that decision. Yet this positive perception by Gulf Arabs of Iranian intentions *vis-á-vis* their interests was short-lived. Within a year it was vitiated substantially by Iran's actions in the Abu Musa and Tunbs islands disputes. Tehran has yet to regain the standing it previously enjoyed in the eyes of those Arab leaders with whom Iran's goal of establishing a relationship of confidence and trust remains as elusive as it is earnestly sought.

Of the factors contributing to the uneasy *modus operandi* between Iran and these states, the islands issue plus the continued military presence in Oman remain the most irritating, while the relentless arms build-up, combined with militance and rising violence within Iran itself, had become the most alarming until the revolution. The overall effect in terms of an Arabian assessment has been and continues to be one of dissuading many of the elites in these states from engaging in open, and in some cases even private, collaboration with Iran.

Examples of the obstacles that Iran has created in the trend towards greater co-operation and integration of the Arabian Penin- sula states may be found in its recent relations with the Sheikhdom of Dubai and the Sultanate of Oman. The former is a key member of the United Arab Emirates; the latter, comprising the second largest country in the Arabian Peninsula, has been the scene of the greatest challenge to regional security to date. Both states, though vastly dif- ferent in size, location and international status (Dubai, as a member of the UAE, is not a fully sovereign state), have strategic, economic and other interests that parallel those of Iran.

In Western terms Iran's relationship with Dubai can be likened to the United States' with the State of New York, i.e. as a whole to a part. In this case the ties between the two entities are of considerable importance to both for several reasons. Not the least is the fact that a substantial proportion of Dubai's population is of Iranian origin and that much of the emirate's highly lucrative entrepot trade has long been with Iran. Moreover, in the late 1970s Dubai was receiving oil revenues approximating $1 billion annually from an offshore field which Iranian officials claimed privately extends into Iranian territory. This income is vital to the prospects for success of Dubai's ambitious economic schemes. Indeed, anticipated future revenue from this and nearby oilfields comprises the emirate's most impor- tant means for repaying the numerous international loans under- taken to finance its costly development programme.

In addition to these conditions, the long-standing and excep- tionally close personal relationship between the Shah of Iran and UAE Vice-President Sheikh Rashid of Dubai has frequently given cause for suspicion and distrust among other more affluent and ambitious rulers in the area. As a state known to prefer autonomy in UAE affairs and long suspected of harbouring secessionist notions, Dubai has frequently been a source of frustration to those respon- sible for creating a viable union out of the loosely organised con- federation. In their view, Dubai's less than wholehearted support for the federalist idea remains possible mainly because it holds the important UAE posts of Vice-President, Prime Minister, Minister of Finance and Minister of Defense and because it possesses veto power denied all the other states except Abu Dhabi. The effect of implicit Iranian support for the emirate's independent courses of action has not only been to weaken rather than strengthen the hands of the federalists. More specifically, it has been to encourage instead of inhibit separatist tendencies in a federalist state constitutionally bound to unified action on most international matters, including those of defence and security.

In the case of Oman, the situation is substantially different. The common interests supportive of the Sultanate's willingness to collaborate with Iran are not so much commercial or economic as military and strategic. The most important dimension of Iranian-Omani ties to date was manifested by the intervention, noted earlier, of Iranian forces in the Dhofar insurrection. Numerous other states supported Sultan Qabus in his efforts to defeat the guerrillas, but it was undeniably the role of the Iranian expeditionary force that helped to end the military phase of the conflict in 1975.

In addition, a unique factor in the relationship between Iran and Oman, but one necessitating intimate collaboration on strategic and regional security matters, is the overlapping of their respective territorial seas in the Straits of Hormuz. From the perspective of Tehran and Muscat, the presence of Iranian troops in the Sultanate long after the fighting in Dhofar had ceased was linked as much to this mutual interest as much as to any other consideration. The administration of this special aspect of the relationship, however, has on occasion contributed to a deterioration of Oman's relations with certain of its Arab neighbours: namely Southern Yemen and the UAE, not to mention Libya and Algeria. Here again the effect, particularly since the end of the Dhofar war, has been to undermine rather than bolster the prospects for greater regional security.

In the late 1970s the actual and potential weight of Iranian influene in the balance of intra-regional security affairs was further demonstrated in an east Arabian border dispute that, to date, has received scant attention in the literature. The dispute in question erupted in late 1977/early 1978 and involved Oman's Musandam Peninsula enclave that overlooks the Hormuz Straits on one hand, and the neighbouring UAE state of Ra's al-Khaimah on the other. Oman advanced a claim to part of Ra's al-Khaimah — like Dubai, an emirate with less than sovereign powers in international affairs — soon after reports that Ra's al-Khaimah had discovered oil offshore. This territorial dispute between two resource-poor states might well have been resolved with despatch and a measure of equity by the parties most directly concerned but for Iran's private assertion of support for Oman. That Iran interfered in this manner in an essentially inter-Arab dispute only complicated and delayed the prospects for an early settlement. That it supported, (even privately) a state's claim which, *ipso facto*, represented a clear challenge to the political and territorial *status quo* in the area — against the positions of both the state of Ra's al-Khaimah and the UAE government as well — was viewed with consternation not only by many in the UAE but by outside powers with a stake in the outcome.

Moreover, when Dubai was reluctant to endorse the hard-line

reaction of the Ruler of Ra's al-Khaimah as well as a similar response by the UAE government, Western strategists and policy-makers were quick to assume Dubayan complicity, by virtue of its special Iranian connection, with Omani *cum* Iranian designs. These and other analysts, however, were slow to acknowledge that something other than a mere power play or grab for additional territory along the lines described earlier might be involved. Information which might otherwise have been dismissed as biased or irrelevant became essential for insight into the behaviour of an important actor in lower Gulf and east Arabian affairs. What escaped the notice of many observers was the fact that half of the immediate blood relations of the Ruler of Dubai hailed from the disputed territory and that he held title to land in the same area. Furthermore, unknown to many analysts was the fact that, elsewhere in Oman, Sheikh Rashid held sovereignty over — and therefore rights of access to — the Wadi Hatta, an area rich in costly construction material vital to the building of Dubai's burgeoning economic infrastructure.

Iranian interference has on occasion thus been seen to have a deleterious and generally disquieting consequence. Senior officials of the Omani, UAE and emirate governments have repeatedly complained that whatever Tehran's ultimate intentions in the area may be, Iranian policy in practice remains vulnerable to the charge of pursuing a divide and rule approach in the course of supporting some states while opposing or being less supportive of others. Such a policy, these officials acknowledge, might be valid were Oman, individual emirates or the UAE as a whole seriously to pose a credible threat, either real or potential, to Iran. However, this is not the case, nor does such an eventuality seem remotely possible in the foreseeable future.

These officials allege, in short, that Iranian interference of the kinds discussed above has tended both to hinder the forces of unity in the lower Gulf and eastern Arabia, and to alienate and antagonise a significant segment of the politically aware in the area as a whole. In emphasising this point, these officials are not begrudging the successful Iranian role in deterring others from interfering in the area. On the contrary, they remain grateful for what Iran had achieved in this regard and they acknowledge the fact that the task has not been easy. Rather, their concern is that insufficient emphasis has been given to the view that the blessings of Iranian hegemony in regional affairs can only be seen as mixed. For in their eyes, Iran has been as much a negative and disruptive force as a positive factor in the cause of promoting stability and security.

Local awareness of this dimension of intra-Gulf political dynamics is much more sophisticated and widespread than many outsiders appear to appreciate. It is also true that many among the elites of these states linked the policies of Western governments together with Iranian policy. Their reasoning, though simplistic, is none the less seductive. A widespread local perception, for example, is that Iran, no less than Israel, could not have successfully engaged in the activities described above for as long as it had without the endorsement and support, active or passive, of these governments.

Whether separately or collectively then, individual states and groups of states have undermined efforts to achieve greater stability and co-operation, if not integration, among the states on the Arab side of the Gulf. The growing frustration of many of the region's inhabitants with their leaders who they view as powerless in the face of these foreign-directed activities is but one consequence of such activities. From the perspective of the majority of the Arab states in the Gulf such externally supported divisiveness in their ranks has been and remains a source of continuing concern. This is especially the case in view of the fact that official policy among Arabs and Iranians alike has been painstakingly designed to create a milieu in which their common interests in greater regional security and stability would be enhanced.

Postscript

In the air of uncertainty which characterised the first year following the ousting of the Shah, the policies of the Pahlavi dynasty *vis-à-vis* the Gulf seem, from the perspective of the emirates, Oman and Saudi Arabia, benign in comparison to those of the Iranian revolutionary leaders.

That it has precipitated great unease in everyone's minds and especially among governmental decision-makers in the area is only obvious and a natural consequence of the fluidity and unpredictability of the situation.

Most immediately, the unease has taken the form of heightened co-operation at the level of intelligence-sharing on a broad range of matters pertaining to regional and internal security. The state of organisation and the grievances of various minorities and other groups in these states which are deemed potentially susceptible to revolutionary overtures from Tehran are two topics with respect to which a greater degree of information has been shared among those governments than ever before. It has even heightened the aura of seriousness which some of the states, for example such previously erstwhile adversaries as Iraq and Saudi Arabia, have conferred upon matters pertaining to regional security.

On the other hand, contrary to the hopes of various Western strategists, it has not fostered even a remotely comparable willingness among these states to submerge a measure of their sovereignties into some kind of regional security organisation, which, in the eyes of a number of interested Westerners, might lend greater substance to the credibility of those states' concern.

Although not comparable to Iran, in many ways the Arab Gulf states have been profoundly affected by Iran's upheaval, not least by the manner in which it occurred. Common to all the Gulf states are their vulnerabilities in these issues where Iran's leaders have been able to pick up substantial revolutionary support across wide social strata. These issues are corruption, ostentatious display of wealth, dubious development schemes and the less than *quid pro quo* basis of the relationship between these states and the US on matters pertaining to the Arab-Israeli dispute and the Palestinian problem.

On the other hand, these states are in several ways dissimilar to Iran. Politically, most are characterised by a ruling family that is at once more numerous and in several instances more competent as well as more solidly rooted in the local milieu than were the Pahlavis.

Socially, each adheres in general to the egalitarian ethos of traditional Arabia. This ethos lends an air of unpretension and softness to the relationship between rulers and ruled. The relative lack of pretension, moreover, stands in contradistinction to the pomp and ceremony and air of aloofness, bordering on isolation, which characterised the relationship between the Pahlavi sovereign and his subjects.

Economically, moreover, nearly all of the Gulf states are blessed with comparatively greater prospects for successful development in the foreseeable future than was the case in Iran — owing to their later economic start and, collectively, to their more prodigious oil reserves. Even the exceptions with respect to oil reserves — for example Bahrain, Oman, Dubai and some of the other emirates — have demonstrated a remarkable aptitude for resilience in dealing with some of the more disruptive forces for change in the area. At the same time, these states have exhibited an aptitude for economic diversification that, given their limited resources, is impressive.

Most telling of all, however, is the psychological mood and attitude of the citizenry in these states *vis-à-vis* their present and future prospects. It is this which differs so markedly from the situation which existed in pre-revolutionary Iran. To wit: there exists throughout these states a certainty of almost unlimited social and economic opportunity that arguably never existed for many in Iran. This has gone far in helping to defuse local grievances and political dissent. The most impressive evidence supporting this assessment has been the high rate of return of those students in the emirates and elsewhere who have left the area for advanced training abroad. Again, the persistence of this phenomenon — a bell-wether for gauging the degree of citizen disaffection towards a particular regime — contrasts vividly with the record of the last fifteen years of Pahlavi Iran, where annually thousands of additional young Iranian men and women swelled the ranks of their alienated countryfolk who chose to remain abroad rather than return to their country.

The Iranian upheaval has had its most direct and immediate impact on Iraq. Most importantly, it has served to accelerate a 'redefinition' of Iraqi foreign policy which was already in process. The post-Camp David Accord (between Israel and Egypt) milieu, plus continuing differences of opinion and policy between Iraq and neighbouring Syria, along with mounting unease within the Baghdad regime over United States-Soviet rivalry in the Gulf would have been sufficient, in themselves, to bring about changes in the nature and orientation of Iraqi policies *vis-à-vis* the outside world. The occurrence of a revolution next door, however, has been the source of most immediate concern.

One effect of Iran's incapacity has been to make Iraq, temporarily, the number one military force in the Gulf. For the first time it can be assumed that in any armed conflict with Iran, Iraq would emerge as the clear victor.

The ascendancy of a revolutionary government in Tehran has also alienated the Iraqi leadership from its counterparts in Iran to a far greater extent than was the case during most of the Pahlavi period. While Iraqi Ba'thists never 'liked' the Shah, he was an individual with whom the Baghdad regime could strike a bargain, whereas with the Ayatollah Khomeini — whom they expelled from their midst — appeared to be the opposite.

Further afield, Iraq has undertaken to improve its relations with and image in the United States. Indeed, one of the more significant trends became Iraq's tendency towards a 'pro-West tilt'. Baghdad officials remarked with increasing frequency that events in Iran served to put Iraq inside the circle of the so-called 'Arc of Crisis', rather than leaving it outside in its previous role as an 'encircler'.

The PDRY

The PDRY regime, led by its Marxist President 'Abd al-Fattah Isma'il, entered the 1980s with a close, almost patron-client, relationship with the Soviet Union. Although many outsiders viewed the relationship in terms of its alleged potential for undermining Arabian Peninsula and Gulf security, tangible evidence supportive of the thesis that this has in fact been a goal of the Aden government, remained much less persuasive than during the 1967–75 period, when the PDRY was the principal external source of assistance for the insurrection in Oman's southern province of Dhofar.

Admittedly, Oman remained vulnerable, but this was not only from attacks by radical leftist forces, but arguably even more so from Arab nationalist influences emanating from conservative states. The primary reason was Oman's willingness to flaunt the consensus of all the other Gulf states by being the only Arab state to endorse the Egyptian-Israeli peace treaty. By pursuing such policies which accentuated its isolation the Omani regime hoped primarily to be able to establish a strong strategic and defence relationship with the United States. In the process, it also hoped to find a means whereby Egyptian troops might manage to serve as an effective substitute for the Iranian contingent in Dhofar, which had been the principal foreign force helping to quell the Dhofar rebellion in the mid-1970s, but which had been withdrawn just prior to the overthrow of the Shah. Whether Oman had thereby significantly enhanced either its external or internal security situation through these measures, or whether by such policies it had merely hastened the inevitability of an eventual uprising against the Al Bu Sa'id dynasty remained to be determined. The latter prospect seemed greater were Oman to deepen its relationship with the United States government which gave every indication of continuing to drag its feet on the issue of overriding importance to Oman's immediate neighbours as well as one to the peoples of the Gulf as a whole: namely, a just and lasting settlement of the Palestinian problem.

10   IRAQ: EMERGENT GULF POWER
Edmund Ghareeb

Iraq, or ancient Mesopotamia, where the Tigris and the Euphrates nurtured the most ancient human civilisation, has often been portrayed in the West as a xenophobic land plagued by violent political upheavals and instability.

Recent developments, however, tend to show that Iraq, under the leadership of the Arab Ba'th Socialist Party is, by Iraqi standards, emerging as a stable land that is seriously backing its bid to lead the Arab world and become a prominent force in the non-aligned movement. Furthermore, Iraq has, in the wake of the Camp David accords and of the Iranian Revolution, emerged as a regional power that is destined to play a pivotal role in the Arab/Persian Gulf region in the coming decade.

But while much attention has been focused on the growing economic, political and strategic importance of the Gulf countries, little attention has been paid to Iraq's role in this sensitive region. Iraq has received scant coverage as a Gulf state with legitimate interests of its own in the area. Despite its vast economic potential (unlike a number of other oil-rich states, Iraq has a rich agricultural and industrial potential as well), geographic position and population, it has either been ignored or briefly covered in the context of its relations with Iran and Kuwait.

Iraq's chronic instability, its tough anti-Israel positions and its reputed closeness to the Soviet Union may have contributed to colouring Western attitudes, but the main reason lies elsewhere. Iraq, until recent years, lacked the interest or the means to become involved in Gulf affairs.

Iraq was conquered by the Ottoman Turks in the sixteenth century. For the next four hundred years, it served as a buffer between the Ottoman and Persian empires. The constant violence of these years contributed much to the fragmentation of the society which continues to have effect to this day.

But while much of Iraq suffered under this period, it was the southern Iraqi province of Basrah bordering the Gulf which suffered the most.[1] For in addition to the economic stagnation that befell the whole area, southern Iraq suffered for sectarian reasons.

The Ottoman Persian struggle was waged as a Sunni v. Shi'i struggle. The Ottomans, who were Sunni Muslims did not allow the Shi'i Muslims who were in the majority in southern Iraq to partici-

pate fully in the military or political affairs of the area.[2] Consequently, whatever economic and political development took place
occurred in central and northern Iraq.

In 1917–18 British forces occupied the province of Basrah and
most of Iraq in order to protect their oil and commercial interests in
the region as well as the road to India. Faced with mass protests that
developed into a full-scale revolt, the British declared that it was
their intention to form an independent Arab government under
British trusteeship. In an attempt to assuage popular feeling, the
British chose Prince Faisal, the son of Sharif Husain of Mecca and
leader of the Arab Revolt, as King of Iraq. Faisal's appointment was
welcomed by the majority of Iraqis.

Faisal's kingdom, however, was plagued by many problems, new
and old. The Ottomans had not only left behind a stagnant economy
and deep-seated sectarian cleavages, but they had also failed to
develop any unifying political institutions or a viable central administration.

Among the new problems facing the country were those of British
control and the question of Kurdish and Arab nationalism. Faisal
was aware of the sectarian, ethnic, tribal and religious problems
facing the new state. In a secret memorandum published after his
death, Faisal concluded: 'Iraq is one of those countries which lack
the most important force necessary for social cohesion: a common
sectarian, religious and intellectual bond. As a result the country is
fragmented and divided.'[3]

The new Iraq did not, however, inherit any long-standing
economic and political interests in the Gulf, although some commercial activity did exist with neighbouring countries.[4]

Under the monarchy, Gulf affairs had little or no role in the
thinking of Iraqi leaders, with the exception of half-hearted calls for
uniting Kuwait with Iraq issued by some Iraqi parties and King
Ghazi in the 1930s.[5] These calls were quickly squelched by the
British, who enjoyed *de facto* control over Kuwait and some other
Gulf countries.

The attention of King Faisal and his associates focused on the
Fertile Crescent area. The King and many of his top aides had led the
Arab Revolt in the hope of uniting the Arabian Peninsula and the
Fertile Crescent into a single independent state. Faisal's ouster from
Syria by the French did not lessen the desire or the interest of the
King and his successors to continue to seek unity with Syria.[6]
Geographic, economic and religious ties also required close and
friendly relations with Turkey and Iran.

The nature of the Iraqi economy reinforced this trend. The
economy was primarily agricultural and what little industry existed
was concentrated in the centre of Iraq.[7] Date exports were the major

source of revenue and these were mainly produced in southern Iraq and shipped through the port of Basrah, but the loading, shipping and marketing were handled by foreign companies.[8] And while the port of Basrah was a major trading centre, the area did not have much impact on the country's policies towards the Gulf because the institutions which handled the trade, such as the Basrah Port Authority, acted independently.[9] The lack of funds created difficulties for the government and prevented the initiation of major development projects. The situation improved slightly in 1951 when Iraq signed a new contract with the Iraq Petroleum Company (IPC) giving it 50 per cent of the profits from oil sales.[10]

The increase in oil revenue and the growing importance of the oil industry began to affect Iraq's relations with the Gulf because the government became more attentive to the oil-producing areas, particularly when operations began in the southern oilfield of Rumaila. Nevertheless, production in the northern oilfields of Mosul and Kirkuk far exceeded that of Rumaila. In addition, the oil from these fields was transported to Mediterranean ports through Syria and Lebanon.

Thus Iraq's oil, trade and industrial development oriented the government's policies more towards the Fertile Crescent, Turkey and Iran than towards the Gulf.

Another major reason for Iraq's lack of interest in the Gulf at this stage was British domination and influence over the Gulf. Iraqi rulers who looked towards Britain as a protector were aware that Britain would not allow any political or military intervention in the region. Iraq's small armed forces were strategically dependent on the British and when the Iraqi Army challenged British control in 1941, the Iraqis lost. The country also lacked the surplus financial revenues, the merchant marine or the navy necessary for it to play the role of a regional power.

After Faisal's death, the monarchy began to lose its popularity. His successors lacked his intelligence, prestige, popularity and ability to work with various factions. On 14 July 1958 a successful revolt under the leadership of General Abd al Karim Qasim brought a bloody end to the Hashemite monarchy.

The major reasons for the revolt were the impatience of the young generation with the slowness of reform; the disenchantment with the way the country was being ruled; the growth of Arab nationalism as a radical ideology; and the opposition to the Baghdad Pact and the Arab union between Jordan and Iraq were seen as deterrents to Arab unity.[11]

The 1958 Revolution did not, however, succeed in advancing Arab unity, nor did it bring stability and prosperity. Instead the revolution introduced new elements of instability. The period from 1958 to

1968 was marked by instability and violence. A struggle for power ensued among the Arab nationalists and between them and the Iraqi Communist Party (ICP) and the Kurdistan Democratic Party (KDP).

Qasim's unwillingness to join the United Arab Republic alienated the Nasserites and the Ba'thists and led to greater reliance on the KDP and ICP.[12] He allowed Kurdish leader Mulla Mustafa al-Barzani to return from exile in the Soviet Union. Relations with Barzani began to deteriorate, however, when Qasim refused to grant autonomy to the Kurds, and fighting ensued.[13]

The conflict with the Arab nationalists and the Kurds weakened Qasim's grip and allowed the Ba'th Party and a group of conservative officers to mount a successful *coup* against Qasim on 8 February 1963.

Beset with internal rivalries and weakened by the war against the Kurds, the Ba'th Party was unable to maintain itself in power and was ousted by General Abd al-Salam Arif. Following his death in a helicopter crash in 1966, his brother was appointed President until he was ousted by the Ba'thists on 17 July 1968.

The country's political instability following the 1958 Revolution virtually paralysed economic development. One important change, however, left an important impact on Iraq's interest in the Gulf — the oil industry. The new government faced serious economic difficulties when it sought to improve living standards and to increase military capability. As a result, it turned to the Iraq Petroleum Company (IPC) for increased revenues.[14] For political as well as economic reasons, IPC refused to accede to demands for increased production and a share of the profits on each barrel produced.

While government pressure failed to get IPC to allow it a share in the operation of the company, it nevertheless forced the company to promise to double its production in 1962. This development forced the oil companies to build new handling, transport, loading and storage facilities.[15] Most of these facilities were built in the south in order to avoid interruptions similar to the one that occurred in 1956 in Syria.

The Qasim government also made efforts to advance commercial activity in the south. Work started on a rail line connecting Baghdad and Basrah, bidding opened for the reconstruction of a new port at Um Qasr on the Gulf, funds were allocated for the expansion of the port of Basrah and a modest shipping company was established to conduct foreign trade.[16]

Another indication of the regime's growing interest in Gulf affairs was the Iraqi claim of sovereignty over Kuwait. Iraq's claim was based on the fact that Kuwait was administered as a part of the province of Basrah during the Ottoman period. Domestic political factors as well as Kuwait's substantial oil revenues may have played a part in Qasim's decision. Arab and British opposition prevented Qasim from carrying through his threats of annexing his small but wealthy neighbour. While not immediately observed, the impact of these efforts on the economy of southern Iraq was substantial. It ultimately influenced the growing interest in Gulf affairs of the present government. Active Iraqi involvement in Gulf affairs, however, did not emerge until the return of Ba'th Party to power in 1968.[17]

On 17 July 1968 the Ba'th Party, with the help of some military officers, staged a bloodless *coup d'état* against the government of General Arif. Less than two weeks later, on 30 July, the party succeeded in ousting its military allies and began to work towards the implementation of the goals it had failed to achieve during its brief seizure of power in 1963. Tariq Aziz, Iraqi Deputy Prime Minister, member of the national (Pan-Arab) and regional (Iraqi) commands of the party and a leading Ba'thist theoretician, stressed the distinguishing feature of the Ba'thist take-over of power when he wrote, 'it is important that the revolution should be seen as a Ba'th Party revolution and that the Party should not be a facade for other apparent or hidden forces.'[18]

The 17–30 July Revolution, as Ba'thists prefer to call it, did in fact bring to power in Iraq one of the most unique, home-grown political parties to emerge in the Arab world. The Ba'thist take-over in 1968 was not simply a military *coup d'état* similar to others that have occurred in many Arab and Third World countries. It was instead a revolution backed by an ideological party with concrete programmes, goals, leaders and members whose commitment to Ba'thism was tested by many years of underground activity and ṣtruggle.

In order to understand Iraq's domestic and foreign policy, particularly the nature of its response to new realities in the Gulf, it is necessary to understand some of the Ba'th Party's basic tenets. The Ba'th Party, according to Patrick Seale, 'has outstripped in influence even Nasser, the greatest Arab leader of the postwar period and its chief rival in the pan-Arab states. It provided — and continues to provide — a working definition of that most elusive of all notions: Arabism'.[19]

Founded in 1940 by Syrian intellectual Michel Aflaq, the party holds the view that the Arab nation extends from the Atlantic Ocean in the west to the Arab Gulf in the east. Aflaq and his associates believed that centuries of Ottoman and Western control led to Arab decline, division and confusion. The party advocated the view that regional boundaries among Arabs were artificial and will disappear with the 'awakening of Arab consciousness.'[20] Theoretically the Ba'thists preached nationalism as open to all inhabitants of the Arab land, who consider themselves a part of the 'Arab Nation' regardless of religion, sect or ethnic origin. Aflaq called for a revitalisation of Arab society in order to achieve the Arab nation's goals of 'unity, freedom, and socialism'. The party's goals can only be achieved through revolution and struggle and not by reliance 'on slow evolution and contentment with superficial and partial reforms which threaten these aims with failure and extinction'.[21] Unlike other Arab parties, with the exception of the Communists, the Ba'th did not depend on the charismatic leadership of an individual. Collective leadership is stressed and the party's structure is well organised and disciplined.

Another distinguishing feature of Ba'th Party rule in Iraq is the existence of a built-in dualism in the power structure. This is manifested in the maintenance of separate state and party institutions. The Ba'thist state, as Professor Khadduri aptly put it, 'is only the means to an end, while the party is the agency which provides leadership and direction for action'.[22] The party is responsible for the broad outlines which govern the policy orientation of the regime, while the state is seen as an instrument for the implementation of the party's objectives.

Ba'thist ideas began to reach Iraq in the late 1940s, particularly among students and intellectuals. But a regional branch of the party was not founded until 1954. In the 1950s the party in Iraq waged a two-sided struggle against the monarchist regime, which it considered reactionary and subservient to Western interests, and against the ICP, its main rival — which it considered hostile to Arab nationalism.

Following its ouster from power in 1963, the party faced a series of crises and setbacks. Internal schisms and repression by the Arif regime were followed by a more serious schism within the Syrian branch of the party. In 1966, the military wing of the Syrian branch of the party, which had come to power in 1963, succeeded in ousting the historic civilian leadership of the party (headed by Aflaq and his associate Salah al-Din al-Bitar) and their military allies, while the Iraqi branch remained loyal to Aflaq's leadership. This schism caused serious divisions within the party, leaving it with deep and bitter internal conflicts that have persisted to this day.

Mindful not to repeat their earlier mistakes, the Ba'thist leaders were determined to maintain their authority and to create the prerequisites for stability. Tough, pragmatic and secular in their outlook, they were convinced of the justness of their cause and determined to make Iraq, in the words of now President Saddam Hussein, a 'model state' and a leader of the Arab world.[23] The leaders realised that the establishment of a stable regime had to be ensured before their ideology could be implemented. Consequently, the regime set for itself four major objectives: (1) consolidation of Ba'thist authority; (2) achieving economic independence by gaining control over natural resources, particularly oil; (3) broadening the regime's popular base by inviting independent nationalists, Communists and Kurds to enter into a national front coalition with the Ba'th; (4) resolving the Kurdish problem.[24]

In foreign policy the party was primarily concerned with ending all traces of foreign control over the various parts of the 'Arab homeland'. Arab unity was to be achieved through protracted struggle against 'imperialism, Zionism and Arab reaction'. The Ba'thists advocated non-alignment in the Cold War between East and West and, as the party of the 'liberated Arab vanguard' which has come to 'objectively recognize the tie between the struggle of our people and the struggle of other colonized and oppressed people in the world'.[25] The regime's preoccupation with the task of warding off plots against it and consolidating its authority, and its conflict with the Kurdish rebels continued to limit Iraq's foreign policy options during the first six years.

The return of the Ba'th to power, however, coincided with a number of other factors which led to increased emphasis on Gulf affairs in Iraqi foreign policy. These factors included:

(1) Britain's declaration of its intention to withdraw from East of Suez by 1971 increased Iraq's concern about the future power structure in the Gulf. The Ba'thists believed that this action was going to lead to 'tightening of imperialist, political, economic, and military control of the area'.[26]

(2) the decline of Nasserism in the Gulf region following the 1967 defeat left the field open for the Ba'thists to carry the mantle of pan-Arabism and to co-operate with Arab nationalist and radical forces in the Gulf.

(3) the growing importance of oil, particularly after the energy crisis and the 1973 oil embargo. Oil in the area ceased to be merely a target for foreign investment. It also became a matter of great strategic importance. Lines of transportation and communication became as important as the oil itself. American efforts to get Iran to fill the vacuum supposedly created by British withdrawal was seen by Iraq as an imperialist attempt to change the Arab character of the Gulf by encouraging non-Arab immigration; to continue to control the area and its natural resources; to isolate and if possible liquidate the Iraqi and South Yemeni regime in order to strike the Arab revolutionary movement inside and outside the

Gulf; and to impose an American solution on the Arab-Israeli conflict.[27]

(4) the bitter Iraqi-Syrian feud which greatly constrained Iraqi efforts to project its influence into the Fertile Crescent area.

Iraq's interest in the Gulf was further enhanced by the growing economic and strategic importance of the Gulf to the Iraqi government. In its frantic search for stability the government was aware that this goal could only be acquired by improving the living standards of its people by establishing a strong army, and by diversifying the sources of revenue by promoting Iraq's vast industrial and agricultural potential. In order to achieve this, the government needed new revenues. The only area in which the government could quickly increase its revenue was its substantial oil wealth (Iraq is today the second-largest producer and its reserves are estimated to be the second-largest within OPEC after Saudi Arabia).

The major goal of the government in 1970 became the nationalisation of oil. In the fifties the Ba'thists had raised the slogan of 'Arab oil belongs to the Arabs' and called for the nationalisation of this resource. IPC's failure to increase production as requested by the government was interpreted as an effort 'to contain the Revolution by delaying tactics to gain its downfall'.[28] Another reason for nationalisation was the reported attempts to overthrow the regime by opponents suspected to have been encouraged by foreign interests.[29] Negotiations with the oil companies failed to yield results. Instead, the oil companies reduced production. . . The government responded by giving the oil companies a two-week ultimatum in May 1972. When IPC refused to negotiate, the government nationalised its northern oilfields. In the meantime, Iraq had fully prepared for this battle by signing a 15-year treaty of friendship with the Soviet Union in April 1972. Confronted by hostility from its neighbours and by a Kurdish rebellion at home, Iraq needed to show that it was not isolated or friendless. It also needed Soviet technical and economic aid for political development and political backing during the nationalisation of the IPC. The government also needed Soviet arms and political support in dealing with the KDP and the ICP. US, Dutch and Gulbenkian oil interests were nationalised during the 1973 Arab-Israeli war because of US and Dutch military and economic aid to Israel. Iraq nationalised the remaining shares of the Basrah Petroleum Company in 1975 when it felt it was able to produce and market all of its oil.

The nationalisation of oil and the increased revenues left a dramatic impact on Iraq's economy and consequently changed its attitude towards the Gulf. These changes were reflected in the following developments: (1) the increase in the construction of oil industry facilities inside Iraq and particularly in the southern area bordering on the Gulf; (2) the construction of new strategic pipelines for the shipping of oil linking the pumping station of Haditha with the new al-Bakr port on the Gulf and with Turkey. Iraq wanted to avoid dependence on the pipelines carrying oil to the ports in Syria and Lebanon. The interruption of Iraqi oil flow in 1956 and 1967 following the Syria-IPC conflict caused great difficulties for the Iraqis. Iraq also faced difficulties with the Syrian government when the Syrians, following the IPC nationalisation, doubled the transit fee and threatened to block oil shipments if Iraq did not pay.[30] (3) Development of Iraq's industrial and commercial capabilities. The Ba'th government built various road and railway networks to link the various parts of Iraq with the Gulf ports. The ports of Um Qasr and Basrah were expanded. The number of industries established near the Gulf increased greatly and included oil and sugar refineries, fish and paper processing factories, cement and chemical fertiliser plants and a floating dry dock. Iraq also began to exploit its rich sulphur, natural gas and phosphate deposits through the Gulf ports. The government also greatly expanded its fishing and merchant and marine capabilities.[31]

Iraq's growing economy greatly increased not only the economic importance of the Gulf, but its strategic importance as well. Iraq is confined to 38 miles of coastline on the Gulf and shallow water ports. Consequently, Iraq's economic security became vulnerable to the increasing power of neighbouring Gulf states, particularly Iran.

Iraq's growing economic and strategic interests in the Gulf led it to put forth its claim to the Kuwaiti islands of Warba and Bubyan which dominate the estuary on which Iraq's new port of Um Qasr is located. Hence the Gulf became a major factor in Iraq's foreign policy for ideological, economic and strategic reasons.

From 1968 to 1975 the Ba'thists were unable to play a major role in expanding their ideology to other Gulf states, in preventing Iran from posing as policeman of the Gulf, and in getting the Arab states to join it in a common Arab stand against Iran. The reasons for this failure were: (1) the preoccupation of the regime in domestic affairs; (2) the absence of strong economic and political ties with the other Arab Gulf states; (3) the suspicion of the conservative Gulf states toward the Ba'th regime because of its conflict with Kuwait and for ideological reasons; (4) the weakness of nationalist and radical movements in the area; (5) the increased military and political aid given to Iran and Saudi Arabia, Iraq's main rivals, by the United States in order to fill the 'vacuum' created by the British withdrawal. During the first two years of its rule, the Ba'th regime sought, without much success, to get a unified Arab position to preserve 'the Arab character of the Gulf' against Iranian claims. When this failed, the Ba'th followed a policy of ideological confrontation, not only against Iran, but against the conservative Arab regimes as well. Since 1975, however, Iraq has embarked on a policy of *rapprochement* and *détente* towards its Gulf neighbours, including Iran. Relations with Iran, however, began to deteriorate rapidly following the first few months of the Iranian Revolution.

Iraq's relations with her Arab neighbours were greatly affected by the return of the Ba'th to power. The Ba'thist advocacy of a radical ideology bent on altering the prevailing configuration of power and committed to radical social and economic change did not appeal to their more conservative neighbours.

The Ba'thists viewed the continued fragmentation of the Arab world, the humiliation of the Arab defeat in the 1967 war, the championing by the West of Iran's hegemonic role in the Gulf and the increased foreign (non-Arab) immigration to the Gulf as parts of a deliberate effort by Western imperialism, Zionism and their regional allies to divide the Arabs and to continue to exploit their oil wealth.[32]

Iraqi leaders called on the Arab Gulf states to adopt a united stand. The appeals were couched in nationalist terms. Iraq, for example, supported the creation of a federation among the seven emirates and Qatar and Bahrain, which it viewed as 'a fence protecting the Gulf from imperialism'.[33] Dynastic, tribal and territorial conflicts prevented the formation of the federation. Iraq also tried, without much success, to check Iran's growing role in the Gulf by co-operating with Saudi Arabia, which was emerging as a major regional power in the Arabian peninsula. Iraq had hoped to build on the strained relations between Iran and Saudi Arabia over the Shah's claims to Bahrain.[34] The Shah had cancelled a visit to Bahrain in March 1968 as a protest against the Saudi reception of the Amir of Bahrain as head of state. The Ba'thist revolution, however, prompted the two monarchies to move closer together. The Shah paid official visits to Saudi Arabia and Kuwait in 1968 and early in 1969 renounced his claims to Bahrain if its people favoured independence.[35]

Iraq also advocated non-interference in the internal affairs of the Gulf states and offered to mediate the dispute between South Yemen and Saudi Arabia without much success.[36]

When Iraq proposed a military agreement with Saudi Arabia in May 1969, during a visit by the Saudi Minister to Baghdad, it was rejected. And when Baghdad failed to get Saudi support in its confrontation with Iran following the latter's abrogation of the Shatt-al-'Arab treaty in 1969, it began to reassess its position towards co-operation with the conservative Gulf states and to look elsewhere for support.

A number of developments occurred in the region in 1970 which

further fuelled Iraqi suspicions and feelings of isolation and encirclement. The most important of these was the visit by US Under-Secretary Elliott Richardson to Iran to meet US Gulf ambassadors to
assess US policy towards the region. Richardson invoked the Nixon
Doctrine of reliance on regional allies to defend regional security,
and hinted that Iran might play the role of the guardian of Gulf
security.[37] The exchange of visits between the Saudi Foreign
Minister's visit to Tehran in April 1970 and the return visit by the
Iranian Foreign Minister amidst talk of a US-backed security
arrangement served to heighten Iraqi suspicions further.[38]

These developments led Iraq to reassess its policies and to look for
support from the Soviet Union. In July 1970 an Iraqi delegation
went to Moscow to seek military aid. The favourable Soviet response
and the increasing co-operation between the two countries led to
further polarisation between Iraq, Saudi Arabia and the other conservative Arab Gulf states. Iraq's backing for the Dhofar Liberation
Front against the Sultan of Oman and its backing of the People's
Democratic Republic of Yemen did not improve relations with Saudi
Arabia. In the meantime, Saudi Arabia, with US encouragement,
began a major arms build-up. In 1970, the Saudi government
announced that it would spend billions of dollars on modernising its
armed forces. Relations between Saudi Arabia and the other Arab
Gulf states and Iraq were further worsened by Iraq advancing her
claim on Kuwait's Warba and Bubyan islands.

In 1974 and 1975, however, Iraq's relations with Saudi Arabia
began to improve. Saudi Arabia was becoming increasingly concerned over Iran's role in the Gulf and her stationing of Iranian
troops in Oman. Saudi Arabia was also interested in reducing Iraq's
reliance on the Soviet Union. Consequently, when Iraqi leaders
sought to improve relations again with the Saudis, they were told
that there were a number of bilateral issues which must be solved
before a common agreement could be attempted. The issues
included the question of frontier delineations, the neutral zone,
tribal migrations, smuggling and other issues. The Iraqis agreed and
visits were exchanged between Crown Prince Fahd and Saddam
Hussein in 1974 and 1975. The atmosphere was further improved by
the Iranian-Iraqi agreement of 1975. Negotiations between the two
countries led to an agreement in the summer of 1975 providing for an
equal division of the neutral zone.

Another agreement was signed in February 1979, during a visit by
then Iraqi RCC member and Minister of the Interior, Izzat Ibrahim
al-Duri to Saudi Arabia to meet with the Saudi counterpart, Prince
Naif, who declared that the agreement would lead to 'positive results
for the security of the two countries. Our viewpoints concerning the
issues discussed were identical.'[39] The agreement is believed to deal

with border control, tribal migrations, smuggling, exchange of criminals and other technical and administrative matters. There were, however, some disagreements between the two countries. One was Iraq's refusal to attend the Riyadh Summit Conference which agreed on sending Arab deterrent forces to Lebanon. The Iraqis were extremely critical of Syria's role in Lebanon and the Middle East conflict. The two countries also disagreed over the question of oil prices.

In 1979–80, Iraq and Saudi Arabia moved even closer to each other, mostly as a result of the Iranian Revolution and their opposition to the Camp David peace agreements. In addition, the Saudis have appeared increasingly to share Iraq's determination to keep big powers out of the Gulf.

On the question of oil, Iraq began moving closer to Saudi Arabia. Iraqi Oil Minister Teyeh Abdul Karim described the relations between 'the first and second producers of oil' as 'excellent'.[40]

The Iraqis appeared to be working towards easing Saudi Arabia out of America's embrace. The Saudis and the Iraqis feel the attempts by the West to acquire military bases and facilities in the Gulf region will invite Russian meddling. At the same time they are both equally opposed to Soviet attempts to play a more active role in the Horn of Africa and in the Gulf and in Afghanistan.[41]

Ba'thist relations with Kuwait have served to isolate them among the other countries in the Arab Gulf and to increase suspicions about their ambitions in the region.[42]

The situation began to deteriorate in 1969 when Kuwait acquiesced under Iraqi pressure to allow Iraqi troops to be stationed on her side of the border. Iraq needed to place her troops on the Kuwaiti side in order to protect the Iraqi port of Um Qasr from possible Iranian attack following the worsening of Iraqi-Iranian relations over the Shatt-al-'Arab dispute.

Iraq's hostile relations with her neighbours and the increased arms build-up in the area, combined with its attempt to expand Um Qasr, show its determination to demonstrate to the other states that it wants to play a role in the region. As a result, Iraq attempted to enforce her garrison at Um Qasr and one month later demanded the Kuwait surrender or lease to her the islands of Warba and Bubyan which straddle the shipping channel to Um Qasr. When the Kuwaitis rejected the Iraqi demand, minor clashes ensued. Following Arab pressures and mediation attempts, Iraq agreed to withdraw its troops, but stated that the matter was one of direct negotiation between the two countries.

With the resolution of the Iraqi-Iranian conflict, Iraqi arguments began to lose weight in Kuwait. The Iraqis admitted that the threat of war was no longer prevalent but continued to hold the view that Um Qasr needed to be defended against future threats. Iraq stated that it would be willing to accept the *status quo* if Kuwait allowed her to use the islands of Warba and one-half of Bubyan. Iraqi Foreign Minister Sa'dun Hammadi said that 'such an arrangement is a reasonable demand in view of Iraq's security needs'.[43]

Kuwait rejected these arguments and minor clashes were reported again in 1976. But while the dispute has not been resolved, the nature of the dispute itself has changed. Professor Abdullah al-Nafisi aptly put it when he stated that the claim to Kuwait itself has ended and it has become

> a conflict over Warba, Bubyan and deep water ports needed to allow Iraq to have an opening to the Gulf. The conflict is now over borders and not over the entity of Kuwait and this is a common problem among the countries of the region.[44]

Subsequent negotiations, however, led to an improvement in relations between the two countries and to the signing of an agreement for joint economic co-operation in 1977 and 1978.

Kuwaiti Crown Prince Saad al Abdullah visited Iraq on 12 May 1980 and met with RCC Vice-Chairman Izzat Ibrahim al-Duri. Both sides agreed to work towards agreements in the fields of water, power links, railway links, land, industrial and agricultural co-operation.[45]

It is, however, Iraq's relations with Iran which have assumed critical importance in Ba'thist Iraq's foreign policy, particularly in the Gulf. Relations between the two countries from 1968 to 1975 were characterised by suspicion and hostility. The quarrel between the two countries was deep and complex. It was one between a conservative, non-Arab monarchy whose ruler was seeking to both preserve his throne and play an important role in the region, particularly in the Gulf, and an Arab nationalist and socialist regime aiming at maintaining itself in power, spreading its ideology to other Arab regions and thwarting Iran's aims in the Gulf. The reasons behind the conflict were not limited to ideological factors, but had historic and territorial causes as well. The roots of the historic trouble date back to the political struggle between the Ottoman and Persian dynasties which manifested itself in clashes over the border. British and Russian mediation helped in reaching a border agreement between the two states in 1937 over Shatt-al-'Arab and the land boundaries. Following Iraq's emergence as an independent state, Iran began to question the agreement, claiming that it was made under pressure when Iran was weak and had no choice but to accept. Border incursions by Iran occurred in the early 1930s but Turkey helped to mediate the problem, which led to a treaty fixing the frontier between the two countries in 1937. The 1937 treaty between Iran and Iraq had given Iraq control over the Shatt — which is formed by the confluence of the Tigris, the Euphrates and the Karun Rivers as they intersect and flow into the Gulf — except for the area near Abadan and Khuramshahr.

Iraq retaliated by claiming the whole eastern bank of the Shatt, since it was primarily inhabited by Arabs and was annexed to Iran in the 1920s by Reza Shah. But as soon as Iraq's relations with Nasser's UAR began to deteriorate, an improvement occurred on the Iraqi-Iranian front. The situation began to worsen again when the Ba'th came to power in 1963 and as talks of a union between Iraq, Syria and Egypt began to surface again. Relations improved slightly when the Aref government exchanged visits between Foreign Ministers of the two countries in 1967 and 1968.

Relations, however, reached a new low following the return of the Ba'th to power. Iran viewed the socialist and Arab nationalist regime which advocated the preservation of 'Gulf Arabism' and the rejection of security arrangements dominated by Iran with hostility and suspicion. The Ba'thist position stressed the existence of a deliberate plan by Zionism and imperialism to fragment the Arab homeland. Iran was seen as a third partner in this coalition. Iraq viewed the Iranian immigration to the Gulf countries as a part of a systematic and well organised plan sponsored by the Shah to alter the Arab character of the Gulf. Ba'thist aspirations ran directly counter to the Shah's goals 'to regain our historic and natural position in the Persian Gulf'.[46]

The conflict between the two countries was fuelled also by Iran's support for the Kurdish rebels led by Mulla Mustafa al-Barzani in its collusion in a conspiracy to overthrow the new regime in February 1969. Minor clashes erupted between the two sides in March 1969. One month later, on 15 April, Iraq decided to enforce its territorial right in Shatt-al-'Arab under the 1937 treaty which had been violated by Iran in previous years and required Iranian ships to pay entry tolls to the Iraqi port authority. Iran refused and began to send naval units to accompany its ships. On 19 April 1969 Iran unilaterally abrogated the treaty, claiming that it had been imposed on Iran by the British.

Iraq's inability to take effective action was a source of humiliation for the regime. Efforts at negotiation by King Hussein failed. Iraq, however, retaliated by expelling thousands of Iranians living in Iraq, by boycotting Iranian goods, and by giving asylum to leftist and religious opponents of the Shah. In addition, support was given to groups calling for the liberation of Arabistan and Baluchistan.

Iraqi-Iranian hostilities were also influenced by the following factors:

(1) Iraq's efforts to strengthen its ties to Arab nationalist and radical forces in the Gulf area;

(2) the Iranian claim to Bahrain and its occupation of the two Tumb and Abu Musa Islands belonging to the newly formed United Arab Emirates in November 1971 (Iraq was the only Arab country to break relations with Tehran over this issue);

(3) Iran's intervention in Oman against the Dhofar Liberation Front;

(4) Iranian-supported *coup* attempts against Iraqis;

(5) Iranian-sponsored efforts to isolate Iraq among the conservative Arab governments fearful of Iraq's ideology and aspirations.

Isolated and feared by her neighbours, Iraq, from 1970 until 1972, took a number of initiatives aimed at increasing the security of the regime and at widening its support at home and abroad. These actions included the following.

(1) The 11 March 1970 Manifesto offering autonomy to the Kurds and a peaceful solution to the costly Kurdish problems. Iraq's Kurds had waged a bitter ten-year struggle for autonomy against Iraq. For ideological as well as pragmatic reasons, the government offered the Kurds a limited form of self-rule guaranteeing Kurdish cultural and national rights within an autonomous Kurdish region. Despite its limitations this offer conceded more to the Kurds than any other Iraqi or Middle Eastern government has been willing to offer. This measure allowed the government to get wider backing from Arabs and Kurds as well as from the Soviet Union, which had been urging a negotiated settlement of this thorny problem.

(2) Internally, the Iraqi government solidified its position following the failure of several attempted *coups*. Internal rivalries among the Ba'th leaders led to the demotion or ouster of leading Ba'thist military figures and concentrated power in the hands of the civilian wing of the party led by Saddam Hussein and backed by then President General Ahmed Hassan al-Bakr.

(3) The proclamation of the National Action Charter in 1971 which brought the IPC and the KDP as well as independent figures to participate in the political process along with the Ba'th Party.

(4) The conclusion of the fifteen-year treaty of friendship between the Soviet Union and Iraq, and the consolidation of its ties with the socialist bloc.

(5) IPC was nationalised.

As the government solidified its control within the Arab areas of Iraq and as the chances of a successful *coup* decreased, the possibility of creating economic, social and political prerequisites for stable government increased. The rise in oil income became an additional factor in helping the government achieve stability, modernise its army and increase its leverage in the Arab arena. These developments, which were seen as major gains for the regime, were viewed with increasing alarm by Iran, Israel and the United States.

Expecting hostilities from each other, Iran and Iraq searched for and responded to opportunities to act against each other. For Iran, the Kurdish question offered a real opportunity to destabilise or overthrow the government. The US secretly offered military and economic aid to Barzani in the summer of 1972, and Israel and Iran increased their aid. Encouraged by promises of aid from three countries, the Kurdish leader Mulla Mustafa al-Barzani escalated his demands. He insisted that the Kurdish region include Kirkuk and its rich oil-wells and that the Kurds have the authority to maintain their own army and to conduct their own foreign affairs. The Iraqi government, at times backed by the Soviets, made several attempts to reach an agreement with Barzani, but did not threaten Iraq's sovereignty. When these efforts failed, Iraq, on 11 March 1974, unilaterally implemented the 11 March Manifesto in the Kurdish areas under its control. Heavy fighting between the Iraqi Army and the Kurdish rebels took place throughout 1974 and early 1975. The Iraqi armed forces, better trained and better equipped, were able to make costly but steady advances against the rebels. The Iraqi Army was able to hold its ground during the winter and did not retreat as in previous campaigns. Iraqi forces reached the outskirts of Galala, the headquarters of the Kurdish leadership. Iran, which had escalated its aid to the Kurdish forces, was confronted with the choice of increasing the military aid, possibly permitting the Kurds to hold for one more year, or doing nothing and allowing the Iraqis to win. Such a development would have led to political and military realities not favourable to Iran or would have forced her to escalate her intervention, thus becoming involved in direct or indirect war with Iraq. One Iraqi Ba'th leader told this writer in 1976 that Iraq would have considered such an escalation a *cassus belli* and a direct and open war between the two countries would have been triggered, with serious consequences for both themselves and the world.

An Iraqi-Iranian war would have meant, in addition to the heavy human and material losses for both sides, the shelling of each other's oil-wells. In a speech in February 1975 at the Baghdad conference of the Arab Popular Organization held in solidarity with Iraq, Saddam Hussein hinted at this when he declared that oil is a very flammable matter. A war between the two countries would have meant a serious crisis for the industrialised countries. The conflict was also becoming costly to both sides.[47]

The growing seriousness of this situation led to mediation efforts by King Hussein, President Sadat and Algerian President Boumedienne. The mediation efforts succeeded and on 6 March 1975 Saddam Hussein and the Shah signed an agreement which netted gains for the two sides. For Iran, the agreement meant Iraq's acceptance of the demands that the boundaries between the two countries and Shatt-al-'Arab run along the thalweg line and ending the Iraqi aid to Iranian dissidents and Arab and Baluchi secessionists. For Iraq the agreement meant the end of the Kurdish rebellion and the agreement upheld the *status quo* concerning the land frontiers. Furthermore, both sides avoided any disruption of oil production and established a strong front within OPEC calling for increasingly higher prices.

The agreement between the two sides was of major importance in the Gulf area, since they both pledged to work for normalised relations among the Gulf countries. The Iraqi-Iranian *rapprochement* and the resolution of the Saudi-Iraqi border problems served to minimise tensions among the Gulf states and to create a more conducive atmosphere for communication and co-operation between Iraq and her neighbours. Nevertheless, the Gulf states were still unable to reach an agreement on a common decision towards Gulf security.

Following the Algiers Agreement, Iraq followed a friendlier but nevertheless cautious policy toward the Shah's Iran. Saddam Hussein declared in 1976 that 'Iranian-Iraqi *rapprochement* has permitted discussions for establishing a collective Gulf security agreement',[48] but that the spirit of the accord means that Iran 'must respect the national sovereignty of all Arab countries'.[49]

Following the ouster of the Shah, Iraqi leaders welcomed the statements issued by Iranian Prime Minister Shahpur Bakhtiar concerning the declaration that Iran will no longer play the role of Gulf policeman. Foreign Minister Hammadi praised this stand as a 'positive step toward the establishment of cordial relations toward the Arab Gulf states'.[50]

Iraqi leaders continued to express hopes for co-operation with Iran after the fall of Bakhtiar's government. On 13 February 1979 Iraq sent a memorandum to the new Prime Minister Mahdi Bazargan stressing Iraq's desire to establish 'the strongest fraternal relations on the basis of respect and non-interference in domestic affairs'.[51] It indicated Iraq's 'special view' of relations with Turkey and Iran, who are 'linked to the Arabs by historic and religious ties', and expressed sympathy and support for the struggle of the Iranian people for 'freedom and progress'.

Similar views were echoed by Saddam Hussein who told an Iraqi magazine:

we are keen on cooperation with Iran in a way that will ensure the interests and security of the people in the area as well as preserve the historic ties based on non-interference and respect for national sovereignty. . . . Any system which does not side with our enemy, respects our independence and whose oil policy is consistent with the interest of our two peoples will certainly command our respect and appreciation.[52]

Iraqi hopes for better relations did not materialise. Deep conflicts of national interest exist between the two countries regardless of the nature of the regime in power. This conflict is further sharpened by ideological antagonism between a secular, nationalist (pan-Arab) regime in Baghdad and a theocratic, internationalist (pan-Islamic) regime in Tehran.

The bad blood between the leaders of the two countries may have started with Iraq's expulsion of Iranian leader Ayatollah Khomeini after he began to escalate his activities against the regime of the Shah in the spring of 1978. In accordance with the Algiers Agreement, Iraq asked Khomeini to cease his activities or leave the country after Iranian protests.[53] The unfolding events in Iran coincided with President Sadat's US-backed efforts to reach accommodations with Israel, and consequently with Iraqi attempts to unify Arab ranks in opposition to these policies. Iraq wanted to avoid re-opening the conflict with Iran at a time when it was by no means certain that the Shah's regime was about to collapse. Khomeini and his followers interpreted this move as a hostile act against their revolution and harboured resentment against the Iraqi leadership and believed that 'every opponent to the Imam must be punished'.[54] Iraqi Deputy Prime Minister Tariq Aziz charged that 'leading Iranian figures began attacking Iraq since the first day [of the Iranian Revolution]'.[55] The first major Iranian propaganda campaign, however, did not start until June 1979. It followed repressive measures against Iranian Arabs demanding cultural and administrative rights in Khuzestan in May 1979 and the strafing by Iraqi planes of two Iranian border villages.[56] The organ of the Islamic Revolutionary Party in Tehran charged that Iraqi leaders 'seem to think they can prevent their suppressed people from encountering Islamic ideology and open a path for their [Soviet] masters to warm water ports in the Persian Gulf'.[57] Admiral Ahmad Madani, the governor of Iran's oil-producing Khuzestan province, which originally was populated exclusively by Arabs, and which the Iraqis call Arabistan, accused Iraqi leader Saddam Hussein of receiving money 'from the ex-shah's agents and [running] arms into Iran'.[58] Foreign observers in Tehran saw this campaign as an attempt to divert attention from Iran. The Iraqi Ba'th Party organ *Al-Thawrah* responded in a series of articles dealing with Iraqi-Iranian relations. The paper warned the Iranian leaders 'as we did in 1969: Do not play a dirty game with Iraq' and expressed Iraq's 'ideological and political sympathies with the Arab people of Arabistan'.[59]

Relations deteriorated rapidly in late 1979 and early 1980. In March 1980 Iran unilaterally downgraded its diplomatic ties to the chargé d'affaires level, withdrew its ambassador, and requested Iraq to do the same. The situation reached a new level of threats and counter-threats following the attempted assassination of Deputy Prime Minister Tariq Aziz on 1 April by an Iraqi of Iranian origin. Pars news agency claimed at first the attack was carried out by an Iranian group, but later on Radio Tehran attributed it to the Iraqi Muslim Mujahidin, a previously unknown organisation.[60] Three days later, bombs were thrown at the funeral procession of some of the students who had died in the earlier attack. The Iraqis blamed the attack on resident members of the Iranian community and began expelling thousands of them.[61] The rapid deterioration of relations led many observers to expect the eruption of war between the two countries.

The conflict between these two neighbours is based on ideological, political and territorial issues.

Ideologically, the two countries are at opposite ends of the spectrum. Iraq is ruled by a secular nationalist and socialist regime. Hussein said in a speech in 1977 that Ba'thists, while opposing atheism, also oppose the 'use of religion for political purposes' and the adoption by the state of religious policies in dealing with secular affairs because it will only lead 'to sectarian and religious conflicts and result in national diversion and disunity'.[62] Iran, on the other hand, is run by a theocratic regime whose leaders insist on implementing and interpreting the Shari'a as the supreme law of the land. They also make no attempt to hide their intention of exporting their Islamic ideology to other countries.[63]

Furthermore, Iraq did not trust Iranian talk about exporting the revolution, since this could not occur except through interference in the ethno-sectarian structure of their society. Khomeini's long stay in Iraq and his close association with some of the Shi'ite religious leaders might have encouraged some of these leaders to emulate his example with direct or indirect Iranian aid. An Iraqi spokesman has recently charged that Iran has 'certain groups operating in Iraq on behalf of al-Da'wah party which receives orders from Khomeini. . . The Iraqi communists have been collaborating with these groups.'[64] Iranian leaders have explicitly called on Iraq's Shi'ite community to overthrow the Iraqi regime.[65] Other Iranian leaders, including Ayatollah Khomeini, Iranian President Bani Sadr and Iranian Foreign Minister Ghotzbadeh, have accused the Iraqi leaders of being 'evil and atheist' and called for a 'holy war' to overthrow the regime.[66]

Attacks by Iranian leaders on Arab nationalism have added fuel to the fire. Sadr has accused Arab nationalism of containing 'Zionist but not Islamic characteristics'.[67] Following his becoming President, Bani Sadr told a French correspondent, 'we are the true heirs of liberating Islam, not this wretched Saddam Hussein who deceives the public when he portrays himself as a good Muslim. Ba'thist ideology is an amalgamation of Nazi, Fascist, and Marxist doctrines which his people abhor.'[68]

The Iraqis in turn accuse Khomeini of being a 'turbaned Shah' and of using Islamic slogans to cover 'Persian racist' designs on the Gulf countries and of attempting to avenge the battle of Qadisiyya, when a small Arab army defeated the larger Sassanid Persian army in 637 AD.

The territorial dispute focuses on the old dispute between the two countries. President Saddam Hussein told Iranian Foreign Minister Ibrahim Yazdi during a meeting at the Havana non-aligned summit conference in autumn 1979 that normal relations between the two countries are dependent on: (1) putting an end to the 'unjustifiable vilification and transgressions' against Iraq; (2) revision of the agreement on Shatt-al-'Arab which 'was concluded under special circumstance in 1975 in which you took a part of Shatt-al-'Arab that must be returned to Iraq'; (3) return of the Tumbs and Abu Musa islands seized by Iran in 1971 because 'they are Arab and must be returned to their owners'; (4) 'the granting of national rights to Iran's Arab Kurdish and Baluchi minorities'.[69]

Iraq has accused Iran of supporting Communist and Kurdish opponents of the regime and of financing and arming al-Da'wah Islamic Party to commit acts of sabotage and assassinations in Iraq.

Iran in turn has accused Iraq of supporting Kurdish, Arab and anti-regime Persian groups in Iran. In addition, both sides appear to be locked in a dispute over oil-wells in Ilam on the Iraqi-Iranian border.[70] Iran has also accused Iraq of sabotaging its oil production.

Despite the talk of an imminent Iranian-Iraqi military confrontation and of continued border clashes, it is unlikely that a major war will erupt between the two sides as long as both sides have the ability to attack each other's oil-wells. The vulnerability of oil-wells of both sides continues to deter a major confrontation. It is expected, however, that both sides will continue to support internal opposition forces and exploit each other's internal problems. Nevertheless, it is more than likely that controlled border clashes between the two sides will continue.

Iraq's perception of Gulf security remains the same even after the Iranian Revolution. This perception could be summarised as follows.

(1) Iraq is a Gulf country and needs the Gulf for exports as well as imports. Consequently Iraq insists on freedom of navigation in the Straits of Hormuz and would oppose any attempts by foreign powers to control this strategic area.[71]

(2) Iraq calls for co-operation among the Arab Gulf states on the basis of the Arab national interest. And despite some doubts about Iraq's ultimate goals by some of the conservative Arab Gulf states because of its ideology and its dispute with Kuwait, the Ba'ath regime positions have been characterised by flexibility and willingness to develop cordial relations with all Arab countries. President Hussein has said that Iraq would 'fight to defend the [Arab] people and land, against the foreigner regardless of the nature of the [Arab] regime and the rulers, and regardless of the kind of relations we have with this or that foreigner'.[72]

(3) Iraq has constantly rejected regional military pacts. Iraq's Foreign Minister Sa'dun Hammadi declared Iraq's opposition to such arrangements in April 1975. Iraq has recently opposed Omani proposals for a Gulf security pact.

(4) Iraq has constantly favoured bilateral agreement among the countries of the region. This position has been manifested in Iraq's agreements with Iran, Saudi Arabia and Kuwait.

(5) Iraq has favoured joint co-operation among the Arab Gulf states through various commercial and economic projects. This became apparent following the 1975 Muscat summit conference.

(6) Iraq has favoured the eradication of foreign bases in the region, be they Western- or Soviet-sponsored. A high-ranking Iraqi official told this writer in April 1979 that

Iraq is opposed to the establishment of American bases in Masira and Bahrain, which are disguised as facilities. We are also opposed to the establishment of any naval land bases in the Gulf or Red Sea. We believe foreign bases must be liquidated regardless of the country they represent.

Iraq's Arab and regional policy has recently been articulated further in a Charter of National Principles announced by Iraqi President Hussein on the anniversary of the Ba'thist revolution of 8 February 1963. In introducing the charter he said that Iraq 'should work with our Arab brothers on any level agreed upon between us and them so as to prevent the partitioning of the Arab homeland into shares among the superpowers'. The Charter of Principles, which was supported by the majority of the Arab states, is believed to have emerged out of Iraqi leaders' fears for regional security and stability. Iraqi leaders believe that the Tehran hostage affair gave the USSR the chance to intervene in Afghanistan and that the US in turn is taking advantage of the situation.[73] The Iraqis feared that this dangerous situation might lead the 'two superpowers to a new Yalta by which they will redivide the world'.[74]

The charter contained the following points: (1) the banning of arms of foreign military presence in the Arab world; (2) the rejection of the use of force as a means of settling Arab conflicts; (3) banning the use of force as a means of settling disputes with neighbouring countries except in self-defence; (4) solidarity with Arab states against all foreign aggression; (5) respecting international laws and customs concerning the use of international waters and air space; (6) commitment to non-alignment and neutrality in international conflicts; (7) development and strengthening of a common base to develop Arab economies; (8) Iraqi commitments to these principles and its willingness to open a dialogue concerning them.[75]

While some of the principles of this charter are simply an extension of or elaborations on Iraq's stated policies, it is nevertheless the first clear attempt to formulate a common Arab strategy and to offer the Arabs a third way in opposition to tutelage to the superpowers, and to guide Arab relations with the superpowers and with their neighbours.

In its relations with the United States Iraq has consistently been influenced by the Palestinian question, which occupies a central place in Ba'thist ideology, and US support for Israel. Israel is seen as a colonial settler state created by the West to keep the Arabs divided. The Ba'thists see relations between the US and Israel as organically linked. US support for Israel is seen as a manifestation of US aggressiveness and hostility to the Arabs. Iraqi Ba'thists have opposed the peaceful settlement plans espoused by the US and accepted by some Arab states. The convergence of Iranian, Israeli and US interests in encouraging and backing the Kurdish rebellion and in attempting to destabilise and isolate Iraq adversely affected US-Iraqi relations. Iraq, which broke diplomatic relations with the US during the 1967 war has rejected repeated American attempts at resuming diplomatic relations. In a statement to a group of Arab students in 1974, Saddam Hussein discussed the question of resuming ties by saying:

> The breaking of diplomatic relations is a stand, but not a permanent stand, a position but not a permanent position. It is a stand in which one country expresses its anger over a certain issue in its

relations with another country. This position will change when the circumstances change and for basic political reasons. They won't change just because Kissinger might come over and kiss us on this cheek and this cheek. We resumed diplomatic relations with Britain and Germany when we saw that it was in our [Arab] national interests to neutralize Europe.[76]

In February 1979 Hussein revealed that the US had been sending mediators to relay its interest in normalising relations. 'Our unambiguous answer', he pointed out, 'is that our policy is connected to the national interest of the Arab nation and those of Iraq. Once normalization of relations can serve these interests we will not need mediators.'[77]

One year later, and in the wake of the hostage crisis in Iran, rumours began to surface in various publications about a secret attempt made by US national security adviser Zbigniew Brezinski to improve relations with Iraq.[78] On 27 March, Saddam Hussein told an Arab conference in Baghdad that the US had been making 'monthly or at least yearly attempts' during the past five years to restore relations with Iraq, but that his country will 'continue to view the US as an enemy of the Arabs as long as Israel, with US backing, continues to occupy Arab lands'.[79]

This response, however, did not deter two high US officials from issuing new calls for normalising relations. Under-Secretary of State David Newsom declared in a speech on 11 April in Washington that the US is prepared to 'resume diplomatic relations with Iraq at any time. Our approaches to Iraq, however, have not met with success.'

Three days later, Brezinski made a similar appeal. He told the *McNeil-Lehrer Report*:

It's been our position for quite some time that we neither deplore nor fear the Arabic renaissance. The Arab world has come alive again, after several centuries of dormancy. We desire good relations with all Arab countries. We see no fundamental incompatibility of interests between the United States and Iraq. We feel that Iraq desires to be independent, that Iraq wishes a secure Persian Gulf, and we do not feel that American-Iraq relations need to be frozen in antagonism. . .we do not wish to continue the anomalous state of US-Iraq relations, though we recognize that the road towards improvement is a long one.[80]

In another gesture the US approved of the sale of American engines to be used in warships sold by Italy to Iraq.[81] These moves are not likely, however, to lead to a resumption of diplomatic relations.

In May Iraqi Deputy Premier Na'im Haddad responded to a question on the state of Iraqi-American relations by saying that 'US imperialism was and still is the basic enemy of the Arab nation'.[82] He accused the US of continuing to support Israel, of plundering Arab oil, and intensifying its military presence in the Gulf region and the Red Sea. He also said that 'Iraq did not see any change in US policy, but an intensification of its hostility to the Arab nation through continuing its Camp David foul plot. . .US imperialism was and still is the basic enemy of the Arab nation.'

But while political relations with the US remain strained, economic ties have improved greatly since 1973. 'The US has a friend and an enemy in its relation with Iraq. The enemy is its backing for Israel, and the friend is US technology', the Director of the Minister of Planning told this writer in 1976.

Iraq appears to have a pragmatic approach to development. Iraqi officials have said that there is room for expanding trade relations with the US.[83] American companies have participated in various industrial and construction projects. Co-operation is expected to continue in the areas of irrigation, agriculture, capital goods and technology.

Iraq's relations with the Soviet Union were substantially improved and consolidated as a result of its disenchantment with US policy. This relationship reached its zenith when Iraq concluded a twenty-year treaty of friendship and co-operation with the Soviet Union in 1972. Iraq's feeling of isolation and encirclement was reinforced by her disputes with Iran, Kuwait and Syria and its perception of external threats to the regime as manifested by foreign-supported *coup* attempts and by aid to the Kurdish rebellion.

Iraq has also needed the Soviet Union for continued supplies of modern weapons and substantial (but declining) commercial trade, economic co-operation and technology. Iraq further relied on the Soviet Union for help in securing co-operation from the Iraqi Communist Party and the Kurdish Democratic Party in 1971–3. Relations between the two countries, however, have been marred by traditional and deep-seated hostility between Ba'th and Communist ideology. These differences have not disappeared despite participation by the ICP in the National Front, as the conflict between the Ba'th and the ICP show.

Disagreements between the two focus on a number of issues. The Soviets sold Iraqi oil to third parties for three times the cost they paid to Iraq. Soviet failure to respond to Iraq's urgent appeals for weapons and ammunition during the last months of the Kurdish rebellion severely strained ties between the two countries and contributed to Iraq's arms shopping in the West.[84]

The real breakdown in Soviet-Iraqi ties and in the Ba'th-ICP coalition emerged in the spring of 1978 when Iraqis arrested and executed a number of Iraqi Communists for establishing cells in the armed forces, an act prohibited to non-Ba'thists by agreement with the KDP and ICP. The *coup* in Afghanistan is reported to have alarmed the Iraqis and led the army to check on local Communists. They discovered that the ICP has infiltrated the miltary.[85]

Iraq also differed with the Soviets over their military aid to Ethiopia in its fight against Eritrean guerrillas. Iraq's Information Minister criticised Soviet policy on Eritrea, and added that Iraq's position on the Middle East conflict differed from that of the Soviet Union. Soviet policies in Afghanistan and Ethiopia greatly alarmed the Iraqis and raised serious questions about Soviet intentions. On 9 July Saddam Hussein told *Newsweek* magazine that the 'Soviet Union will not be satisfied until the entire world becomes Communist'. He also warned that the execution of 21 Communists should be viewed as a warning against outside interference.

A slight thaw in relations followed the Camp David accords. On 17 October 1978 Saddam Hussein spoke in a friendlier tone about the Soviets:

> The Soviets are our best friends. The USSR always sides with the Arabs. We act accordingly. But we should not fall in love with the Soviet Union if it renounces us. Well, this has never happened, even though our views differ, for example on Eritrea's conflict with Ethiopia.[86]

In December 1978 Hussein and some of his top aides visited the Soviet Union and signed two new economic and technical co-operation agreements. In a joint communiqué the two sides expressed opposition to the Camp David agreements, and the Soviets expressed their willingness to strengthen Iraq's defences.

The increased oil revenues have lessened tremendously Iraq's dependence on the Soviets for arms and economic and technological aid. Since 1975 Iraq has made an attempt to diversify its purchases of Western arms, goods and technology. This policy is not likely to make the Soviet leaders happy with Iraq's policies.

In an interview in January 1979 Iraqi Foreign Minister Hamadi said that Soviet relations are 'subject to the principles of independence and friendship'. He added that Iraq 'practices and not only preaches' an independent and non-aligned foreign policy.

> We are linked to the Soviet Union through ties of friendship. The practical translation of this is that we should cooperate and participate in matters in which we have common interests. Our relations do not become hostile because of matters we disagree upon.

This is what the policy of independence and friendship means. The best way to describe our relations with the Soviet Union is to say that our relations follow an upward but zigzagged line.[87]

In December 1979 Iraqi RCC member Tariq Aziz expressed Iraq's fears of superpower ambitions by telling an American journalist: 'We are concerned by political or military action in the region by superpowers. We believe all big powers to be expansionist.'[88]

Iraq joined the Islamic summit conference at Islamabad in January 1980 which condemned the Soviet invasion of Afghanistan. The Ba'th Party has charged that the Soviet intervention 'represents a violation of Afghanistan's sovereignty', and the 'right of peoples to self-determination'.[89]

Iraq believes that this Soviet action invites US adventurism. Tariq Aziz told a Turkish newspaper, *Tercuman*, on 7 March:

> We vehemently condemn Soviet intervention in Afghanistan. This intervention is totally unjustifiable. We openly express our disapproval and demand Soviet withdrawal. The biggest attraction for the superpowers to this region is oil wealth. It is high time that the states possessing this wealth form their defense system in order to protect this wealth. Threats connected with oil are creating unrest in the area. All superpowers should stop threatening the Gulf and the oil-producing Gulf states.

New attempts have been made to improve relations. A Soviet delegation visited Iraq early in April to celebrate the signing of the Soviet-Iraqi treaty of friendship. During the latter part of the month Iraq signed an economic agreement to provide for the expansion of cooperation in the fields of oil, industry, agriculture and irrigation.[90]

RCC member Na'im Haddad said that his country still considered the Soviet Union as

> a friend and was linked to it by a treaty of friendship and cooperation. However, through this friendship we always stress the principle of balanced relations and mutual respect for sovereignty and non-interference in the internal affairs of the two countries.[91]

In short, Iraq cannot be viewed as a satellite of the Soviet Union, and despite friendly relations between the two, there is nothing permanent or inevitable in their ties, but they will depend on Iraq's perception of its regional and pan-Arab interests.

The Iraqi policy of *rapprochement* which prevailed among the Gulf countries since the Algiers agreement has been based on the principles of non-interference in the domestic affairs of each other.

In regard to security Iraq has defined it in terms of self-reliance and the exclusion of any superpower role in the region. Iraq's increased oil revenues, which are expected to reach $30 billion in 1980, have allowed the government to modernise its armed forces. Iraq has nearly doubled the strength of its air force since 1973. It has signed a $1 billion arms deal with the Soviets to buy Soviet fighters and bombers, including MIG 23s, Sukhoi 20s and Tupolov 22s, as well as modern tanks and missiles. Iraq has also sought to diversify its forces by purchasing tanks, missiles, French Mirages, patrol boats, personnel carriers and Gazelle helicopters at about $1 billion.[92]

Iraq has an armed force of about 190,000 men. It has in its arsenal 2,600 Soviet tanks, of which 1,000 are Soviet T62; 2,120 pieces of artillery, and assorted missiles. Iraq also has an air force of 30,000 men and a navy of 4,000, and is reported to have firmed up a $2 billion deal with a number of Italian naval and marine supply firms for warships and complete outfitting of naval bases and facilities, in a bid to become the naval power in the region.[93]

In addition, Iraq's popular army, which is organised of party members and supporters who are trained to use light and heavy weapons, is reported to reach 225,000 men and women.[94] Iraq is reported to be the only Arab country attempting to develop nuclear capacity, with the help of Italy and France, but it has signed the nuclear non-proliferation treaty.[95]

Internally, the economy is in high gear. Multi-million dollar projects are under way in development schemes and industrial and agricultural projects. This year's budget is expected to reach 14 billion Iraqi dinars.[96] The ordinary Iraqi is already beginning to share in the nation's wealth. The government finances free education and provides medical care.[97] United Nations statistics show that about one-third of the population is in school or university. Secondary school students have increased by 15.6 per cent. Vocational school enrolments have increased by 10 per cent. The government started a major campaign in 1979 to eradicate illiteracy.

Non-alignment to Iraq means alignment with those countries which seek to avoid superpower entanglement. Iraq has also expanded its trade, financial and oil transactions with France, Brazil, India, Spain and African countries which it considers friends, and has also made a major bid to improve relations with Europe since they see that it is in the interest of non-aligned countries to have a strong and independent Europe as an alternative to reliance on the superpowers.

Strengthening Iraq's military, economic, cultural and technical ties with Western Europe is a cornerstone of Iraq's policy. The acceleration of the trend in late 1979 and early 1980 appears to be linked to Iraq's bid for military leadership in the Gulf and its attempt to counter the growth of US and Soviet influence in the region.

Sadun Hammadi told a press conference in Bonn that the Arab states were ready to discuss how to guarantee future oil supplies to the EEC countries. He pointed out that economic co-operation was linked to political considerations. European countries must support the ending of Israeli occupation of Arab lands and oppose super-power hegemony.[98]

Iraq has also given more economic aid proportionately to developing countries than any other OPEC country, according to Oil Minister Abd al-Karim.[99] He also said that Iraq has provided $1.2 billion in grants and low-interest loans to four countries. He added that Iraq broke new ground by providing $254 million to some twenty underdeveloped countries to demonstrate his country's concern for the world's poorest nations.

Such actions fit in well with Iraq's pan-Arab policy and its desire to keep the Gulf area free of superpower control, be it Soviet or American. As a result of Iraq's increased military strength and its flexibility in its relations with its Gulf neighbours, it began to emerge out of isolation and to become a credible regional power in 1978. This trend has been strengthened greatly by the growing turmoil in Iran following the overthrow of the Shah's regime, which had been perceived outside the region as a bastion of stability and as a guardian of Gulf security.

Iraq's emergence as a key player in Middle East and Gulf politics was manifested in a number of events.

(1) Iraq's successful call for the convening of an Arab summit conference in Baghdad in the autumn of 1978 to reach an agreement on a minimum common Arab stand against the Camp David agreement and against the peaceful settlement advocated by the United States. The attendance of Saudi Arabia and other conservative Arab states reveals the changing political circumstances in the region and the growing acceptance of Iraq's role. This was manifested clearly during the Arab Foreign Ministers' conference held in Baghdad following the signing of the Egyptian-Israeli peace treaty and which led to the adoption of certain measures against Egypt. The hesitancy of some to implement these measures was ended when Iraq, Syria, the PLO and Libya threatened to take tough measures against any country that continued to give financial aid to Egypt.

(2) The signing of an agreement of co-operation in internal security matters, including border, technical and administrative issues between Saudi Arabia and Iraq in February 1979.

(3) The joint Iraqi-Syrian efforts to bring a prompt halt to the conflict between North and South Yemen in March 1979.

(4) The selection of Saddam Hussein as the new head of the non-

alignment movement to replace Fidel Castro in 1982. Since his assumption of office in July 1978, Husain has undertaken a major effort to expand economic and cultural ties with African and Latin American countries. Many Third World leaders have visited Baghdad in recent months.

(5) The announcement of a 'Charter of Principles' which is seen by Hussein as an attempt 'to establish a new type of Arab relations, now that the Arabs know that no one can protect them and that US protection is mere talk'.[100] But despite the growing concern about Soviet actions and intentions in the region the Iraqis do not appear to be ready to end their treaty of friendship with the Soviets. The reason for this is that by over-reaching they might play into Washington's hands. They are greatly concerned that the US will use the prospect of Gulf instability and Soviet actions in Afghanistan as a pretext for intervening to protect their oil supplies.[101]

(6) The implementation of long-delayed plans to hold Iraq's first elections since the 1958 revolution as a part of the Ba'thist concern for internal reconciliation and democratisation. The elections are for a legislative assembly for Iraq and a separate legislative council for the Kurdistan region. Hussein has described these measures as a 'model for completing and deepening democratic practices and institutions'.[102] Candidacy is open to all Iraqis over 25 years of age except those who oppose the principles of the Ba'th Party. The RCC is expected to have a veto power over the decisions of the assembly.

The question about Iraq's future role in the region is one of great importance in the wake of the Egyptian-Israeli agreement and the continuing convulsion in Iran. Saudi Arabia, which in the early seventies began to play a leading role in Arab affairs, has been forced, following the revolution in Iran, to keep some distance from the United States and to oppose the peace treaty. Its balancing role between Cairo, Damascus and Baghdad has altered and continues to alter. Its manoeuvrability has been limited. It is possible that Iraq will step in to fill the power gap and to establish its own influence in the Gulf. It is unlikely, however, that Iraq will change its policy of *détente* with its neighbours during the next few years, unless these countries follow a policy similar to President Sadat or attempt to interfere in Iraq's internal affairs. In this event, it is likely that Iraq will work to isolate or bring down these governments.

Otherwise, Iraq is likely to continue on its present course of non-interference in the internal affairs of other states in the Gulf. If Iraq attempts to fill the gap created by the absence of Egypt and Iran, it is apt to damage its relations with Saudi Arabia. These relations, for political as well as economic reasons, are too important to damage for a minor edge over Saudi Arabia. If Iraq tries to reassert itself in a menacing manner, it will again become isolated in the Gulf. Iraqi leaders are anxious not to raise the suspicions of their more conservative neighbours, now that these suspicions have decreased in the past few years.

The Iraqi leadership appears to have larger ambitions. Ba'thist ideology could play a more prominent role as an energiser, or catalyst, among Arab and Third World nations. Iraq also has the financial resources and the agricultural and the industrial potential to become a leader of the non-aligned movement. Furthermore, the peace treaty between Egypt and Israel appears to have led to greater cohesion among its Arab opponents. Iraq, Syria and Saudi Arabia will go through a period in which they will search for a proper balance of exercising regional influence. The failure of Syrian-Iraqi attempts at uniting the two countries has been a serious set back for Arab unity schemes. Nevertheless Iraq continues to provide the $520 million subsidy to Syria as well as aid to Jordan and the PLO in accord with the Baghdad summit conference. Relations with Jordan appear to be excellent.

In the Gulf and Arab arena Iraqi ideology will continue to have appeal as long as it continues to emphasise keeping the superpowers out of the area and the advancement of pan-Arab goals. Iraq has emerged as the major power in the Gulf following the overthrow of the Shah. The immobilisation of Iran, as a result of the revolution there and the continuing turmoil, as well as the announcements of the new Iranian government that it will not play the role of the policeman in the Gulf, has and will continue to enhance Iraq's Gulf position.

In the wake of the Iranian Revolution, some experts have forecast growing troubles for Iraq as a result of the Islamic revolution and its possible spread. Such a prognosis, however, appears highly unlikely. The Iraqi regime is different from that of Iran for the following reasons:

(1) Iraq is led by a well disciplined and well organised political party with ideological content whose numbers and partisans reach close to a million, and whose security apparatus is well run and ready to take immediate action against any opponent of the regime;

(2) the Iraqi regime has dealt firmly with corruption at all levels, including high government officials;

(3) Iraq has done a better job than most oil-rich countries of spreading the wealth to its people and raising their living standards.

These actions have helped give the population increased confidence in the regime. Pockets of opposition against the regime exist. A loose alliance 'to end Ba'th rule' appears to have been made between the ICP, Kurdish factions led by Jalal Talibani and Mas'ud Barzani, and religious fundamentalists belonging to al-Da'wah Party.[103] It is unlikely, however, that these groups will pose a serious threat to the regime. During the last thirty years, the Ba'th Party has embedded itself deeply among various sectors of the Iraqi population. The most serious threats to the regime have in fact come from within Ba'thist ranks. It is true that the ICP also has strong roots in Iraq, but the Ba'th has been able to implement many of the programmes advocated by the ICP. Inter-party factionalism and government purges have made an impact on the party's growth and effectiveness. Iraq's granting of a limited autonomy to the Kurds, its tough security measures and the huge development schemes taking place in Iraqi Kurdistan have gone a long way towards stabilising the Kurdish region. Iraq has also been able to take advantage of Iranian rejection of Kurdish demands for autonomy to improve its position *vis-à-vis* its own Kurds and to undermine any appeal that Talibani and Barzani factions may have by pointing to their ties with the Khomeini regime. Iraqi religious leaders do not enjoy the support or the drawing power of their Iranian counterparts. Generally speaking, Iraq's youths are better educated and more secular than Iran's. The religious links which might pull some Iraqis in Iran's direction are matched, if not surpassed, by the ethnic pull of pan-Arabism. The regime is also well known for its quick and harsh measures against anyone seeking to use religion as a political weapon. This attitude was clearly manifested in the reaction to the Najaf and Karbala incidents in 1977 and 1979, and in the recent execution of Ayatollah Muhamed Baqir Sadr who was accused of leading al-Da'wah Party and co-operating with Iran. While sectarian and ethnic tensions continue, they nevertheless appear to be manageable and containable.

The Arab centrality appears to have shifted from the Nile to the Euphrates. In addition, Iraq's huge oil reserves, its resolution of its major internal problems and regional co-operation with the Gulf countries secure its future in the Gulf. Consequently Iraq has an interest in stability, particularly with the present instability in Iran. Its role is apt to be determined by the absence of internal and external factors limiting its options.

Furthermore, if Iraq's legitimate interests in navigation, in off-shore oil exploration, in preserving the Arab character of the Gulf and its independence from foreign control are recognised, then the country's role will be constructive. If, however, it is dealt with and viewed as a hostile power, its role will be destructive. In fact, Iraq never has had, in its recent history, such a fortunate opportunity to play a leading role in Gulf and Arab affairs.

Notes

1. Richard Coke, *Baghdad the City of Peace* (Thornton, Butterworth, London, 1927), pp. 211–80. See also Kathleen Langley, *The Industrialization of Iraq* (Harvard University Press, Cambridge, Mass., 1961), p. 8.

2. Fahim Qubain, *The Reconstruction of Iraq* (Frederick Praeger, New York, 1958), p. 2.

3. Abd al-Razzaq al-Hasani, *Tarikh al-Wazarat al-Iraqiyya* (Dar al-Kutub, Beirut, 1974), vol. 3. pp. 323–30.

4. Qubain, *Reconstruction*, pp. 2–3.

5. Majid Khadduri, *Independent Iraq* (Oxford University Press, Oxford, 1951), p. 141. See also Mustafa al-Najjar, *al-Tarikh al-Siyassi li — 'Alaqat al-'Iraq al-Dualiyya bil-Khalij* (Basrah University Press, Basrah, 1975).

6. Majid Khadduri, *Republican Iraq* (Oxford University Press, Oxford, 1969), p. 12. He states that Iraq was looked upon by Arab nationalists as the Arab Prussia that would unify Arab lands. See also Patrick Seale, 'The United Arab Republic and the Iraqi Challenge', *World Today* (July 1960), p. 298.

7. Qubain, *Reconstruction*, pp. 164–5.

8. Langley, *Industrialization*, p. 201.

9. International Bank for Reconstruction and Development, *Economic Development of Iran*. (Johns Hopkins University Press, Maryland, 1952), pp. 46–7 and 305–15.

10. Khadduri, *Independent Iraq*, pp. 352–5.

11. Khadduri, *Republican Iraq*, p. 2.

12. Edmund Ghareeb, *Al-Haraka al-Qawmiyya al-Kurdiyya* (Dar al-Nahar, Beirut, 1973), pp. 38–40.

13. Ibid., p. 47.

14. For details of the oil negotiations see Khadduri's *Republican Iraq*, pp. 160–8.

15. Chronology, *Middle East Journal* (Spring 1962), pp. 193–4.

16. Ibid., p. 183.

17. For background on the Ba'th Party see Kamel Abu Jabir, *The Arab Ba'th Socialist Party* (Syracuse University Press, Syracuse, 1966); John Devlin, *The Ba'th Party* (Hoover Institution Press, Stanford, Conn., 1976); Majid Khadduri, *Socialist Iraq* (The Middle East Institute, Washington, DC, 1978); and Gordon Torrey, 'The Ba'th: Ideology and Practice', *The Middle East Journal* (Autumn 1969), pp. 445–70.

18. Tariq Aziz, *A Revolution of the New Way* (Iraq, 1974), p. 33.

19. Patrick Seale, 'The Ba'th in Government', *Middle East International* (May 1977), p. 11.

20. The Constitution of the Ba'th Party, 1947, quoted in Tariq Ismael, *The Arab Left* (Syracuse University Press, Syracuse, 1976), p. 37.

21. Ibid., pp. 128–9.

22. Khadduri, *Socialist Iraq*; p. 37.

23. See *Revolutionary Iraq: the Political Report adopted by the Eighth Regional Congress of the Ba'th Arab Socialist Party* (Baghdad, October 1974).

24. Edmund Ghareeb, 'Iraq's Development Policy', Gannett News Service, 3 April 1975.

25. Interview with a high Ba'thist official, *al-Nahar, Al-Arabi was al-Duali*, 22 January 1979.

26. *Revolutionary Iraq*, p. 206.

27. Ibid., pp. 207–8.

28. Ibid., p. 89.

29. For details of the oil negotiations see ibid., pp. 80–100 and Khadduri, *Socialist Iraq*, pp. 125–9.

30. See *Christian Science Monitor*, 6 April 1973 and *Al-Thawra*, 7 April 1980.

31. *Al-Thawra*, 1 March 1979.
32. Interview with Dr Zayd Haydar, July 1976. Dr Haydar was a Ba'th Party National Command member and then head of the Foreign Relations Department.
33. *al-Jumhuriyya*, 13 October 1969.
34. *Christian Science Monitor*, 16 March 1968.
35. *Arab Report and Record* (London) 1–15, 19 January 1969, p. 2.
36. Chronology, *Middle East Journal* (Fall 1969), p. 513.
37. *Christian Science Monitor*, 25 April 1970.
38. *Arab Report and Record*, 16 July 1970, p. 410.
39. *Al-Nahar*, 26 February 1979.
40. *The Washington Post*, 13 April 1980.
41. *The New York Times*, 9 March 1980.
42. For details see Khadduri, *Socialist Iraq*, pp. 153–9.
43. Khadduri, *Socialist Iraq*, p. 158.
44. Abdullah al-Nafisi, *Kuwait Al-Wajh al-Akhar*, p. 47.
45. Baghdad Radio, Foreign Broadcast Information System (FBIS) 12 May 1980.
46. S. Chubin and S. Zabih, *The Foreign Relations of Iran* (University of California Press, Berkeley and Los Angeles, 1974), p. 195.
47. *New York Times*, 11 January 1975.
48. *Al-Siyassah*, Kuwait, 4 April 1976.
49. *Baghdad Observer*, 5 October 1975.
50. *Al-Hawadith*, 18 April 1980.
51. For the text see Iraqi News Agency, 13 February 1979.
52. Cited in *Baghdad Observer*, 27 February 1979.
53. *Al-Thawra*, 12, 13 and 14 June 1979.
54. *Al-Hawadith*, 8 April 1980.
55. *Al-Watan al-Arabi*, 25 April 1980.
56. *The Washington Star*, 6 June 1979.
57. Ibid.
58. Ibid.
59. *Al-Thawra*, 12, 13 and 14 June 1979.
60. *The Economist*, 12 April 1980. See also AP despatches, 2, 3 and 4 April 1980.
61. *Christian Science Monitor*, 15 April 1980.
62. *Al-Thawra*, 6 June 1977. Hussein has declared that Iraq does not distinguish between Iraqis be they 'Muslim or Christian, Arab or Kurdish, Shi'i or Sunni' (*Al-Thawra*, 29 April 1980). Tariq Aziz has also stressed that Iraq believes in Ba'thist goals, and that it is a 'nationalist, not an internationalist system'. (*Al-Watan al-Arabi*, 2 April 1980).
63. President Bani Sadr expressed Iran's 'principled stand to help any liberation movement in Islamic countries' (*Al-Nahar*, 30 March 1980). Top Iranian religious leaders, including Ayatollahs Muntazeri and Ruhani, charged that the Gulf states were 'un-Islamic and oppressive' and Ruhani expressed his willingness to lead a revolt against the government of Bahrain (*Al-Nahar*, 24 September 1979).
64. Milliyet, 14 April 1980. Cited in Foreign Broadcast Information System, 18 April 1980.
65. See statement by Iranian Defence Minister Mustafa Chamran, broadcast on Radio Tehran, 25 April 1980. Cited in FBIS, 28 April 1980.
66. Tehran Radio, 9 April 1980.
67. *Al-Nahar*, 23 December 1979.
68. *Le Monde*, 8 April 1980.
69. See Hussein's speech following the bomb attack on Tariq Aziz by an Iraqi of Iranian origin, 2 April 1980.
70. Tehran Radio, 31 March 1980.
71. See Ba'th Political Document submitted by the Ba'th Party to the Arab

People's National Conference in Baghdad on 25 March 1980. See also *al-Hawadith*, 9 May 1975.

72. Speech by Saddam to the Arab People's National Conference, *al-Thawra*, 28 March 1980.

73. Political Document and *al-Thawra*, 28 March 1980.

74. *Le Monde*, 1 February 1980.

75. *Al-Thawra*, 12 February 1980.

76. Edmund Ghareeb, 'Iraqi-US Relations', Gannett News Service, 3 April 1975.

77. *Baghdad Observer*, 27 February 1979.

78. *The Wall Street Journal*, 8 February 1980.

79. *Al-Thawra*, 23 March 1980.

80. *The McNeil-Lehrer Report*, 19 April 1980.

81. *Al-Khalij*, 16 May 1980.

82. KUNA, Kuwait, 8 May 1980.

83. *The New York Times*, 18 February 1980.

84. *The Washington Post*, 9 February 1975.

85. Ibid.

86. Baghdad Radio, 17 October 1978.

87. *Al-Nahar*, 22 January 1979.

88. *The Washington Post*, 24 December 1979.

89. Political Document.

90. INA, 24 April 1980.

91. KUNA.

92. Study by the International Institute of Strategic Studies, London. Cited in *al-Ittihad*, April 1980.

93. John Cooley, 'Neutral Iraq Proves Detractors Wrong', *Emirates News*, 22 March 1980.

94. *Al-Jumhuriyya*, 4 February 1980.

95. *The Washington Post*, 19 March 1980.

96. *Middle East Economic Digest*, 15 February 1980.

97. Cooley, 'Neutral Iraq'.

98. *8 Days*, 23 February 1980.

99. *The Washington Post*, 12 April 1980.

100. INA, 2 March 1980.

101. Political Document.

102. *Al-Jumhuriyya*, 4 February 1980.

103. Interview with ICP First Secretary Aziz Muhammad, *Morning Star*, 28 December 1979.

11   THE IRANIAN REVOLUTION: TRIUMPH OR TRAGEDY?

L. P. Elwell-Sutton

According to the history books, Iran has undergone three 'revolutions' during the present century. Yet, if we take the term 'revolution' in its traditional sense as implying the violent overthrow of a despotic and reactionary regime by a spontaneous popular uprising, followed by the charting of a new and progressive course for society, then none of them fit the pattern. The first, the 'Constitutional Revolution' of 1906, carried out by a small heterogeneous group of merchants, religious leaders, intellectuals and tribal chiefs, aimed at no more than bringing an already weak and declining monarchy under the control of an elected parliament. Its only achievement was an acceleration of the country's drift into chaos and disorder, a drift halted only by the *coup d'état* of Reza Khan in 1921.

The second revolution, the 'White Revolution' of 1963, was of an entirely different character. Indeed it had begun long before, with Reza Khan's accession to power and finally to the throne in the 1920s. Here certainly we had the 'charting of a new and progressive course', but there was no uprising either spontaneous or popular, and the planning and direction of the reforms that sprang out of it came entirely from the top. In spite or because of this, according to one's point of view, the changes in Iranian society were fundamental, and some consideration of the Pahlavi regime is necessary if we are to understand the nature of the third revolution, the 'Islamic Revolution' of 1978/9, to which the title of this chapter refers.

The Pahlavi era, from 1921 to 1979, fell historically into three clearly defined phases — 1921–41, a period of stabilisation and modernisation under autocratic rule; 1941–53, restoration of parliamentary government and a slackening of the pace of reform; and 1953–79, a steadily accelerating resumption of the drive towards modernisation and what the Shah was pleased to call the 'Great Civilisation'. Yet from a long-term historical point of view the whole epoch may be seen as a single phase, with the middle period a mere pausing for breath rather than a change of direction. Certainly there were differences of detail and even of substance between the first and third periods, but the ruling trend remained constant. This was based on the belief that Iran's salvation, its escape from the vicissitudes of the nineteenth and early twentieth centuries and from

231

domination by foreign great powers riding roughshod over the country's interests, could only be achieved by a policy of Westernisation, of breaking with the restricting traditions of the past, of building an Iran that could compete on equal terms with the 'advanced' societies of the West. Both Reza Shah and his son therefore pursued this policy with a ruthless disregard of the social problems that such a drastic reorientation was bound to bring. For both rulers internal security loomed large, justified in the former's case by the prevailing disorder, the breakdown of centralised authority, the centrifugal tendencies of a country composed of variegated and often mutually incompatible social, ethnic and economic elements. Indeed a considerable degree of success was achieved in welding this heterogeneous conglomerate into a national unity, and it might have been thought that the time had come by the sixties and seventies for a measure of relaxation. Whether or not this was the case (and the events of 1979 suggest that the unity may not have gone very deep), Mohammad Reza Shah continued the practice begun by his father of building up the centralised security forces — army, police, gendarmerie and, finally, the iniquitous secret police SAVAK — to the point where they took on an autonomy of their own. Universal conscription, excessive expenditure on sophisticated weaponry, suppression of independent political activity and imprisonment of dissidents were among the negative aspects of this policy.

On the positive side, Reza Shah concentrated his earlier efforts on the creation of an industrial base for the Iranian economy, and it is perhaps a measure of the success that this policy achieved that, whereas in the initial stages the pace of industrialisation was criticised for being too slow, towards the end many observers felt that it was moving too fast. Between these two extremes Iran had progressed from an almost wholly non-industrial society in 1920 to one in which about 250,000 plants employed 2.5 million workers, about a quarter of the total working population. From the early sugar-beet refineries, canning plants, tobacco and match factories and cotton mills that were Reza Shah's pride, Iran had by the seventies a very wide range of industries manufacturing domestic appliances, electrical goods, motor vehicles and other light and heavy industries. Above all, it had won back control of its oil industry, run by foreign interests since its inauguration at the beginning of the twentieth century. Certainly the situation was not as rosy as this somewhat superficial picture suggests. Most of these industrial workers were employed in very small units of less than ten employees, and output per man, though increasing rapidly, was still comparatively low. Much sophisticated equipment was acquired, but too often before the necessary technical expertise was available to use it properly. But perhaps most serious of all was the relative neglect of agriculture.

In Reza Shah's time the need for industrialisation, improvement of communications, establishment and centralisation of security and development of urban life was so acute that it was almost inevitable that the rural areas should have taken second place. Some attempt at settlement of the nomadic tribes took place, but the lot of the peasant remained much as it had been for centuries. It was not until the White Revolution of 1963 that any serious attempt was made to bring the villages into line with the towns, and it was both the successes and failures of this programme that created the problems at the root of the critical events of 1978. The idealism behind the Land Reform, largely the inspiration of the Minister of Agriculture, Hasan Arsanjani, saw it as a means of releasing the peasants from the tyranny of a centuries-old land ownership system that deprived them of all but a fraction of the fruit of their labour, and turning them into small-scale landed proprietors. That the Shah also saw it as a means of destroying the power of the landed aristocracy is undeniable; but this in no way detracts from the more idealistic aspects. The failure of the Land Reform lay less in its principles than in the difficulties inherent in carrying out such a massive reform at the pace demanded, which in turn led to twists and deviations of policy that produced results satisfactory to no one. On the positive side, apart from the redistribution of ownership, were the allied measures to improve rural life — the formation of rural co-operatives, the nationalisation of pasture-lands, the creation of the Literacy, Health and Development Corps, and the establishment of the Houses of Equity. But the regime never learned how to reconcile its ambitions for the peasants with the need for cheap food for the urban populations. It made no provision for the large class of landless peasants who, never having been tenants, did not qualify for participation in the land distribution, and it actually re-created the problems of the 'large estate' by encouraging the formation of large-scale mechanised agri-business corporations. It failed to allow the rural co-operatives to develop into a channel for the expression of peasant grievances, it could not restrain the corruption that survived as an heirloom from less progressive times, and it did not appreciate how the closer contact with and awareness of urban life and conditions would lead to a revolution of rising expectations in the villages. In consequence the land reform, far from stemming the drift from the country into the towns, turned that drift into a torrent; whereas in 1963 the peasants accounted for about two-thirds of the total population, only fifteen years later the balance was beginning to turn in favour of the urban dwellers.

The main consequence therefore of the economic reforms of the Pahlavi regime was the creation of a new industrial proletariat swollen by an influx of landless peasants who found work in building and construction and other casual labour of the kind. At the same time the concentration of population in the cities and towns, especially the capital Tehran, which grew from 200,000 in 1920 to 4,500,000 in 1976, created a new middle class composed of professionals, doctors, teachers, lawyers, businessmen, engineers, technicians, journalists and bureaucrats. It is not surprising therefore that the first steps towards the provision of social services were taken in the urban areas, ranging from housing and health through schools and universities to factories and labour conditions. That immense strides were taken in all these fields can be denied only by the most prejudiced. That they were inadequate to cope with the demands made on them is equally true. This inadequacy was reflected particularly in the growth of shanty towns on the outskirts of the main cities, which in this sense could only be said to have been created by the Pahlavi regime. From a long-term point of view, however, the most serious by-product of the regime's social measures was the need to override and break down traditional attitudes and patterns of life. This of course has always been associated with social reform; in Iran's case the rapidity with which the changes were carried out did not leave time for new attitudes and patterns to develop in their place. There was therefore much admirable legislation, but no solid foundations. This was particularly noticeable following the two abdications of 1941 and 1979, and nowhere more than in the field of female emancipation. Both rulers adopted this as a main plank of their social policies, and took substantial steps in that direction. Reza Shah abolished the veil, admitted girls to school and university, and encouraged the participation of women in jobs and professions. The events of 1941 slowed down, though only temporarily, the incursion of women into the public sphere; but the veil returned, even if not on the former scale. Mohammad Reza Shah gave women the vote, and in 1967 the Family Protection Law climaxed a long series of measures designed to place women on a more equal footing with men in respect of marriage, divorce and inheritance. Women were indeed still allowed to vote in the post-Pahlavi elections of 1980, but the Family Protection legislation was dropped, and in other respects the position of women became subject to traditional religious rules and practices.

The social effects of the Pahlavi regime may then be summed up as a process of weakening or destroying the traditional classes of society and creating new ones. The landowning class became separated from the land and joined the growing business classes, the relatively wealthy entrepreneurs with international connections and interests in banking and insurance. The growth of this 'big business' sector led in turn to the weakening of the traditional 'bazaar' class, the small merchants operating on a personal basis and with their own methods of finance. The decline of this class began to erode the economic base of the religious hierarchy, who were already as a result of Pahlavi policies losing their domination of education and the law. In their place was appearing a new professional class of teachers, lawyers, bureaucrats, technocrats — and students. Meanwhile the peasant class, released from the domination of the old landlord class, failed or was not allowed to play a significant role in the new society, and having no sound economic base on the land joined, ironically, its quondam masters in the movement into the cities to swell the ranks of the new industrial proletariat. Here they came into contact with the higher material standards of the city-dwellers, while access to the educational facilities of the towns gave them a basic literacy that was only slowly becoming available to the rural areas in the final stages of the White Revolution, through the agency of the Literacy Corps. In short, the sixty years of the Pahlavi regime changed Iran from a predominantly rural society based on the produce of the land to a substantially urban society drawing its strength from a new and somewhat shaky industrial structure.

The events of 1978 and 1979 are to be explained not so much in terms of the erroneousness of Pahlavi policies as in their failure to achieve the strength that would have enabled them to stand up to the challenge of the late seventies, and the nature of which we shall have to look at in some detail. But before we do this, we must examine and identify the weak points in the regime's policies that underlay this failure. Several writers have drawn attention to the economic aspects — the false euphoria that followed the massive increases in oil revenues after 1973, the doubling of the 1974 budget, the runaway expenditure on sophisticated technology without first ensuring the necessary infrastructure and skilled personnel. Not enough emphasis has perhaps been laid on the role of international finance in this stage. The United States has of course been blamed for supporting the regime, and equally for having abandoned it at the last moment. But there is some reason to think that this was only one facet of the situation. America was by no means the only country involved, and anyone who has studied the machinations of the international financiers will be aware that their role is 'supranational' rather than international. Whether there is a conscious and consistent policy may be questioned, but it can hardly be doubted that the interests of the supranational finance houses, oil companies, armaments manufacturers and shipping trusts are not linked to those of any particular nation. During the seventies Iran may well have seemed to these eyes to be on the point of becoming a maverick, a danger to the carefully balanced structure of the supranational system. The vigorous line pursued by the Shah in OPEC may have been seen as threatening. At the same time Iran, by excessive reliance on foreign financial and technical aid and by allowing external finance houses and multinational companies to dominate its economy, made itself extremely vulnerable to external intervention on the economic level. It would not have been difficult, while seeming to support and encourage the Shah's ambitions of turning his country into the 'Japan of the Middle East', so to manipulate its finances as to bring about the weakening and collapse of its economic foundations. Whether there was or not such a conscious plot, there can be little question that the massive scale of 'aid' supplied from the United States, Western Europe and the Eastern bloc was largely responsible for the 'overheating' of the economy.

To say this is not to underrate the natural problems that faced the country — a harsh climate, shortage of water, lack of vegetation, absence of exploitable natural resources other than oil, and above all centuries of neglect. Inevitably, too, these physical problems have brought with them social and psychological obstacles. The insecurity of life for the peasantry has made them conservative, reluctant to experiment with new techniques or to take risks. The corresponding feature in the urban dweller is an unwillingness to make decisions and to take responsibility, a tendency to 'pass the buck' to higher authority, and even to assume that faults and failures are the result of intrigues by others rather than matters calling for re-examination of methods and attitudes. The same outlook spills over into politics. It was a long-standing joke among Iranians as much as among foreigners that all ills, from inflation to the breakdown of the telephone system and the inclemency of the weather, were held to be the fault of the British (and later of the Americans); and it was not always said in jest. An ardent supporter of the new regime, writing recently to a Scottish newspaper, exclaimed indignantly: 'Quite simply, if Iranians do not blame the Shah and America for the many shortcomings and deficiencies in the country, whom should they blame?' It would be easy enough to give a short answer to that question; but in fairness it must be remembered that, ever since the beginning of the nineteenth century, Iran has been subject to intervention and pressure from the great powers that surround its frontiers — Britain, Russia and, later, America. It is less than paranoid, though it may be mistaken, to assume that such interventions, because they are primarily of benefit to the intervening power, must therefore be detrimental to the interests of Iran. But, understandable as this attitude may be, it has only served to reinforce the tendency of many Iranians to blame others for their own faults.

It is the same psychology no doubt that leads many Iranians to seek relief in following a charismatic leader. This has never been more evident than during the seventy-odd years since the granting of the Constitution. One of Iran's misfortunes has been the failure to establish on a firm basis any form of parliamentary or representative government. Iranian politicians therefore lack the experience needed to make such institutions work. The first period of 'constitutional' government, from 1906 to 1921, plunged the country into such disorder that most people were only too glad to welcome the strong hand of Reza Shah. The 1941–53 period was hardly more successful, and opened the way for the restoration of what was seen at first as a benevolent autocracy. Nevertheless the failure of Mohammad Reza Shah to establish a viable political party system through which individuals could acquire a sense of participation in the process of government was another disruptive factor, even though it may have affected a fairly narrow layer of the politically conscious elite.

This brings us to the role of the Shah, who as the autocratic leader of the regime cannot be absolved of personal responsibility for the developments of the past twenty-five years. Mohammad Reza Shah was a different man from his father, who was a bluff, self-educated, strong-willed soldier who pulled himself up by his own bootstraps. Reza Shah had little knowledge of the outside world (he left Iran before his abdication only twice, once to Iraq and once to Turkey), but he was possessed of an insatiable curiosity and a gift for grasping essentials. He believed firmly that Iran had to break with the restrictive obscurantism of its Islamic past, and knowing his countrymen he was convinced that this could only be achieved by the use of draconian measures. He knew what he wanted, and was impatient of obstruction and incompetence. His son, on the other hand, had none of his forcefulness. Mohammad Reza Shah was trained from an early age for his future role as ruler, given a sound European education in Switzerland, and taken round with his father on the latter's many tours of inspection. But he was never allowed any independence, and when suddenly, at the age of twenty-one, he was called on to take over the reins of government, he was only marginally better off than the Safavid and Qajar heirs who were obliged to spend their formative years in the harem, lest they should become a focus for opposition to the sovereign.

During the early years of his reign, hampered as much by his own personal inadequacies as by the inhibiting presence of foreign occupying forces, he took little or no part in the affairs of the country; but there is no reason to doubt his own claims that, then as later, he had a genuine desire to carry on the reforming work of his father, and to work for the greatness of his country. The charge commonly echoed in the West that the Shah was 'corrupt' is largely meaningless in the context of Iranian politics. In earlier days the monarch in Iran was virtually the proprietor of his country, and the constitutional and political developments of the twentieth century had done little to undermine this assumption in the minds of all but an intellectual elite. The Shah himself has claimed that the greater part of his personal wealth was at the disposal of the Pahlavi Foundation, a charitable organisation engaged in a variety of social, educational, literary and cultural projects. There seems little evidence that the Shah diverted to his personal use much more than would be regarded as appropriate to a ruler in his position — in Iran or indeed in some other countries with a monarchical tradition. The charge of corruption was more justly levelled at some of his relatives, but this was all part of the general structure of corruption that, though nowhere near as all-pervading and harmful as in Qajar times, was and still is a regrettable feature of Iranian life and society.

The Shah's failures stemmed more from weakness of character than from the despotic qualities that were so often attributed to him. The most obvious evidence of this was his inability to cope with major crises such as those of 1946, 1953 and 1978, when he was easily persuaded to abdicate authority rather than to take firm action himself. But the combination of indecision and over-reaction, of vacillation between strong measures and conciliatory concessions, of erratic changes of direction and excessive dependence on sycophantic and incompetent advisers, is characteristic of the whole of his reign. The wave of optimism that swept him along after the triumphal celebrations of 1971 contrasted with the total collapse of 1978, when close intimates reported him as incapable of giving any guidance at all. Like many weak men, he was afraid of opposition, mistrustful of political debate, incapable of delegating or giving away power, and all too prone to rely on repression as an answer to every problem. Fatally, he was suspicious of the intellectuals, who might have been his strongest and most reliable supporters, and preferred to put his trust in the unlettered masses, whom he saw as malleable and responsive to the grand gesture. With all this he was contemptuous of personal popularity, and believed himself charged with a divine mission, a frame of mind that developed in later years into megalomania.

He seems never to have understood or realised the degree and variety of opposition that was building up against him. Yet by 1978 he had lost the support of virtually every section of society. One group indeed neither he nor his father had ever won over or seriously attempted to do so — the religious hierarchy; and since it was this group that for the time being emerged triumphant from the chaos surrounding the Shah's departure at the beginning of 1979, it is necessary to look in some detail at the role of Shi'a Islam in Iranian society.

It is part of conventional thinking in the West to consider religion as a 'reactionary' social force — the 'opium of the people' — and it is equally conventional for observers of the Iranian scene to riposte that in that country's history religion has as often as not been associated with revolutionary movements. In fact, of course, neither statement represents the whole truth. The question that has to be asked is how Islam in Iran can be both encouraging to dissident and even subversive movements and resistant and inimical to fundamental social change? To begin with, we must search back into the history and development of Shi'ite political theory, bearing in mind that Shi'ism — the form of Islam that prevails in Iran — began as a minority movement in Arabia and, until the establishment of the Safavid dynasty in Iran at the beginning of the sixteenth century, had had very little experience of temporal authority. It was not surprising, therefore, that the Shi'ite doctrine of authority grew up in a vacuum. From the first, Shi'ism derived its legitimacy not from any temporal source, but from the Imam of the Age, the direct descendant of the Prophet, and it is symbolic of the whole situation that since the ninth century the Imam has had no physical existence on Earth.

Owing no allegiance, for the greater part of its existence, to any earthly authority, but rather to a spiritual figure represented on Earth by his agents (the Shi'ite theologians), the Shi'ite community was able to develop a legal system that was both more rigid and more flexible than its Sunni counterpart. Both sects of course recognised the Koran (the Word of God) and the Traditions (the sayings and actions of the Prophet Mohammad and his immediate companions) as the two principal pillars of the holy law; but whereas Sunnism supplemented these with 'popular concensus', Shi'ism continued to insist on the ultimate authority of the Imam as the only justification for deviations from the strict letter of the Koran and the Traditions. This in practice meant the consensus of the theologians as the earthly agents of the Imam, and this in turn allowed the development of the doctrine (*ejtehad*) of the continuous reinterpretation of the will of the Imam by his agents.

Contained in this doctrine was the flexibility necessary to enable the religious hierarchy to adapt to changing social and economic conditions. It was during the nineteenth century that it led to the recognition of the status (it was not more specific than that) of the *mojtahed*, someone recognised as having the authority to interpret the law in this way. And among the mojtaheds there was generally (but not necessarily) one recognised not by official appointment, but by general consensus of the theologians, as the *marja-at-taqlid*, the Source of Authority, the Spokesman of the Hidden Imam. In this way the principle of authority was re-established and maintained within the Shi'ite community. In contrast to Sunnism, where the religious institution conferred legitimacy on, and so was closely associated with, the temporal power, the Shi'ite theologians derived their legitimacy from the Imam, and so were wholly independent of the state, regardless of whether this was strong or weak. Thus the position of the theologians in Iranian Shi'ite Islam became greatly enhanced, both because of their firmly centralised organisation (none the less firm for being informal and unwritten) and because of the exclusive right conferred on their head to give a final interpretation of the holy law.

The separate development of the religious and secular powers in the Shi'ite areas of Islam, in particular Iran, accounts for the underlying hostility of the Shi'ite hierarchy towards temporal authority. In Shi'ite thinking the religious power, equated with justice, must always be at war with the temporal, equated with injustice. On this basis there can be no compromise; the state, whatever its policies, must be oppressive, and the role of the Imam, and so of his agents, is the protection of the oppressed. This sense of 'unjust persecution' has permeated Shi'ite thinking ever since Shi'ism emerged at the outset of the Islamic era as the political support of the martyred Caliph Ali and his sons Hasan and Hosein, the first three Imams, and was encouraged by the failure in general of Shi'ite rulers to attain temporal power until the sixteenth century, nine hundred years later. The history of Islam is seen by Shi'ism as a progressive decline, to be explained by the steady corruption of the holy law through the incorporation by illegal and oppressive secular governments of extraneous non-Islamic elements not having the sanction of the Imam. It is the duty therefore of all Muslims to fight governments, or at least to abstain from collaboration with them; such an injunction contains no value judgement on the activities or intentions of such governments. The actions of a secular government must be bad because they do not carry the authority of the Imam. The fact that particular measures are likely to prove popular is all the more reason for opposing them, for in the Shi'ite view a secular government cannot be allowed to acquire a spurious authority based on popular support. The contradictions and tensions inherent in this view are evident. On the one hand the religious leadership must remain independent of the secular government; on the other hand it must seek to ensure that Islamic principles prevail and that social reforms are in accord with such principles. But if such reforms do not issue from the authority of the Imam, they cannot be held to be valid.

The problem of reconciling these contradictions is not a new one. It emerged very clearly during the Constitutional Revolution of 1906, which was to begin with supported by the religious institution because it was seen as an attack on an oppressive secular power. But very soon it became apparent that the intention of the Constitutionalists was to replace one temporal authority — the monarchy — with another — the people (the parallel with today is inescapable). From this point there developed a clear split in the religious hierarchy between those who saw the constitution as a means, albeit secular, of restricting the activities of an 'illegal' temporal power and those who believed that collaboration with the monarchy was necessary to ensure that the holy law was fully implemented. This division of the hierarchy into those who support the established government and those who take up a dissident or detached position has not wholly disappeared even at the present day, though the political circumstances and the particular bones of contention have.

We may therefore start our consideration of the religio-political situation in Iran prior to 1978 by positioning two linked but often mutually antagonistic groups — the independent religious hierarchy and the state-supported hierarchy.

During the period up to 1921 the independent hierarchy was making the running. It was of course a period of intense political activity, and the religious institution made full use of the opportunity of giving a religious guise and sanction to political opposition. The two main strands in Shi'ite political thought were dominant and indeed in close association — fear of the corruption of Islamic law and teaching, and hostility to secular government. The Qajar regime was condemned both for its oppressive conduct and for its association with foreign interests, and especially for its readiness to dispose of Iranian resources to foreign concessionaires — measures which, as in the case of the 1891 Tobacco Regie, were held to be encouraging the infiltration of corrupting non-Islamic ideas and attitudes. Religious influence in the Constitutional movement ensured the passage of the Supplementary Constitutional Law of 1907, which specified a particular form of Shi'ism as the established faith of Iran and provided for the formation of a committee of five mojtaheds to vet legislation and ensure that it was in conformity with the holy law. It seems that this provision was never implemented; certainly there were from the first mojtaheds and mollas in the Majlis (parliament), but if a formal committee ever existed it lapsed shortly after Reza Khan assumed full powers in the twenties.

The beginning of the Pahlavi reign in 1925 marked a sharp decline in the power of the independent hierarchy, but it is probable that this had begun earlier. The break-up of the Constitutionalist alliance meant that the religious hierarchy withdrew into itself and to a large extent abandoned its always superficial support for political and social reform. The years from 1910 onwards show an increasing obscurantism, and so it is not surprising that, faced with a vigorously reforming secular government enjoying widespread popular support, the reactionary attitudes of the hierarchy cut little ice. It is true that to begin with the religious institution had some apparent success. It managed to stop the republican movement of 1924 in its tracks, and even put up some opposition in the Majlis to the deposition of the Qajar dynasty in October 1925. But the tide was running strongly against it, and once Reza Shah had got into his stride it was clear that the religious hierarchy was not going to stop him. The educational and legal reforms left it without authority in these two important fields, and though there were murmurs of protest against many of the Shah's Westernising innovations, not least the unveiling of women in 1936 and the encouragement of female participation in education and a wide range of occupations, they attracted little popular support and were certainly quite ineffectual. It is true that Islam still retained its influence over the lower social classes, but this was on the whole welcomed by the regime as an antidote to revolutionary Communism, which was seen as a more serious threat. Among the Westernised intellectual middle and upper classes, those who formed the backbone of the new order, the Islamic religion was despised as one of the main causes of Iran's backwardness. It was in general a period in which popular feeling was behind the regime and its reforms, and the religious hierarchy had little alternative but to go along with this. Even the eventual abdication of Reza Shah in 1941 under external pressures was as great a surprise to them as it was to the rest of the population. They had not been working for it any more than the minor left-wing opposition.

The abdication of Reza Shah thus found the religious institution in some disorder, less prepared to take advantage of the new situation than their rivals on the political left. To begin with, the changed atmosphere was shown mainly in such things as the resumption of the veil by women of the lower classes, the revival on a limited scale of religious ceremonials such as the Moharram processions and passion plays, and a growth of interest in religious questions. Religious teachers gained access to the media; Koran recitals became a regular feature of radio programmes, and radio preachers gained wide audiences. Overt political activity developed with the formation of the National Will Party in 1944; strongly oriented towards tradition, it provided a natural haven for the more conservative-minded religious, and although few clerics were high in the counsels of the party, it gained the support of 'political' theologians and religious newspapers. For the time being they were content to serve as a counterweight to the growing power of the left. But with the end of the war and the foreign occupation, the Azerbaijan crisis of 1946, the collapse of the left and the consequent restoration of power to the central government and increasingly to the Shah himself, the religious hierarchy began to resume their old role of opposition to the temporal power, and this of course brought them into uneasy association with other 'opposition' forces of all shades and colours. The post-war period in Iran, and particularly that phase of it associated with the premiership of Mohammad Mosaddeq, witnessed the zenith of the power of the religious hierarchy, and with it the rise of extremist movements at both ends of the spectrum — the Fedaiyan-e Islam and the Mojahedin on the one hand, and on the other the range of left-wing groups associated with the Tudeh Party. The one thing they had in common was opposition to foreign imperialism, symbolised by the Anglo-Iranian Oil Company. Although the hierarchy drew back from the brink in time, and so were not dragged down with the left after the fall of Mosaddeq in 1953, the legacy was an atmosphere of mutual suspicion between the independent religious institution and the government, which became all the more noticeable when the Shah embarked on his programme of reforms in the sixties.

The events of 1953, when the government of Dr Mosaddeq was overthrown by a CIA-aided *coup d'état* that raised the Shah once again to the pinnacle of power, returned the religious institution to something like the position it had held during the reign of Reza Shah. This was not immediately obvious, since religious activity continued to play a much more overt role in post-1953 Iranian society than it had during the years between the wars. Nevertheless much of this outward show belonged to that section of the religious institution that had thrown its lot in with the establishment. The independent institution maintained its financial independence from the state, relying almost entirely on popular support from the traditional merchant class. Moreover, it was able to keep its loose but effective organisation, particularly as the seat of the marja-at-taqlid was for most of the period in the holy cities of Najaf and Kerbela, across the border in Iraq. This withdrawal beyond the reach of the secular authority (which is by no means a form of exile, but a convenient method of maintaining independence during periods when the temporal power is strong) is a traditional practice going back at least two centuries, and has enabled the Shi'ite hierarchy to survive where a nationally based one would have had to bow to the political establishment. That it does not constitute a derogation of authority is clear from the restraints that it was able to impose from this vantage-point on, for example, the Shah's family protection legislation, which for all its progressive outlook was unable to incorporate the abolition of polygamy or even of the 'temporary' marriage sanctioned by Shi'ite law.

But such superficial successes merely underline that the general situation of the religious institution is characterised by failure to keep up with the times. More than ever in the present environment the traditional training and outlook of the Shi'ite theologians has made it impossible for them, in spite of the use of ejtehad, to adjust to changing conditions. They are completely out of touch with current intellectual developments even in their own country, let alone in the world. On the political plane this lack of adaptability showed itself in more or less indiscriminate opposition to social reform, in so far as this stemmed from the policies of the secular power. Even in the case of such obvious targets as American military and financial penetration or economic relations with Israel, but more especially over land reform, female suffrage and the other points of the 'White Revolution', the main force of the criticisms was not of the reforms or measures themselves but of the fact that they were being carried out by a temporal government which, according to traditional Shi'ite doctrine, was illegal and therefore oppressive in all its actions, whatever these might be. There is an ironic resemblance between this stance and the posture of the Marxists, who reject any revolution, however fundamental, if it has not come about in strict accordance with the Marxist interpretation of history.

The policy of the Pahlavi shahs towards the religious institution varied in intensity, but was fundamentally consistent. In general the Pahlavi regime found itself strongest when the religious institution was weakest. The advent of Reza Shah in the twenties saw the initiation of a series of reforms, many of which, even if not expressly so designed, had a severe impact on the position and power of the hierarchy. Most important was the removal of the fields of law and education from the hands of the religious authorities. In both cases this meant a good deal more than a mere transfer of responsibility. The new civil and criminal codes made gestures in the direction of conciliating ecclesiastical opinion, but in general they were based firmly on European models, and the committee of mojtaheds envisaged in the Constitution played no part in their formulation. Though religious education was not entirely dropped from the schools, it ceased to be compulsory after 1930, and the courses were planned by the Ministry of Education. Other measures, though not specifically designed to strike at the religious institution, showed up its weakness in the face of a powerful reforming regime. The education of girls, vigorously promoted by Reza Shah's government, had hitherto been hotly opposed by the hierarchy. Even such matters as the unveiling of women and the Europeanisation of dress could be seen as blows at traditional religious attitudes, while more specific slights included the ban on the traditional Moharram mourning ceremonies.

Reza Shah's attitude towards the religious institution derived from his view of the theologians as an obstacle to the rebuilding of the country's society on a foundation of patriotic rather than religious unity. He seems personally to have been a man of average piety, but he felt that Iran's history showed that Islam was an inadequate basis for national rebirth, and so he aimed at the creation of a secular state. Throughout his reign the hierarchy were forced to take a back seat, and occasional rumblings of revolt (as, for example, against female emancipation) were put down ruthlessly. The nationalisation of the religious endowments in 1940 removed the financial prop that had hitherto given some reality to religious independence, while the marriage of the Crown Prince (later Shah) to the Sunni Egyptian princess, Fawziya, in 1939 merely served to underline the extent to which the views of the Shi'ite hierarchy were ignored in the implementation of measures of state.

Though in essence Mohammad Reza Shah's religious policy was a continuation of his father's, his method was a more conciliatory and perhaps weaker one. He was at pains to cultivate an Islamic exterior by attending the mosque regularly, performing pilgrimages and so on. He seems to have regarded Islam in its popular form as a safe-guard against revolutionary Communism, which he feared more than anything else as a threat to the new society he was trying to build. He evidently felt that by adopting this line he could appeal over the heads of the intellectual middle class directly to the masses. But the effect was to strengthen the religious hierarchy without reconciling it to his regime. There was in any case a built-in con-tradiction which merely served to increase the tension. Religion in the Shah's view should be separated from political activity; at the same time it should be a factor in the achievement of social stability and to that extent subservient to state policy. So it became necessary to develop a state-approved hierarchy that would not only provide a viable alternative to the traditional independent hierarchy, but would also have the freshness of outlook that would enable it to collaborate in programmes of social reform. That this policy was based on a serious miscalculation is clear from subsequent events. In spite of marginal reforms in the theological training centres and the encouragement of intellectual theologians, the general effect was to restore the centre of Shi'ite power to the external headquarters in Iraq, where its leaders were more free to voice their opposition and to build up their strength for the confrontation of 1978.

The political strength of the religious hierarchy was reinforced by the economic backing of the bazaar. The bazaar religion of the towns comes nearest to being a part of the independent religious institution and, by the same token, has been least influenced by the state hierarchy. The bazaar society is characterised by an almost paradoxical blend of intense individualism and a propensity for corporate organisation, and this makes it an ideal instrument for the public expression and implementation of policies favoured by the independent hierarchy. The religion that acts as a cement binding together the bazaar organisation is not a personal but a corporate religion, and it is a commonplace that demonstrations against the policies of a secular government have occurred first within the bazaar environment. However, it would be inaccurate to regard the bazaar as no more than the political arm of the religious hierarchy. Bazaar religion is even less open to change and adjustment than the religious institution, and there are many aspects of it that have survived in the face of active disapproval not only from the state but also from the hierarchy itself. Though the mosque is one centre of corporate activity, the craft guild also survives, and associated with this is the religious discussion group (*hei'at*), which can take a number of different forms and provides a forum for the formulation of political as well as religious ideas. These groups are particularly patronised by the smaller bazaar merchants, who are more conservative and traditional in their attitudes. It is at this level in particular that support comes for the traditional religious practices and observances that the more sophisticated religious authorities would prefer to see abandoned. Apart from the observance of Ramazan, most of these are associated with the mourning ceremonies performed annually in commemoration of the martyrdom of Hosein at Kerbela in 680. Most widespread is the *rouzé-khani*, the recitation of verses describing the events of Kerbela and other linked stories; this takes place for the most part in private houses, the rouzé-khan being paid a fee for his services. The Moharram processions and passion plays are no longer performed on the scale that used to prevail before their banning by Reza Shah, but they still retain a good deal of popularity, especially in the smaller towns. The story of the Kerbela tragedy, the crushing of a tiny minority by an oppressive tyrant, provides scope for the whipping up of feeling against tyrannies in general, and from this it is only a short step to particular application to the current secular authority, in conformity with Shi'ite doctrine about temporal rulers; this happened frequently under both the nineteenth-century Qajar and the twentieth-century Pahlavi regimes. But the bazaar religious organisation is beginning to crumble under external political and social pressures. The hei'at, and the other observances associated with it, appeal less and less to the younger generation, and to this natural dichotomy between the generations have been added the pressures of the mass media.

The next important source of opposition to the Pahlavi regime was of an entirely different character. It is ironical that the intelligentsia as a class was largely the creation of the Pahlavi regime. Indeed the earlier stages of the modernisation programme under Reza Shah could hardly have been carried out without the co-operation of the new educated and foreign-trained engineers, administrators and economists who were the product of his educational reforms. These men, forming the core of the new middle class, had no quarrel with Reza Shah's anti-clerical policies; under the influence of the Europe-oriented outlook of the time, whether the social-democratic views of Britain, America and France, or the Fascism and national socialism of Italy and Germany, they acquired a dislike of religious dogmatism, and shared his view that Islam was an obstruction to progress, a reactionary creed to be discarded on the road to modernity. Religious faith gave way to progressive idealism, narrow nationalism to cosmopolitanism, a desire to break down the cultural boundaries between East and West. But in the course of time they became disillusioned as well with the increasing repression of Reza Shah's reign; and when the 'democratic' interlude of 1941–53 failed to meet their aspirations, and was finally replaced by an even more severe policy of repression, they began more and more to come under the influence of the left. They developed a concern for human rights, which they saw as flouted by the regime, and took the line that they could not co-operate with an illiberal government, no matter how admirable some of its actions might seem to be. For the most part, if we except the small groups who engaged in guerrilla activity, they preferred not to go beyond non-cooperation, and contented themselves with standing on the sidelines and barracking. Some indeed, the more technocratically minded as well as the less courageous, fell in with the technocratic tendencies of the Pahlavi regime and gave their services while refusing to sell their minds. The antagonism was mutual. Mohammad Reza Shah never trusted the intelligentsia, especially after the events of 1951–3, and came to believe that the only way to deal with them was repression. This was the class that was the main victim of the secret police, and it was unfortunate for the Pahlavi regime that they were also the most articulate, the most closely in touch with the outside world. It was easier to shock foreign audiences with horrific accounts of the methods of the loathsome SAVAK, the arrests, secret trials, imprisonments, tortures and executions than to impress the Iranian public, some of whom could still remember the conduct of the secular and religious authorities in Qajar times, as exemplified by the treatment of the heretical Babis or of the Constitutionalist rebels. Thus the views of the dissidents soon came to dominate the scanty references to Iran in the foreign press to the exclusion of the more constructive aspects of the regime; in consequence the Shah found little sympathy abroad when disaster struck in 1978.

Meanwhile the intellectuals, while instinctively attracted to the political left, nevertheless were also painfully aware that political power did not lie there, and that the religious hierarchy, with its economic base in the bazaar and its numerical strength in the peasants and urban proletariat, was in spite of its apparent weakness and disorganisation the most hopeful instrument with which to

topple the Shah. Islamic dogmatism was all the same a hard pill to
swallow; and it was the self-imposed task of a group of theoreticians,
of whom the best known was Dr Ali Shari'ati (who died in London in
1977), to attempt a reconciliation between Islamic and Marxist doctrines. Whether this attempt to merge opposites was a success may be
doubted, but at least it was sufficient to salve the consciences of the
intellectuals who were now seeking the collaboration of the mollas in
the grand objective of overthrowing the Pahlavi regime.

The Shah meanwhile needed a power base. He had never had
much hope of the religious institution, of whose automatic opposition he was fully aware; he distrusted the intelligentsia; and he knew
that he could not expect support from the bazaar merchants, whose
position had been undermined by the growth of big business and the
multinational corporations. As far back as 1963 he had decided to
appeal over the heads of these groups to what was then still the
largest section of the community, the peasants. To begin with the
Land Reform was in this respect a success; the peasants welcomed
the disappearance of the absentee landlords and of landlord control
generally, but they soon found that their place was taken by government officials, who were not only less efficient but also less conscien-
tious. As the years rolled by and the great expectations were not
fulfilled, the peasants began to turn back to their traditional guard-
ians and protectors, the mollas. This applied as much to those who
migrated to the towns as to those who remained in the villages. By
1978, as a result of migration, the poorer areas of the cities were
overflowing with a rootless proletariat, of mainly peasant origin,
concerned more with basic needs of food, warmth and shelter than
with abstract questions of human rights, and above all predominantly young (the 1976 census showed that 53 per cent of the
population was under 20, and 45 per cent under 16). Neither the
Shah nor the intellectuals had any message for these people. The
Shah's promises had failed, and he seems not to have understood
that, while immediate benefits might temporarily win their allegiance, his Westernising policy, by riding roughshod over traditional
practices, could only in the long run alienate them. The steady infiltration of Western and particularly American methods and values
was arousing the hostility of many sections of society apart from the
traditionally xenophobic religious classes, even among the middle
class who were the prime beneficiaries of his policies. Foolish and
unnecessary concessions to American demands, such as the granting
in 1963 of extra-territorial rights to United States personnel, an
action reviving memories of the hated 'capitulations' abolished by
Reza Shah, merely served to fan the flames. At the same time the
intellectuals' idealism was too abstract to make any appeal to disillusioned migrants in search of a better life. Only the religious leaders,

themselves often of peasant origin, had the kind of charisma that would bring out mass support when the time came.

By 1978 the Shah had lost the backing even of his regular supporters. The court was riddled with corruption. The armed forces were weakened by the Shah's deliberate policy of divided command. He had consciously destroyed the landed classes, but the big entrepreneurs who had taken their place were too dependent on American and other international interests, too vulnerable to the manipulation of supranational financial organisations, to offer a reliable base. American support for the regime, as we have seen, was based primarily on strategic, commercial and political considerations, and apart from not necessarily being in Iran's interests, could be and was withdrawn without notice on purely pragmatic grounds. The middle classes, materialist in outlook but frustrated and disillusioned, were not* impressed by the half-hearted gestures in the direction of 'liberalisation', and were ready to go along with any change. By the middle of 1978 the Shah was completely isolated.

This total loss of confidence in the Shah's ability or will to carry through his programme of reform threw the field wide open to all the elements for the right to lead the attack on the Pahlavi regime. The intellectuals, especially those on the left, regarded themselves as the natural heirs to this position; but their methods and aims were too intellectual, too out of touch with the ordinary people, to carry any weight. They found it hard to shake off their long-favoured stance of non-participation and non-cooperation; they could not simplify their objectives sufficiently, and remained hopelessly split between left, centre, right, anti-clerical, pro-Islamic. By seeking the collaboration of the religious hierarchy they may well have envisaged that they would still remain as leaders of the movement; but this was to display a serious miscalculation of the nature and strength of the religious institution. Other elements in the middle class,·particularly those who had derived benefits from the Pahlavi regime and were turning away from it only now when it had failed, had no basis on which to give a lead to the masses, and ended up by throwing in their lot with the religious leaders in spite of their instinctive distrust of them. So it was that the mollas found themselves thrust into the position of leadership.

It would be wholly mistaken, nevertheless, to describe subsequent events as an 'Islamic revival', a resurgence of Islam. This is an intellectual, middle-class concept, and can only have applied, if at all, to a limited upper- and middle-class group — and even here it had political rather than religious overtones. There was certainly a reaction on the part of the younger generation in this class against the materialist outlook of their parents, just as the latter in their turn had reacted against the Islamic commitment of *their* parents. The pendulum had swung from Islam to secularism and now back again. We would be unwise to see in this any more than the natural rejection by the young of the attitudes of their parents. The Islamic Marxists, the young men sprouting beards, the girls taking to the veil, were merely indulging in a form of political protest, and this would fade away once the novelty had worn off. On the other hand, in the lower middle, bazaar and working classes, Islam had always been, and continued to be, a powerful influence; there was no revival here because there had never been, in spite of the efforts of the Pahlavi regime, any slackening of allegiance. Perhaps the peasants were less influenced than the city-dwellers; in their daily lives immemorial custom and superstition were more potent than religious doctrine, but they too turned naturally to the mollas when they felt the need for some kind of political leadership. In this sense Islam became a weapon, an effective instrument ready to the hand of any power-seeker who could pick it up. It had happened before — in 1906, in 1951; but there had never previously been a time when all other possible leaders had been reduced to impotence. The religious leaders too had stronger motives than ever for taking drastic and decisive action. The Pahlavi regime had been steadily eroding their position, and even though that threat now seemed to have been removed, the anti-clerical tendencies among the intellectual left were sufficiently strong for the mollas to distrust any strengthening of the left's position. They saw that they must act at once or not at all.

In spite of the loose, negative, even directionless nature of the religious institution's organisation, they had the means of concentrating their power and influence on a limited objective. By focusing the attack on the Shah, by setting before the people the single aim of removing him and his family from the throne, by refusing to plan or speculate about the future, they succeeded in rallying round themselves support from all sections of society. Certainly their power over the masses was their trump card. Only the mollas could have called out the mass demonstrations and parades of the latter half of 1978, and it was the sheer weight of these that in the end proved stronger than the Shah's military machine.

In laying so much emphasis on the political power of the religious institution we must not wholly dismiss the personal role played by Ayatollah Khomeini. Ever since 1963, when he had spoken out against the Shah's land reform and emancipation of women, he had been growing in influence as the one religious leader of standing who was not prepared to compromise in his hostility to the Shah. We do not need to seek personal reasons for this hostility — though it is true that his father had been a victim of Reza Shah's regime. It is more likely that he foresaw that single-minded adherence to an uncompromising view would stand him in better stead when, as he hoped, the regime began to show signs of collapse. It was a political stance, not a religious one, though it could be justified — as in fact it was in his book *Velayat-e Faqih*[1] — on the grounds that the only legal government was that supervised by the successors of the Imams, that is to say, the religious hierarchy. Khomeini was never formally appointed as head of the hierarchy — such an office does not exist; but from the Shi'a base in Iraq, whither he retired after his temporary arrest in 1963, he kept up a steady flow of statements, decrees and broadsides, many of them subsequently smuggled into Iran in the form of recorded cassettes, that kept his name before the public. He owed his charisma less to any personal qualities than to the fact that he was becoming acknowledged as the natural leader of a movement that was steadily gaining ground. It was the position that created the charisma rather than the reverse.

So the Shah fell. But now the weaknesses of the 'limited objective' method began to appear. With the objective once achieved, the various elements in the revolutionary movement found themselves without any other common interest. The collapse of the Pahlavi regime was indeed so sudden and unexpected that the momentum of the movement that overthrew it continued unchecked for a time. It was this perhaps that accounted for what seemed at times to observers as an almost lemming-like mass race along a path that led nowhere but to the destruction of all that had been achieved in the past fifty years. But very soon the coalition began to fall apart, and the religious leaders were faced with the problem of holding on to the following that they had acquired with such misleading ease. In the long run the masses would prove to be the most difficult. But for the time being they could be distracted by appeals to xenophobia, particularly directed against the Americans, as well to the Shi'a traditions of martyrdom and self-sacrifice. Khomeini was reminding his followers of this when he wrote in *Velayat-e Faqih*, 'Blood must be shed to preserve Islam! The blood of the Imam Hosein, the most precious blood of all, was shed for Islam!' For other sections of society cruder methods were needed. The middle classes had already exposed their fear of the masses, and this fear could easily be maintained by the methods of revolutionary terrorism, by the arrests, secret trials, imprisonments, tortures and executions that seemed little different from those practised by the preceding regime. For many confiscation and expropriation were sufficient to drive them into exile with such vestiges of their possessions as they could salvage. Some of the younger middle class could, as we have seen, be swayed by idealism; but it was an idealism that was acquiring an unpleasant tinge. The words and actions of the students occupying the American Embassy, for instance, reminded older observers of the language and style of the Nazi storm-troopers of the 1930s.

The most obvious failure of the religious hierarchy, as of the Shah, was to secure the allegiance of the intelligentsia. The alliance was an uneasy one at best. The triumph of the religious leaders brought about a situation which was the reverse of everything the intellectuals had hoped for. Instead of the free democratic society they desired, they saw the life of the community dominated by reactionary clerics to whom democratic methods and concern for human rights were meaningless phrases. They saw their colleagues maltreated solely for having worked, however reluctantly, for the deposed regime. They listened to propaganda pouring from the state-owned television and radio every bit as biased and sycophantic as its predecessors. Feminists saw the gains of the past fifty years thrown away, the family protection legislation discarded, women of all classes thrust back into the subordinate position they had occupied for so many centuries. Many people were inclined to revert to the view that Islamic Shi'ism was an alien growth on the body of Iranian culture, a reactionary force holding Iran back from progress, a destroyer of cultural values and civilised attitudes. One writer even compared the disaster to the Arab conquest of Iran in the seventh century. Academics pointed to the closure of educational institutions, the suspension of scientific and technical courses, the withdrawal of funds for study abroad, the threat to 'purge' university professors who had contacts with Europe and America, the ban on study and research into Iran's pre-Islamic culture. But again, characteristically, many intellectuals chose the path of exile in the more congenial atmosphere of the West rather than face the prospect of fighting the entrenched power of the mollas.

Further difficulties for the new regime seemed likely to come from Iran's traditional tendency towards factionalism. During the first twelve months after the departure of the Shah the country continued to be torn by separatist movements — tribal, linguistic and ethnic groups like the Kurds, the Arabs, the Azerbaijanis, Turkmans and Baluchis, religious minorities like the Sunnis, who have powerful allies across the border. The alienation of non-Muslim minorities like the Baha'is, Armenians and Chaldaeans is not likely to result in open opposition, but rather in withdrawal from public life; and this will mean a further drain on the better-educated sections of the population, which could also have serious implications for the practical running of the country. All this, combined with the disillusionment of the intelligentsia, the resentment of the middle classes at the country's economic decline and the deliberate rejection by Khomeini and his followers of the support offered by the left is likely to put the leaders of the Islamic Republic into an isolation as destructive for their aims as that in which the Shah found himself.

It is not as if they will be able to count much longer on the support of the masses. An anti-materialist policy is well enough for the 'haves', but it makes little appeal to the hungry millions who followed their religious leaders in the belief that they would march them into a better world. Diversionary tactics such as the occupation of the American Embassy or demands for the extradition of the Shah may whip up enthusiasm for a while, but they are no substitute for a concrete policy of economic and social reconstruction, and this so far the regime has signally failed to produce. For the time being the economy may continue to 'tick over', run by the technocrats who have survived from the Pahlavi regime. But their co-operation with the new rulers will be unenthusiastic at best, and could before long turn into non-cooperation or even outright obstruction and sabotage. Initially perhaps it will be only the more affluent sections of society who are affected by the general economic breakdown, by inflation, by inefficiency and corruption. The unemployed peasant in the Tehran slum has nothing to lose but his hopes, but once these have gone he will look for new leaders — and he will not care very much whether these come from the extreme left or the extreme right. What is certain is that whatever new regime comes into power will be as unsympathetic to the aims of the religious hierarchy as the latter were to the Pahlavi 'White Revolution'.

The political inexperience and ineptitude of the religious hierarchy is nowhere more evident than in their treatment of foreign policy. In an ideal world a declaration of intent to remain free from foreign intervention and involvement might be sufficient. But in the practical world of the present day the maintenance of such a policy calls for a degree of astuteness and understanding of world affairs that is certainly not shared by Iran's present rulers. In the past Iranian politicians have very well understood the implications of a 'policy of balance', and have brought to a fine art the game of playing off one great power against another. For the present this skill seems to have been lost. A tactic of 'thumbing the nose' may produce dramatic results for a while; but it can never serve as a long-term policy. Iran is still, as it has been for more than two centuries, at the crossroads of great power rivalries, and its leaders, if they are to avoid a repetition of the disasters of 1914 or 1941, will have to play their cards much more carefully than so far they have shown any disposition to do. They appear to believe that they are in a position to make the running; instead they are indulging in a display of brinkmanship that is altogether beyond their capacity to control. This may have consequences far outside the Iranian sphere. For some time it has been evident that the balance of power is slowly shifting from Europe and America towards Asia, and if this trend continues, the rest of the world will hope for and expect from Asian countries a measure of responsibility in world affairs that the present regime in Iran has so far failed to show.

The unpredictable collapse of the Shah's regime precipitated the religious leadership into a situation that they had never expected, and for which they were quite unprepared. The dichotomy between state-supported and independent hierarchies had disappeared. The latter not only took over the headship of the state, but at one time were in danger of having to take over the task of government as well. This would have been contrary to Shi'a doctrine, which has always seen the role of the religious hierarchy as that of the final arbiter of the actions of a secular government. They shrank in time from that precipice, but only to the extent of permitting the appointment of a secular government that they were not prepared to support whole-heartedly and whose actions they could disown at will. Since no politician of integrity could allow himself to be placed in such a position, the work of government had to be left in the hands of second-rate men of doubtful ability. Inevitably there resulted a breakdown of centralised administration; the writ of the govern-ment scarcely ran in the capital, and local power was left largely in the hands of irresponsible revolutionary committees. At the same time the involvement of the religious leaders was still too close for them to escape the consequences of the inevitable failure. The task that they had set themselves was the staggering one of reversing the whole direction taken by Iranian society over the past sixty years. Such a task called for leaders of the highest ability and integrity; but at the time (April 1980) there was no sign of such leaders. The mollas, trained according to the narrow principles of the theological colleges, were incapable of rising to the challenge. The result was an authoritarian regime without power, direction or principle, res-ponding helplessly to one stimulus after another, and clinging desperately to power for its own sake.

The tragedy is that, in such an atmosphere, the true and enduring Islamic qualities — humanity and compassion, respect for the individual, personal responsibility, honest dealing and respect for obligations, tolerance and open-mindedness, affirmation of the brotherhood of mankind — are in danger of betrayal.

Note

1. It is difficult to find a precise equivalent for this in English, but 'theocratic guardianship' comes somewhere near it.

12 REVOLUTION AND ENERGY POLICY IN IRAN: INTERNATIONAL AND DOMESTIC IMPLICATIONS

Fereidun Fesharaki

The Iranian Revolution of February 1979 served to bring about fundamental changes in domestic and foreign policy. One of these fundamental changes concerned energy, and specifically oil policy. Indeed, it may not be an exaggeration to argue that oil was the central theme in the struggle to overthrow the Shah. Ever since the discovery of oil in Masjid-e-Soleiman in 1908, oil has played a major role in shaping the destiny of Iran. Iranian politics and nationalistic sentiments have for long been associated with a struggle against foreign domination of the Iranian oil industry. That the 1953 US-backed *coup* which brought the Shah back to power was motivated primarily by the Western interest in Iran's oil was a factor which plagued the Shah for twenty-five years, denying him the legitimacy of an independent political leader.

After the anti-Shah demonstrations started in 1978, the oil workers were the first organised group to go on strike, in November. Their strike was particularly effective because it attacked the regime's weakest point. Not only did it destroy the image of its invincibility and paralyse the economy, but it also sent the message abroad that the Shah could no longer be relied upon as a stable and reliable ally to deliver oil to the international economy. In fact, the Western thirst for Iranian oil and the Shah's grandiose plans for economic development through industrialisation were a perfect match. It required little or no pressure to persuade the Shah to run the oilfields at maximum capacity. When OPEC was formed in 1960, Iran was the smallest producer in the organisation. By 1970, Iran had risen to the rank of the second-largest producer in OPEC and the second-largest exporter of oil in the world after Saudi Arabia. The expansion in productive capacity required large investments by the oil companies with the encouragement of their parent countries. Indeed, investments in Iran's oil industry came at the expense of other Middle East producers, particularly Iraq. The Western world found it preferable that oil production be expanded in Iran and Saudi Arabia, who seemed to enjoy long-term stability. However, it must be borne in mind that, except for Iraq, few oil producers had the potential to expand production beyond 4 million barrels per day.

By 1978 Iran's productive capacity had risen to 7 million barrels per day, of which 6.2 million was located in the southern oilfields of Khuzistan. This was considered peak capacity which could be sustained with heavy gas injection investments for 8 years before an inevitable decline. In the 1974–8 period Iran's actual production ranged between 5.2 and 6.0 milion b/d, leaving over 1 million barrels of shut-in (spare) capacity which could be relied upon in any emergency. Such large expansion in the rate of production and capacity in a supposedly stable country made the world extremely vulnerable to supply interruptions of Iranian oil when the Shah fell.

In the following pages this chapter will examine two main issues: first, the impact of the Iranian Revolution on the industrial countries and, second, the actual and likely changes in the Iranian energy sector which will ultimately affect world energy supplies.

Impact on Industrial Countries

The impact of Iran's oil supply interruptions on the industrial countries can be assessed from four different perspectives: world petroleum supplies; international trade; oil prices; inflation and balance of payment problems.

First, the importance of Iran's oil in the world petroleum context can be seen in Tables 12.1, 12.2 and 12.3. Iran's proven petroleum reserves constitute 10 per cent of the world reserves, while Iran's oil production in 1978 was around 9 per cent of the world oil output. However, the real importance of Iranian oil must be assessed through export performance rather than production, since most of the large producers in the industrial world are also large consumers themselves (for example the US, the USSR, the UK). In 1978 Iran provided 15 per cent of the world trade in petroleum, second only to

Table 12.1: Iran's Oil in International Perspective, 1978

		Percentage of OPEC	Percentage of World
Proven reserves (billions of barrels)	65	16	10
Production[a] (million barrels per day)	5.64	18	9
Exports: Crude and product (million barrels per day)	5.00	18	15

Note: a. For January-September 1978, before political disturbances reduced production.

Source: *BP Statistical Review of the World Oil Industry*, 1978; *CIA World Oil Market in the Years Ahead* (August 1979); *OPEC Annual Statistical Bulletin*, 1978; and National Iranian Oil Company announcements.

Table 12.2: Iran's Oil Production[a] (millions of barrels per day).

| | | | | | | | | | 1979 | | | | |
1974	1975	1976	1977	1978		Jan.	Feb.	Mar.	Apr.	May	Jun.	Jul.	Aug.	Sept.	9-Month Average
6.0	5.35	5.88	5.67	5.2		0.40	0.76	2.18	3.8	4.10	3.95	3.75	3.60	3.75	2.9

Note: a. Iran's exports equal production minus domestic consumption. Domestic consumption rose from 500,000 b/d in the early 1970s to 650,000–700,000 b/d in 1979.
Source: US Department of Energy, *International Energy Indicators (October 1979)*.

Table 12.3: Industrial Countries' Dependence on Iranian Oil, 1978 (thousands of barrels per day of crude and refined products)

	Oil Imports from Iran	Percentage of Total Oil Imports	Percentage of Iran's Exports	Iran's Rank in Oil Imports
US	771	9	17	4th
Japan	852	16	19	2nd
Canada	110	17	2	2nd
Western Europe	2,053	16	46	2nd
W. Germany	347	12	8	1st
France	209	8	5	3rd
UK	185	12	4	3rd
Italy	294	12	6	4th
Netherlands	325	19	7	1st
Spain	173	17	4	2nd
Other W. Europe	520	14	12	2nd
Total	3,786	16	84	2nd

Source: *CIA International Energy Statistical Review* (September 1979); *OPEC Statistical Bulletin,* 1978.

Saudi Arabia, which provided 24 per cent of the world oil trade. Iran's 15 per cent share must also be viewed within the international oil supply context. With political and physical constraints on OPEC oil production and with little possibility of increasing production elsewhere, a delicate balance between supply and demand was maintained in 1978. In such a situation, Iran's oil cut-off placed a severe strain on the world supplies, leading to long gasoline lines in some countries, price increases and confusion. In fact, some industrial countries had foreseen the Shah's possible downfall and had built up large oil stocks before the revolution. They drew heavily on their stocks when the cut-off came to cushion the impact. However, running down stocks is a temporary measure and the long-term reduction of Iranian oil require major adjustments — often found unpleasant in the industrial world. Table 12.2 shows the pattern of production in Iran. In January and February 1979 all production went to domestic consumption, virtually denying the world of any Iranian oil. For the first nine months of 1979 production and exports averaged 2.9 and 2.2 million b/d respectively. Thus compared to the same period a year before around 8 per cent of the world petroleum trade was lost due to the revolution. Even if Iran's production can be sustained at 4 million barrels per day, as announced by the new regime in Iran, the loss to the world trade still would be around 6 per cent on a permanent basis. Table 12.3 shows the dependence of the industrial countries on Iran's oil in 1978. In 1978 Iran was the second-largest supplier of oil to Western Europe and Japan, and ranked fourth as oil supplier to the US. Nearly half of Iranian exports went to Western Europe, providing one-sixth of total imports for these countries.

Second, the industrial countries' trade relationship with Iran was affected by the revolution. Iran has consistently been a major market for the exports of the industrial nations (Table 12.4). In 1978 Iran imported $13.3 billion of goods from the seven largest industrial countries, while the same countries imported $13.9 billion of Iranian oil, leaving Iran with a modest $0.6 billion trade surplus. That Iran ploughed back its oil revenues of over $21 billion annually into the industrial countries in imports was also a great source of comfort to these countries who did not have to worry about accumulation of large surpluses and possible monetary destabilisations. Indeed, Iran was the single largest export market for the industrial world among developing countries. Although Saudi oil revenues were larger than Iran's, these revenues were not all spent. As can be seen, in the first quarter of 1979 trade with Iran was significantly down from previous years. The impact is likely to remain severe for 1979 and 1980, affecting balance of payments and unemployment in the industrial world.

Third, the cut-off of Iranian oil led to supply shortages which in turn placed an upward pressure on prices. The calendar of oil price changes triggered by the Iranian Revolution is provided in Table 12.5. The price of Iranian light crude rose from $12.81/b in December 1978 to $23.50 in October 1979, an increase of 83 per cent. Libyan and North Sea crudes rose by 90 and 93 per cent respectively. The first big jump came after the OPEC 'consultative' meeting in March 1979 which was scheduled in the aftermath of chaos and panic created by the Iranian oil cut-off. Thereafter, prices increased not only through official OPEC conferences but mostly on a free-for-all basis. The prices rose in 1979 and will continue to rise in the future, not only because of reduced production in Iran or Iran's hawkish attitude in OPEC, but because of the inherent instability of the new regime in Iran which could lead to further supply interruptions — this time with perhaps less advance warning than before. The oil embargo imposed on the US is just one example of the unpredictability of the new Islamic leaders in Iran. Still, the prices shown in Table 12.5 are not truly representative, since they do not take account of spot prices. While the highest official price is just over $26/b, spot prices reached $45/b in the last quarter of 1979. With 10 to 15 per cent of the world oil trade in the spot markets in late 1979 and with the possibility of the spot market occupying 25 per cent of world trade in 1980, prices will be yet higher. Currently, Iraq and Iran are asking for large 'entry payments' of around $10/b as a price to get a term contract in 1980. Other states will quickly follow.

Table 12.4: Industrial World's Trade with Iran (millions of US $).

	US	Japan	West Germany	France	UK	Italy	Canada	Total
Exports to Iran (f.o.b.)								
1975	3,244	1,853	2,107	632	1,102	565	144	9,647
1976	2,776	1,709	2,295	655	921	806	152	9,314
1977	2,731	1,942	2,741	682	1,142	912	138	10,288
1978	3,684	2,719	3,381	881	1,440	1,067	134	13,306
1979[a]	245	54	359	92	210	80	6	1,046
Imports from Iran (c.i.f.)[b]								
1975	1,579	4,978	1,469	1,265	1,553	1,140	819	12,803
1976	1,631	4,454	1,988	1,440	1,880	1,271	744	13,408
1977	3,045	4,269	1,868	1,098	1,370	1,493	556	13,699
1978	3,164	4,256	2,101	1,202	1,021	1,563	576	13,883
1979[a]	248	207	297	145	195	102	2	1,196
Trade Balance								
1975	+ 1,665	-3,125	+ 638	- 633	- 451	- 451	-675	- 3,156
1976	+ 1,145	-2,745	+ 309	- 785	- 959	- 465	-592	- 4,094
1977	- 314	-2,327	+ 873	- 416	- 228	- 581	-418	- 3,411
1978	+ 520	-1,537	+ 1,280	- 321	+ 419	- 556	-442	- 577

Notes: a. First quarter only.

b. Ninety-seven per cent of Iran's export earnings are from oil.

Source: IMF Direction of Trade.

This has led to a new type of oil sale invented by the Iranians which is termed 'two-tier spot market'. Thus, to get a true picture of oil prices one should add $2–4 per barrel to the official prices in order to reflect the impact of the unofficial spot market. It is important to note that although the Saudis refused to raise their prices beyond $18/b until November 1979, in the hope of slowing down the price spiral, they did not succeed. The ultimate consumer had to pay OPEC prices and the difference was pocketed by the major oil companies which are members of Aramco, Saudi Arabia in effect thereby losing revenues for its moderation on prices.

**Table 12.5: Calendar of Oil Price Changes for Selected Crudes[a]
(US$ Per Barrel)**

	1978 31 Dec.	1979 Jan.	1979 Apr.	1979 May	1979 June	1979 July	1979 Oct.-Dec.	Percentage Annual Increase
Iranian Light 34°	12.81	13.45	16.57	17.17	18.47	22.80	23.50	83
Iranian Heavy 31°	12.49	13.06	16.04	16.64	17.74	19.90	22.77	82
Arabian Light 34° [b]	12.70	13.34	14.54	14.54	18.00	18.00	18.00	42
Arabian Medium 34°	12.32	12.88	14.05	14.05	17.54	17.54	17.54	42
Libyan ES-Sider 37°	13.68	14.52	18.08	18.78	21.09	23.28	26.05	90
North Sea Forties 36.5°	13.50	15.00	17.60	17.60	20.00	22.50	26.02	93

Notes: a. Official prices. Does not include spot prices.
b. Marker crude.
Prices in January and July 1979 reflect OPEC Ministerial Conference decisions. Other price changes were on a free-for-all basis.
Source: *Petroleum Intelligence Weekly*, different issues, 1979.

Fourth, the rate of inflation and balance of trade position of the industrial countries is affected by the snowballing impact of the Iranian Revolution. Not only did the Iranians raise the price of their oil, but through their actions the world oil price was raised significantly. It is too early to estimate the inflationary impact of the recent oil price increases, but simple calculations point to a *direct* impact of 1–2.5 per cent on the rate of inflation in the industrial world. Higher prices mean higher oil import bills. The United States, for instance, paid $41.6 billion for petroleum imports in 1978 (compared to $7.5 billion in 1973 and $26.5 billion in 1975), which amounts to just under a quarter of its total import bill. In 1979 the US oil import bill could rise to $70–85 billion, with a significant deterioration in its balance of trade and payment. In 1980 most industrial countries can be expected to have to double their oil import bill, compared to 1978.

What is the margin of tolerance for the industrial world regarding oil prices? How far can oil prices go before it becomes economically intolerable? This is not easy to answer, since much depends on the willingness and success of the industrial countries in restructuring their economies and accepting a lower standard of living until alternative sources of energy can be found. The critical factor here is time. If there is indeed a tolerance limit, the oil-induced recession of the early 1980s with rising unemployment and inflation might suggest that further disruptions of oil supplies and new large price increases in the 1980–2 period might stretch that tolerance to the limit.

With Iran as the pivotal factor in the likely oil supply disruptions in the next few years, the following pages will be devoted to a detailed examination of the new energy policy in Iran in order to get an insight into the workings of the energy sector and the likely developments in the future.

Iran's Domestic Energy Policy

Organisation

The organisations responsible for energy production and distribution in Iran are likely to remain intact. Water and power will remain the responsibility of the Ministry of Energy. Despite initial calls for the integration of the National Iranian Oil Company (NIOC) with the National Iranian Gas Company (NIGC) and the National Petrochemical Company (NPC), it seems that they are not going to be integrated as such. The leaders of the three giant ventures are inexperienced and unaware of the general problems of the industry, but fortunately a handful of able and experienced directors who have remained at their posts have managed to persuade their superiors to moderate their attitudes. However, the majority of capable technocrats have either been forced out or have decided to leave because of repeated abuse, leaving behind only a thin layer of expertise.

The petrochemical industry is by its nature very different to the oil industry, and even if integration was forced upon it, NPC would still have to operate as a separate entity. A number of important officials in the industry believe that NIGC should be dissolved and its functions carried out by NIOC. They point out that there is no need for a separate gas company because:

(a) gas production is undertaken by NIOC and not NIGC;
(b) future gas export plans are cancelled and NIOC could itself handle IGAT I sales;

    (c) for distribution, NIOC's outlets and longer experience will be of great value and will lead to major cost savings.

This way of thinking is in the minority within the industry today, but it is possible that in the short term NIGC will be totally absorbed within NIOC.

In the past, each of these entities represented an empire within the national government. They failed to co-ordinate their policies, despite a nominal High Energy Council, and the Prime Minister exercised little control over them. They reported individually to the Shah, obtained his approval on an issue and then carried on as they wished. Now the co-ordination of the policies is far greater and there is no evidence of disregard of the government line by the industry chiefs. Smaller boards of directors at NPC and NIGC have made co-ordination far easier than in the past.

Generally speaking, the operational problems of the energy sector in Iran today are great. Foreign technicians and experts required particularly for the secondary recovery projects and petrochemical operations are not welcomed. The more experienced and able Iranians have been dismissed or forced into early retirement. Nevertheless, the energy sector is at least still working at a slow pace, which is more than can be said for other public or private organisations. It is understood that the industry chiefs are well aware of the problems created by the shortage of skilled manpower, but are unable to do much in the tense, revengeful political environment.

The possibility of industrial problems at the energy sector is ever present. The workers with leftist tendencies, particularly in the oil-fields, refineries and power plants, pose a serious threat to the future of the Islamic regime in Iran. The leftists are mainly white-collar workers, who are a minority numerically but command a great deal of influence among the workers; their co-operation is essential for the continued operation of the oil sector and power plants. The leftist oil workers have a great deal of sympathy for autonomy-seeking ethnic minorities, particularly the Arab population in Khuzistan, which has been active in blowing up pipelines and sabotage at refineries. However, the Arab community is concentrated in Khoramshahr, Ahwaz and Abadan. Very few Arabs are employed in the oilfields or refineries.

The oil workers seemed to have come to an understanding with the first NIOC chief after the revolution: Hassan Nazieh — a social democrat and human rights activist who is now a fugitive after being dismissed from his post for challenging the clergy on the issue of human rights. With total support declared for Nazieh by the oil industry workers and threats of strike in case of his dismissal, many expected a confrontation after he left. But except for a short-lived strike at the Tehran headquarters of NIOC, nothing happened. It would be a mistake to conclude from this that Ayatollah Khomeini's supporters are in control of the oil industry. The leftists are waiting for the right opportunity to provoke a serious confrontation. Indeed, the leftists had seriously opposed the re-start of oil exports last March, and it was only after prolonged negotiations with Nazieh that they agreed to let the oil flow. Seven of the leftist oil leaders have been detained without charge since early summer and the new regime is prepared to deal harshly with opposition in the oilfields. But the recent physical attack on the new Oil Minister, Ali Akbar Moin-Far, a close aide of Khomeini and a member of the ruling Revolutionary Council, for opposing the welfare demands of workers drawn up by leftists, is just another sign that the troubles are yet to come. Indeed, it is reasonable to speculate that the downfall of the Islamic regime will start with the closure of the oilfields as it did with the Shah. The timing of the confrontations will depend on Khomeini's domestic policy — late 1980 may be a time to look for such troubles. All oil workers, and not leftists alone, feel that they have been let down after the revolution. Instrumental in the Shah's downfall, they demanded a seat on the Revolutionary Council, one or two Ministerial portfolios and major welfare benefits. They received nothing.

So far as OPEC affairs are concerned, there has been a transfer of authority from the Ministry of Economic Affairs and Finance to the Ministry of Oil. This is a logical step. In the past, rivalries between Finance Ministers and NIOC chiefs made co-ordination impossible. Indeed, Iran was the only OPEC member without an Oil Minister. The creation of a Ministry of Oil is thus a welcome decision. There has long been a need for a Cabinet Minister to co-ordinate the activities of NIOC, NIGC and NPC. Without a total reorganisation of the industry, the Oil Ministry will become just one more bureaucratic device. The present constitution of the companies allows them unusual authority and there is always the danger of them becoming empires again, unless restructuring is started and given the sanction of law.

Under the present rules all companies are registered as private joint stock companies whose shares are fully owned by the government. The representative of shareholders are seven Cabinet Ministers (including the Prime Minister) who will meet annually to discuss and approve the operational budget. All questions have to be asked and answered in one or two sessions. Without access to details of billions of dollars of investments and receipts, these meetings tend to become a formality. Indeed, there are parts of the NIOC constitution which run contrary to the laws of the land. Under Article 53, NIOC is empowered to take the oil income, spend what it needs and return the remainder to the treasury, while national law requires all funds to go to the treasury for allocation by the government. This means that no government control can really be exercised under present laws, and industry chiefs are not as such answerable to anyone.

At the same time, since these companies are registered as private companies, salary levels are not governed by the general rules for government employees. This may not be a bad thing, as higher salaries are awarded for the specialised work in the hydrocarbon sector. But, at the same time, inefficiency and over-staffing in these companies are even worse than other government departments. These companies will have to decide to behave either as a public or a private company, but not both. To avoid past mistakes and to maintain a firm grip on the industry with its multi-billion dollar incomes and expenditures, the new Ministry must seek a totally new set of rules for a complete overhaul of the organisations.

Oil

The oil industry in Iran today is operating under abnormal conditions. The continued threat of strikes implicit in the political and welfare demands of the NIOC employees in the south has significantly reduced the authority of the Tehran head office. The real power lies in the oilfields of the south and at the refineries.

Iran's former capacity of 7 million b/d is not being utilised and it is not even certain what the capacity will be in a couple of years. Some published US intelligence reports expect the capacity to fall to 2.9 million barrels a day in early 1980s, as part of a deliberate Iranian policy. I view this estimate as on the low side and expect a capacity of 3.5–4 billion b/d will be maintained well into the 1980s. I certainly do not think that Iran is *deliberately* following a policy to reduce capacity.

It was only natural that after the revolution the rate of production be reduced to make a dwindling asset last longer. Even under the Shah, many people within the industry had called for production of 4 million b/d. These calls were swept aside by the Shah, who was in a rush to arm Iran and to achieve industrialisation with indiscriminate and over-ambitious development projects. The present production rate is around 4 million b/d with 3–3.5 million coming from the Khuzistan area and the rest from four joint ventures (IPAC, IMINICO, LAPCO, SIRIP) and one service contract (SOFIRAN).

Barring any changes in the government's instructions, NIOC plans to maintain production at around 4 million b/d for the remainder of 1979. It is doubtful that production will ever exceed that rate again, even if the present regime in Iran falls. Indeed, one may expect a lowering of production in the near future. I shall elaborate on this issue later.

From a total production of 4 million b/d, around 700,000 b/d are used domestically and the remainder exported. The exported volume includes 250,000–300,000 b/d of products (light and heavy distillates) from the Abadan refinery. This leaves roughly 3 million b/d of crude exports, which is divided into 2.8 million b/d of 9-month term contracts, and 100,000–200,000 b/d of spot oil. NIOC was previously selling around 600,000 b/d of crude in the frenetic spot market of April-June 1979. But increasing commitments to sell oil at official prices to some poorer Muslim countries who could not afford to pay for spot prices as well as new term contracts, meant that the available spot crude was significantly reduced by the beginning of the fourth quarter of 1979. The Iran US oil embargo released over half a million b/d for spot sales from November 1979. Since the embargo against the US will be a temporary measure when new term contracts are signed in early 1980 it is expected that no more than 20 per cent of Iranian oil will be sold on the spot market.

The recipients of Iranian oil can be classified as follows (9-month term contract, crude and product):

(1) 21 contracts with independent companies from Belgium, Switzerland, West Germany, France, the USA and Japan (total delivery 950,000 b/d);

(2) 6 contracts with the state oil companies from Romania, Brazil, Philippines, Finland, Portugal and Bangladesh (total delivery 270,000 b/d);

(3) 8 contracts with major international oil companies (total delivery 1–1.1 million b/d);

(4) 20 contracts with companies, the nature of which are not specified, from India, Spain, Sweden, West Germany, Sri Lanka, Italy and Eastern Europe (total delivery 700,000 b/d).

The recipients of Iran's oil, except for the last category, are listed below (except for the US firms temporarily embargoed since November 1979).

(1)	Mitsubish	(10)	Kanomatsu
(2)	Mitsui	(11)	Japan Line
(3)	Marubeni	(12)	Nichimen
(4)	C. Itoh & Co.	(13)	Kyodo
(5)	Showa Oil	(14)	BP
(6)	Idemitsu	(15)	CFP
(7)	Somitomo	(16)	Gulf Oil
(8)	Dai Kyo Oil	(17)	Exxon
(9)	Nissho-Iwai	(18)	Caltex

(19) Texaco	(28) Marathon
(20) Charter	(29) Nesteoy (Finland's state oil co.)
(21) Marco	(30) Petrofina
(22) Union	(31) Petrol Export (Romania's state oil
Rheinische	co.)
(23) Fillipin	(32) Ashland
(24) Petrogal	(33) Amerada Hess
(Portugal's state	(34) Petrobras (Brazil's state oil co.)
oil co.)	(35) Arco
(25) Marcrich	
(26) Bangladesh	
(27) Sun Oil	

It can be seen from the above figures that 40 per cent of Iran's contract sales go to the major oil companies which were part of the Iranian consortium. This compares with the 60 per cent share of the consortium members of Iran's exports agreed upon by both parties when negotiating for the revision of the 1973 Sales and Purchase Agreement just before the outbreak of strikes in the oilfields in the last quarter of 1978. Iran's sales of crude to all purchasers are devoid of any discounts or fees and the majors are treated in the same way as other companies. No one has seriously been looking for discounts in the tight market.

There are pressures from the left wing, clergy, media and even some government Ministers to force NIOC gradually to eliminate crude sales to the consortium members. Preference, they think, should be given to spot sales and state oil companies. Here is a typical case of political forces, with little knowledge of the industry, trying to force the technocrats to toe their line. To fight off this pressure an internal report was prepared within NIOC and submitted to its chief to justify the present sales structure. It was pointed out in the study that:

(1) spot prices are not always above OPEC prices, indeed they have traditionally been below the official price and Iran cannot totally be dependent on spot sales;

(2) sales to smaller companies involves inefficiencies and higher costs, particularly in the transport sector. Such sales, particularly on the state-to-state deals provide pressure points when prices tend to rise. At the same time all trade between Iran and the purchasing state may be affected when direct contact is made.

(3) major oil companies as tax collecting agents provide a cushion between the producer and the purchaser. As the largest purchaser of OPEC oil they provide an easy outlet for the exporter.

Fortunately the stand of the technocrats within NIOC has meant that there is unlikely to be a drastic change in the sales pattern. I expect that the role of the international oil companies in the Iranian oil exports will remain more or less at the same level in the next few years.

One of the side-effects of the revolution has been the complete shut-down of gas reinjection programmes for secondary recovery, which was expected to increase the enhanced recovery factor from 18 per cent of the oil-in-place to 25 per cent. One cannot over-emphasise the importance of this programme, as each percentage point of recovery will add 3.5 billion barrels or 5 per cent to Iran's present proven reserves of 60–70 billion barrels. Every few percentage points means an additional North Sea or Alaska in terms of recoverable oil available on the world market.

The gas re-injection programme which got off to a slow start in 1974 and encountered some technical difficulties during 1976/7 was far behind schedule in early 1978, when the disturbances in the country began. With the strike at the oilfields, the programme was halted. There are no signs of any plans to restart the project. The secondary recovery programme requires advanced technology and is very much dependent on foreign experts. Not only have the latter left Iran, but also one or two Iranian firms (such as Iran-Texas, fully owned by the Iranians) capable of designing parts of the project are in the process of closing down. It seems obvious and ironical that the lack of attention to Iran's small indigenous skilled manpower will eventually lead to an even greater foreign dependence than formerly.

The amount of gas necessary for the programme was previously estimated at 12.8 billion c.f.d. optimally and 6.5–7 billion c.f.d. at a minimum. This gas is, of course, available under the ground, but not yet developed. Part of the required gas was to be supplied from the 'associated' gas, of which around 50 per cent is now being flared, with the rest coming from the gasfields of the south near Bushehr. These estimates were based on maintaining a production capacity of around 6.2 million b/d from the Khuzistan area. With the present (and quite possibly future) production target of around 4 million b/d the re-injection rate and the astronomical $8 billion cost of the project will be revised downwards. Nevertheless, despite the apparent lack of urgency due to the prospects of reduced capacity needs, if capacity is not to fall quickly it is imperative that the programme is restarted as soon as possible, otherwise, through negligence, even present rates will not be maintained in the near future. At the same time, increasing the capacity will prove to be far more costly.

Iran's oil income in the first quarter of the Iranian year (commencing 21 March) was estimated to run at around $20–21 billion annually. After the June 1979 OPEC conference the estimates were raised to around $24–25 billion for the country's first post-revolution year — the highest ever oil income in current prices. At the same time, the government's economic policy of tightening import controls, defence and nuclear energy cuts, foreign exchange restrictions as well as a serious economic recession, has meant that the government will be left with a large surplus of foreign exchange this year. The government finds it politically inexpedient to revert to the large-scale import of goods and services from the West, or to ease exchange restrictions.

Here we have a major dilemma facing the present government in Iran, or for that matter a future government or a new regime. Obviously Iran has given some kind of undertaking to its OPEC partners to produce at about the present rate for a period of time. Its foreign reserves are bulging and it finds it politically unacceptable to import goods. At the same time, the government finds it embarrassing to admit that large reserves are being kept at an American bank and lent out to its customers. It is therefore quite possible that around 1 million b/d may have to be taken off the market in early 1980 for domestic political reasons. This will obviously push the marginal oil market towards higher prices for spot and official sales.

Another major problem which will affect the production rate in Iran is the lack of maintenance and servicing of oil facilities. *Regular* periodic maintenance carried out by foreign and Iranian experts as in the past is now totally ignored. With capacity already falling to 4.5–5 million b/d and without proper systematic care for the oilfields and complex refineries, it is likely that production will be forced down by 1 million b/d by late 1980, for purely technical reasons.

The trend in the future is towards a lowering of production, irrespective of which political group rules the country. Had the Shah survived the revolution he would have been forced himself to follow a more or less similar line on production. At the same time, domestic consumption is expected to rise to nearly 1.5 million b/d by 1985 and to just under 2 million b/d by 1990. It is doubtful whether more than 1 million b/d of Iranian oil will be available for export by the end of the 1980s. Budgetary needs are, of course, important. Less reliance in the future on oil proceeds is to be expected, not because the country's industrialisation programmes are going to succeed or import needs reduced, but because political forces will have to be the dominant consideration.

A brief discussion of the general state of the Iranian economy and the budget may prove useful at this point. Because of the disorganisation within the government hierarchy no actual data on the economy are available, except for inflation and unemployment, and these are subject to disagreement among various political groups.

Unlike the last few years of the Shah's reign where inflation was mainly caused by excessive purchasing power, the current impetus behind inflationary pressures is the shortage of imported goods and domestically produced goods exacerbated by very poor distribution. Many food items, particularly meat, are hard to find and their prices have risen by more than 100 per cent. The Minister of Agriculture has announced a 7–10 per cent growth in agricultural production, but most observers question this. Worst hit is the service sector, which has been put on the brink of total destruction by the 'Islamic way of life' as practised by the new regime. The industrial sector is also suffering because of the shortage of imported raw materials, labour and management problems. While the government claims that industrial capacity utilisation is between 60 and 80 per cent, many observers think that the actual figure is closer to 30 per cent. The rate of inflation which was brought down from 30 per cent to around 12 per cent by the autumn of 1978 has risen sharply. Official central bank statistics show an average of 12.8 per cent increase in the wholesale price index for April–August 1979, rising to 18 per cent in August. No official figures for the retail price index representing inflation are available; unofficial estimates range from 30 to 50 per cent. The official level of unemployment is around 1–1.5 million, but unofficial estimates, more reliable for employment, put the figure at 3–4 million out of an active work-force of over 9 million.

As for the budget, an official announcement of a highly aggregated nature was made for the current year's budget (March 1979 to March 1980). Figures are shown in Table 12.6.

Table 12.6: Iranian Budget: Sources and Uses of Funds (billions of US $)

Sources	1979–80	1978–9
Oil and gas	21.0 (61%)	21.7 (47%)
Taxes	5.1 (15%)	8.5 (18%)
Other revenues	3.6 (10%)	3.5 (8%)
Deficit financing	4.7 (14%)	12.4 (27%)
Total	34.4 (100%)	46.1
Uses		
Current expenditures	22.2 (65%)	24.7 (53%)
Development expenditures	12.2 (35%)	17.3 (38%)
Other	0	4.1 (9%)
Total	34.4	46.1

The proposed budget shows a decline of 25 per cent over the previous year. It also shows heavier reliance on oil as a revenue source and a 30 per cent cut in development expenditure. The budget also implies the need for 2.6 million b/d of oil exports to meet budgetary needs.

Anyone familiar with the process of budgeting in Iran would not attach too much importance to the budget. There is seldom any adherence to budget guidelines at all. The policy implication of the budget, that Iran needs to produce 3.3 million b/d of oil at the minimum to satisfy its budgetary needs, is extremely misleading. The planning authorities in Iran are convinced that they could easily manage with $12–15 billion of oil revenues corresponding to 1.5–1.9 million b/d of exports. This is possible due to (1) cancellation of arms imports, (2) cancellation of prestige projects such as the purchase of nuclear power reactors, (3) major restrictions on imports, particularly consumer goods, (4) foreign exchange restrictions and (5) the general slow-down of economic activity, reducing demand for imported items. This analysis is difficult to fault. It is fruitless to assume for policy purposes that the Islamic regime will have to produce a certain amount of oil.[1] If there is a need, it is fair to assume that the government in Iran could function with far less oil revenue for a year or two. At the same time the foreign exchange reserves of Iran, at over $12 billion, provide a cushion for the Iranian leaders to function even without oil production for a year or so. The US freeze of Iranian assets, after all, can only be temporary.

Gas

The impact of the revolution has been particularly severe as far as exports are concerned. In fact, in the last two years before the revolution, strong objections were raised by Iranian technocrats against gas export plans. After much debate the Shah agreed to order a freeze on any new gas export agreements. The reasoning was based on the low netback of gas sales compared to oil. For instance, in a typical LNG export plan, it was estimated that the netback at the wellhead would be around 30¢ per thousand cubic feet (assuming an 18 per cent return on investment). This would correspond to 20–25 per cent of the similar BTU export of crude. Given the expected energy shortage of the 1980s and 1990s and the immense reinjection needs, it was thought unwise to export gas.

After the revolution, as a result of political and technical considerations several projects were cancelled. Future export plans now include the following.

1 Kalingas Project — involving 1.2 billion c.f.d. of LNG exports for three separate projects aimed at three different markets: USA, Japan and Western Europe. The strategic choice of markets and relatively small size of the exported volume were basically looked on as a market penetration tactic rather than wholesale export of gas. The NIGC agreement with the US firm Columbia Gas was well advanced and the agreement involved innovative clauses worked out by NIGC men which made it one of the best contracts ever drawn up between the host country and the purchaser. This contract was faced with *de facto* cancellation through the refusal of the US federal authorities in the last quarter of 1978. The Japanese deal was moving ahead with $6 million of Japanese investment in the initial stage. This is understood to be on the verge of cancellation with 'reasonable' compensation for the foreign investor. And the European export plan never got off the ground in the first place.

It seems that the Kalingas project is dead and buried until at least the end of the next decade. Indeed it was precarious even before the revolution. LNG exports will not be major foreign exchange earners for Iran and in the future more and more gas will be consumed domestically to release oil for exports. Early next century might be a good time to look for Iran's gas in the world market. Again, it should be emphasised that the political leadership in the future will have to follow broadly the same strategy, irrespective of who rules the country.

2 IGAT II Project — for export of 1.65 billion c.f.d. to Europe via the Soviet Union through a swap deal. The total cost of the pipeline was reported unofficially to be around $3–4 billion, of which $400–500 million has already been spent. In fact, the constructed pipeline can easily be connected to IGAT I pipeline for domestic gas consumption. IGAT II has been attacked by many technocrats in Iran since its inception. It was difficult to see the economic justification of gas delivered at the Soviet border for around $1 per thousand cubic feet at the time, when exploration and transportation costs were close to that figure. Any reasonable 'intrinsic value' for gas added to other cost would have yielded a negative netback. Let us remember that this was not the associated gas with perhaps zero opportunity cost, but gas from the Pars gasfield. Still, this contract was far superior to IGAT I. As far as the Shah was concerned, the political advantages of making Europe dependent upon Iran via the Soviet Union was the important consideration and he overruled all purely economic arguments against it. The new Iranian government's first ambassador to the Soviet Union came out strongly in favour of continuing this contract, even advocating an IGAT III for the future. Nevertheless, the industry stood firm and a final decision was made to cancel the project altogether and to accept the losses. IGAT II has thus been cancelled.

3 IGAT I — involving direct gas exports to the Soviet Union of just under 1 billion c.f.d. The terms of the contract at the time it was sealed and particularly as it involved the construction of Iran's first 600,000-ton steel mill, could be termed as acceptable. But in today's circumstances this contract is highly detrimental to Iran's interests. The last official price for gas was around 75¢ per thousand cubic feet. Under the contract gas prices were linked to the movements of bunker oil price posted by the majors at the Iranian ports. The gas price could only be revised if bunker prices went up by over 30 per cent and only then negotiations could start. Since the major oil companies of the former consortium handed the Abadan refinery back to NIOC only Mobil oil posts prices there and this will come to an end soon. The yardstick would then have to be NIOC postings. The Soviets objected to relying on NIOC postings, ignoring the simple fact that NIOC has to compete in the Persian Gulf with many other sellers. They insisted that postings by Aramco members at Ras-Al-Tanura in Saudi Arabia should be taken as the yardstick. The Soviets were not even prepared to accept a formula of average postings by national oil companies in the region. Clearly Iran could not depend on a foreign country for its gas prices, and subject to continuing haggling on the 'correct' posted price. Iranian officials, angered by this unreasonable stand, wanted a high-level warning sent to the Soviets. When the Tabriz riots started in early 1978, the government decided not to pursue its arguments further for fear of Soviet political reaction in the disturbances. Another problem was that the Soviets paid for gas in their domestic (soft) currency, which because of the inferior quality of their goods the Iran government was unable to use. There resulted an accumulation of rubles ($250 million a year) which were unspent. After the revolution gas deliveries to the Soviet Union fell to around 500–550 million c.f.d. or 60 per cent of the former deliveries due to the decline in oil production. Despite the flaring of half the associated gas for technical, if not political, reasons, the exported volume has been limited to the above level. With the increase in oil prices, it is expected that corresponding new gas prices will be around $1–1.10 per thousand cubic feet. Iranians now hope to couple the price increase with a Soviet commitment on the expansion of the Isfahan steel mill from 600,000 to 1.9 million tons, on a barter basis. This is an excellent way to spend the accumulating roubles, far preferable to price increases in a currency that cannot be spent.

An interesting idea unofficially debated with regarding to the future of IGAT I is to try to impose IGAT II terms on IGAT I. This would have advantages for both sides.

(1) The Soviets would be assured of a twenty-year supply of Iran's gas. The present IGAT I contract will end in about five years and Iran may well decide not to agree to the optional renewal.

(2) Perhaps 50 per cent of the volume received could be ear-

marked for Europe with the other half being used in the Soviet Union's energy-deficient south. Like IGAT II, a transit fee could be charged by the Soviets. Indeed, it is just possible to increase the deliveries to the Soviet Union slightly to around 1.1 billion c.f.d. If the already completed section of IGAT II is to be used for domestic gas transport, it will even be possible to allocate more gas to IGAT I deliveries to the Soviet Union.

(3) With the gas price delivered at Astara on the Soviet border at around $1.50–1.70 per thousand cubic feet, under the original agreement (with necessary escalations and foreign exchange adjustment between D-marks and US dollars), all Iranian income would be in hard currency.

(4) Iran's flared gas would go to the Soviet Union and the remainder would be used domestically and earmarked for reinjection.

There are good reasons why Iran should insist on such an agreement. Soviet negotiators may be the least flexible in the world, but this time the incentive to agree would be considerable if they knew that the IGAT I contract would not be renewed.

Petrochemicals

After the revolution, two major decisions were made on the petrochemical plants. First, all the small petrochemical plants were merged together under the direct control of NPC. Second, the Iran-Japan Petrochemical complex (IJPC) survived with practically identical terms originally set out in the agreement. This 50–50 joint venture, involving around $3 billion joint investment, which with associated investment comes to around $5 billion, is one of the few major projects which escaped the axe: outright cancellation or nationalisation. The reasons for its survival are twofold. First, 85 per cent of the work is completed and the terms of the agreement seem reasonable. Second, and perhaps most important, some extremely knowledgeable people in the industry were able to persuade the government that IJPC should be retained in the national interest.

The present leaders of NPC have a more realistic outlook on the future of the petrochemical industry in Iran than their predecessors. They are convinced that for a long time the petrochemical industry will not be economically viable compared to the West (in terms of the price of gas input). Manpower shortage, dependence on foreign skills, inefficiency and infrastructural problems are expected to remain with the industry for a long time.

With the expected expansion of the domestic markets it is thought that 50 per cent of volume and 25 per cent value of the IJPC products will be used domestically in Iran. Petrochemicals are no longer looked at as a major source of foreign exchange earnings in the 1980s as oil exports are reduced. Also, it is unlikely that new major petrochemical plants will be constructed in Iran over the next decade.

Again, as with other projects in the energy sector under the Shah, strong objections had been raised by government technocrats on the emphasis on, and false expectations from, the petrochemical industry. These objections, often reported to the highest authorities, were based on:

(1) the high capital costs in Iran for plant construction;
(2) incorrect value — added calculations based on the erroneous assumption of zero gas cost;
(3) an unclear export market, given the extremely confused future of the export markets as well as the likelihood of imposition of high tariff walls by the US and EEC;
(4) the problem of excess capacity on the order of 30–35 per cent internationally and the need carefully to study the similar plans by SABIC (Saudi Arabia) as well as other Gulf states before embarking on large projects.

These objections were often overruled as a result of the personal relationship of the NPC chief and the Shah. Nevertheless, the Shah was reconsidering the project just before the unrest started in Iran, and it is likely that a reappraisal would have come about gradually.

Atomic Energy

In the early 1970s a Canadian consultancy firm forecast that Iran's electricity demand would be 55,000 megawatts by 1993. For some reason not made clear it was thought that around 40 per cent, or 23,000 megawatts, should be generated from atomic power through the acquisition of twenty large-size reactors (PWRs):

(1) two 1,190-megawatt plants from the German firm Kraftwerunion (KWU) at Bushehr (Halilch);
(2) two 935-megawatt plants from the French firm Framaton near the Karun river (Darkhouin);
(3) four 1,200-megawatt plants by KWU: two near Isfahan and two at another site;
(4) two 1,200-megawatt plants by the German firm Brown Boveri;
(5) two other plants from Framaton;
(6) eight plants from Westinghouse (US).

Iran's Atomic Energy Organisation (IAEO), headed by an Assistant to the Prime Minister, was one of the empires referred to earlier. Though the Atomic Energy Council, made up of the Prime Minister, the Minister of Economic Affairs and Finance and the Director of Plan and Budget Organisation was to make final decisions on the IAEO policy, in fact IAEO took instructions from no one but the Shah. In many circumstances it would not even reply to a simple inquiry from the Prime Minister's office. All data relating to costs and future plans were kept out of reach of the other government departments. IAEO grew with dizzying speed, but only in a superficial manner. Many graduates in unrelated areas were recruited at salaries two to five times the government range. Expensive large buildings acquired or rented by IAEO mushroomed all over Tehran. The educational budget of IAEO of 10 billion rials exceeded that of Tehran University. Corruption in the organisation became widespread and some of the contracts awarded contravened the most basic government laws.

In such circumstances the technocrats in other departments who were forced to use covert action to get estimates of costs and learn what was happening inside the organisation undertook a number of studies and reports about the organisation. With the help of academics and experts in the energy field studies were prepared which underlined the urgency of bringing IAEO under strong government control. The objections against the programmes of IAEO can be summarised.

(1) Costs per kilowatt were \$3,000–4,000 compared to \$800–1,000 in other countries.

(2) There was no clear need for twenty reactors and the original estimate of electricity demand had been exaggerated.

(3) Vast gas reserves with an electricity generation cost of \$300–500 per kilowatt made atomic energy at best a long-range option.

(4) Plants were too big for Iran's national grid. The national grid today has an installed capacity of 6,800 megawatts, an available capacity of 4,500 megawatts and operative capacity of 2,500 megawatts. To bring in two plants at 2,400 megawatts onstream would lead to destabilisation of the grid and chaos in the cases of frequent shutdowns which are expected for large plants.

(5) Transmission lines would be incapable of connecting such a large electrical flow to the grid.

(6) The plants at Isfahan, where water is scarce, would call for several monumental cooling towers unmatched in the world, and hence untested.

(7) The strong *turnkey* nature of the contracts allowed for little participation of Iranians and hence no real technological benefit would be passed on in terms of training or technique.

The steady flow of negative reports finally influenced the Shah, who had looked on atomic energy as his pet project. By the summer of 1978 IAEO was put under the direct control of the Ministry of Energy. By late October 1978, it was decided to cancel sixteen of the plants which were in the planning stage. The two KWU plants at Bushehr were 50 per cent completed and the foundations had been laid for the two Karun plants. It was decided that the two KWU plants should go ahead and the other two be studied again. By December 1978 even the two Karun plants were curtailed and there remained only two plants to go onstream in the 1980s.

After the revolution, a decision had to be made on whether the two remaining reactors, for which 5.8 billion DM had been spent, should go ahead or not. Surprisingly, from within the IAEO there were great objections to these two plants. Finally it was concluded that:

(1) it is not possible to bring these two plants by transmission lines onstream and connect them to the national grid;
(2) by going through the complicated calculations of escalation clauses the total cost would be nearer 18 billion DM and that it was best to cut the losses and terminate them;
(3) based on the clauses of the contract, the demonstrable cost plus reasonable loss of profits should be paid to KWU. IAEO calculated that costs came to 3 billion DM and 1 billion loss of profit, a total of 4 billion DM. On the basis of this Iran expects to get 1.8 billion DM back from KWU. Iranians also claim that the agreed standards were not fully carried out and point to 30 items of breach of contract due to lower standards. At the same time KWU claims an additional 1 billion DM for the work carried out. Both claims are negotiation stands and a compromise will probably be reached.

Atomic energy, however, is not totally dead and buried in Iran. There are two forces which have emerged in support of nuclear power. First, there are the university professors and technocrats who believe that Iran should not be left behind in nuclear technology. This group does not look at atomic energy as a major source of electricity in the next two decades, but they advocate 25 to 100 MW research reactors and possibly a 250–300 MW plant for electricity generation with a view to learning about the operational problems of the technology. Second, there is a group of clergymen associated with the leading Islamic party who have declared that it is the Iranian scientists' 'religious duty' to pursue nuclear power in search of an atomic bomb. These clergymen, who command a lot of popular influence, consider the control of nuclear bombs by non-Moslems of East and West a threat to the future of Islam. There is no evidence that this idea is supported by the top religious leaders, but at the same time neither has there been an explicit rejection of such proposals. It is not certain whether the government could withstand pressure from the clergy, if the clergy really promoted the bomb as a goal of national-religious duty.

OPEC Affairs

Iran's attitude as far as OPEC is concerned will clearly be consistently in favour of price increases, joining the group of hard-liners such as Iraq, Algeria and Libya. But the hawkish attitude may be more on the surface than in depth. While Iran will push for higher prices whenever possible, the general irrational demands of some members will not be shared by Iran. Though an OPEC member, Iran is a Gulf country and will no doubt have to adopt policies which can be operational within the Persian Gulf region. Thus the regional location will, I believe, be more dominant in Iran's oil stand than the OPEC consideration as a whole. However, Iran's 'moral' influence in OPEC has increased as that of Saudi Arabia has declined.

The reduced rate of production from Iran has severely limited the Saudis' previously powerful role as the swing producer. Saudi Arabia is no longer able to threaten to flood the market with cheaper oil in its efforts to dictate price moderation. Most recent reports indicate Saudi Arabia's sustainable capacity at 9.5 million b/d,[2] the rate at which it has been producing in the last half of 1979. The Saudis have initially said that they would reduce production to their previous ceiling of 8.5 million b/d from early 1980. They may yet extend the period of higher production for a few months,[3] but they are finding it futile to over-extend themselves fighting a losing battle against supply restrictions and price rises. A good example of their new weakness in the wake of the Iranian reduced output is their stand in regard to oil prices in the last half of 1979. They pumped oil at peak capacity with prices of $4–5 per barrel below other OPEC and non-OPEC export prices. Not only were the OPEC prices maintained in the international market, but also many countries were able to raise their prices again during October and November of 1979. The Saudis will find it politically difficult within OPEC to maintain their isolated and conspicuous position as the defender of the West.

The Iranian Revolution has changed the balance of power in OPEC in favour of small producers by stretching to the limit the output potential of Saudi Arabia. It is now likely that any of the smaller producers could effect major price increases on their own without having to consult others, by some kind of supply restriction. It is, however, unlikely that output restriction will spread from Iran to other countries on a large-scale basis, since most of these countries have had some kind of a ceiling for some time. As noted earlier, Iran is likely to take a million b/d off the market sometime in 1980 for political-technical reasons. This will provide the grounds for an average (official and spot) price of $30–35 in 1980. If the Saudis revert to production of 8.5 million b/d or less, then the pressure on prices will be intense.

Iran needs to pay more attention to the staffing of her OPEC team. Another matter which requires attention is the Ministerial Committee on long-term OPEC strategy. The idea for such a committee was generated in early 1978 and at the June 1978 OPEC Ministerial conference, the Ministerial Committee of the six most important members met formally for the first time. The idea had generated a lot of interest in Iran particularly, because it was thought that OPEC should not wait for the outcome of the North-South dialogue to work out a strategy. With the expected dramatic changes which were to come in the 1980s, OPEC had to be prepared with a set of its own options and strategies. It was thought that OPEC as an organisation may have to play a different kind of role with new functions. After a great deal of discussion a working paper was presented by Iran to the Ministerial Committee which formed the basis of the future research. Each country introduced one person who would be a national representative/consultant and outside consultants were also employed. The Committee voted Sheikh Zaki Yamani chairman of the group of experts. The topics under study were: future of Soviet oil, future of Chinese oil, future relationships with developing nations to help increase their indigenous oil supplies and relations with developed countries; Mexican oil, the future pricing strategy, OPEC's bargaining position, etc. These studies were completed in the first quarter of 1979 and a co-ordination of studies meeting took place in Taief, Saudi Arabia during late July/early August 1979. Another meeting in October of 1979 was expected to complete the proposals which were to be submitted in December 1979 at the OPEC conference.

After the revolution, the Iranian authorities seemed to have washed their hands of their long-term strategy meeting. They withdrew their representative, suspecting this to be a trap in which the past regime was involved. This lack of interest in OPEC affairs is short-sighted. It is the result of ignorance about the contents and importance of the final report, which will have its influence whether or not Iran signs it. This short-sightedness may be excusable in the immediate aftermath of the revolution, but it should not become part of government policy. Revolutionary militance and ideological purity combined with wishful thinking will only create problems for the efficient use of the country's resources. Attention to the technical underpinnings of the nation's economy and its relationship to the international oil market will require clear thinking devoid of emotional reactions and responses to perceived or imagined injustices. In some ways the new regime in Iran has already shown a readiness to confront Iran's problems realistically. It is to be hoped that in the process OPEC, and indeed the international community, are seen for what they are: part of an interdependent system which, if disrupted, affects producer and consumer alike. Iran's revolution has shattered the international oil market without so far reinvigorating Iran's approach to its own future energy problems. How far it serves as a model for other oil producers and how far it reflects its own indigenous circumstances remain to be seen.

Notes

1. Cf. Theodore Moran's study for the Congressional Research Service.
2. This may increase to over 12 million b/d by the early 1980s.
3. The Saudi authorities announced in December 1979 their intention to maintain production at the 9.5 million b/d level until April 1980.

Bibliography

Articles

Iran Ali, Mehrumisa 'Iran's Relations with the US and USSR', *Pakistan Horizon*, (3rd Quarter, 1973)

Barang, Marcel 'L'Iran: renaissance d'un empire', *Le Monde Diplomatique* (May 1975)

Bill, James 'Iran and the Crisis of 1978', *Foreign Affairs* (Winter 1978/9)

Bozeman, Adda B. 'Iran: US Foreign Policy and the Tradition of Persian Statecraft', *Orbis* (Summer 1979)

Burrell, R.M. 'Iranian Foreign Policy during the Last Decade', *Asian Affairs* (February 1974)

—— 'Iranian Foreign Policy', *Journal of International Affairs* (Fall 1975)

Campbell, John C. 'Oil Power in the Middle East', *Foreign Affairs* (October 1977)

Canot, Frederic 'L'Iran sur la breche 1968/78', *Défense Nationale* (July 1978)

Chubin, Shahram 'Iran: Between the Arab West and the Asian East', *Survival* (July/August 1974)

—— 'Iran's Security in the 1980s', *International Security* (Winter 1978)

—— *Soviet Policy towards Iran and the Gulf*, Adelphi Papers, no. 157 (IISS, London, 1980)

Cooley, John K. 'Iran, Palestinians and the Gulf', *Foreign Affairs* (Summer 1979)

Cottrell, Alvin J. 'Iran, the Arabs and the Persian Gulf', *Orbis* (Fall 1973)

—— 'The Foreign Policy of the Shah', *Strategic Review* (Fall 1975)

—— and Hanks, R.J. 'The Strategic Tremors of Upheaval in Iran', *Strategic Review* (Spring 1979)

Elwell-Sutton, L.P. 'The Iranian Revolution', *International Journal* (Summer 1979)

Freymond, Jacques 'La Crise Iranienne', *Politique Etrangère*, no. 2 (Summer 1979)

Griffith, William E. 'The Revival of Islamic Fundamentalism: the Case of Iran', *International Security* (Summer 1979)

Halliday, Fred 'The Genesis of the Iranian Revolution', *Third World Quarterly* (October 1979)

Hottinger, Arnold 'Die Krise in Iran', *Europa Archiv*, 25 January 1979

Kaiser, Karl 'Iran and the Europe of the Nine: a Relationship of Growing Interdependence', *World Today* (July 1976)

Laquer, Walter 'Why the Shah Fell', *Commentary* (March 1979)

Lenczowski, George 'The Arc of Crisis', *Foreign Affairs* (Spring 1979)

Macdonald, Charles G. 'The Role of Iran and Saudi Arabia in the Development of the Law of the Sea', *Journal of South Asian and Middle East Studies* (Spring 1978)

Majidi, Abdol-Majid 'Iran 1980–85', *World Today* (July 1977)

Moghtadar, Houshang 'Iran's Oil Revenue and Economic Development', *Aussenpolitik* (Fourth Quarter, 1977)

—— 'Iran's Foreign Economic Relations', *Aussenpolitik* (1st and 2nd Quarter, 1978)

Moran, T.H. 'Iranian Defense Expenditures and the Social Crisis', *International Security* (Winter 1978/9)

—— 'Still Well-Oiled?', *Foreign Policy* (Spring 1979)

Mozafari, Mehdi 'Les Nouvelles Dimensions de la Politique Etrangère de l'Iran', *Politique Etrangère*, no. 2 (1975)

Neuman, Stephanie 'Security, Military Expenditures and Socio-economic Development: Reflections on Iran', *Orbis* (Fall 1978)

Parvin, Manoucher 'Political Economy of Soviet-Iranian Trade', *Middle East Journal* (Winter 1977)

Petrossian, Vahe 'Dilemmas of the Iranian Revolution', *World Today* (January 1980)

Pryor, Leslie M. 'Arms and the Shah', *Foreign Policy*, no. 31 (Summer 1978)

Ramazani, Rouhollah K. 'Emerging Patterns of Regional Relations in Iranian Foreign Policy', *Orbis* (Winter 1975)

—— 'Iran's Search for Regional Cooperation', *Middle East Journal* (Spring 1976)

—— 'Iran and the United States: the Dilemma of Political Independence and Political Participation', *Journal of South Asian and Middle Eastern Studies* (Winter 1978)

Iraq Bari, Zohurul 'Syrian-Iraqi Dispute over the Euphrates Waters', *International Studies* (April/June 1977)

Catudal, Honore M. 'The War in Kurdistan: End of a Nationalist Struggle?', *International Relations* (May 1976)

Cockburn, Patrick 'Iraq: Special Report', *Middle East Economic Digest* (*MEED*), 3 June 1977.

Djalili, Mohammed Reza 'Le Rapprochement Irano-Irakien et ses Consequences', *Politique Etrangère*, no. 3 (1975)

Kedourie, Elie 'Continuity and Change in Modern Iraqi History', *Asian Affairs* (June 1975)

Rondot, Philippe 'L'Irak d'aujourd'hui: de la Fermeté au Réalisme', *Politique Etrangère* no. 3 (1978)

—— 'Irak-Syrie: Divergences et Reconciliation', *Défense*

Nationale, February 1979

Shawi, Hamid al 'Le Ba'ath et l'armée en Irak et en Syrie', *Maghreb Machrek* (January/March 1976)

Wright, Claudia 'Iraq — New Power in the Middle East', *Foreign Affairs* (Winter 1979/80)

Anon. 'Irak — Cinq Ans de Revolution Baasiste', *Le Monde Diplomatique* (July 1975)

Anon. 'Irak — Neuf Ans de Pouvoir Baasiste', *Le Monde Diplomatique* (April 1977)

Saudi Arabia Aulas, Marie-Christine 'Petrodollars et Stabilisation du Monde Arabe: la Diplomatique Saoudienne a l'Epreuve', *Le Monde Diplomatique* (April 1977)

Balta, Paul 'L'Arabie Sauoudité de la Tribu l'Etat', *Défense Nationale* (May 1973)

Bonnenfant, Paul 'Utilisation des Recettes Petrolières et Strategie des Groupes Sociaux en Peninsule Arabe', *Maghreb Machrek* (October/December 1978 and January/March 1979)

de Bouteiller, Georges 'L'Arabe Saoudité, Aujourd'hui et Demain', *Défense Nationale* (November and December 1978)

Brabanti, Ralph and Al Farsy, Fouad Abdul-salam 'Saudi Arabia: a Development Perspective', *Journal of South Asian and Middle Eastern Studies* (Fall 1977)

Campbell, John C. 'Oil Power in the Middle East', *Foreign Affairs* (October 1977)

Dawisha, Adeed I. 'Internal Values and External Threats: the Making of Saudi Foreign Policy', *Orbis* (Spring 1979)

Hemsay, Nicolas 'L'Immigration dans le Peninsule Arabique', *Maghreb Machrek* (July/September 1979)

Hoagland, J., and Smith, J.F. 'Saudi Arabia and the United States: Security and Interdependence', *Survival* (March/April 1978)

Martin, Christian 'Puissance et Evolution du Royaume Saoudite', *Le Monde Diplomatique* (February 1974)

Morano, Louis 'Multinationals and Nation States: the Case of Aramco', *Orbis* (Summer 1979)

Rustow, Dankwart A. 'United States-Saudi Relations and the Oil Crisis of the 1980s', *Foreign Affairs* (April 1977)

Salame, Ghaosane 'Development et Dependence: Quelques Remarques Dérivés du Cas Saoudien', *Oriente Moderno* (September/October 1978)

Shirreff, David 'Saudi Arabia: Special Report', *Middle East Economic Digest* (June 1979)

Soulce, G.J.L., and Champenois, L. 'La Politique Extérieure de l'Arabie', *Politique Etrangère*, no. 6 (1977)

Turner, Louis 'Oil and the North-South Dialogue', *World Today*

(February 1977)

—— and Bedore, James 'Saudi Arabia: the Power of the Purse', *International Affairs* (July 1978)

Anon. 'Saudi Arabia: Special Issue', *MEED* (August 1978)

Kuwait Khader, Bichara 'Les Palestiniens au Khoweit', *L'Afrique et L'Asie Modernes* (October 1977)

Mackie, Alan 'Kuwait: Special Report', *MEED* (August 1977)

Tixier, Gilbert 'Evolution Politique et Constitutionelle du Koweit', *Revue Juridique et Politique* (January/March 1974)

Trojanovic, Radmilo 'The Internal Development and International Activity of Kuwait', *Review of International Affairs*, 20 June 1976

Anon. 'Koweit: Developpement et Democratie', *Le Monde Diplomatique* (February 1976)

Oman El Mallakh, Ragaei 'Economic Requirements for Development, Oman', *Middle East Journal* (Autumn 1972)

Kelly, J.B. 'Hadramaut, Oman, Dhufar: the Experience of Revolution', *Middle East Studies* (May 1976)

Peiriss, Denzil, 'Oman: Vital Link to Asia's Security', *Far East Economic Review*, 28 July 1978

Whelan, John, and Shirreff, David 'Oman: Special Report', *MEED* (September 1978)

Anon. 'Oman: Special Survey', *Africa* (November 1973)

Anon. 'Oman vers un état moderne', *Le Monde Diplomatique* (March 1977)

United Arab Emirates Dallaporta, Christian 'Les transferts institutionnels et politiques dans l'Emirat d'Abou Dhabi', *Politique Etrangère*, no. 6 (1974)

Duke Anthony, John 'The Union of Arab Emirates', *Middle East Journal* (Summer 1972)

Qureshi, Khalida 'The United Arab Emirates', *Pakistan Horizon* (4th Quarter, 1973)

Anon. 'UAE — Special Report', *MEED* (July 1977, December 1978, December 1979)

Qatar Kawar, Suleil 'Qatar's Increased Economic Earnings Permit Major Economic, Social Development', *International Monetary Fund* (IMF) *Survey* (August 1977)

Naklek, Emile 'Labor Markets and Citizenship in Bahrayn and Qatar', *Middle East Journal* (Spring 1977)

Bahrain Barth, Robert 'Bahrain Takes Steps to Diversify Industry through Projects Financed by Oil Revenue', *IMF Survey* (November 1977)

Moghtadar, Hooshang 'The Settlement of the Bahrain Question: a Study in Anglo-Iranian-UN Diplomacy', *Pakistan Horizon* (2nd Quarter, 1973)

Anon. 'Bahrain — Special Report', *MEED* (March 1978)

Gulf Region Bey, Franke Heard 'The Gulf States and Oman in Transition', *Asian Affairs* (February 1972)

—— 'Social Changes in the Gulf States and Oman', *Asian Affairs* (October 1972)

Burrell, R.M. 'Politics and Participation where Britannia Once Ruled', *New Middle East* (December 1972)

Chubin, S. 'The International Politics of the Persian Gulf', *British Journal of International Studies* (October 1976)

—— 'The Repercussions of the Crisis in Iran', *Survival*, vol. XXI, no. 3 (May/June 1979)

Cottrell, Alvin 'The Political Balance in the Persian Gulf', *Strategic Review* (Winter 1974)

Djalali, Mohammed Reza, and Kappeler, Dietrich, 'Persian Gulf — Contrasts and Similarities', *Aussenpolitik* (2nd Quarter, 1978)

Hurewitz, J.C. 'The Persian Gulf, British Withdrawal and Western Security', *Annals* (May 1972)

—— 'The Persian Gulf: After Iran's Revolution', *Foreign Policy Association* (Headline Series 244) (1979)

Kennedy, Edward M. 'The Persian Gulf: Arms Race or Arms Control', *Foreign Affairs* (October 1975)

Khan, M.A. Saleem 'Emerging Power Patterns in the Persian Gulf', *Economics and Politics Weekly*, 4 March 1972

—— 'Oil Politics in the Persian Gulf', *India Quarterly* (January/March 1974)

Knapp, Wilfred, 'Stabilité et Instabilité dans le Golfe Arabo-Persique', *Maghreb Machrek* (July/September 1977)

Nye, Roger P. 'Political and Economic Integration in the Arab States of the Gulf', *Journal of South Asian and Middle Eastern Studies* (Fall 1978)

Peretz, Don 'Foreign Policies of the Persian Gulf States', *New Outlook* (January-May (three parts) 1977)

Razavian, M.T. 'The Population Problem in the Persian Gulf Area', *Iranian Review of International Relations* (Fall 1976)

Rondot, Pierre 'Tensions Autour du Golfe', *Défense Nationale* (February 1976)

—— 'Le Mouvement des Nationalistes Arabes et ses Manifestations dans le Monde Arabe d'Aujourd hui', *Défense Nationale* (December 1976)

Wright, Dennis 'The Changed Balance of Power in the Persian

Gulf', *Asian Affairs* (October 1973)

Singh, K.R. 'Conflict and Cooperation in the Gulf', *International Studies* (October/December 1976)

Anon. 'Growth Problems in Wealthy Developing Countries', *Afro-Asian Review* (September/October 1972)

Anon. 'The Persian Gulf and the Indian Ocean', *Iranian Review of International Relations*, no. 8 (Fall 1976)

Books

Amirsadeghi, Hossein (ed.) *Twentieth-century Iran* (Heinemann, London, 1977)

Abdullah, Muhammed Morsy *The United Arab Emirates: a Modern History* (Barnes and Noble, New York, 1978)

Anthony, John Duke *Arab States of the Lower Gulf* (Middle East Institute, Washington, DC, 1975)

Burrell, R.M., and Cottrell, A.J. *Iran, the Arabian Peninsula and the Indian Ocean* (National Strategy Information Center, New York, 1972)

—— *Iran, Afghanistan, Pakistan: Tensions and Dilemmas* (Sage, Beverley Hills, for the Center for Strategy and International Studies, Georgetown University, 1974)

Chubin, Shahram, 'Implications of the Military Build-up in Non-industrial States: the Case of Iran' in Uri Ka'anan, Robert Pfaltegraff and Geoffrey Kemp (eds.), *Arms Transfers to the Third World: the Military Build-up in Less Developed Countries* (Westview Special Studies in International Relations, 1978)

—— and Zabih, Sepehr *The Foreign Relations of Iran: a Developing State in a Zone of Great-Power Conflict* (University of California Press, Berkeley, 1974)

Daniels, John *Abu Dhabi: a Portrait* (Longman, London, 1974)

Ehrenberg, Eckehart *Rustung und Wirtschaft am Golf: Iran und seine Nachbard (1965–78)* (Deutschen Orient-Institut, Hamburg, 1978)

Fenelon, Kevin G. *The United Arab Emirates, an Economic and Social Survey* (Longman, London, 1976)

Gabbay, Rony *Communism and Agrarian Reform in Iraq* (Croom Helm, London, 1978)

Graham, Robert *Iran, the Illusion of Power* (Croom Helm, London, 1978)

Halliday, Fred *Arabia without Sultans* (Penguin, Harmondsworth, 1974)

—— *Iran, Dictatorship and Development* (Penguin, Harmondsworth, 1979)

Khadduri, Majid *Socialist Iraq: a Study in Iraqi Politics since 1968* (Middle East Institute, Washington DC, 1978)

Khouja, Mohamed W., and Sadler, Peter *The Economy of Kuwait* (Macmillan, London, 1979)

Luckner, Helen *A House Built on Sand: a Political Economy of Saudi Arabia* (Ithaca Press, London, 1978)

Mann, Clarence *Abu Dhabi: Birth of an Oil Sheikhdom* (Klayots, Beirut, 1964)

Monroe, Elizabeth (ed.) *The Changing Balance of Power in the Persian Gulf* (American Universities Field Staff, New York, 1972)

Nakhlel, Emile A. *Bahrain, Political Development in a Modernizing Society* (Heath, London, 1976)

Osborne, Christina *The Gulf States and Oman* (Croom Helm, London, 1977)

al-Otaiba, Mona Saeed *Petroleum and the Economy of the United Arab Emirates* (Croom Helm, London, 1977)

Penrose, Edith, and Penrose, Ernest *Iraq: International Relations and National Development* (Benn, London, 1978)

Pranger, Robert J., and Tahtinen, Dale *American Policy Options in Iran and the Persian Gulf* (American Enterprise Institute, Washington, DC, 1979)

Ramazani, R.K. *The Persian Gulf, Iran's Role* (University Press of Virginia, Charlottesville, 1972)

—— *Iran's Foreign Policy 1941–73* (University Press of Virginia, Charlottesville, 1975)

—— *The Persian Gulf and the Straits of Hormuz* (Center for the Study of Marine Policy, University of Delaware, Delaware, 1979)

Reppa, Robert B. *Israel and Iran: Bilateral Relationships and the Effect on the Indian Ocean Basin* (Praeger, New York, 1974)

Sadiq, Muhammed T., and Snavely, William *Bahrein, Qatar and the United Arab Emirates* (Heath, Lexington, Mass., 1972)

Skeet, Ian *Muscat and Oman, End of an Era* (Faber and Fox, London, 1974)

Tahtinen, Dale *Arms In the Persian Gulf* (AEI, Washington, DC, 1974)

—— *National Security Challenges to Saudi Arabia* (AEI, Washington, DC, 1978)

Townsend, John *Oman: The Making of a Modern State* (Croom Helm, London, 1977)

Winstone, H.V.F., and Freeth, Z. *Kuwait, Prospect and Reality* (Allen and Unwin, London, 1972)

Yodfat, Aryeh, and Abir, Mordechai, *In the Direction of the Persian Gulf: the Soviet Union and the Persian Gulf* (F. Cass, London, 1977)

Zahlan, Rosemarie S. *The Creation of Qatar* (Croom Helm, London, 1979)

NOTES ON CONTRIBUTORS

Hossein Amirsadeghi, a leading expert on Iran and the Persian Gulf, writer, editor, and political commentator, resigned from the Shah's court in 1973 as an early advocate of balance and retrenchment in national policies. In the last stages of the Shah's regime he was called upon to act as chief advisor and was instrumental in attempting a bloodless resolution to the massive crisis of late 1978. Overtaken by the sudden collapse, he escaped the turmoil and settled in Europe, becoming one of the leading opposition figures to the Khomeini regime.

John Duke Anthony is Associate Professor of Middle East Studies at the Johns Hopkins School of Advanced International Studies (SAIS) in Washington, DC. He is also President of Middle East Educational Trust, Inc. and a consultant on Arabian Peninsula and Gulf affairs to the US Treasury, Defense and State Departments. In 1980 he was appointed Chairman of the Advanced Area Studies Program for the Arabian Peninsula countries and Iran, Foreign Service Institute, Department of State.

John C. Campbell was Vice President of the Middle East Institute, Washington, DC from 1967 to 1979 and Member of the Board of Governors. From 1955 to 1978 he was Senior Fellow and Director of Studies at the Council on Foreign Relations and was in the Department of State for a period of twelve years.

Steven L. Canby is a defence consultant and President of C. & L. Associates Inc., Maryland. A graduate of the US Military Academy Command and General Staff College, he was for six years a serving soldier and is the author of numerous studies on military strategy, techniques, organisation and manpower.

C.D. Carr has taught in the USA and is currently at work on a large project covering US-Iran relations since the Second World War.

Shahram Chubin has been at the International Institute for Strategic Studies since 1977 and from 1974 to 1976 worked at a Research Institute in Iran. He is currently engaged in supervising a project on Regional Security, the first stage of which deals with the Gulf.

Lewis A Dunn is a member of the senior professional staff at the Hudson Institute, New York. He has served as a project leader for studies of nuclear proliferation for various US agencies, and is at present completing a book on nuclear proliferation for the Twentieth-century Fund.

L.P. Elwell-Sutton is Professor of Persian at the University of Edinburgh and has been connected with oriental studies for the past fifty years. He has served in such varied organisations as the Anglo-Iranian Oil Company, the School of Oriental and African Studies, London, the BBC Eastern Services and the British Embassy in Tehran.

Fereidun Fesharaki is a Research Associate at the Resource Systems Institute of the East-West Center in Honolulu and an Adjunct Associate Professor of Economics and Geography at the University of Hawaii. From 1977 to 1978 he served as the Energy Advisor to the Prime Minister of Iran and as a delegate to the OPEC ministerial conferences and has been consultant to such international organisations as the United Nations and the State of California Energy Commission.

Edmund Ghareeb is a writer and consultant on Middle Eastern affairs. He is a former columnist and correspondent for the Beirut *Daily Star* and *al-Ittihad* newspaper of Abu Dhabi and a former assistant editor of the *Journal of Palestine Studies.*

Richard Haass is Special Assistant to the Deputy Under-secretary of Defense/Policy Review in the Department of Defense, Washington, DC. His chapter was written while he was a Research Associate at the International Institute for Strategic Studies.

Geoffrey Kemp is Associate Professor of International Politics at The Fletcher School of Law and Diplomacy, Tufts University, Massachusetts and has written extensively on Middle East military affairs.

Stephanie C. Neuman is a Senior Research Associate in the Institute of War and Peace Studies, Columbia University. She is currently working on a research fellowship awarded by the Ford Foundation to investigate the relationship between arms transfers and socio-economic development of less industrialised countries.

INDEX

Abu Dhabi 18, 23, 172, 173, 174, 184, 185, 186, 190
Abu Musa 171, 172, 173, 188, 189, 211, 216
Acheson, Dean 60
Afghanistan 8, 9, 11, 12, 15, 17, 24, 30, 45, 46, 49, 53, 54, 112, 121, 153, 208, 218, 221, 222, 225
Aflaq, Michel 201-2
Africa 22, 23, 59, 223, 225; Horn of 153, 161, 208
aid, economic (Gulf) 23, 24, 178, 181, 189, 212, (Soviet) 14, 204, 221, (US) 2, 10, 64-7, 73, 205; military 181, 212, (Soviet) 61, 207, (US) 2, 14, 58, 62-9, 185-6, 205, see also arms supplies
Ajman 171
Algeria 23, 187, 191, 278
Algiers agreement 182, 213, 214, 222
America, Latin 22, 225
Anglo-Iranian Oil Co. 243
Anthony, John Duke 170-96
Arab-Israeli conflict 6, 27, 34, 53, 162, 163, 170, 180-7, 194, 204
Arab League 17; — Military Industries Organisation (AMIO) 181-2
Arabism 179, 201-2, 203, 210, 224, 226, 227
Arabistan 210, 214, 215
Aramco 180, 261, 273
Arif, General Abd al-Salam 200, 201, 202
arms, limitation 11-12; race 85, 90-1, 93, 98, 158-60, 166; sales/supply 4, 7, 11-13, 15, 17, 27, 34, 46, 52, 54, 57, 62-4, 71-4, 79, 131-50, 158-60, 163, 204, 207, 219, 221, 223, 271, embargo 32
Arsanjani, Hasan 233
Asia 22, 43, 46, 59, 90, 91, 97, 98, 153, 155, 253; South-East 57, 71, 160; see also individual countries
Azerbaijan 58, 242, 252
Aziz, Tariq 201, 214, 215, 222

Baghdad Pact 4, 10, 13, 15, 64, 65, 68, 199

Bahrain 5, 16, 30, 48, 160, 171, 172, 173, 174, 177, 178, 179, 182, 184, 186, 187, 188, 189, 194, 206, 211
Bakhtiar, Shahpur 213
al-Bakr, President Ahmed Hassan 211
Baluchistan/Baluchis 46, 93-4, 210, 216, 252
Bangladesh 266
Bani Sadr, President 216
Baqir Sadr, Ayatollah Muhamed 227
Barzani, Masud 227
al Barzani, Mulla Mustafa 200, 210, 212
bases 18, 217, (Soviet) 14, 29, (US) 2, 15, 70, 217
Ba'thism 201-3, 206, 210, 215-16, 218, 226
Bazargan, Mahdi 213
Belgium 266
Bell Helicopter Co. 140
Bhabha, Homi 92
Bhutto, Zulfikar Ali 90
al-Bitar, Salah al-Din 202
Bloomfield, Lincoln 79
Boumedienne, President 213
Bowles, Chester 68, 69
Brazil 96, 154, 223, 266
Brezhnev, Prime Minister 49
Britain 1, 3, 5, 13, 14, 30, 33, 54, 63, 64, 74, 86, 152, 153, 160, 171, 172, 183, 198, 199, 203, 205, 219, 235
British Aerospace Corporation 140
Brzezinski, Zbigniew 219
Bubiyan 171, 176, 205, 207-9

Campbell, John C. 1-25
Camp David Accord 195, 197, 208, 220, 221, 224
Canby, Steven L. 100-30
Carr, C.D. 57-84
Carter Administration 11, 34, 44; President 9, 10, 24
Castro, Fidel 225
Central Treaty Organization 5, 6, 10, 17, 18, 45, 68
change, social and economic 30, 47, 151-2, 232-5, see also modernisation